Islamic Schooling in the West

Mohamad Abdalla • Dylan Chown
Muhammad Abdullah
Editors

Islamic Schooling in the West

Pathways to Renewal

palgrave
macmillan

Editors
Mohamad Abdalla
University of South Australia
Adelaide, SA, Australia

Dylan Chown
University of South Australia
Adelaide, SA, Australia

Muhammad Abdullah
University of South Australia
Adelaide, SA, Australia

ISBN 978-3-319-73611-2   ISBN 978-3-319-73612-9 (eBook)
https://doi.org/10.1007/978-3-319-73612-9

Library of Congress Control Number: 2018935692

© The Editor(s) (if applicable) and The Author(s) 2018
This work is subject to copyright. All rights are solely and exclusively licensed by the Publisher, whether the whole or part of the material is concerned, specifically the rights of translation, reprinting, reuse of illustrations, recitation, broadcasting, reproduction on microfilms or in any other physical way, and transmission or information storage and retrieval, electronic adaptation, computer software, or by similar or dissimilar methodology now known or hereafter developed.
The use of general descriptive names, registered names, trademarks, service marks, etc. in this publication does not imply, even in the absence of a specific statement, that such names are exempt from the relevant protective laws and regulations and therefore free for general use.
The publisher, the authors, and the editors are safe to assume that the advice and information in this book are believed to be true and accurate at the date of publication. Neither the publisher nor the authors or the editors give a warranty, express or implied, with respect to the material contained herein or for any errors or omissions that may have been made. The publisher remains neutral with regard to jurisdictional claims in published maps and institutional affiliations.

Cover illustration © Ville Palonen / Alamy Stock Photo

Printed on acid-free paper

This Palgrave Macmillan imprint is published by the registered company Springer International Publishing AG part of Springer Nature.
The registered company address is: Gewerbestrasse 11, 6330 Cham, Switzerland

Contents

1 **Introduction**   1
Mohamad Abdalla, Dylan Chown, and Muhammad Abdullah

2 **The Emergence of Islamic Schools: A Contextual Background**   11
Shaikh Abdul Mabud

3 **Muslim Schools in Australia: Development and Transition**   35
Jan A. Ali

4 **Towards a Hybrid Approach to the Governance of Islamic Schools in NSW**   63
Ayda Succarie, Wayne Fallon, and Gabriela Coronado

5 **What Else Do They Teach in an Islamic School?**   97
Peter Jones

6 **Islamic Worldview and Curriculum Development**   117
Freda Shamma

7 **Muslim Ethos Within Muslim Schools**   129
Abdullah Trevathan

8 Enacting a Vision in a Faith School: Putting
   Word into Action   151
   Anne McDonald

9 Islamic Pedagogy: Potential and Perspective   169
   Nadeem A. Memon and Mariam Alhashmi

10 A Pedagogical Framework for Teacher Discourse
   and Practice in Islamic Schools   195
   Muhammad Abdullah

11 Attaining the 'Islamic' in Islamic Schools   227
   Abdullah Elleissy

12 The Importance of Islamic Studies from
   an Islamic Worldview in Australia   239
   Ibrahima Diallo

13 Islamic Studies in Islamic Schools:
   Evidence-Based Renewal   257
   Mohamad Abdalla

14 Arabic Teaching at Australian Islamic Schools:
   A CALL Framework   285
   Nadia Selim

15 Conclusion   315
   Mohamad Abdalla, Dylan Chown, and Muhammad
   Abdullah

Index   323

Notes on Contributors

Mohamad Abdalla is Professor of Islamic Studies and the Founding Director of the Centre for Islamic Thought and Education (CITE) at the University of South Australia (UniSA). Over the last 20 years, Professor Abdalla has played a leading role in establishing Islamic studies as an area of academic interest in Australia. Prior to joining UniSA, he was the Founding Director of the Griffith University Islamic Research Unit (GIRU), and Director of the Queensland Node of the National Centre of Excellence for Islamic Studies (NCEIS). Abdalla's publications include: *Leadership in Islam: Processes and Solutions in Australian Organizations* (Palgrave Macmillan, co-authored with Nezar Faris) and *Islam and the Australian News Media* (co-edited with H Rane and J Ewart).

Muhammad Abdullah has a Bachelor of Arts (Hons) in Arabic and Middle Eastern Studies, a Diploma of Education in Secondary Mathematics and a Graduate Diploma of Education (English Literacy). He teaches mathematics at a Government K–12 school in an inner suburb of Sydney. He has been Chief Examiner of Aboriginal Studies for The Higher School Certificate in New South Wales and is currently the Supervisor of Marking for the same subject. His PhD research focuses on 'The Formulation of a Pedagogical Framework for Islamic Schools in Australia'.

Jan A. Ali (PhD) is a religious sociologist specialising in Islam. He is Senior Lecturer in Islam and Modernity at the School of Humanities and Communication Arts, Western Sydney University. His main sociological focus is the study of existential Islam. Ali is working on two separate research projects. His first project is a study of the causes and consequences of Muslim terrorism and in his second project, Ali is collaborating with Shahadat Hossain from Dhaka University to examine Global City Formations and Transformations: *The Case of the Global City of Sydney*.

Mariam Alhashmi is an assistant professor in the College of Education at Zayed University, UAE. Her academic interests include the philosophy of Islamic education and its implications for curriculum development and teacher professional learning. She has extensive expertise in the areas of international education, teacher professional development, and Arabic and Islamic education teaching and learning.

Alhashmi started her career in the field of education as a teacher, and then as an assistant head of a kindergarten school. She also worked as a head of the national curriculum for a group of schools focusing on the teaching and learning of the Arabic, Islamic Studies, and UAE Social Studies curricula. Prior to joining Zayed University, she worked as the Director of Curriculum and Instruction at Emirates National Schools, responsible for overseeing all areas related to teaching and learning of 20 schools across the United Arab Emirates (UAE). Alhashmi has trained hundreds of teachers and principals in the UAE, Kuwait, Kingdom of Saudi Arabia, and Kenya. She also presented Arabic and Islamic education teaching and learning in conferences and symposiums in the UAE, Bahrain, Jordan, Morocco, and Spain.

Dylan Chown is a research fellow and Program Director for Islamic Education at the Centre for Islamic Thought and Education/School of Education, University of South Australia. Chown is a member of the University of South Australia Centre for Research in Education and Social Inclusion (CRESI) and Pedagogies for Justice and Wellbeing Research group. He coordinates the accredited teacher education and professional learning degree programmes, the Islamic pedagogy specialisation in the Master of Teaching (secondary) and the Graduate Diploma and Graduate Certificate in Education (Islamic Education). Chown has 20 years' experience in the field of education combining roles of teacher, principal, consultant, researcher and lecturer. He is a passionate advocate for Islamic schools and Islamic education in Australia. He was also a member of an international network of educators on the Islamic Teacher Education Program, a project of Razi Education (Canada, UAE). He completed a Master of Education (Leadership) through the National Centre of Excellence for Islamic Studies (NCEIS), Griffith University, where he examined school vision in an Islamic school with implications for education leadership. Chown was instrumental in the establishment of the now annual whole-of-field Islamic education gatherings in Australia, the Islamic Education Forum and the Islamic Schooling Conference. His PhD research focuses on Islamic pedagogy in Australian Islamic schools and aims to further efforts towards Islamic school renewal, teacher education and more broadly, equitable and inclusive educational practice. This complements his other areas of interest, including character education and culturally and religiously responsive pedagogy.

Gabriela Coronado is a Mexican anthropologist with a PhD in Social Inquiry from Western Sydney University, Australia. From 2002 to 2012 she was senior lecturer in the School of Management, Organisation Studies. Previously in Mexico she researched for 28 years on different aspects of Mexican culture, language, and identity, focusing on issues of intercultural communication and politics between Indigenous and non-Indigenous peoples. She is an adjunct fellow in the Institute for Culture and Society at Western Sydney University.

Ibrahima Diallo is a senior lecturer and Convenor of the Francophone Studies at the University of South Australia, Australia. Diallo obtained his PhD in Applied Linguistics from Griffith University. His research interests include, among others, language policy and planning, Islamic literacy and education, and intercultural pedagogy and teaching.

Abdullah Elleissy commenced his teaching career in 2001. He completed his schooling in Australia, and obtained a double degree in Islamic Theology/Islamic Sciences and Arabic language in Damascus. He has also obtained an Ijaza in Hadeeth from the late renowned scholar Moulana Abul Hasan Ali Al-Nadwi. Prior to that, he had completed the memorisation of the Holy Qur'an in Pakistan. Upon his return to Australia, he completed a Diploma in Secondary Education, and in 2008 he completed his Masters of Education. Elleissy commenced his career at Darul Ulum College where he initially coordinated the Arabic Department, the Islamic Studies Department and thereafter the VCE Department. He also served as the senior secondary level coordinator for few years. Since 2016, he has been assigned the rather challenging yet engaging role of Head of School for the male wing of the college.

Wayne Fallon Wayne is Associate Dean International in the School of Business, Western Sydney University focusing on India and South Asia more broadly, with substantive position as Senior Lecturer in Management.

His work in South Asia involves developing and supporting institutional and corporate relationships, and supporting South Asian students studying Business at Western Sydney University.

Peter Jones teaches comparative religion and modern world history at The Friends' School in Hobart, Australia. He has a Graduate Diploma in Islamic Studies from the University of New England, New South Wales and his PhD thesis was on Islamic schools in Australia. He has also lived and travelled through many parts of Africa and Asia, and taught Asian studies at the University of Tasmania for a number of years.

Shaikh Abdul Mabud is Associate Professor of Islamic Spirituality, Ethics and Education at the Sultan Omar 'Ali Saifuddien Centre for Islamic Studies (SOASCIS), University of Brunei Darussalam. He is also the honorary Director General of the Islamic Academy in Cambridge, UK, where he has been based since 1983. Previously, he taught at the University of Rajshahi, Bangladesh, and the University of Utah, Salt Lake City, USA. His main academic interests are in the areas of education, religion and Islamic philosophy. He is the editor of Cambridge-based educational journal, *Muslim Education Quarterly*, which deals with the problems of Muslim education in various countries of the world. He holds a PhD and a Postgraduate Certificate in Education (PGCE), both from the University of Cambridge.

Anne McDonald has been an educator within the Victorian Catholic education sector for over 40 years. She has taught in Catholic single gender and coeducational primary and secondary schools, holding a number of leadership positions including Deputy Principal. McDonald moved from schools to system level working in the areas of school reviews, strategic planning, leadership development and teacher professional enrichment. In 2007, she was appointed Principal of Nazareth College—a multi-cultural school. As educator, she engaged in continual studies including courses at Harvard University and Boston College which have enabled her to build a school of "faith, wisdom and knowledge." McDonald concluded her role as Principal at the end of 2016. She is now semi-retired and works as a private educational consultant.

Nadeem A. Memon is a senior research fellow at CITE, School of Education, UniSA, Australia. His research focuses on teacher education with particular emphasis on Islamic pedagogy, comparative faith-based schooling, philosophy of religious education and culturally relevant and responsive teaching. He is the co-editor of two books: *Philosophies of Islamic Education: Historical Perspectives and Emerging Discourses* (2016) and *Discipline, Devotion, and Dissent: Jewish, Catholic, and Islamic Schooling in Canada* (2013).

Nadia Selim is an Arabic language teacher. She taught at the Institute of Modern Languages, University of Queensland, Australia, from 2012 to 2016. With a Master's degree in Applied Linguistics from the University of Queensland and a vocational graduate certificate in TESOL and English language development from the Southbank Institute of Technology (SBIT), Queensland, Selim turned her attention to Arabic and focuses on methods that improve the effectiveness, relevance and attainment rates of Arabic programs. Selim is interested in computer-assisted language learning, rhythm for memory and the rediscovery of Islamic thought on Arabic teaching. Selim continues to work on the development of an Arabic program for non-native speakers, an Arabic website, mobile app, and social networking sites and content. Selim is working on a PhD thesis at UniSA (CITE) that examines Arabic at Islamic schools in Australia.

Freda Shamma is an educator who has worked on developing Islamic curriculum on three continents. She received her MA from the University of California, Berkeley, and her EdD from the University of Cincinnati. She has travelled widely collecting Muslim literature from as far away as China, and as close as the nearest used book store. She has been a book content editor for American Trust Publications, and has long been active in the educational activities of the Islamic Society of North America, which, in 2010, honoured her life commitment and service to Islamic education.

Ayda Succarie is Lecturer in Human Resource and Management, and a PhD candidate in the School of Business at Western Sydney University, Australia. Succarie is the unit coordinator for enterprise leadership and has teaching experience in organizational behavior, corporate governance, and social entrepreneurship. Her teaching philosophy draws on critical and reflective thinking, and experiential learning. Succarie's doctoral thesis is in the area of governance in the independent schooling sector, professional identity, and the professionalism of boards in Islamic schools in New South Wales. Her research is in the areas of organizational behavior, leadership, governance, and ethics. Her research interest is in the management practices of boards in independent schools and the not-for-profit sector, with a particular interest in Islamic school boards. Prior to joining academia, Succarie worked in a number of Islamic schools as an administration officer and business manager.

Abdullah Trevathan has worked in the education sector for over 30 years, having taught in all levels: primary schools, secondary schools and in higher education. He has been the Director (head teacher) of two different schools in London and of a school in Morocco. He has taught at the university level for ten years, initially lecturing in education at Roehampton University, London, for seven years and thereafter in academic skills, comparative religion, and philosophy at Master's level at the Al Akhawayn University in Ifrane, Morocco. He has a Bachelor of Education degree, an RSA Diploma in Teaching English to Bilingual Children, Master's degree in Philosophy of Education, and a PhD in Philosophy and Theology. In conjunction with and under the auspices of the University Polytechnic Mohammed VI in Benguerir, he has headed up the team to set up the International Green School in Benguerir.

List of Figures

Fig. 3.1	Utopian muslim school model	44
Fig. 3.2	Model of neoliberalism	47
Fig. 3.3	Corporate muslim school model	53
Fig. 4.1	Hybrid model of governance	79

LIST OF TABLES

Table 3.1	Australian Muslim population by state/territory	39
Table 4.1	Case studies of Islamic schools	72
Table 6.1	Islamic or secular—some basic principles that orient teaching materials	121
Table 10.1	A Prophetic Pedagogical Framework (PPF)	204
Table 10.2	Examples of additional Hadith	208
Table 10.3	A possible synthesis of Productive Pedagogies and a Prophetic Pedagogy (initial part of the framework)	211
Table 10.4	A possible synthesis of Productive Pedagogies and a Prophetic Pedagogy (continuation of the framework)	213
Table 13.1	Views of coordinators of IS	264
Table 13.2	Views of IS staff	265
Table 13.3	Views of IS students (Years 10–12)	266

CHAPTER 1

Introduction

Mohamad Abdalla, Dylan Chown, and Muhammad Abdullah

Historically, the dissemination of knowledge held a prominent place across the breadth of Islamic civilisation. The emphasis on education found in the Qur'an and Hadith is fundamentally premised on the seeking and imparting of knowledge. The Qur'an, Islam's primary source of knowledge, contains many imperatives on the topic (for example Qur'an 96:1–5; 76:10; 39:9; and 20:114). The Hadith, Islam's secondary source, is equally replete with instructions and maxims about the value of knowledge, its teaching and imparting. A few examples will suffice to elucidate the point. The Prophet Muhammad (Peace and blessings of God upon him) said, 'Envy is permitted only in two cases: A person whom God gives wealth, and he/she disposes of it rightfully, and a person to whom God gives knowledge which he/she applies and teaches it'. Moreover, 'God makes the way to paradise easy for one who treads the path in search of knowledge'.[1]

M. Abdalla (✉) • D. Chown • M. Abdullah
University of South Australia, Adelaide, SA, Australia
e-mail: mohamad.abdalla@unisa.edu.au; dylan.chown@unisa.edu.au; muhammad.abdullah@mymail.unisa.edu.au

© The Author(s) 2018
M. Abdalla et al. (eds.), *Islamic Schooling in the West*,
https://doi.org/10.1007/978-3-319-73612-9_1

The emphasis on seeking and imparting knowledge was a significant impetus for the rise of an Islamic civilisation known for its love and pursuit of knowledge. This motivation allowed it to appropriate the knowledge of ancient (*ʿulum al-ʿawaʾil*) civilisations, such as those of the Greeks and the Indians, and spend almost three hundred years translating it into classical Arabic, and subsequently editing and adding to it significantly. The translation movement, perhaps one of the most powerful yet overlooked intellectual movements in history, masterfully rendered the ancient texts into accessible scholarly works that influenced the course of history.

A direct consequence of this immense outpouring of knowledge was the establishment of educational institutions capable of absorbing and disseminating it. Hence, the first universities in the world were established in Morocco (859 CE) and Egypt (970 CE), in addition to thousands of *maktab* (*Kutab*) and *madrasas* (plural of *madrasa*), where various branches of knowledge were taught. These educational institutions were sophisticated, structured and had their own intelligible logic. The result was a universal, cosmopolitan and highly sophisticated educational system that influenced the East and the West alike.

This rich heritage of Islamic education provides tremendous motivation for contemporary Islamic education proponents and practitioners. After disruption and stagnation resulting in an oft-recognised malaise, Islamic education as a field of study is enjoying a revival of sorts. At the same time, waves of migration have seen increased numbers of Muslims living in 'Western' contexts, a by-product of the colonial period and the current era of modern imperialism affecting Muslim-majority countries. As these new waves of Muslim peoples have settled and matured among long-standing local Muslim communities in Western contexts, the desire to educate their children and young people in ways that honour their religious, cultural and linguistic traditions has inspired the founding of Islamic schools in the West.[2] This book is therefore a timely contribution for educators, academics and students. This book brings forward an international collaboration of leading scholars, academics and educationalists as they expound on the theme of renewal of Islamic schools in the West.

The following Prophetic dictum beautifully captures the essence of renewal: 'Faith wears out in your heart as clothes wear out, so ask God to renew the faith in your hearts.'[3] This narration calls for people to renew their faith in their hearts, cautioning that faith wears out as clothes wear out.

When extended beyond faith at the personal level, this narration also captures the essence of renewal in Islamic schools in both Western and non-Western contexts. Islamic schools, having to negotiate change in context, have arguably inspired Muslim communities locally, regionally and globally to renew their connections with their educational tradition. In this book, we argue for a renewal, not a reformation, of Islamic schools.

Renewal is not a 'reformation' nor an effort to impose an imagined ideal past model on the present.[4] We do not call for 'reform' because the label is 'redolent of a well-articulated political and ideological position that inherently assumes [the Islamic tradition] contains deficiencies that need correction and modernizing rectification' (Hallaq 2007). As summarised succinctly by Professor Wael Hallaq (2007):

> 'Reform' thus clearly insinuates not only a transition from the pre-modern to the modern, but also passes an un-appealable verdict on an entire [Islamic] history and a legal culture that is perennially wanting and thus deserving of displacement, and—no less—eradication, from memory and the material world, respectively. If the study of 'reform'—as a field of academic endeavour—is thus engulfed by these ideological associations, then the scholarly trajectory and agenda can safely be said to have been predetermined.[5]

Instead, for us, renewal is a recognition that a robust heritage of education has been inspired and shaped within the Islamic tradition. It is a recognition that Islam offers an ideal theory for education, the gap being its translation into practice.[6] Renewal is also an expression of gratitude for the tradition, and gratitude for the pioneers, in Islamic schools specifically, and Islamic education generally, in the Western context.

This book argues that Islamic schools in Western contexts have negotiated the establishment phase and must next embrace a period of renewal. Renewal relates to a purposeful synthesis of tradition with contemporary educational practice and greater emphasis on empirical research to substantiate best practices in Islamic schools. This renewal must reflect teaching and learning practices consistent with an Islamic worldview, an Islamic vision of education and appropriate pedagogy, and thereby inform all aspects of the school including character education, classroom management models and relevant and contextual Islamic and Arabic studies. This book hopes to include the reader in the conversation and acquaint them with the contemporary challenges and opportunities facing Islamic schools in the Western context.

Inspiration for the Book

The inspiration for this book arose out of a watershed event, the Inaugural Australian Islamic Schooling Conference held in Melbourne in 2016. In the Australian context, member principals of the Islamic School Association Australia (ISAA) had been meeting annually for a number of decades.[7] Never before, however, had international and local scholars, academics, educationalists, educational leaders, policy specialists, educational practitioners and teachers from inside and outside Islamic schooling been brought together. The aim of the conference was to start a national and international conversation in relation to the challenges, issues and opportunities facing Islamic schooling, particularly within Western contexts. The conference was aptly themed *Continuity and Change: Envisioning the Way Forward for Islamic Schooling in the West*.

One outcome of the conference was the idea of producing a ten-year road map for the field. This strength-based approach is to be characterised by a willingness to study and understand deeply the challenges in Islamic schools and apply evidence-based solutions, consistent with tradition and worldview, and a willingness to evaluate their effectiveness. It calls for increased collaboration and a willingness to share stories of hope. This book captures the themes presented at this conference by scholars, academics, educationalists and thought leaders.

Islamic Schools in Western Contexts

Searching for positive, alternative schooling for their children, Muslim parents living in Western countries turn toward 'Islamic' schools. Accordingly, Islamic schools are growing rapidly in Western countries. Islamic schools have not been free of criticism, however, some of it superficial and some of it more incisive.

A significant criticism of Islamic schools is that they are relatively 'conventional', implementing a schooling model that was intended to be secular, arguably enacted and experienced as an out-of-context hybrid model, with an external Islamic ethos in a manner that is 'stale', 'irrelevant' and 'decontextualized'.[8] The era of renewal calls for a rethinking of purpose and a reconceptualising of the models offered by Islamic schools. Islamic schools have not been immune to the dominant discourse of neo-liberalism and neo-conservatism, particularly in the USA, UK and Australia,[9] and the dogged pursuit of academic results as the yardstick, as a sign of legitimacy, as the measure of success, which has arguably been a distraction from the process of rethinking.

How much do we really know about the success of 'Islamic' schools in Western contexts? Should this success be measured against academic performance or against the vision of each Islamic school? To what extent does a school's vision influence its future direction? How do we attain the 'Islamic' in Islamic schools and how do we measure it? Are teachers trained to impart the 'Islamic' in these schools? Do these Islamic schools implement an 'Islamic' classroom management or character education model, or do they imitate 'secular' models? Are the Islamic studies programmes relevant and contextual? Do Islamic studies programmes meet students' needs and aspirations? Do Islamic schools equip young Western Muslims with the necessary and relevant knowledge and skills to navigate the modern world? This book seeks to address the above questions and offer valuable and practical insights into the future of Islamic schools in the West.

Structure and Purpose of the Book

The intent behind this book was to expand and build upon the contemporary intellectual, religious and spiritual rigour driving Islamic schools. The chapters herein seek to address many of the questions raised in Islamic schools in the West. The editors offer this book as a 'pathway to renewal'.

Chapter 2 provides a contemporary account of the emergence of Islamic schools during the last thirty years. It makes a comparative study of the philosophical principles of Islamic and secular schools and highlights their distinctive features. This chapter also discusses how to develop an educational curriculum that encourages pupils to practise Islamic values and develop mutual respect.

Chapter 3 focuses on the development and transition of Muslim schools in Australia. The global pervasiveness of neo-liberalism as an economic philosophy brought about fundamental changes in the way Muslim schools operate and empower their students with knowledge. Muslim communities have seen schools transform and transition from a Utopian Muslim School Model to a Corporate Muslim School Model. The chapter argues that this transformation and transition has made Muslim schools spaces for commercial activities and in the process rendered Islamic education itself a commercial transaction.

Chapter 4 proposes an approach that draws on a hybrid model of governance for Islamic schools. The chapter outlines an empirical study of the governance and management practices in Islamic schools in New South Wales, Australia. The Islamic worldview was used to guide this chapter, and governance theories form the theoretical framework. The chapter argues that the issues of compliance, accountability and transparency of Islamic schools' registration and stakeholder needs are influenced by confusion between a stewardship model of governance and directors' sense of ownership of the institutions. The chapter proposes a hybrid approach to the governance of these schools, by adopting a combination of the theoretical attributes of stewardship and an Islamic worldview.

Chapter 5 examines what is taught in Australian Islamic schools. It argues that there is considerable variation in what is taught in Islamic schools in Australia (and other similar contexts), depending on the policies of the particular school and whether or not it has the relevant staff available.

Chapter 6 explores the underpinning features of humanism, which, according to the author, make the 'academic' subjects in most Islamic schools decidedly 'un-Islamic'. A comparison of basic Islamic principles with humanistic principles illustrates the problem. It argues that a number of key questions are posed for further consideration, which should underpin the foundation of a curriculum based entirely on Islamic principles.

Chapter 7 examines the 'culture of managerialism' which many claim pervades the contemporary educational sphere. The non-materialist and iconoclastic nature of the Muslim dynamic is at odds with such managerial paradigms. Nonetheless, this culture has been deeply absorbed not only into contemporary Muslim educational discourse but also into the theology of Islam, leaving modern Muslim education counterproductive in the Foucauldian sense. The chapter contends that in standardising and commodifying, the bureaucratisation of education requires the reifying of concepts such as 'School ethos' to be employed for marketing purposes. This chapter examines these issues and the influence they may have upon the ethos within Muslim schools, followed by options afforded by classical thought.

Chapter 8 argues that renewal of a school's vision and mission is vital to ensure its growth as an effective learning community within a specific tradition. Renewal cannot be achieved overnight, nor can it reside with one person. When approached strategically and owned by the school community, renewal leads the school to a new means of achievement and celebration of identity and values. Within a faith and cultural community, renewal ensures that our children are successful, value our traditions and grow up to be great people within our community. This chapter follows the work of one Christian school as their community identifies their specific vision and their goals and strategies to take them to renewal and their preferred outcomes.

Chapter 9 argues that religious traditions embody inherent pedagogical perspectives—a way of teaching religion. Among Muslim scholarship, conceptual aspects of a philosophy of education rooted in Islam have been articulated but often in a piecemeal fashion, making it inaccessible to Islamic schools today. The challenge has been in synthesising philosophies of Islamic education, or better termed Islamic pedagogy, in a way that is relevant and applicable to contemporary schools. The chapter aims to establish some semblance of an Islamic pedagogical framework. The concepts and perspectives identified may serve as a rubric for Islamic schools to renew their conceptions of Islamic education for a deeper connection between religious education as a subject and pedagogy rooted in a religious tradition.

Chapter 10 argues that there is no pedagogical framework for teacher discourse and practice in Islamic schools, which is consistent with the Australian/Western Islamic context. The chapter therefore presents a synthesis of a pedagogical framework that is responsive to contemporary educational research embedded in a prophetic pedagogy. The chapter proposes that this could enable consistent teacher quality in Islamic schools, thereby enabling the achievement of Islamic education and enhanced student outcomes.

Chapter 11 stipulates that the reasons behind the establishment of Islamic schools in the West vary, as do the factors that influence the decisions of parents and guardians. However, irrespective of motives, there is a dire need to revisit the whole notion of what the 'Islamic' entails so that its interpretation and manifestation are not left to the mercy of cultural practices or prevalent understandings. The chapter argues that a sincere and genuine approach to analysing the notion of the 'Islamic' in existing Islamic schools compels us to go back in history to contemplate the prevalent norms, practices and pedagogies that were embraced by our predecessors who played a significant role in shaping the society as a whole and in reforming individuals.

Chapter 12 explores the importance of Islamic studies in Islamic schools, and contends that despite the prejudices against Islam and Muslims, Australian Muslims show strong attachment to Islamic studies, to developing an Islamic worldview constructed on Qur'anic teachings and prophetic traditions. The chapter describes and analyses data collected from among

61 members of the Islamic community in Adelaide and Darwin, which found that Australian Muslims place a high value on Islamic studies in their Islamic community schools in order to develop an Islamic worldview. In addition to providing details about the sample represented in this case study, the chapter discusses the ways in which Islamic studies contribute to the Islamic worldview of Australian Muslims.

Chapter 13 examines the strengths and challenges of Islamic studies at an Australian Islamic school as experienced by senior students and teachers. The findings are based on empirical research undertaken for the first time in Australian (and possibly other Western) Islamic schools. Data collected from focus groups and classroom observations demonstrate that while there are some strengths associated with the teaching of Islamic studies, overall there are many challenges that need attention. The chapter provides recommendations for renewal in Islamic studies for Islamic schools based on empirical findings.

Finally, Chap. 14 discusses the role of Arabic in the lives of Muslims, and the challenges faced in teaching Arabic in Islamic schools. It argues that the Arabic teaching profession is challenged by a diminishing supply of professionals, use of ineffective methodologies and the absence of school textbooks designed for learners of Arabic as a foreign language (AFL), as well as the fact that many textbooks are not guided by the field of second language acquisition (SLA). In fact, Arabic teaching has reached crisis level, with the distaste for Arabic lessons evident among Australian students arguably unresolvable in the near future. However, while most solutions require huge amounts of funding and time, this chapter suggests that the strategic use of computer-assisted language learning (CALL) can assist in forging a way forward.

Notes

1. Sahih Muslim collected by Muslim b. al-Hajjaj (d. 875).
2. Muslim schools and Islamic schools both appear in the literature, often interchangeably. This book will adopt the term Islamic schools in the main. The authors acknowledge that 'Muslim' and 'Islamic' are problematic and contested terms when attached to schooling. In many contexts, including the Australian one, all schools are inclusive so the term 'Muslim' school would seemingly exclude those who do not identify as Muslim. The term 'Islamic' is problematic given the weighty connotations it holds and the tendency to debate what is and what is not Islamic. This can lead to a divisive and exclusive discourse which is unhelpful. In Australia, a precedent has been set with labels such as Catholic or Christian schools, meaning the term 'Islamic' is widespread.

3. Narrated by al-Haakim in his *Mustadrak* and al-Tabaraani in his *Mu'jam* with a Saheeh *isnaad*.
4. Niyozov Safaroz and Nadeem Memon, 2011. "Islamic Education and Islamization: Evolution of Themes, Continuities and New Directions," *Journal of Muslim Minority Affairs* 31 (1):5–30.
5. Wael Hallaq, What is Sharia? 2007. https://www.academia.edu/11170698/_What_is_Sharia_.
6. Amjad Hussain, 2008. "Recent Western Reflections on Islamic Education," *Religious Education* 103 (5):579–585.
7. The Islamic Schools Association of Australia (ISAA) are a representative body for Islamic schooling.
8. Nadeem Memon, 2013. "Between Immigrating and Integrating: The Challenge of Defining an Islamic Pedagogy in Canadian Islamic Schools." In *Discipline, devotion and dissent: Jewish, Catholic and Islamic Schooling in Canada*, edited by Graham P. McDonough, Nadeem A. Memon and Avi I. Mintz, 73–97. Canada: Wilfrid Laurier University Press.
9. Bruce Johnson and Anna Sullivan, 2016. "Understanding and Challenging Dominant Discourses About Student Behavior at School." In *Challenging Dominant Views on Student Behaviour at School*, edited by Anna Sullivan, Bruce Johnson and Bill Lucas. Singapore: Springer.

Bibliography

Hallaq, W. What Is Sharia? 2007. https://www.academia.edu/11170698/_What_is_Sharia_.

Hussain, Amjad. "Recent Western Reflections on Islamic Education." *Religious Education* 103, no. 5 (2008): 579–585.

Johnson, Bruce, and Anna Sullivan. "Understanding and Challenging Dominant Discourses About Student Behavior at School." In *Challenging Dominant Views on Student Behaviour at School*, ed. Anna Sullivan, Bruce Johnson, and Bill Lucas. Singapore: Springer, 2016.

Memon, Nadeem A. "Between Immigrating and Integrating: The Challenge of Defining an Islamic Pedagogy in Canadian Islamic Schools." In *DISCIPLINE, DEVOTION and DISSENT: Jewish, Catholic and Islamic Schooling in Canada*, ed. Graham P. McDonough, Nadeem A. Memon, and Avi I. Mintz, 73–97. Canada: Wilfrid Laurier University Press, 2013.

Niyozov, Sarfaroz, and Nadeem Memon. "Islamic Education and Islamization: Evolution of Themes, Continuities and New Directions." *Journal of Muslim Minority Affairs* 31, no. 1 (2011): 5–30.

Shamma, F. "The Status of Islamic Curriculum," 2004. Accessed August 6. www.4islamicschools.org.

CHAPTER 2

The Emergence of Islamic Schools: A Contextual Background

Shaikh Abdul Mabud

INTRODUCTION

Many Muslim schools have been set up in both Western and Muslim countries during the last few decades in response to the dominant secular education of these countries.[1] Generally speaking, they take two forms, those that are independent and privately funded and those that are voluntary aided and state funded. They have been set up with a certain ideal in mind—to impart education in the Islamic framework within an Islamic ethos while taking full advantage of the secular education of the country. These schools are different from *madrasas*, which are purely Islamic institutions with an Islamic curriculum aimed at producing specialists in Islamic sciences. These Muslim schools, now often referred to as 'Islamic schools', are unique in the sense that they are neither like *madrasas* nor like mainstream secular schools (also known as 'common schools'), nor do they represent an institution that has succeeded in integrating both the systems of Islamic and secular education. Rather, they incorporate religious education into a secular structure, and thus these Islamic schools still suffer from

---

S. A. Mabud (✉)
Universiti Brunei Darussalam, Bandar Seri Begawan, Brunei Darussalam
e-mail: shaikh.mabud@ubd.edu.bn

a dichotomy resulting from the juxtaposition of the two conflicting systems of education. Islamic schools have achieved varying degrees of success in their attempt to eradicate this dichotomy by adopting different strategies such as critically analysing secular ideas from the perspective of their deep-seated beliefs and values, teaching Islamic texts and engaging in their most important task, that of character building in their pupils.

Muslims in Western countries are still experimenting to find the best form of education for their children. To establish schools where all subjects are taught from an Islamic perspective and where an organically developed, unified system of Islamic education operates at all levels of the educational structure requires a substantial change in the systems of education that Muslims are currently experiencing. So far, Muslims have been only partially successful in achieving this goal. Even when they are able to establish such schools, gaining government recognition is another hurdle they need to overcome. A shortcut whereby some kind of integration can be achieved between the Islamic system of education and the existing secular system of education is the establishment of Islamic schools. It is assumed that in these schools children's Islamic values will be respected, their self-confidence as Muslims will be strengthened and they will learn the basics of Islam. Such schools aim to provide 'the best way of preserving the way of life of the Muslim community while at the same time giving Muslim children the benefits of a modern education'.[2]

Such schools are a praiseworthy step towards integrating the two sources of knowledge—religious and secular—but they are still far from the kind of Islamic institutions where both systems have merged into a unified Islamic system of education with its own principles and philosophy. One of the challenges facing the integration of religious and secular subjects is the teaching of the national curriculum. All state-funded Islamic schools must follow the national curriculum, but private Muslim schools are not required to do so, although according to the Association of Muslim Schools most do.[3] Muslim schools have sought to meet these and other challenges in different ways. This chapter is presented in support of such 'Islamic schools' with the full knowledge that they do not represent an ideal system of education from the Islamic perspective.

Both liberals and humanists have contested the demand for state-run Islamic schools in pluralist liberal democratic societies on the basis that such schools are sectarian, divisive and parochial.[4] Others find them too dogmatic, intolerant and indoctrinating to meet the educational needs of the modern world.[5] This debate has been ongoing in the UK since

Muslims' demand for separate religious schools for their children gathered momentum in the 1980s. McLaughlin has argued for the compatibility of at least certain forms of separate schools with the liberal democratic conception of religion.[6] Ashraf has supported the establishment of separate voluntary-aided schools for Muslims in the UK.[7] Halstead has examined some arguments for and against the establishment of Islamic voluntary-aided schools and concluded that such schools provide the best means for Muslims to achieve the double aim of the preservation, maintenance and transmission of their religious faith and the provision of a high standard of general education for their children.[8]

The Aim of Islamic Education

The content of education—that is, the body of knowledge—can be divided into two categories: that which is concerned with the development of skills or technical or scientific knowledge whose nature is not constant but changes with time and place, and the other category which is based on permanent values that are not subject to change. For Muslims, the latter category is embodied in the Qur'an and Sunnah, which provide the principles that determine the validity and applicability of any knowledge that comes under its purview. As far as the question of values is concerned, these two domains of knowledge are governed by the unitary (*tawhidic*) principle of Islam, leaving no scope for a false dichotomy, as the separation between religious education and secular education has no place in Islamic education. One can speak of different aims and objectives of specific aspects of education, but the fundamental aim of education from the Islamic perspective reflects the purpose for which human beings have been created.[9] Generally speaking, this fundamental aim has remained essentially unchanged throughout Islamic history, although different scholars have expressed it differently. Sufis,[10] philosophers,[11] educationalists[12] and social scientists[13] have tried to explain the aims and purposes of education using their own vocabulary. Some of these ideas have been challenged as not being Qur'anic enough.[14]

The great Islamic educationalist Al-Zarnuji (d. 1223 CE) stated that the aim of education is to strive 'for the pleasure of God, the abode of the Hereafter, the removal of ignorance ... the revival of religion, and the survival of Islam'.[15] For Al-Ghazali, education is the disciplining of the self through religious knowledge and moral values: 'The knowledge about (*ma'rifah*) God is the end of every cognition (*ma'rifah*) and the fruit of every knowledge (or science, *'ilm*) according to all schools of thought.'[16] For him, *'ilm* (knowledge) and *'amal* (action), which form the principle theme of Muslim ethics, are the only way to happiness.[17] He is more sympathetic towards religious knowledge, although 'he retains his practical attitude toward secular learning'.[18]

In recent times, Husain and Ashraf have stated that the true aim of education is 'to produce men who have faith as well as knowledge, the one sustaining the other ... Islamic education ... insists that piety and faith must be clearly recognized in syllabuses as an aim to be systematically pursued.'[19] This fundamental aim of education has been captured by Nasr as a process that 'prepares man for felicity in this life, its ultimate goal is the abode of permanence and all education points to the permanent world of eternity (*al-akhirah*) beyond the transient vacillations of this world of change'.[20] Al-Attas believes that the correct term to denote education in Islam is by using the word *ta'dib*, that is, the instilling and inculcation of *adab*—the discipline of body, mind and soul—in man.[21] He defines the concept, content and process of education as 'recognition and acknowledgement, progressively instilled into man, of the proper places of things in the order of creation, such that it leads to the recognition and acknowledgement of the proper place of God in the order of being and existence'.[22] According to Hadi Sharifi, Islamic education aims to prepare pupils for the attainment of the state of *al-insan al-kamil*, 'the perfect man'. He identifies Islamic education as a process that has a beginning but no end—which is immersed in the Infinite—as the state of the perfect man is identified with the realisation of the Unity of Being, and hence the Truth as Absolute.[23] There are some common ideas embedded in the above definitions of Islamic education, which were succinctly expressed as the aim of education at the First World Conference on Muslim Education held in Makkah in 1977, in which all the scholars mentioned in this paragraph participated:

> Education should aim at the balanced growth of the total personality of Man through the training of Man's spirit, intellect, the rational self, feelings and bodily senses. Education should therefore cater for the growth of man in all its aspects: spiritual, intellectual, imaginative, physical, scientific, linguistic, both individually and collectively and motivate all these aspects towards goodness and the attainment of perfection. The ultimate aim of Muslim education lies in the realization of complete submission to Allah on the level of the individual, the community and humanity at large.[24]

Academic, religious and social goals of education have been expressed in this passage. According to this, education is aimed at achieving a balance among the physical, rational and spiritual aspects of human beings, its final goal being 'the realization of complete submission to Allah', which embodies a number of concepts all at once, that is, the attainment of servitude (*'ubudiyyah*), cognisance of God (*ma'rifah*), piety (*taqwa*) and God consciousness (*ihsan*). Education can never be complete unless it involves the education of the body, intellect and spirit: it is educating the whole person. Corresponding to these three components of human beings, we have physical aims (*ahdaf jismiyyah*), intellectual aims (*ahdaf 'aqliyyah*) and spiritual aims (*ahdaf ruhiyyah*) of education, whose fulfilment prepares human beings to become the vicegerents of God (*khalifatullah*).[25] The purpose of education is not just to transmit knowledge, or to attain knowledge for its own sake, but to translate it into purposeful and worthwhile activities. Islamic education focuses on both individual and social development in accordance with the divinely ordained moral imperatives embodied in Shari'ah. The following sayings of the Prophet peace and blessings of God be upon him (henceforth abbreviated as p.b.u.h.) urge men to transform their knowledge into action: 'Woe to the ignorant man once, for he has not acquired knowledge! But woe to the learned man a thousand times, for he has not acted in accordance with what he learned!'[26] Knowledge, therefore, is a responsibility which must not be taken lightly. Education is not divorced from belief (*iman*), nor is belief divorced from action (*'amal*), nor action from virtue (*ihsan*): 'Whoever increases in knowledge and does not increase in guidance, only increases in distance from God.'[27] True education fulfils the purpose for which human beings have been created.

Secular Education

Secularism is the strict separation of the state from religious institutions. It is a belief system that disregards all forms of religious faith and worship and holds that religious considerations should be totally excluded from the functions of the state, including public education. This is a philosophical position whose understanding of life and the world does not require presupposing the existence of God. This position is one of indifference to, or rejection or exclusion of, religion or religious considerations from state or public affairs. A truly secular state does not express religious beliefs or preferences and does not fund or promote religious activities, including religious education, whether through 'religious affiliation of schools, curriculum setting, organised worship, religious instruction, pupil selection or employment practices'.[28]

General education systems in Western countries have many features of secularism, and although they are not completely secularised, their liberal approach stands in sharp contrast to religious schools in its fundamental philosophical principles. The dominant theories of education, being almost entirely rationalistic in tone, consider values as free standing and conceive of educational activities without reference to religion. Liberal education does not align itself with any fixed notion of the good, adopts a stance of neutrality on the diversity of religious views, and encourages pupils to question their assumptions, values and beliefs. To Muslims this represents a great challenge to the foundation of their faith, but Muslim children are experiencing this type of education throughout their lives at school. The sharp contrast between the Islamic and secular approaches to education and schooling has been depicted by Professor Syed Ali Ashraf in the following way:

> They [Muslims] want their children to grow up as good Muslims and they find the secularist state schools creating non-believers in spite of religious education. All subjects are taught from a secularist point of view. Children are encouraged to be critical of their own traditions and values and even of faith. Doubts are encouraged. Whereas a Muslim teaches a child to pray to God for forgiveness and to strengthen his/her faith, the rationalist teacher teaches the student to explore on his/her own or with reference to other faiths and ideologies. The Islamic method of removing doubts and the strengthening of faith is completely ignored. It is desirable for a Muslim child to be open-minded and be ready to admit the truth in other religions and ideologies, but it would be wrong to be critical of one's own religion without any norm to judge which is true and which is false. Who will provide the child with that norm? Parents? Teachers? Their own unguided reason?[29]

According to Ashraf, 'their own unguided reason' is the only criterion that has taken the place of revelation in the secular ideology. However, the experience of spiritual masters of various religions over the centuries shows that there is knowledge beyond the domain of sense, reason and imagination. For Muslims, the certainty of the revealed truth is unquestionable and intellectual and rational sciences, being products of the human mind, occupy subsidiary places. According to McLaughlin, public education in liberal societies is not based on a particular philosophy of life, nor can it promote one. Public education takes a neutral stand on religion, and at times can ignore it completely or undermine it deliberately or by default.[30]

A unifying vision that brings all aspects of human beings together and integrates their various faculties under a unitary principle is non-existent in the liberal concept of education. The cultures of the common school in many ways militate against maintaining an Islamic identity as they are required to promote certain teachings that are against their faith, because, for example, the school 'must not give a viewpoint that certain lifestyles are wrong', nor 'should the school promote a particular lifestyle'.[31] Even the activities that do go on in school assemblies 'continue to expose Muslim children to un-Islamic values on a daily basis'.[32] Muslim children cannot take part in certain school functions, for example, some religious festivals such as nativity plays and Diwali celebrations, without compromising their religious and cultural values. The common school speaks of celebrating the diversity of cultures, but at the same time it promotes the philosophy of developing shared values, shared culture and shared citizenship at the cost of the distinctive identity of each community. The tension between these two is apparent and a balance is rarely achieved.

THE PURPOSE OF ISLAMIC SCHOOLS

A Muslim school provides an environment where Islam is a lived way of life, and where pupils experience a culture similar to the one they enjoy at home. The primary purpose of establishing Islamic schools is to teach Muslim children about their religion, to instil in them Islamic values and attitudes which will help them grow as practising Muslims and prevent them being assimilated into anti-Islamic cultures, and to encourage them to continue to adhere to their faith. Such schools, ideally and among other outcomes, could provide a high standard of teaching and learning, and produce pupils who will have academic credentials in accordance with conventional educational practices as well as being fully functioning members and upright citizens of society.

Numerous studies conducted during the last twenty years have looked into the reasons why Muslims have been dissatisfied with mainstream schools and have felt the need for separate schooling for their children. What emerges from the study of McCreery, Jones and Holmes is that parents are convinced that the state is not providing a suitable setting for the education of their children, which has prompted Muslims to challenge Western educational beliefs and values on a range of issues, especially 'diversity, inclusion, parental rights and ultimately the aims of education'.[33] Hewer has identified four concerns that have prompted the establishment of Islamic schools, namely, (1) to provide a 'safe' environment for post-pubescent girls, (2) to provide an integrated faith-based education that would educate the whole person in an Islamic environment, (3) to offer specialist training in Islamic sciences alongside general education that would help boys especially to serve the community as religious leaders, and (4) the desire to set higher standards of expectation and achievement for Muslim pupils.[34] Rizvi's research shows that parents prefer Muslim schools because of underachievement in state schools, racism and difficulties in meeting religious obligations.[35] Saeeda Shah argues that Islamic schools are seen by Muslims as a means to gain an updated education in conformity with their perception of Muslim identity, as well as a venue for an agenda of resistance to challenge racism and existing power relations. Muslim schools foster the *Muslimness* of Muslims, which helps them counter the marginalisation they experience in 'secular' societies.[36] Muslim schools are a safe haven from 'moral permissiveness and lower academic achievement' and a necessity to protect their children from public schools that 'ignore the cultural and religious identities of Muslim children'.[37]

Islamic schools are a place where pupils can be taught from an Islamic perspective, and where they can be given the opportunity to appreciate their own faith, traditions and cultures instead of doubting them. Such schools can assert the transcendental dimensions and the spiritual nature of human life and our relationship to God. In some cases, by their teaching they may be able to convey to the wider society the limitations of seeing social and political life in secular terms.

Islamic schools generally have an open policy vis-à-vis modern knowledge, but Islamic scholarship requires that all forms of knowledge be assessed critically before they are accepted, modified or rejected. The criterion by which any piece of knowledge will be judged is no less than the Qur'an—another name for which is *Furqan*, that is, the Criterion—and the Sunnah of the Prophet (p.b.u.h.). The importance of being critical about modern knowledge has been stressed by McLaughlin:

> [Catholic] schools need to avoid a merely *de facto* or pragmatic acceptance of, or conformity to, educational norms and circumstances in the world as a whole, where there is a danger of acquiescence in the face of pressures which may not support, and in some cases may undermine, the properly Catholic

aims and values of the school. Catholic education, after all, is an enterprise which is in significant respects conducted 'against the grain of the world' ... this process requires discernment about which features of the general educational landscape need to be resisted and rejected and which are to be seen as compatible with, or maybe even expressions of, Catholic values.[38]

What McLaughlin is saying about Catholic education is applicable to Islamic education as well, although the Islamic criteria for identifying what is 'against the grain of the world' may be different. Muslim scholars, by resisting and rejecting those features that threaten to militate against the principles of Islamic education and the aims and values of the Islamic schools, and integrating those that are in concordance with Islamic values, will help develop a strategy for Islamic schools appropriate for the present time.

Muslims should carefully monitor what is being taught to their children in the name of education, because the vision of liberal education rules out the 'uncritical presentation of any concept of the good or of any understanding of the world and human life'.[39] Pupils are encouraged to question their assumptions, family values and worldviews and to engage in rational debate about all issues of interest, including religion. Doubt as a tool to seek the truth is a positive value, but to generate and nurture doubt as a perpetual state of mind is destructive for the development of the human self. Doubt as a way of life precludes the possibility of attaining certainty and that is against the Islamic concept of knowledge (*'ilm*), belief (*iman*) and certitude (*yaqin*).

Islamic schools, like other faith schools, are concerned with the cultural and spiritual needs of all pupils irrespective of their faith. The ethos of such schools will be Islamic but the pupils, who will be of all faiths and none, will be given the opportunity to reflect upon the multicultural nature of the Western society in which they live while being aware of the distinctive role played by the individual faith communities. The presence of pupils of other faiths and no faith in such schools will provide an opportunity to develop interpersonal skills beyond their own groups. The school curriculum should be more inclusive so that all pupils are able to know other people's faiths and cultures. If Muslim faith schools operate on Islamic principles—which recognise people's freedom to pursue their faith—then there will be cultural interaction, as is testified by the history of Islam.

The Formation of an Islamic Identity

Whereas cultural identity is based on many factors including religion, ethnicity, tradition, language, race and nationality, religious identity is formed primarily by religion and religious traditions. The formation of an Islamic identity is one of the most important tasks of any Muslim school. Ameen and Hassan observe that 'Secular Eurocentric schooling in the UK can no longer masquerade as an ideologically neutral space when it affirms particular identities and discourses and marginalises others'.[40] In the Muslim consciousness, religious identity is more deeply rooted than any other identity, and Muslims believe that their religious identity is the primary identity that permeates their whole life. For those communities that take their religious membership seriously, Halstead notes that 'It is their religious commitment, rather than their citizenship, which determines the primary identity of these religious minorities'.[41] Muslim faith schools help pupils form and develop their sense of Muslim identity, which in turn develops their confidence and self-esteem. The religious nature of the school, that is, its faith-centred curriculum, school assemblies, daily school practices, teachers sympathetic to the Islamic religion and the overall school ethos, will form the child's individual identity and secure his or her place in society in a way that is not possible in a state school.

Fostering a Sense of Belonging

Irrespective of differences of race, ethnicity, language and location, Muslims all over the world constitute one community (*ummah*), as the Qur'an says: 'This *ummah* of yours is a single *ummah*.'[42] The concept of an *ummah*—the global community of Muslims—transcends all racial and tribal barriers and is upheld by the common faith in Allah and the prophethood of Muhammad (p.b.u.h.). It plays a dominant role in forming Muslim identity, so much so that the Prophet (p.b.u.h.) said 'The believers, in their love, mutual kindness, and close ties, are like one body; when any part complains, the whole body responds to it with wakefulness and fever'.[43] The social responsibility taught by Islam is embedded in the *ummatic* (communal) aspects of Muslims' existence. Islamic schools should develop in children an emotional attachment to the *ummah* and make them aware of their responsibility towards it. The notion of the solidarity of the *ummah* derives from the communal nature of the Islamic faith and encourages pupils to understand the importance of participating in the Islamic community. Students' critical reflection should be directed not only to theological issues but also to social and political contexts so that they are able to see how justice can alleviate miseries and dissatisfaction among members of a society and bring them together. Students must learn to challenge negative traits in their own character and in the wider society.

Muslims' concern for the *ummah* follows from their grasp of the rich tradition of Islamic values, history and cultures. Differences in tradition, culture, history, hopes and aspirations among Muslims do not negate the concept of the *ummah* as enshrined in the Qur'an and Hadith. It is a tragic fact of life that divisions do exist among Muslims due to sectarianism, inequality, brutal treatment of others and so on, which should be viewed as human weaknesses; but it is their beliefs and practices, enshrined in the Qur'an and the teachings of the Prophet (p.b.u.h.)—which they have accepted as their faith—that place them on the same path to God in their terrestrial life. This is what gives Muslims their Islamic identity and a sense of belonging which should be situated in the context of the *ummah*. Living as a minority in a multicultural society, they understand that they will need to adjust their own culture to a certain extent, but they cannot compromise the fundamentals of their religion.

Moral and Spiritual Development

Islamic educational principles and practice insist that teachers should be of the Islamic faith or at least of good moral character (*akhlaq*), as their character will affect the development of the pupils. As the examples set by teachers can influence the upbringing of the pupils under their care, it is important that Muslim teachers who understand the pupils' problems, and who can take on pastoral care roles and positively influence the character of the pupils by their own actions and behaviours, are appointed at Islamic schools. As faith (*iman*), knowledge (*'ilm*) and action (*'amal*) are integrally related, education cannot be divorced from its effect on the character of the pupils, the formation of their attitudes and the development of their perspectives on life and the world. Both teachers and pupils participate in the process of preserving and passing on the tradition of knowledge and learning as well as the essential traits of ethics and morality. Through a proper curriculum and Qur'anic pedagogy, Islamic schools are meant to nurture innate goodness in pupils and encourage them to establish a relationship with God and live with the consciousness of God's presence. The religious ambience of the school should have a lasting effect on the physical, mental, moral and emotional development of the pupils, who will learn to develop their faculties and uphold their own dignity. Teachers will enable pupils to reflect on their personal and social situation and accept the responsibility to do good work, and ultimately situate their thoughts and actions in terms of God.

Moral and spiritual developments are integrally related in Islam, as one cannot stand without the other. Muslim schools should foster the development of a strong set of positive values, derived from the Qur'an and Sunnah, as a necessary element in spiritual development. Pupils should also be taught to avoid such negative traits as lying, cheating, bullying, selfishness, intolerance, discrimination and the like. The decision by the British government (and other Western governments) to establish more faith schools will widen the opportunity to provide a moral ethos based on faith and give pupils and the community a sense of spirituality in a society that is becoming increasingly secular. These schools will facilitate the provision of a moral and spiritual structure to life and learning which is currently missing in ordinary state schools. Even though the British Education Act 1988 speaks of spiritual development, in practice there is a noticeable vacuum in this area. As I have argued elsewhere,[44] secular education cannot impart spirituality in its essential form. This is because spirituality is beyond its comprehension. What it can conceive of, at best, is a veneer of spirituality or a limited kind of spirituality, as spiritual values can only be understood against the backdrop of a revealed religion and sacred law that impose restrictions on its followers and help maintain social equilibrium. Religion creates a sense of accountability to God and hence the realisation that there is a need to purify the soul. This, ideally, puts a check on prejudice, selfishness and hatred, and promotes love, tolerance and understanding among people.

CITIZENSHIP EDUCATION

Citizenship is one of the compulsory national curriculum subjects in the UK, so the question for Islamic schools is not whether to engage in citizenship education, but rather what sort of citizenship education they wish to develop. In a liberal society where religion does not occupy a prominent place, the relationship between citizenship education and religion is a problematic one. Citizenship education should develop in pupils the skills to live well in a family and community, to negotiate in a fair and friendly way, and to have respect for people's rights irrespective of their faith. It should show them how to become good citizens and take part in the flourishing of the society as responsible and active citizens. It should be made clear to them how religion can play a part in attaining these goals. Too often the role that religion can play has been underestimated and ignored in the modern secular discussion of citizenship, and religion is even portrayed as an obstacle to responsible citizenship. It would be a very defective citizenship education that encouraged pupils to see it purely in secular terms and ignore the fact that many of their fellow citizens draw inspiration and guidance from religion. Moral education is indissolubly linked to political education. The concept of citizenship must be placed in relation to the concepts of justice, freedom, loyalty, fairness and compassion, to each of which religion has many positive contributions to make. Islam has clear moral principles or norms, which it shares with other revealed religions, and many of these are upheld by those who profess no religion; when put into practice, these can help our society flourish and progress, which should be central to citizenship education in Islamic schools. To ignore the spiritual and moral imperatives of religion in the discussion of citizenship can have far-reaching consequences not only for one's own country but also for the wider world, especially as more people are engaged positively with others across the globe and international links are intensifying.

In principle, the aims of secular public schools are to achieve social justice, equality, fairness and non-discrimination in order to create citizens with common values and shared loyalties. According to Pring, the arguments for public schools are based on 'the principles of equality, including equal respect for persons, and the preparation for living in a community that requires a common culture to overcome divisions arising from "wealth and birth and social position"—and, one might add, religion'.[45] The common school's aim of promoting a set of shared values and a sense of common citizenship and providing equal opportunities is laudable, but the liberal concept of adhering to common values and shared loyalties can lead to tension between the notion of assimilation into the broader society and careful adaptation to its culture. Akgündüz observes:

> Generally speaking, Muslim minorities—once admitted as full citizens in a European country—cease to be minorities (of foreigners) according to the law, although they will always be a minority in terms of culture and, above all, ethnic and religious background. They should not be singled out and should not be considered second or third class citizens. After all, with the obtaining of their new citizenships, they are accorded equal rights and obligations towards their new homeland, and humanity at large.[46]

Children should be made aware of the full participation and equal rights of the various ethnic and religious communities present in our society, as well as the principles of social justice towards all, so as to engender in them a sense of equal and full citizenship. They should also be made aware of the benefits this bestows and the obligations it entails. Muslims must adhere to the laws of the country in which they live, whether in the West or the East, whether under Islamic rule or not, as long as the law is not in contradiction to the religion of Islam. According to a saying of the Prophet (p.b.u.h.), 'It is necessary upon a Muslim to listen to and obey the ruler, as long as one is not ordered to carry out a sin. If he is commanded to commit a sin, then there is no adherence and obedience.'[47] When loyalty to certain principles of the state conflicts with loyalty to one's religion, societal tensions and disagreements can arise, in which case one should try to resolve the problem through the exercise of great caution and wisdom—through dialogue, negotiation, having recourse to law and patience (*sabr*)—so that any attempt to solve the problem does not lead to greater harm.

ISLAMIC SCHOOLS AND OTHER RELIGIONS

Through a strong pastoral care programme, Islamic schools should promote understanding among people so that they learn to develop good relationships with all other cultures and religions. One of the aims of the Association of Muslim Schools (AMS), which is an umbrella organisation looking after the interests of some 150 Muslim schools in the UK, is:

> [To] promote better understanding and positive relationships between different faiths and cultural traditions within the UK and contribute to the creation of a harmonious and cohesive society that is based on principles of mutual respect, justice and sound acquisition and application of holistic education.[48]

To be nurtured in the Islamic faith requires pupils to learn that Muslims believe that Abraham, Moses, David and Jesus—who conveyed God's message to people—are the prophets of God. The messages they conveyed—the Torah, the Psalms and the Evangel (Gospels)—are revelations from God. We are not suggesting that schools should promote a syncretic approach to religion or consider all religions to be of equal worth. There are sharp theological differences between Islam and other religions of which the pupils should be made aware so that the unique identity of Islam becomes clear to them. Theistic religions believe in the Absolute attributes of God, but the manifestations and expressions of those Absolutes are different in different communities, which gives them their distinctive identities. An Islamic school will prepare its pupils to be aware of the existence of distinctive and different styles of life inspired by various religious or non-religious beliefs. However, instead of conflicts, Islamic schools should use these differences to provide opportunities to know and cooperate with one another for the common good. Students of Islamic schools should be taught that the roots of the fundamental values of religions are the same. By demonstrating a unity of moral purpose, Islamic schools can contribute to the enrichment of the larger community, thus playing an important role in bringing together different religious groups to overcome any sense of disharmony and reinforce a shared common citizenship.

The Curriculum of Islamic Schools

In order to realise the aims and objectives of Islamic education it is necessary for Islamic schools to have an Islamic curriculum. A curriculum reflects the concept of human beings in which the society believes, the cultures and traditions it has inherited and the goals it wants to achieve. In an ideal Islamic curriculum, different branches of knowledge are seen not in segregation but in the context of unified Truth, which raises the question of how to integrate Islamic beliefs and traditions with the statutory national curriculum of the country. We immediately encounter a number of problems. Firstly, teachers have not yet succeeded in developing such a curriculum due to various reasons. Some work in this area has already been done and much more is needed, which can perhaps be undertaken by various Muslim educational organisations across the country. Secondly, one needs to consider whether the integrated or 'Islamicised' national curriculum—assuming one has been developed—will also deliver what is legally required. A carefully developed and delivered curriculum should be able to achieve this, but probably at the cost of longer school hours, a greater workload and a larger workforce. Thirdly, the Islamic unified approach may appear to impinge on the autonomy of each discipline, in accordance with the Western liberal concept of education. The Islamic unitary principle requires that all branches of knowledge be integrated into a coherent whole, and the concept of 'autonomy' must operate within this unified concept of knowledge. The problem of introducing Islamic ideas into a largely secular curriculum without changing the ideological basis of the latter is that any correctives applied will not be entirely satisfactory.

The secular philosophy is deep rooted and permeates all aspects of the curriculum and the school ethos. As secular education is rooted in the philosophy of the Enlightenment, it does not endorse the concepts of monotheism (*tawhid*), prophethood (*risalah*) and the hereafter (*akhirah*).[49] An Islamic curriculum, on the other hand, will introduce these Islamic doctrines wherever possible in such a way that pupils fully understand their meanings and their bearing upon the individual and social life.

Islamic schools should teach Qur'anic recitation and memorisation, Arabic, Islamic studies and basic Islamic rules in the area of *'ibadah* (worship) in addition to the compulsory national curriculum subjects. Wherever possible, Islamic beliefs and values should be incorporated into the national curriculum. Sadaf Rizvi's research shows that teachers in some schools in the UK have developed 'Islamicised' lessons to bring in an Islamic interpretation of the topics taught in the national curriculum.[50] In the area of health and physical education in the Australian context, Chown and Barry have successfully integrated religious values, beliefs and traditions with the *Original Version of Health and Physical Education for the Australian Curriculum* in order to assist teachers and pupils in a variety of physical and health learning contexts.[51] Islamic schools should try to achieve coherence between the key national priorities in education and the Islamic understanding of the issues involved.

It is beyond the scope of this chapter to present a comprehensive discussion on how Islamic values and beliefs can be integrated with the national curriculum. The process of Islamicisation of the national curriculum requires teachers to be engaged in the task of identifying those elements that are openly or subtly damaging to the Islamic development of children and presenting alternative Islamic views so that they can see the difference between the secular and Islamic approaches. For example, in addition to presenting the theory of evolution as required by the national curriculum, the school should also present the Qur'anic view of creation. Any Eurocentric bias in history and geography curricula should be countered by a balanced and honest presentation of contributions of various communities to the making of the world's civilisations. Likewise, Islamic values must be reflected in the teaching of sex education, music, art and physical education.

Conclusion

Muslim parents feel that the mainstream state school cannot provide for their needs. Their desire for the establishment of Islamic schools has been prompted by many concerns, such as protecting the religious beliefs and values of Muslim children, imparting Islamic education, and avoiding discrimination and racism. The common school's concept of shared national identity does not give due weight to the diverse cultural identities of its pupils. Muslim parents want to send their children to schools where they will receive a good education but in an environment where they can maintain their identity, cherished religious values and cultures. They realise there will inevitably be some clashes between the values of the school and those of the home, but as they do not want their children to be educated at the cost of their religious values and traditions, they expect the conflict to be kept to a minimum. Many unnecessary tensions can be avoided in an Islamic school, where children will be exposed to an environment on a daily basis where they will feel at home and where they will have greater opportunities to discover their own identity and sense of belonging. They will realise that they are Muslims but are also part of British society. Their sense of citizenship will be properly formed as they see that their cultures and values are being respected by the wider society. There will be more acceptance and less dissatisfaction, more cooperation and less radicalisation, more religious tolerance and less hostility, and more social harmony and less tension. Eventually, a British Muslim identity will emerge that Muslims will be able to accept as their own. Anything other than this will simply create tensions, confusions and conflicts. To be educated in a secular school in whose ethos God has no or little role to play, day after day, for many years at an impressionable age, will surely mould the attitude of the children in a way that might far outweigh the influence of the home and the mosque. On the other hand, through the proper delivery of an integrated Islamic curriculum, and by providing opportunities for prayer and worship, the school will strengthen students' relationship with God and foster a sense belonging and commitment to being together.

While mainstream educationalists need to understand what it is like to see the world from a Muslim perspective, Muslim parents and teachers must understand and contribute to the discourse that is emerging about the place of Islamic schools in Britain. As Lawson has noted, significant progress needs to be made in the mutual understanding between Islamic schools, Muslim communities and the wider society as a whole. The success of Islamic schools will depend on their management, leadership and vision.[52]

NOTES

1. Ruhul Ameen and Nasima Hassan, "Are Faith Schools Educationally Defensible?," *Research in Teacher Education* 3, no. 1 (April 2013): 11–17.
2. J. Mark Halstead, *The Case for Muslim Voluntary-Aided Schools: Some philosophical reflections* (Cambridge: The Islamic Academy, 1986), 65.
3. "Q & A: Muslim schools", accessed 15 February 2017, http://news.bbc.co.uk/2/hi/uk_news/education/6338219.stm. (Archived by WebCite® at http://www.webcitation.org/6oMvYeCvU.)
4. Michael Swann, *Education for all: The Report of the Committee of Inquiry into the Education of Children from Ethnic Minority Groups* (London: Her Majesty's Stationery Office, 1985), 509.
5. Humanist Philosophers' Group, *Religious schools: The case against* (London: British Humanist Association, 2001). Liz Lightfoot, "Muslim schools accused of 'undermining our society'," accessed 16 February 2017, http://www.telegraph.co.uk/news/uknews/1481425/Muslim-schools-accused-of-undermining-our-society.html. (Archived by WebCite® at http://www.webcitation.org/6oMw2aLrU.)
6. Terence H. McLaughlin, "'Education for all' and religious schools," in *Education for a Pluralist Society. Philosophical Perspectives on the Swan Report—Bedford Way Paper No. 30*, ed. Graham Haydon (London: London Institute of Education, University of London, 1987). Terence H. McLaughlin, "The Ethics of Separate schools," in *Ethics, Ethnicity and Education*, ed. Mal Leicester and Monica Taylor (London: Kogan Page, 1992).
7. Syed A. Ashraf, "The Islamic Response: faith-based education in a multi-faith multicultural country," in *Agenda for Educational Change*, ed. John Shortt and Trevor Cooling (Leicester: Apollos, 1997), 276–278.
8. J. Mark Halstead, *The Case for Muslim Voluntary-Aided Schools: Some philosophical reflections* (Cambridge: The Islamic Academy, 1986).
9. The Qur'an, 51:56.
10. Annemarie Schimmel, *Mystical Dimensions of Islam* (Chapel Hill, NC: The University of North Carolina Press, 1975).
11. Seyyed H. Nasr, "The Islamic Philosophers' Views on Education," *Muslim Education Quarterly* 2, no. 4 (1984): 5–16.
12. Burhan al-Din Al-Zarnuji, *Instruction of the Student: The Method of Learning*, trans. Gustave E. Von Grunebaum and Theodora M. Abel (Chicago: Starlatch Press, 2003), 6.
13. Syed F. Alatas, "Ibn Khaldun on Education and Knowledge," Oxford Scholarship Online, accessed 16 February 2017, http://www.oxfordscholarship.com/view/10.1093/acprof:oso/9780198090458.001.0001/acprof-9780198090458-chapter-3.

THE EMERGENCE OF ISLAMIC SCHOOLS: A CONTEXTUAL BACKGROUND   29

14. 'Abdul-Rahman S. 'Abdullah, *Educational Theory: A Qur'anic Outlook* (Makkah: Umm Al-Qura University, 1982).
15. Al-Zarnuji, *Instruction*, 6.
16. Al-Imam al-Ghazzali, *Mizan al-'amal*, ed. Sulayman Dunya (Cairo: Dal al-Ma'arif Press, 1964), 351.
17. al-Ghazzali, *Mizan*, 328.
18. Franz Rosenthal, *Knowledge Triumphant: The concept of knowledge in medieval Islam* (Leiden: Brill, 2007), 95.
19. Syed S. Husain and Syed A. Ashraf (eds.), *Crisis in Muslim Education* (Kent: Hodder and Stoughton, and Jeddah: King Abdulaziz University, 1979), 37–38.
20. Seyyed H. Nasr, "The Islamic Philosophers' Views on Education," *Muslim Education Quarterly* 2, no. 4 (1984): 7.
21. Syed M. Al-Naquib Al-Attas, *The Concept of Education in Islam: A framework for an Islamic philosophy of education* (Kuala Lumpur: ABIM, 1980), 28.
22. Al-Attas, *The Concept*, 22.
23. Hadi Sharifi, "The Islamic as Opposed to the Modern Philosophy of Education," in *Crisis in Muslim Education*, 49–50.
24. King Abdulaziz University, *First World Conference on Muslim Education: Conference Book* (Jeddah: King Abdulaziz University, 1977), 78.
25. 'Abdullah, *Educational Theory*, 119.
26. Al-Imam Al-Ghazali, *Al-Ghazali on Islamic Guidance*, trans. Muhammad Abul Quasem (Kuala Lumpur: Universiti Kebangsaan Malaysia, 1979), 20.
27. Ahmad Ibn Hanbal, *Musnad*, II, 371, 441.
28. The National Secular Society, "Secular Charter," accessed 17 January 2017, http://www.secularism.org.uk/secularcharter.html. (Archived by WebCite® at http://www.webcitation.org/6na88of7m.)
29. Syed A. Ashraf, "Foreword" to *The Case for Muslim Voluntary-Aided Schools*, vi.
30. Terence H. McLaughlin, "The Distinctiveness of Catholic Education," in *The Contemporary Catholic School: Context, Identity and Diversity*, ed. Terence H. McLaughlin, Joseph O'Keeffe S.J., and Bernadette O'Keeffe (London: Falmer Press, 1996), 145–146.
31. Hilary White, "UK gvmt to faith schools: promote homosexuality and other religions or face closure," 2 February 2015, accessed 16 February 2017, https://www.lifesitenews.com/news/uk-gvmt-to-faith-schools-promote-homosexuality-and-other-religions-or-face. (Archived by WebCite® at http://www.webcitation.org/6oMwbTon4.)
32. J. Mark Halstead, "In Place of a Conclusion: The Common School and the Melting Pot," *Journal of Philosophy of Education* 41, no. 4 (2007): 840.

33. Elaine McCreery, Liz Jones, and Rachel Holmes, "Why do Muslim Parents want Muslim Schools?," *Early Years: An International Journal of Research and Development* 27, no. 3 (2007): 203–219.
34. Chris Hewer, "Schools for Muslims," *Oxford Review of Education* 27, no. 4 (2001): 518.
35. Sadaf Rizvi, "Muslim faith schools are teaching tolerance and respect through 'Islamicised' curriculum," *The Conversation*, accessed 15 February 2017, https://theconversation.com/how-muslim-faith-schools-are-teaching-tolerance-and-respect-through-islamicised-curriculum-32239. (Archived by WebCite® at http://www.webcitation.org/6oLRcqKGU.)
36. Saeeda J. A. Shah, "Muslim schools in Secular Societies: persistence or resistance!," *British Journal of Religious Education* 34, no. 1 (2012): 51–56.
37. Michael S. Merry and Geert Driessen, "Islamic Schools in Three Western Countries: Policy and Procedure," *Comparative Education* 41, no. 4 (November 2005): 426.
38. McLaughlin, "The Distinctiveness," 137–138.
39. J. Mark Halstead, "Should Schools Reinforce Children's Religious Identity?," *Religious Education* 90, no. 3–4 (1995): 360.
40. Ameen and Nasima Hassan, "Are Faith Schools," 16.
41. Halstead, "Should Schools Reinforce," 366.
42. The Qur'an, 21:92.
43. *Muslim*.
44. Shaikh A. Mabud, "Editorial," *Muslim Education Quarterly* 17, no. 3 (2000): 1–4.
45. Richard Pring, "The Common School," *Journal of Philosophy of Education* 41, no. 4 (2007): 505.
46. Ahmet Akgündüz, "A Position on the Islamic Concept of Citizenship and Muslim Minorities," *Islam and Civilisational Renewal: A journal devoted to contemporary issues and policy research* 1, no. 1 (2009): 158.
47. *Sahih al-Bukhari*, no. 2796.
48. The Association of Muslim Schools, UK, "The AMS Brochure," accessed 17 January 2017, http://ams-uk.org/wp-content/uploads/2013/12/AMS-Brochure.pdf. (Archived by WebCite® at http://www.webcitation.org/6nShVEB32.)
49. William Chittick, "The Goal of Islamic Education," in *Education in the Light of Tradition*, ed. Jane Casewit (Indiana: World Wisdom, 2011), 85.
50. Rizvi, "Muslim Faith Schools."
51. Dylan Chown and Graeme Barry, *Introduction to the Alternate Version of Health and Physical Education for the Australian Curriculum* (Cambridge: Cambridge University Press, 2016).

52. Ibrahim Lawson, *Leading Islamic Schools in the UK: A challenge for us all* (Spring 2005), accessed 16 February 2017, http://webarchive.nationalarchives.gov.uk/20130401151715/http://www.education.gov.uk/publications/eOrderingDownload/RASLAW05.pdf.pdf. (Archived by WebCite® at http://www.webcitation.org/6oMtAWGRj.)

Bibliography

'Abdullah, 'Abdul-Rahman S. *Educational Theory: A Qur'anic Outlook*. Makkah: Umm Al-Qura University, 1982.
Akgündüz, Ahmet. "A Position on the Islamic Concept of Citizenship and Muslim Minorities." *Islam and Civilisational Renewal: A Journal Devoted to Contemporary Issues and Policy Research* 1, no. 1 (2009): 142–158.
Alatas, Syed F. "Ibn Khaldun on Education and Knowledge," Oxford Scholarship Online. Accessed 16 February 2017. http://www.oxfordscholarship.com/view/10.1093/acprof:oso/9780198090458.001.0001/acprof-9780198090458-chapter-3.
Ameen, Ruhul, and Nasima Hassan. "Are Faith Schools Educationally Defensible?" *Research in Teacher Education* 3, no. 1 (April 2013): 11–17.
Ashraf, Syed A. Foreword to *The Case for Muslim Voluntary-Aided Schools: Some Philosophical Reflections*, by Halstead, J. Mark, v–ix. Cambridge: The Islamic Academy, 1986.
———. "The Islamic Response: Faith-Based Education in a Multifaith Multicultural Country." In *Agenda for Educational Change*, ed. John Shortt and Trevor Cooling, 269–279. Leicester: Apollos, 1997.
The Association of Muslim Schools, UK. *The AMS Brochure*. Accessed 17 January 2017. http://ams-uk.org/wp-content/uploads/2013/12/AMS-Brochure.pdf. (Archived by WebCite® at http://www.webcitation.org/6nShVEB32.)
Al-Attas, Syed M. Al-Naquib. *The Concept of Education in Islam: A Framework for an Islamic Philosophy of Education*. Kuala Lumpur: ABIM, 1980.
BBC. "Q & A: Muslim Schools." Accessed 15 February 2017. http://news.bbc.co.uk/2/hi/uk_news/education/6338219.stm. (Archived by WebCite® at http://www.webcitation.org/6oMvYeCvU.)
Chittick, William. "The Goal of Islamic Education." In *Education in the Light of Tradition*, ed. Jane Casewit, 85–92. Indiana: World Wisdom, 2011.
Chown, Dylan, and Graeme Barry. *Introduction to the Alternate Version of Health and Physical Education for the Australian Curriculum*. Cambridge: Cambridge University Press, 2016.
Al-Ghazali. *Al-Ghazali on Islamic Guidance*. Trans. Muhammad Abul Quasem. Kuala Lumpur: Uiversiti Kebangsaan Malaysia, 1979.
Al-Ghazzali, Al-Imam. *Mizan al-'amal*. Edited by Sulayman Dunya. Cairo: Dal al-Ma'arif Press, 1964.

Halstead, J. Mark. *The Case for Muslim Voluntary-Aided Schools: Some Philosophical Reflections*. Cambridge: The Islamic Academy, 1986.

———. "Should Schools Reinforce Children's Religious Identity?" *Religious Education* 90, no. 3–4 (1995): 360–376.

———. "In Place of a Conclusion: The Common School and the Melting Pot." *Journal of Philosophy of Education* 41, no. 4 (2007): 829–842.

Hewer, Chris. "Schools for Muslims." *Oxford Review of Education* 27, no. 4 (2001): 515–527.

Humanist Philosophers' Group. *Religious Schools: The Case Against*. London: British Humanist Association, 2001.

Husain, Syed S., and Syed A. Ashraf, eds. *Crisis in Muslim Education*. Kent: Hodder and Stoughton and Jeddah: King Abdulaziz University, 1979.

King Abdulaziz University. *First World Conference on Muslim Education: Conference Book*. Jeddah: King Abdulaziz University, 1977.

Lawson, Ibrahim. *Leading Islamic Schools in the UK: A Challenge for Us All*. Spring 2005. Accessed 16 February 2017. http://webarchive.nationalarchives.gov.uk/20130401151715/http://www.education.gov.uk/publications/eOrderingDownload/RASLAW05.pdf.pdf. (Archived by WebCite® at http://www.webcitation.org/6oMtAWGRj.)

Lightfoot, Liz. "Muslim Schools Accused of 'Undermining Our Society'." Accessed 16 February 2017. http://www.telegraph.co.uk/news/uknews/1481425/Muslim-schools-accused-of-undermining-our-society.html. (Archived by WebCite® at http://www.webcitation.org/6oMw2aLrU.)

Mabud, Shaikh A. "Editorial." *Muslim Education Quarterly* 17, no. 3 (2000): 1–4.

McCreery, Elaine, Liz Jones, and Rachel Holmes. "Why Do Muslim Parents Want Muslim Schools?" *Early Years: An International Journal of Research and Development* 27, no. 3 (2007): 203–219.

McLaughlin, Terence H. "'Education for All' and Religious Schools." In *Education for a Pluralist Society. Philosophical Perspectives on the Swan Report—Bedford Way Paper No. 30*, ed. Graham Haydon. London: London Institute of Education, University of London, 1987.

———. "The Ethics of Separate Schools." In *Ethics, Ethnicity and Education*, ed. Mal Leicester and Monica Taylor, 114–136. London: Kogan Page, 1992.

———. "The Distinctiveness of Catholic Education." In *The Contemporary Catholic School: Context, Identity and Diversity*, ed. Terence H. McLaughlin, Joseph O'Keefe S.J., and Bernadette O'Keeffe, 136–154. London: Falmer Press, 1996.

Merry, Michael S., and Geert Driessen. "Islamic Schools in Three Western Countries: Policy and Procedure." *Comparative Education* 41, no. 4 (November 2005): 411–432.

Nasr, Seyyed Hossein. "The Islamic Philosophers' Views on Education." *Muslim Education Quarterly* 2, no. 4 (1984): 5–16.
The National Secular Society. "Secular Charter." Accessed 17 January 2017. http://www.secularism.org.uk/secularcharter.html. (Archived by WebCite® at http://www.webcitation.org/6na88of7m.)
Pring, Richard. "The Common School." *Journal of Philosophy of Education* 41, no. 4 (2007): 503–522.
Rizvi, Sadaf. "Muslim Faith Schools Are Teaching Tolerance and Respect Through 'Islamicised' Curriculum." *The Conversation*. Accessed 15 February 2017. https://theconversation.com/how-muslim-faith-schools-are-teaching-tolerance-and-respect-through-islamicised-curriculum-32239. (Archived by WebCite® at http://www.webcitation.org/6oLRcqKGU.)
Rosenthal, Franz. *Knowledge Triumphant: The Concept of Knowledge in Medieval Islam*. Leiden: Brill, 2007.
Schimmel, Annemarie. *Mystical Dimensions of Islam*. Chapel Hill, NC: The University of North Carolina Press, 1975.
Shah, Saeeda J.A. "Muslim Schools in Secular Societies: Persistence or Resistance!" *British Journal of Religious Education* 34, no. 1 (2012): 51–65.
Sharifi, Hadi. "The Islamic as Opposed to the Modern Philosophy of Education." In *Crisis in Muslim Education*, ed. Syed S. Husain and Syed A. Ashraf, 47–50. Kent: Hodder and Stoughton and Jeddah: King Abdulaziz University, 1979.
Swann, Michael. *Education for All: The Report of the Committee of Inquiry into the Education of Children from Ethnic Minority Groups*. London: Her Majesty's Stationery Office, 1985.
White, Hilary. "UK Gvmt to Faith Schools: Promote Homosexuality and Other Religions or Face Closure," 2 February 2015. Accessed 16 February 2017. https://www.lifesitenews.com/news/uk-gvmt-to-faith-schools-promote-homosexuality-and-other-religions-or-face. (Archived by WebCite® at http://www.webcitation.org/6oMwbTon4.)
Al-Zarnuji, Burhan al-Din. *Instruction of the Student: The Method of Learning*. Trans. Gustave E. Von Grunebaum and Theodora M. Abel. Chicago: Starlatch Press, 2003.

CHAPTER 3

Muslim Schools in Australia: Development and Transition

Jan A. Ali

INTRODUCTION

As a minority religious group in Australia, Muslims, since first arriving in the country, have been concerned about the education and future of their children. As new arrivals, Muslims placed a priority on securing employment for themselves, but at the same time held grave concerns about the preservation of religious identity and culture. The project of building Muslim schools in Australia has been driven by Muslim enthusiasm for a refined religious identity and the need to preserve Islamic cultural traditions in a plural secular society. The philosophical underpinnings of this nascent approach were to make Muslim schools places for Islamic practices, the nurturing of an Islamic ethos, the inculcation of Islamic moral and ethical behaviour, the preservation of Islamic culture, the Islamisation

This chapter argues that this transformation and transition has made Muslim schools spaces for commercial activities and in the process rendered Islamic education itself a commercial transaction.

J. A. Ali (✉)
Western Sydney University, Penrith, NSW, Australia
e-mail: Jan.Ali@westernsydney.edu.au

© The Author(s) 2018
M. Abdalla et al. (eds.), *Islamic Schooling in the West*,
https://doi.org/10.1007/978-3-319-73612-9_3

of knowledge and the production of "good" Muslims in whom rested the representation and the future of Islam in Australia.

Like in other Western secular democracies, the development of Muslim schools in Australia is an important sociological phenomenon that underscores Muslim dissatisfaction with a national education system built upon secular principles and Judaeo-Christian values. There are some serious concerns around certain subjects, such as sex education and Darwin's theory of evolution, which are taught as part of the standard Australian curriculum. Additionally, there is a perception among some Muslims that the Australian mainstream education system is insensitive to the centrality of Islam in the lives of Muslim pupils.

Some of the Islamic values and practices envisaged for the Islamic education system were the observation of dress codes in school uniform, the offering of ritual prayers, serving of *halal* (permissible) food and a minimum requisite of gender segregation at the senior level of schooling. Additionally, the school curriculum was expected to reflect a strong focus on Islamic studies, the Arabic language, Qur'anic lessons as well as Islamic theology and cosmology. The call was for a spiritually and mundanely balanced education system with a holistic approach to pedagogical practice and learning that gives priority to Islamic values, ideals and morality, which are deeply embedded in the entire school curriculum.

This is the education system infused with Islamic methodology, morality, values, ideals and precepts that the Australian pioneers of Muslim schools imagined. In this view education had resounding religious overtones, embodying Islamic spirituality which was perceived to guarantee the survival of the Muslim community, preserve Islamic culture, Islamise knowledge and produce a distinct Australian Islamic identity. I call this a Utopian Muslim School Model. This, from an Islamic viewpoint, was a noble endeavour which had all the hallmarks of an education revolution.

In this chapter, I want to posit that this much anticipated education revolution in the Australian Muslim community never occurred. What did happen, however, was that Muslim schools were built and filled with Muslim pupils, but as the schools developed, they gradually transformed and transitioned from a Utopian Muslim School Model to a Corporate Muslim School Model. This radical shift, as part and parcel of the new era of neo-liberalism, led to a focus on the adoption of new governance structures to make sure that the schools were operating and being managed better as 'entrepreneurial educational institutions' under the new system of academic capitalism. Muslim schools as teaching institutions were being mobilised for monopoly capitalism and converted into robust for-profit performers in the marketplace, selling Muslims their own faith—Islam—rather than sharing it.

Using the neo-liberalism framework, I will attempt to show the transition of a Utopian Muslim School Model to a Corporate Muslim School Model. I want to argue that Muslim schools have been undergoing significant social change, and Muslims have been feeling the impact on their everyday practices. As the process of marketisation churns the wheels of Islamic schools, it threatens to reduce the significance of Islamic education in the educational and practical lives of young Muslims as well as the role of Islam, within the school as a neo-liberal for-profit institution and outside it. In the process, these attempts have produced commercialisation as a central feature of the Muslim school, which threatens the production of Islamic knowledge and ultimately Islam.

Islam in Australia: A Brief History

Muslim migration to Australia from different parts of the Muslim world has resulted in a diverse Muslim community in Australia. Muslims arrived in Australia much earlier than European settlers, as early as the seventeenth century, when Makassan fishermen from the south-western corner of the Indonesian island of Sulawesi made seasonal trips to the north and north-west coastlines of the Australian continent in search of *trepang*, sea slugs commonly known as *bêche-de-mer*.[1]

Due to their small numbers, temporary residency and the absence of a fully formed community structure, these Muslims made unsystematic and only localised impacts on Australian social and cultural life at the time.[2] Subsequently, cameleers, commonly known as 'Ghans', were brought from the Indian subcontinent during the nineteenth century to help explore the Australian deserts and establish trade and communication routes,[3] and in the process formed small Muslim communities called 'Ghantowns'.[4] The first 'Ghantown' mosque was built in 1889 in Broken Hill in outback New South Wales and the building survives today as a museum occupied by the Broken Hill Historical Society. The Afghans also built mosques in Adelaide in South Australia in 1890, in Perth in Western Australia in 1904, and in 1907 in Brisbane, Queensland, all of which continue to function as mosques to this day.[5] These early mosques symbolised the initial establishment of Islam in Australia. However, the introduction of the railway in the remote interior and the utility truck made camel cartage redundant and hastened the demise of the industry, and with it the gradual public disappearance of Islam.[6]

Post-Second World War Muslim Immigration

After the Second World War, the Muslim population began to increase again in Australia. Australian governments and businesses realised that in order for Australia to be a part of the post-war world development, it had to grow demographically and economically. The sourcing of large numbers of migrant workers, therefore, was related to the dynamics of the global economic position of developed capitalist societies such as Australia.[7] The need for large numbers of migrant workers for Australia was not just a national issue but was directly related to the nature of Australia's economy and its positioning in the global capitalist economy. At the end of the Second World War, Australia was a developing capitalist society that had the necessary preconditions, financial structure, and political and natural resources to develop industrially; however, it did not have adequate labour resources and capital to achieve this development.[8]

While the mass immigration programme initiated in 1947 sought migrants from British origins, the ambitious immigration targets soon saw the net expand and gradually become more global and culturally diverse. As a result, Australia started receiving immigrants from overseas and Muslim immigration was part of this process. Between 1947 and 1971 the Muslim population showed real signs of growth, increasing from 2704 to 22,311.[9] The last quarter of the twentieth century and the first decade of the twenty-first century then saw a steep increase in the size of Australia's Muslim population. For instance, in 1991 there were 148,096 Muslims in Australia, constituting 0.9% of the total population[10]; in 1996 there were 200,902, constituting 1.1%[11]; in 2001 there were 281,578, constituting 1.5%[12]; in 2006 there were 340,392, constituting 1.7%[13]; and in 2011 there were 476,290, constituting 2.2% of the population.[14]

Though Muslims live across the Australian continent, they are mainly concentrated in New South Wales and Victoria (as shown in Table 3.1). In all states and territories, Muslims seem to prefer the capital cities.

In New South Wales, where the largest Muslim population lives, Muslims constituted 3.2% of the total state population.[15] Within New South Wales, over 50% of the Muslim population lived almost entirely

Table 3.1 Australian Muslim population by state/territory

State and territory	Total population	Muslims	% of Muslim population	Muslim % of total
New South Wales	6,917,657	219,378	46.1	3.2
Victoria	5,354,040	152,779	32.1	2.9
Queensland	4,332,738	34,048	7.1	0.8
South Australia	1,596,570	19,511	4.1	1.2
Western Australia	2,239,171	39,116	8.2	1.7
Tasmania	495,351	1708	0.4	0.3
Northern Territory	211,944	1587	0.3	0.7
Australian Capital Territory	357,218	7434	1.6	2.1
Total	21,507,719	476,291	100	2.2

Source: Census 2011 in Riaz Hassan 2015

within a radius of fifty kilometres of Sydney, making it the city with the greatest concentration of Muslims in Australia. The radius has grown over the years and is now certainly more than fifty kilometres.

Given that the events of 9/11 and subsequent upheavals have given a new impetus to migration—migrants, refugees and asylum seekers from the Middle East and other Muslim-majority countries seeking to relocate to the rich 'North', including Australia—it is safe to assume that the number of Muslims has increased since the last census. However, Muslims globally are not a homogeneous people and are divided essentially along national, ethnic and parochial lines. Australia's Muslim population is also very diverse, and Abdullah Saeed notes that, between 1975 and 2000, Muslims have come from over seventy different nations, making them the most ethnically diverse religious group in Australia.[16] Muslims are also divided along sectarian and ideological lines, complicating the diversity even further. According to Saeed,[17] Sunnis make up the majority of Muslims in Australia, followed by the various Shi'a sects such as Zaydis, Ismailis, Druze, Jafaris and Alawites, as well as 'a wide spectrum of [other] Islamic sects'.[18]

MUSLIM SCHOOLS IN AUSTRALIA

Despite sharing the same faith in one single God—Allah—and the prophethood of Muhammad, Australian Muslims are internally a culturally and linguistically diverse community.[19] This diversity is reflected in the way Muslims practise their faith and go about organising and managing the affairs of their individual communities. Peter Jones remarks that 'The ethnic diversity within the Islamic community in Australia prevents it from being a homogenous community, and to this day this is reflected in the diversity of the organisations, let alone the individuals, who started each school'.[20] The secular nature of the Australian state also impacts on this process as it relates to the question of the social integration of Muslim immigrant communities and the notions of citizenship and belonging. Furthermore, unlike Muslim minority communities in some other Western countries, for instance, in the United Kingdom, where provisions existed for Muslim children to receive education about their faith in after-school or weekend programmes in addition to their normal daytime schooling, Australian Muslim communities did not have such provisions for their children in the early 1980s.[21] The emergence of Muslim schools in Australia thus grew out of the concern around Muslim identity, citizenship and belonging and a desire to educate Muslim children about their religious and cultural traditions.[22] Many Muslims felt that in order to preserve a Muslim identity and Islamic culture, and at the same time feel a sense of belonging to broader Australian society as full citizens, they had to create an environment, especially for their children—the future representatives of Islam and their community—in which these could be properly and effectively nurtured.[23]

The first Muslim schools in Australia were started in 1983.[24] King Khalid Islamic College, now called Australian International Academy, was established that year in Coburg, Melbourne. In New South Wales, Al-Noori Muslim School (formerly known as Al Noori Muslim Primary School) was also unofficially started in 1983 in the south-western Sydney suburb of Greenacre.[25] Its origin is rooted in the vision of its husband-and-wife founders Silma and Siddiq Buckley. When their daughter was turned away from Presbyterian Ladies' College in Croydon, an inner-western suburb of Sydney, for wearing hijab (a head veil) in the early 1980s, Silma and Siddiq were given an impetus to realise their vision for a Muslim school.

Since the establishment of the first two Muslim schools in Australia in 1983, the number of Muslim schools has grown manifold and it is estimated that there were thirty-five Muslim schools in Australia in 2014.[26] The demand for Muslim schools that provide for the educational needs of the young Muslim population of Australia is the driver of this rapid increase in the number of Muslim schools in recent decades.

Peter Jones reports that by 2008, 'a total of 15,938 students attended Islamic schools' across the major cities in Australia.[27] It is important to note, however, that this number of Muslim students attending Islamic schools constitutes a very small percentage of Muslim students overall when compared with the vast majority who attend non-Muslim schools—81% of Muslim primary school pupils and 87% of secondary school students.[28] This is due to a variety of social, educational and political factors.

Muslim schools in Australia are independent not-for-profit faith schools that offer Islamic studies, Arabic language and Qur'anic lessons,[29] in conjunction with 'the normal curriculum'[30] set by the Curriculum Council in each Australian state and territory. The additional Islamic studies, Arabic language and Qur'anic lessons constitute only 'six hours a week'[31] of the total curriculum and in the broader scheme of the teaching curriculum account for a meagre percentage.

According to Mah, in 2012 Muslim schools were represented in most states and territories, with the exception of Tasmania and the Northern Territory.[32] There were nineteen Muslim schools in Australia's most populated state, New South Wales, nine in Victoria, three in Western Australia, two in Queensland, one in South Australia and one in the Australian Capital Territory. The vast majority of these schools are providers of both primary and secondary schooling, with only a small number of these registered as primary schools. The teachers in these schools come from a variety of backgrounds, and 'While a few schools have wholly Muslim staff, most have around fifty percent non-Muslim staff'.[33]

The majority of Muslim schools are co-educational, with rare exceptions such as Al Zahra College in New South Wales and the Australian Islamic College in Western Australia, where only girls are enrolled at the secondary level.[34] While many Muslim schools are inclined to segregate girls and boys by the secondary school level,[35] not all schools practise gender segregation, and when gender segregation is practised it differs from school to school, with some schools simply seating girls and boys separately in the same classroom.[36]

A Hybrid Islamic Education

Given that Australia is a secular nation-state, public schools, or what may be described as government-run schools, in Australia do not offer a formal religious curriculum. Religiously inspired Muslim pupils have limited and in some cases no access to learning about their faith in public schools. Regarding Islamic schools in the context of three Western countries—the United States, the Netherlands and Belgium—Merry and Driessen report:

> For the small but growing number of Muslims who seek out an Islamic education for their children, public schools represent moral permissiveness and low academic achievement. Others are dismayed with the extent to which schools ignore the cultural and religious identities of Muslim children.[37]

What Merry and Driessen note in the context of the United States, the Netherlands and Belgium clearly resonates with the Australian situation. Many Australian Muslim parents are concerned that public schools do not provide religious education and that religion is 'left out of the syllabus',[38] and thus that they fail to produce an environment in which Islamic values, ethos, Muslim identity and Islamic social ethics are constantly cultivated and maintained. Muslim parents fear '"losing" their children and future generations to an open, predominantly Christian, but increasingly secular, society'[39] through the public schooling system. Irene Donohoue Clyne has observed that a large number of Australian Muslim parents expect their children to attend Muslim schools instead of state schools so children were kept away from secular influence and identity crisis, and at the same time were taught Islamic cultural and moral values. She says that Australian Muslim parents opt to send their children to 'Islamic schools, outside the existing state-controlled system, to provide an education which reflects Islamic values and practices'.[40] Furthermore, a *Sydney Morning Herald* journalist quoted Donohoue Clyne saying:

> Muslim parents choose Islamic schools because the secular education system is underpinned by Judeo-Christian values that either ignore Islam or present it in a biased manner. Like other Australian parents, Muslims believe private schools deliver high academic standards, discipline and a moral framework consistent with home values.[41]

There is also a perception among many Muslim parents that public schools may have the potential to feed negatively biased or inaccurate understandings of Islam to their children as well as expose them to anti-Islamic textbooks and secular theories and values. 'There were also reservations about some of the subjects taught in the normal Australian curriculum' and fear of losing control over the assimilation process of many Muslim students into unorthodox customs and un-Islamic ways of thinking.[42] Coupled with this, these parents understand that public schools disregard common Islamic rules governing diet, dress, gender relations and fundamental pillars of Islam and that there is an inadequate focus on discipline to keep children respectful and away from narcotics and alcohol. Muslim parents who want their children to have the opportunities of integration, social mobility and success in both the worldly and religious arenas are therefore 'concerned about the overall impact of the secular curriculum with its emphasis on a Euro-centric syllabus and no faith teaching'.[43]

Against this backdrop, many Muslim parents have opted to send their children to Muslim schools. They have done so in search of an authentic Islamic education in what I would like to call the Utopian Muslim School Model(utopian because this model offers a hybrid Islamic education with both secular and Islamic curricula, which Muslim parents want and which has been the goal of the pioneers of Muslim schools; this is a 'win–win' situation with a 'perfect' outcome). For these Muslim parents, an authentic Islamic education denotes 'a total Islamic education in which the values and ethos of Islam are incorporated into the entire school culture and curriculum',[44] in 'some kind of integrated education system whereby their children could not only learn about their faith, but learn about it in a school where Islamic values and practices permeated the whole curriculum'.[45]

For many Muslim parents, an Islam-friendly environment is seen to be critical to the production of an authentic Islamic education. Muslim parents see a close correlation between an authentic Islamic education, embodied in the Utopian Muslim School Model, and an environment in which Islam is both taught and normalised. In this connection, Mah found in her study in Australia that

> Most participants referred to the Islamic studies and the actions of the adults at the Muslim schools as sources from which they drew to develop as a Muslim. Two parents ... [described their] decision for keeping their children in the Muslim schools as essentially due to the all-Muslim environment these schools provided. Yet for other parents, a Muslim school was seen as the one-stop shop they relied upon to meet all of the academic, social and religious needs of their children.[46]

For many Muslims, this is an authentic Islamic education. It is an educational model in which Islamic culture is preserved, Muslim identity is inculcated, knowledge is Islamised, science and technology are taught and the not-for-profit status of the school is assured. Thus, the project of building Muslim schools or the establishment of a Muslim education system in plural secular Australia began with the question: 'How can a hybrid Islamic education be established?' 'Concerned members of the Muslim community then decided to establish a formal *hybrid* schooling option aimed at offering both secular and Islamic curriculum to their school-aged Muslim children' (italics in original).[47] A hybrid Islamic education, with Islam constituting the school's heart, is embodied in the Utopian Muslim School Model. A diagram of the model is provided in Fig. 3.1.

Many Muslim parents who embarked on a search for an authentic Islamic education eventually found it, or more likely thought they had found it, in the Utopian Muslim School Model. The Utopian Muslim

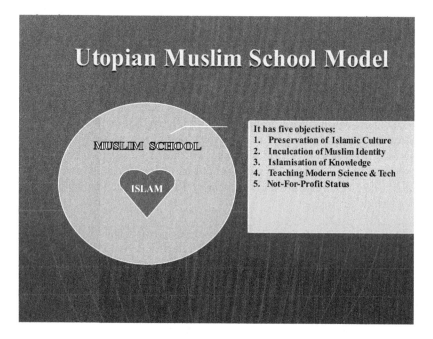

Fig. 3.1 Utopian muslim school model

School Model is not a reality, however. It is a vision, an imagination and a conception that existed in many Muslims' minds, and over time this 'dream' became beyond reach because those responsible for delivering the dream (school management and owners) became consumed by neo-liberalism.

The participants in Mah's study expressed concerns, even disillusionment, regarding the 'dream' not coming true. They dreamed of seeing Muslim schools founded on Islamic principles and reflecting the Islamic spirit through a school culture of compassion, care and fairness. In other words, a great number of participants wanted to see a Muslim school culture that truly reflected the ethos of care, as understood from an Islamic perspective.

What most participants hoped to see was a school that not only implemented Islam in its visible form, but also reflected its spirit internally. They wanted their associated Muslim schools to address the disparity between their initial intent and the direction in which they were heading. Participants from those schools with a strong focus on secular education wished to see a realignment between the intentions that their schools continued to espouse and, in contrast, the importance they gave to academic success over and above everything else.[48]

Instead of realising the vision of an authentic Islamic education in the Utopian Muslim School Model through Islamic pedagogical practice, Islamic moral and ethical values, basic Islamic rituals and practices, an Islamic curriculum and an Islamic cosmology, the school administrators and in some instances the owners opted to de-emphasise these and place greater emphasis on students' academic performance and achievements measured against subjects such as mathematics, physics and chemistry. '*There's no encouragement of non-Maths, Science, English related things I find*' (italics in original).[49] 'Education departments need to know how schools are performing for the purposes of performance management, and identifying what factors contribute to school performance.'[50]

This is critical because when schools score well in terms of their Australian Tertiary Admission Rank, this focus on high academic performance will have a strong impact on the school, particularly in terms of their socio-economic status. For school administrators and owners, this means they can be selective in choosing students and demand high school fees from parents, ultimately guaranteeing a regular and healthy income flow. As Mah notes in her study,

> Much of the information revealed by participants ... indicated an approach of exerting high pressure in order for students to perform academically .... Yet the undertone ... revolved around students' academic performance to maintain the school's ranking status. ... consumers who fed into this system were not all at ease with this approach and some wished that things were different in terms of Islamic studies, the approach and the objective of the institution ...[51]

This has clear implications for school administrators and owners, who make all efforts to improve school education but not necessarily with Islamic fervour. In the following two sections, I will attempt to unravel this conundrum.

Neo-liberalism

In academic and intellectual writings, the term 'neo-liberalism' undoubtedly emerges as polysemic with multiple referents. One observes that 'Neoliberalism seems to mean many different things depending on one's vantage point'.[52] One certainty about neo-liberalism is that it manifests itself as a set of public policies that political scientists, such as Manfred Steger and Ravi Roy,[53] like to call the 'D-L-P Formula', which are focused on deregulation of the economy, the relaxation of government restrictions on trade and industry and the privatisation of state-owned ventures. Neo-liberalism signifies a large range of political settings and socio-economic phenomena,[54] and it is both an ideological and a philosophical confederation.[55] Neo-liberalism was originally an economic philosophy[56] which took root in European liberal scholarship in the 1930s and gradually developed or metamorphosed into a politico-economic philosophy in interwar Europe.[57]

There are various definitions, explanations and models of neo-liberalism. According to Steger and Roy:

> 'Neoliberalism' is a rather broad and general concept referring to an economic model or 'paradigm' that rose to prominence in the 1980s. Built upon the classic liberal ideal of the self-regulating market, neoliberalism comes in several strands and variations. Perhaps the best way to conceptualize neoliberalism is to think of it as three intertwined manifestations: (1) an ideology; (2) a mode of governance; (3) a policy package.[58]

Beginning as a political project in the late 1970s and reaching prominence in the 1980s, neo-liberalism was popularised by Margaret Thatcher in the

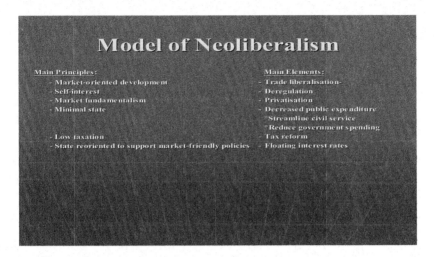

Fig. 3.2 Model of neoliberalism

United Kingdom and Ronald Reagan in the United States in the early 1980s. The neo-liberalism paradigm, as depicted in Fig. 3.2, actively encouraged far-reaching economic liberalisation policies such as privatisation, free trade, deregulation and reductions in state funding in an attempt to mobilise and reinvigorate the private sector of the economy. Neoliberalism as an expression of public policy includes measures such as considerable tax cuts; use of interest rates by independent central banks to control inflation; the downsizing of government; tax sanctuaries for local and foreign corporate investors investing in specific tax-free economic zones; new commercial urban spaces based on market demands; anti-unionisation; removal of restrictions on global financial and trade movement; regional and global integration of national economies; and the establishment of new political institutions.[59]

David Harvey has little faith in neo-liberalism and he succinctly summarises it as follows:

> Neoliberalism is in the first instance a theory of political economic practices that proposes that human well-being can best be advanced by liberating individual entrepreneurial freedoms and skills within an institutional framework characterized by strong private property rights, free markets, and free

trade. ... There has everywhere been an emphatic turn towards neoliberalism in political-economic practices and thinking since the 1970s. Deregulation, privatization, and withdrawal of the state from many areas of social provision have been all too common.

Neoliberalism has, in short, become hegemonic as a mode of discourse. It has pervasive effects on ways of thought to the point where it has become incorporated into the common-sense way many of us interpret, live in, and understand the world.

The process of neoliberalization has, however, entailed much 'creative destruction', not only of prior institutional frameworks and powers (even challenging traditional forms of state sovereignty) but also of divisions of labour, social relations, welfare provisions, technological mixes, ways of life and thought, reproductive activities, attachments to the land and habits of the heart.[60]

Neo-liberalism, as a political philosophy, a political project of machine-like rationality of the market and a laissez-faire economic liberalism, is limiting in its capacity because the political can never cover all aspects of everyday living and comprehensively govern the social, cultural, economic and natural spheres. Nevertheless, we can use the neo-liberalism framework to describe the development and transition of Muslim schools in Australia.

Suffice it to say that Muslim schools in Australia developed with a utopian vision of the Muslim school, as discussed above, in which Muslim students were to find an Islamic home infused with values, principles, teachings, rituals and practices sanctioned by the Qur'an and Hadith (record of sayings and deeds of the prophet Muhammad). The vision was to make true Muslims out of students through an inculcation of an Islamic cosmology, but in the end this vision was rarely realised. I explain the reasons for this in the next section.

THE NEO-LIBERALISATION OF MUSLIM SCHOOLS AND THE COMMODIFICATION OF ISLAM

In Australia, Muslim schools have evolved from being perceived as spaces of Islamic cultural production and inculcation, encounter in worship and generation of spiritual capital, to an arena in which those whom I would like to call 'school entrepreneurs' engage in what David Harvey calls the 'creative destruction' of established institutional frameworks, traditional power relations, normative social exchanges and regular ways of life and thought.[61] There are suggestions in Muslim public discourse that Muslim schools have been reconfigured in the last fifteen to twenty years by their custodians and turned into a marketplace for contractual relations and the exchange of goods and services. Islamic education as the quintessence of the Muslim school, in the eyes of many Muslims, has been fundamentally reformed and transformed by de-emphasising Islam and accentuating the significance of modern secular subjects in the school curriculum and pedagogical practices. Mah claims that in her research finding:

> Common to all Muslim schools was the progressive reduction in time allocated for Islamic studies as the students got older. ... Year 12 students in most schools did not have Islamic studies at all. ... many stakeholders from consumers group alluded to an undertone of dissatisfaction towards both the quality and quantity of Islamic lessons offered by their schools.[62]

Jones adds that 'The main thing was to pass their exams by following the ordained curriculum'.[63] Although Islam does not constitute a major part of the curriculum and is totally absent at the senior level, what makes Muslim parents want to send their children to Muslim schools, as discussed above, is that the environment is perceived to be conducive to Islam (observation of Muslim dress codes in school uniform, availability of halal food in the school canteen, prayer facility, recognition of the Muslim holy month of Ramadan and fasting protocols, celebration of Muslim festivals and practice of gender segregation). Eid notes that 'All Islamic schools confirm in their web sites that ... they are founded to provide Muslim children access to high quality education within an Islamic environment'.[64] School entrepreneurs exploit this situation by calling upon parents to consider the school environment as more critical than the Islamic curriculum in the learning journey of their children. They also emphasise the secular curriculum because parents are made to be believe that it leads to the provision of a sufficient condition for employment. School entrepreneurs cajole parents through 'cognitive mapping' (school brochures, websites, narratives)[65] and stress the importance of executing their duties and responsibilities religiously and diligently when choosing a school for their children, and in doing so render them 'better informed consumers'.[66] With this approach parents are encouraged to behave as partners in the parent–school relationship and as consumers. They are solicited to think and behave in ways that reinforce a consumerist or 'active' orientation to the provision of educational services. Parents are guided into making decisions in a similar manner to consumers in a marketplace—in a rational, deliberative and informed way.

Mah's study found that

> Many participants indicated a phenomenon of dissonance between what they would like Islamic schools to be giving more importance to and what was actually being emphasised in their schools. Some participants perceived that Muslim schools were not operating as they had initially intended. Participants felt that in some schools, too much emphasis on academic achievement had left on the wayside the noble intent of imparting Islamic values to the younger generation.[67]

As a corollary, Islamic education is manipulated to make it attractive to Muslim consumers. The manipulation involves associating Islamic education with piety and Islamic identity and the claim for the development of students' spiritual capital, for instance, by catering for some religious rituals such as prayer. The problem, though, is that 'Just because there is a prayer room doesn't mean the environment is Islamic'.[68] The school produces selective products—Islamic studies, Arabic language and Qur'anic lessons—with supposedly spiritual content. In this context, Muslims consume 'Islam' to create their Islamic identity. Islamic symbolic consumption becomes not only a new source of spiritualism but an important source of religious identification. The blending of Islamic education and piety with capitalism makes Islam a material process rather than a spiritual process in the neo-liberal market economy.

The increased awareness among many Muslims of the importance of Islamic rituals and practices has had a serious impact on the demonstration of social expression, that is, applying the Islamic teachings beyond regular religious rituals to comprehensively permeate everyday living in its entirety. In the neo-liberal market economy, this spiritual elevation and search for an authentic Islamic education influences the Muslim schools and vice versa. Fealy notes that Islamic expression is adopting a commodified form in which Muslims are selectively consuming Islamic products from a growing spiritual marketplace, Muslim schools being one of them.[69] Hasan[70] and Shiraz[71] argue that many Islamic products are inauthentic because they are produced to preserve and exalt religious practice and feeling but are in essence profit-driven.

The growing link between an authentic Islamic education that reflects religiosity and consumption is incentivising Muslim schools to produce selective products—Islamic studies, Arabic language and Qur'anic lessons—with spiritual content. Muslim schools market themselves as 'Islamic' to Muslim consumers in an attempt to meet the demand for 'Islamic products'. In transforming Islam into a symbolic commodity to meet the demands of Muslim consumers—their lifestyle, their modesty, their spirituality and their education—the role of the custodians of Muslim schools or school entrepreneurs assumes great importance.

This is a dismal assessment of Muslim schools, but when Islam is commodified, and as a commodity is maximised by maximising the reach and frequency of market transactions, one cannot help but think of Islam as a commodity for sale and the Muslim school as a marketplace.

The commodification, commoditisation and neo-liberalisation of Muslim schools emanates from the flawed Corporate Muslim School Model. The Corporate School Model is not unique to the Muslim context but is pervasive across the industry. Whether in Australia or elsewhere, and whether in a Muslim context or in another faith-based school context such as Catholic schools, the elected school boards generally operate as 'corporate boards'. Elected boards are often indistinguishable from senior administration and have increasingly come to think, act and react akin to corporate entities, with a proclivity to protect their own interests and defend their schools as their 'personal kingdoms'.[72] In the Corporate Muslim School Model, the following issues are problematic:

- It is in the interests of the school entrepreneurs (board members) to run the school like a business because the wealth generated benefits them directly or indirectly. The school functions as a source of income, a marketplace that generates regular income or wealth.[73] However, the school entrepreneurs are often found to be unqualified and unethical.[74] The school entrepreneurs consciously disregard 'conflicts of interest' and engage in complex business transactions, often under the cover of 'legitimate exchange', but employ family members in order to derive indirect financial benefits. Jones observes, 'Dr Magar received some notoriety for being sent to jail for financial misappropriations but the school continues in his absence with members of his family still involved in running the school'.[75] Hence, due to vested interest, the school entrepreneurs place complex, wide-ranging pressures on the principal and teachers. Jones notes that

'Often the tension has been between the principal and the School Board or sponsoring organisation'.[76]
- Since wealth generation is the school entrepreneurs' primary interest and motivation, the school is a critical source of income/wealth for them and is rendered a factory, involved in producing Islamic education or a marketplace for the exchange of goods and services to satisfy the demands of the consumers (parents and students).
- In order to generate wealth, the school needs to sell selected products—Islamic studies, Arabic language, Qur'anic lessons, Muslim piety and spiritual capital. Muslim parents purchase the product (Islamic education) for their children. Maximising the reach and frequency of this market transaction renders Islamic education a commodity and Islam generally a symbolic commodity in a client–supplier dynamic.
- Education is clothed in spiritual and Islamic garb and sold to unsuspecting Muslim consumers with the promise that it conveys Islamic values, morals, fervour, substance and content. The problem is that the product is inauthentic, of inferior quality and devoid of religious and spiritual content. Unaware of this fact, Muslim parents innocently engage in what may be described as normal consumer behaviour. There is a process of de-Islamisation of knowledge that takes place in many Muslim schools, often in an attempt to make the Muslim school into a marketplace or to turn 'Islamic' education into a business transaction which has to satisfy school entrepreneurs financially. In the end, under such a process, the consumers and Islam both suffer.

Fig. 3.3 illustrates what has become of Muslim schools in the Corporate Muslim School Model in comparison with the Utopian Muslim School Model.

In the Corporate Muslim School Model, Muslim schools are being 'privatised'. I do not deny that, generally speaking, there are benefits to be derived from some forms of privatisation of public goods and services. However, often these benefits are seriously rehearsed and sometimes even exaggerated, and the social costs are conveniently and systematically neglected. Muslim schools are not immune from this kind of neo-liberal mentality. In school policy rhetoric which glorifies 'the private', reflecting a neo-liberal ethos,[77] one could argue that there is a culture of expedient eschewal regarding the role of the profit motive and a systematic neglect

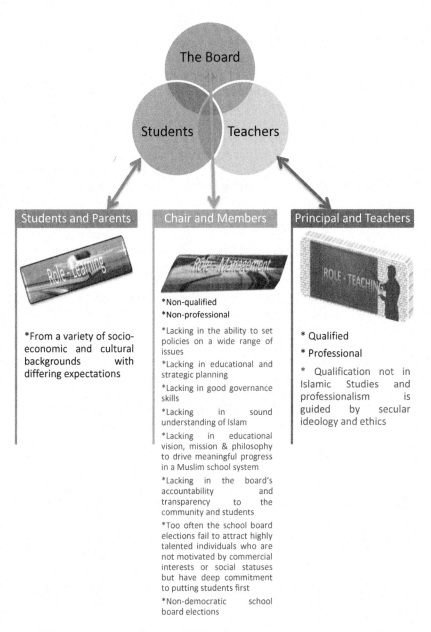

Fig. 3.3 Corporate muslim school model

of Islamic business ethics. In current Muslim school policy and management thinking, 'the private' is idealised and romanticised, while the Islamic notions of *asbab* (social cohesion) and public welfare and good are consistently, and often irrationally and illogically, demonised.[78]

It seems Muslim school custodians engage in 'capitalisation' which turns schools into commodity-producing factories and subjects them to institutional rearrangement based on a capitalist accumulation model.[79] This is a clear example of economic forms of capital concealing the underlying social relations wherein the social exchange between teachers, pupils, parents and school management is conducted in the form of relations between commodities or things. This is a form of reification, or the transformation of human essence, relations and behaviours into things separate from people.

A market-infused approach to education in Muslim schools considers knowledge as a commodity whose exchange value is measured loosely by comparing the cost of completing school with the financial earnings this will facilitate or even guarantee. The assumption here is that the schooling will provide adequate preparation for university and ultimately for employment, and therefore this must be not only cherished but promoted. In the case of Muslim schools, the impetus for commodification comes from administrators or school entrepreneurs who treat schools as money-making machines that must be corporately managed without giving any thought to the social and intellectual enrichment of the students. The objective is to gratify the students and their parents—conceived as consumers—by giving priority to the most quantifiable results: employment supersedes enlightenment.

The school entrepreneurs' mission is to facilitate job security rather than to expand the minds of students to engage in critical thinking, explore possibilities and solve problems. This mentality of school entrepreneurs permeates the school system, so that schools end up being viewed as vocational centres for facilitating job security, rather than as developmental centres for self-discovery, social engagement and enlightenment, and discovering new ideas. Similar to corporate entities battling to win the hearts and minds of consumers, schools now seem to be enveloped in a 'business ontology'.[80]

It is worth noting that in Islam, knowledge of reality facilitates knowledge of the divinity and oneness of God, thus connecting the physical to the metaphysical and the material to the spiritual.[81] In Islam, the emphasis is on the inseparable nature of knowledge and the sacred, something that is not incorporated into Muslim schools' pedagogical practice—in fact, the opposite is true.[82]

The commodification of Islamic education or Islamic knowledge entails both a focus on the naturalisation of pedagogical changes taking place in, and at the same time impacting, Muslim everyday living and consumption patterns, as well as the more general processes of capitalism which reinforce the hunt for new markets, new products and thus new sources of profit. In this fetishising of commodities,[83] Muslim school entrepreneurs deny the superiority and 'humanity' of human relationships that Islam so passionately cherishes. In the pursuit of profit through privatisation of Muslim schools, the commodification of Islamic knowledge and the marketisation of Islamic education there is in effect an eradication of the social, and 'existence' is viewed in terms of quantities and monetary values. In this 'social emptiness' there is no place for spirituality and Islam but plenty of space for unrestrained exploitation and profiteering.

Conclusion

In a globalised world of free-market neo-liberalism, Muslim schools in Australia have undergone a reconfiguration in which the focus has shifted from pedagogical practices that are based on the ideas of the inseparable nature of knowledge and the sacred, and acquisition of knowledge as a means of discovering and establishing nearness to God, to practices that render the production of knowledge a capitalist enterprise. This is evident in the transition process of the Utopian Muslim School Model to a Corporate Muslim School Model.

Muslim schools are factories established by educational entrepreneurs to produce a specific kind of product known as 'Islamic knowledge' or 'Islamic education' for the purposes of exploitation and profiteering. Muslim schools in contemporary Australia are places of free-market contestation where religion is secularised and commodified and social relationships are reduced to a cost–benefit transactional exchange.

Notes

1. Peta Stephenson, *Islam Dreaming: Indigenous Muslims in Australia* (Sydney: UNSW Press, 2010).
2. Bilal Cleland, "The History of Muslims in Australia," in *Muslim Communities in Australia*, ed. Abdullah Saeed and Shahram Akbarzadeh (Sydney: University of New South Wales Press, 2001).

3. Abdallah Mograby, "Muslim Migration and Settlement: The Australian Experience," in *Islam in Australia* (Sydney: Middle East Research and Information Section – New South Wales Anti-Discrimination Board, 1985).
4. Shahram Akbarzadeh, "Unity or Fragmentation?," in *Muslim Communities in Australia*, ed. Abdullah Saeed and Shahram Akbarzadeh (Sydney: University of New South Wales Press, 2001).
5. Qazi Ahmad, "Islam and Muslims in Australia," in *Islam, Muslims and the Modern State: Case – Studies of Muslims in Thirteen Countries*, ed. Hussin Mutalib and Taj ul-Islam Hashmi (New York: St Martin's Press, 1994).
6. Ahmad, "Islam and Muslims in Australia," 317–338.
7. Stephen Castles and Mark Miller, *The Age of Migration: International Population Movements in the Modern World* (New York: Guilford Books, 1993).
8. Harry Field, *Citizen or Resident?: Australian Social Security Provision to Immigrants* (Doctoral Dissertation, University of New South Wales, 2000).
9. Wafia Omar, and Kirsty Allen, *The Muslims in Australia* (Canberra: Australian Government Publishing Service, 1997); A point to note is that between 1947 and 1971, a period when the 'White Australia' policy was very much alive, the Muslim population grew from 2704 to 22,311. This might seem like a substantial increase in the Muslim population, but when the length of this period, which is twenty-four years, is taken into consideration, the average annual growth of the Muslim population is only 930 people.
10. Commonwealth of Australia, *1991 Census of Population and Housing*, Catalogue No. 2722.0 (Canberra: Australian Bureau of Statistics, 1991).
11. Commonwealth of Australia, *1996 Census of Population and Housing*, Catalogue No. 2901.0 (Canberra: Australian Bureau of Statistics, 1997).
12. Commonwealth of Australia, *2001 Census of Population and Housing*, Catalogue No. 2015.0 (Canberra: Australian Bureau of Statistics, 2002).
13. Commonwealth of Australia, *2006 Census of Population and Housing*, Catalogue No. 2068.0 (Canberra: Australian Bureau of Statistics, 2007), 23.
14. Riaz Hassan, *Australian Muslims: A Demographic, Social and Economic Profile of Muslims in Australia 2015*, International Centre for Muslim and Non-Muslim Understanding (Adelaide: University of South Australia, 2015); and in 2016 there were 604,200, constituting 2.6% of the population.
15. Riaz Hassan, "Australian Muslims"; Commonwealth of Australia, "2016 Census of Population and Housing", Catalogue No. 2071.0 (Canberra: Australian Bureau of Statistics, 2017).
16. Abdullah Saeed, *Islam in Australia* (Crows Nest: George Allen and Unwin, 2003).
17. Saeed, *Islam in Australia*.

18. Michael Humphrey, "An Australian Islam? Religion in the Multicultural City," in *Muslim Communities in Australia*, ed. Abdullah Saeed and Shahram Akbarzadeh (Sydney: University of New South Wales Press, 2001).
19. Humphrey, "An Australian Islam? Religion in the Multicultural City."
20. Peter Jones, "Islamic Schools in Australia," *The La Trobe Journal* 89 (2012): 38.
21. Aminah Mah, *Counselling and Wellbeing Support Services in Australian Muslim Schools* (Doctoral Dissertation, The University of Western Australia, 2015).
22. Irene Donohoue Clyne, "Educating Muslim Children in Australia," in *Muslim Communities in Australia*, ed. Abdullah Saeed and Shahram Akbarzadeh (Sydney: University of New South Wales Press, 2001); Mahmoud Eid, *Public Schools or Islamic Colleges? Factors Impacting on Parental Choice of Schooling for Muslim Children* (Doctoral Dissertation, Edith Cowan University, 2008).
23. Irene Donohoue Clyne, "Seeking Education for Muslim Children in Australia," *Muslim Education Quarterly*, 14 (3) (1997): 4–18.
24. Manar Chelebi, *The Australian Muslim Student* (Sydney: David Barlow Publishing, 2008).
25. Silma Ihram, "Director at Diversity Skills Training Pty Ltd." Accessed 4 February 2017. https://au.linkedin.com/in/diversityskillstraining.
26. Mah, "Counselling and Wellbeing," 61.
27. Jones, "Islamic Schools in Australia," 40.
28. Mahmoud Eid, *Public Schools or Islamic Colleges? Factors Impacting on Parental Choice of Schooling for Muslim Children* (Doctoral Dissertation, Edith Cowan University, 2008).
29. Chelebi, "The Australian Muslim Student."
30. Jones, "Islamic Schools in Australia," 42.
31. Jones, "Islamic Schools in Australia," 42.
32. Mah, "Counselling and Wellbeing."
33. Jones, "Islamic Schools in Australia," 40.
34. Mah, "Counselling and Wellbeing."
35. Jones, "Islamic Schools in Australia."
36. Mah, "Counselling and Wellbeing."
37. Michael Merry and G. Driessen, "Islamic Schools in Three Western Countries: Policy and Procedure," *Comparative Education* 41 (4) (2005): 426.
38. Peter Jones, *Islamic Schools in Australia: Muslims in Australia or Australian Muslims?* (Doctoral Dissertation, University of New England, 2012).
39. Mah, "Counselling and Wellbeing," 169.
40. Donohoue Clyne, "Educating Muslim Children in Australia," 117.

41. Linda Morris, "Islam Leads in Rush to Faith Education." Accessed 4 February 2017. http://www.smh.com.au/articles/2003/06/22/1056220477178.html.
42. Peter Jones, "Islamic Schools in Australia," *The La Trobe Journal* 89 (2012): 36.
43. Jones, "Islamic Schools in Australia," 36.
44. Michael Merry, *Culture, Identity, and Islamic Schooling: A Philosophical Approach* (New York: Palgrave Macmillan, 2007), 20.
45. Jones, "Islamic Schools in Australia," 36.
46. Mah, "Counselling and Wellbeing," 88.
47. Mah, "Counselling and Wellbeing," 169.
48. Mah, "Counselling and Wellbeing," 119–120.
49. Mah, "Counselling and Wellbeing," 77.
50. Ian Li and Alfred Dockery, *Socio-Economic Status of Schools and University Academic Performance: Implications for Australia's Higher Education Expansion*, National Centre for Student Equity in Higher Education (Perth: Curtin University, 2014), 7.
51. Mah, "Counselling and Wellbeing," 79.
52. Aihwa Ong, *Neoliberalism as Exception: Mutations in Citizenship and Sovereignty* (Durham, NC: Duke University Press, 2006), 1.
53. Manfred Steger and Ravi Roy, *Neoliberalism: A Very Short Introduction* (Oxford: Oxford University Press, 2010), 14.
54. Tejaswini Ganti, "Neoliberalism," *The Annual Review of Anthropology* 43 (2014): 89–104.
55. Philip Mirowski, "Postface: Defining Neoliberalism," in *The Road from Mont Pelerin: The Making of the Neoliberal Thought Collective*, ed. Philip Mirowski and Dieter Plehwe (Cambridge, MA: Harvard University Press, 2009).
56. Mirowski, "Postface."
57. Ganti, "Neoliberalism," 89–104.
58. Steger and Roy, *Neoliberalism*, 11.
59. Steger and Roy, *Neoliberalism*.
60. David Harvey, *A Brief History of Neoliberalism* (Oxford: Oxford University Press, 2005), 2 & 3.
61. Harvey, *A Brief History of Neoliberalism*.
62. Mah, "Counselling and Wellbeing," 90.
63. Jones, "Islamic Schools in Australia," 45.
64. Eid, "Public Schools or Islamic Colleges?," 80–81.
65. Andrew Wilkins, "School Choice and the Commodification of Education: A visual Approach to School Brochures and Websites," *Critical Social Policy* 32 (2012): 69–85.

66. Department for Children, Schools and Families, *Children's Services: Improvement Support for Local Authorities and Children's Trusts*, A National Prospectus 2009–10 (Nottingham: DCSF Publications, 2009).
67. Mah, "Counselling and Wellbeing," 120.
68. Mah, "Counselling and Wellbeing," 91.
69. Greg Fealy, "Consuming Islam: Commodified Religion and Aspirational Pietism in Contemporary Indonesia," in *Expressing Islam: Religious Life and Politics in Indonesia*, ed. Greg Fealy and Sally White (Singapore: Institute of Southeast Asian Studies (ISEAS), 2008).
70. Noorhaidi Hasan, "Islam in Provincial Indonesia: Middle Class, Lifestyle and Democracy," *Al-Jami'ah Journal of Islamic Studies* 49, no. 1 (2011): 119–158.
71. Faegheh Shirazi, *Brand Islam: The Marketing and Commodification of Piety* (Austin: University of Texas Press, 2016).
72. For detailed analysis of the 'Corporate School Model' see Paul Bennett, 2012 "The 'Corporate' School Board: What Can Be Done to Restore Responsible Trusteeship?" Accessed 4 February 2017. https://educhatter.wordpress.com/2012/11/25/the-corporate-school-board-what-can-be-done-to-restore-responsible-trusteeship/; Andrew Wilkins, "School Choice and the Commodification of Education: A Visual Approach to School Brochures and Websites," *Critical Social Policy* 32 (2012): 69–85.
73. Eryk Bagshaw, 2016, Malek Fahd: Hundreds call for sacking of school board at protest meeting. Accessed 4 February 2017. http://www.illawarramercury.com.au/story/3730155/malek-fahd-hundreds-call-for-sacking-of-school-board-at-protest-meeting/?cs=7.
74. Jones, "Islamic Schools in Australia: Muslims in Australia or Australian Muslims?"
75. Peter Jones, "Islamic Schools in Australia," *The La Trobe Journal* 89 (2012): 41.
76. Jones, "Islamic Schools in Australia," 39.
77. Wilkins, "School Choice and the Commodification of Education."
78. Mah, "Counselling and Wellbeing."
79. Bagshaw, "Malek Fahd."
80. Mark Fisher, *Capitalist Realism: Is There No Alternative?* (Winchester: Zero Books, 2009): 17.
81. John Esposito, *Islam: The Straight Path* (Oxford: Oxford University Press, 2005).
82. Tariq Ramadan, *Islam, the West and the Challenges of Modernity* (Leicester: Islamic Foundation, 2001).
83. Edward Said, *Orientalism* (New York: Pantheon Books, 1978).

Bibliography

Ahmad, Qazi. "Islam and Muslims in Australia." In *Islam, Muslims and the Modern State: Case – Studies of Muslims in Thirteen Countries*, ed. Hussin Mutalib and Taj ul-Islam Hashmi. New York: St. Martins Press, 1994.

Akbarzadeh, Shahram. "Unity or Fragmentation?" In *Muslim Communities in Australia*, ed. Abdullah Saeed and Shahram Akbarzadeh. Sydney: University of New South Wales Press, 2001.

Chelebi, Manar. *The Australian Muslim Student*. Sydney: David Barlow Publishing, 2008.

Cleland, Bilal. "The History of Muslims in Australia." In *Muslim Communities in Australia*, ed. Abdullah Saeed and Shahram Akbarzadeh. Sydney: University of New South Wales Press, 2001.

Commonwealth of Australia. *1991 Census of Population and Housing*, Catalogue No. 2722.0. Canberra: Australian Bureau of Statistics, 1991.

———. *1996 Census of Population and Housing*, Catalogue No. 2901.0. Canberra: Australian Bureau of Statistics, 1997.

———. *2001 Census of Population and Housing*, Catalogue No. 2015.0. Canberra: Australian Bureau of Statistics, 2002.

———. *2006 Census of Population and Housing*, Catalogue No. 2068.0. Canberra: Australian Bureau of Statistics, 2007.

Donohoue Clyne, Irene. "Educating Muslim Children in Australia." In *Muslim Communities in Australia*, ed. Abdullah Saeed and Shahram Akbarzadeh. Sydney: University of New South Wales Press, 2001.

———. "Seeking Education for Muslim Children in Australia." *Muslim Education Quarterly* 14 (1997): 4–18.

Eid, Mahmoud. "Public Schools or Islamic Colleges? Factors Impacting on Parental Choice of Schooling for Muslim Children." Doctoral Dissertation, Perth: Edith Cowan University, 2008.

Esposito, John. *Islam: The Straight Path*. Oxford: Oxford University Press, 2005.

Fealy, Greg. "Consuming Islam: Commodified Religion and Aspirational Pietism in Contemporary Indonesia." In *Expressing Islam: Religious Life and Politics in Indonesia*, ed. Greg Fealy and Sally White. Singapore: Institute of Southeast Asian Studies (ISEAS), 2008.

Field, Harry. "Citizen or Resident? Australian Social Security Provision to Immigrants." Doctoral Dissertation, Sydney: University of New South Wales, 2000.

Fisher, Mark. *Capitalist Realism: Is There No Alternative?* Winchester: Zero Books, 2009.

Ganti, Tejaswini. "Neoliberalism." *The Annual Review of Anthropology* 43 (2014): 89–104.

Hassan, Riaz. *Australian Muslims: A Demographic, Social and Economic Profile of Muslims in Australia 2015*. International Centre for Muslim and Non-Muslim Understanding. Adelaide: University of South Australia, 2015.

Harvey, David. *A Brief History of Neoliberalism*. Oxford: Oxford University Press, 2005.

Hasan, Noorhaidi. "Islam in Provincial Indonesia: Middle Class, Lifestyle and Democracy." *Al-Jami'ah Journal of Islamic Studies* 49 (2011): 119–158.

Humphrey, Michael. "An Australian Islam? Religion in the Multicultural City." In *Muslim Communities in Australia*, ed. Abdullah Saeed and Shahram Akbarzadeh. Sydney: University of New South Wales Press, 2001.

Ihram, Silma. "Director at Diversity Skills Training Pty Ltd." Accessed 4 February 2017. https://au.linkedin.com/in/diversityskillstraining.

Jones, Peter. "Islamic Schools in Australia." *The La Trobe Journal* 89 (2012a): 36–47.

———. "Islamic Schools in Australia: Muslims in Australia or Australian Muslims?" Doctoral Dissertation, Sydney: University of New England, 2012b.

Li, Ian, and Alfred Dockery. *Socio-Economic Status of Schools and University Academic Performance: Implications for Australia's Higher Education Expansion*. National Centre for Student Equity in Higher Education, Perth: Curtin University, 2014.

Mah, Aminah. "Counselling and Wellbeing Support Services in Australian Muslim Schools." Doctoral Dissertation, Perth: The University of Western Australia, 2015.

Merry, Michael. *Culture, Identity, and Islamic Schooling: A Philosophical Approach*. New York: Palgrave Macmillan. 2007.

Merry, Michael, and G. Driessen. "Islamic Schools in Three Western Countries: Policy and Procedure." *Comparative Education* 41 (2005): 411–432.

Mirowski, Philip. "Postface: Defining Neoliberalism." In *The Road from Mont Pelerin: The Making of the Neoliberal Thought Collective*, ed. Philip Mirowski and Dieter Plehwe. Cambridge, MA: Harvard University Press, 2009.

Mograby, Abdallah. "Muslim Migration and Settlement: The Australian Experience." In *Islam in Australia*. Sydney: Middle East Research and Information Section – New South Wales Anti-Discrimination Board, 1985.

Morris, Linda. Islam Leads in Rush to Faith Education. Accessed 4 February 2017. http://www.smh.com.au/articles/2003/06/22/1056220477178.html.

Omar, Wafia, and Kirsty Allen. *The Muslims in Australia*. Canberra: Australian Government Publishing Service, 1997.

Ong, Aihwa. *Neoliberalism as Exception: Mutations in Citizenship and Sovereignty*. Durham, NC: Duke University Press, 2006.

Ramadan, Tariq. *Islam, the West and the Challenges of Modernity*. Leicester: Islamic Foundation, 2001.

Saeed, Abdullah. *Islam in Australia*. Crows Nest: George Allen and Unwin, 2003.
Said, Edward. *Orientalism*. New York: Pantheon Books, 1978.
Shirazi, Faegheh. *Brand Islam: The Marketing and Commodification of Piety*. Austin: University of Texas Press, 2016.
Steger, Manfred, and Ravi Roy. *Neoliberalism: A Very Short Introduction*. Oxford: Oxford University Press, 2010.
Stephen, Castle, and Mark Miller. *The Age of Migration: International Population Movements in the Modern World*. New York: Guilford Books, 1993.
Stephenson, Peta. *Islam Dreaming: Indigenous Muslims in Australia*. Sydney: UNSW Press, 2010.

CHAPTER 4

Towards a Hybrid Approach to the Governance of Islamic Schools in NSW

Ayda Succarie, Wayne Fallon, and Gabriela Coronado

INTRODUCTION

The purpose of boards in Islamic schools, as not-for-profit (NFP) organisations, is to effectively safeguard and pursue the interests of stakeholders. To do this, boards have a civil obligation, through the 'moral ownership of a social contract', to benefit the 'general will' of the community.[1] In governance terms, the aim of a social contract is to safeguard the interests of stakeholders, and the board will do that by establishing a set of policies, protocols and procedures, usually with the agreement of the management in the organisation.[2]

From an Islamic perspective, the activities of board members should be underpinned by the Islamic worldview. This worldview is encompassed by the belief in the existence of one God[3] (Allah, *Subhannah wa Ta'alah* (*SWT*)) and knowledge as interpreted by the revelations found in

---

A. Succarie (✉) • W. Fallon • G. Coronado
Western Sydney University, Parramatta, NSW, Australia
e-mail: a.succarie@westernsydney.edu.au; w.fallon@westernsydney.edu.au; g.coronado@westernsydney.edu.au

© The Author(s) 2018
M. Abdalla et al. (eds.), *Islamic Schooling in the West*,
https://doi.org/10.1007/978-3-319-73612-9_4

the Holy Qur'an and the Sunna.[4] The Islamic worldview provides guidance for Muslims in what is regarded as an authentic understanding of reality (*haqiqah*) and truth (*haqq*) and promotes the phenomena of right action (*adab*) through self-discipline and justice (*adl*).[5] Using the Islamic worldview means that directors ensure the board's compliance, accountability and transparency, and involves engaging in the principles of trust (*amanah*), justice (*adl*), benevolence (*ihsan*) and ethics (*akhlaq*).[6] In addition to this, board members are meant to be moral leaders with a mission to produce and maintain the Islamic vision of their school.[7] These members are also required to add value to the strategic direction of the institution by drawing on their values, attributes, skills and experience.[8]

During the period 2012–2016, a series of media and community debates on issues relating to compliance, accountability and transparency challenged the processes of governance in the boards of a number of Islamic schools in New South Wales (NSW).[9] Compliance with registration and accrediting bodies, such as the Australian Securities and Investments Commission (ASIC), Department of Education and Training (DET) and the Board of Studies Teaching and Education Standards (BOSTES), is an essential part of the governance process for schools.[10]

In addition to compliance, Islamic school boards have a moral obligation to exercise accountability and transparency in their governance practice. Moral obligations ensure that directors apply principles underpinned by the Islamic worldview and help maintain the trust (*amanah*) between boards and stakeholders. The Holy Qur'an states: '*O ye who believe! Fulfill (all) obligations.*'[11] In this verse, Allah (*SWT*) refers to both divine and mutual obligations. For directors, mutual obligations include the 'moral ownership of a social contract',[12] and boards have the responsibility of ensuring this obligation is faithfully discharged.[13]

The recent media debates about the governance-related practices in some Islamic schools specifically reported on a range of issues involving directors. These issues included misappropriation of funds, a lack of professionalism by directors and decision-making that showed a lack of clarity about the responsibilities of board members.[14] Independent audits of some of these schools found board members had acted much like owners of these institutions.[15] Some schools had adopted business practices that indicated they were operated as pseudo for-profit organisations.[16] These audits also found a number of directors had conflicts of interest in their dealings as board members.[17]

Islamic schools are not the only independent schools that have experienced issues in governance, and the independent schools sector continues to face concerns about compliance, accountability and transparency.[18] According to Hamilton,[19] governance issues have also arisen at a 'Methodist Ladies College (MLC)' where, without 'formal mechanisms',[20] directors experienced conflicts of interest and their accountability was challenged. This example, one of many, raised concerns among stakeholder groups about board governance in the independent schools sector more generally.[21] The Minister of Education expressed the need for an inquiry into the governance of independent schools across the country.[22] This prompted amendments to the independent schools registration and accreditation guidelines released by the BOSTES.[23] These developments also suggest the need for further research on governance in the independent schools sector.

To better understand the ongoing issues in the sector, this chapter firstly provides a background to Islamic schools in NSW and reviews governance in these schools. Next, a review of the literature on governance in the sector is discussed. Governance theories and stewardship provide a theoretical framework for this study. Additionally, the chapter identifies the lens used to interpret the data: the Islamic worldview. Findings on the governance of Islamic schools in the study provided an overview of the composition of the boards in these schools and highlighted some of the contemporary challenges faced by school boards. A discussion of the apparent dilemma experienced by some directors between their stewardship responsibilities to their institutions and their perspective of owning these institutions assists in unpacking the nuances of governance in schools. Finally, the chapter proposes a hybrid model for the governance of Islamic schools. It concludes with a suggestion that the hybrid model may assist boards and management to develop approaches that meet compliance requirements and moral responsibilities. This model may also assist in maintaining directors' mutual obligations for the benefit of current and future stakeholder interests and for the general will of the community.

BACKGROUND TO ISLAMIC SCHOOLS IN NEW SOUTH WALES

Primary and secondary schools in Australia belong to either the government or the non-government schools sectors.[24] All government schools operate from a centralised governance framework and are funded by the state and federal governments. Schools in the non-government sector are partially funded by government but also receive funding and support from other stakeholder groups.[25] Most independent schools are affiliated with a religious group, such as Christian, Jewish, Buddhist, Hindu or Islamic groups, although there are a number of special schools, international schools, indigenous schools and community schools with no religious affiliation. These are also part of the independent schools sector.[26]

Islamic schools make up 5% of the independent schools sector and, in 2014, thirty-eight Islamic schools across the country were operating with more than 28,000 students.[27] NSW had the largest Islamic school cohort, and 60% of Islamic schools in Australia operated in South West Sydney.[28] This region is highly heterogeneous and has the largest migrant settlement rates of people from less developed countries or those in conflict, particularly migrants from Muslim backgrounds.[29] Islamic schools are funded by government on a per capita basis and the level of funding is determined according to the population of students from low socio-economic status (SES) backgrounds.[30] Most Islamic schools are located in low SES areas.[31]

In a review of funding for schooling in 2011, the DET recommended priority be given to students residing in low SES areas.[32] The introduction of the National School Resource Standard (NSRS) funding model aimed to improve the quality of education and fairness in the way government funding was distributed across government and non-government sectors.[33] Schools that receive funding under the NSRS are required to maintain a number of governance measures to ensure higher standards of transparency, accountability and administration of funding.[34] In 2015, a media report on Islamic schools suggested that 'as with most private schools, taxpayers contribute 80% of Islamic schools' running costs', with the balance of costs covered by tuition fees.[35]

The Australian Charities and Not for Profit Commission[36] and the DET require that independent schools operate as NFP entities, so Islamic schools are often registered as corporations limited by guarantee. This means that the 'liability of the schools' members … [of the corporation] is limited to the amount the members undertake to contribute to the corporation'.[37] Each Islamic school has a constitution which must comply with the Corporations Act 2001 and which outlines the 'rules and purposes'[38] of the entity. This document articulates requirements about the number of directors and their roles and responsibilities.[39] Directors are required to comply with the Act, including a provision about the misuse of their position.

Section 182 provides that 'A Director, secretary, other officer or employee of a corporation must not improperly use their position to: (a) gain an advantage for themselves or someone else; or (b) cause detriment to the corporation'.[40] In addition to this, according to Carver,[41] a director's civil obligation is to act in the public interest of stakeholders.

Research on Islamic schools in the United States suggests that these schools adopt governance policies that are 'recycled ideas' from other private and public schools and lack a unique vision and purpose for the schools.[42] According to DeCuir,[43] often the founders of these schools are 'patriarchal migrants' who fail to understand the complexity of organisational structures and do not have the educational capacity to organise the policies needed to align with the vision of the school.[44] It is suggested that the dependency of ideas creates an identity crisis for students and staff and confuses the notion of a complete Muslim identity.

The debates specific to some Islamic schools in NSW were similar to those surrounding the governance of Islamic schools elsewhere. DeCuir[45] and Elbih[46] identified that multiple stakeholders (staff and community members) of schools in the United States expressed concerns about board involvement in the day-to-day operations of the schools. There were also concerns about gender bias and patriarchal dominance by boards.[47] Other issues included the selection of board members who lacked an understanding of the roles and responsibilities associated with their directorships. Cases of nepotism and the neglect of public interest (*maslah*) were also raised by stakeholders.[48]

A lack of research on governance in Islamic schools limits understanding of the issues raised in the literature and media reports about NSW schools. Due to the Islamic ideology of these schools, compliance should go beyond organisational rhetoric, and obligations of accountability and transparency need to be centred on the mutual obligation to serve the public interest (*maslah*) of the community. In an Islamic sense, this means that directors are required to safeguard the interests of stakeholders, and exercise the practice of enjoining the good and forbidding the evil (*al amr bil maarouf wa al nahi anil munkar*).[49] This would require boards to adopt the principles of ethics (*akhlaq*), justice (*adl*) and benevolence (*ihsan*), and would help directors to faithfully discharge their responsibilities for the benefit of the community they serve.[50]

Governance and Islamic Obligations

The matter of governance for Islamic school boards has two dimensions. First, these boards are required to comply with the regulations and standards outlined in the Australian Education Act 2014 and the Corporations Act 2001. Second, Islamic school boards have an obligation to ensure that governance adopts Islamic principles, and the boards' mission is to produce an Islamic vision for the school.[51] However, some scholars argue that first- and second-generation boards do not understand the complexity of these two dimensions and that these directors often confuse their Islamic obligations with cultural or Western traditions.[52] According to Al-Attas,[53] applying the Islamic worldview by adopting Western and culturally specific approaches can lead to a mistaken understanding of reality (*haqiqah*) and truth (*haqq*).[54] Although boards may have an ad hoc view of an Islamic vision (by confusing cultural or Western traditions with Islam), the role of directors (as educational leaders) is to maintain a vision that harnesses the principles of right action (*adab*) through justice (*adl*).[55]

Ethical conduct is measured based on good actions (*salihat*) and good intentions (*niyyaat*), and this is central to maintaining justice (*adl*).[56] This ensures relationships of trust are sustained between school policy-makers, management and other stakeholders.[57] To do this, directors should engage in mutual consultation (*Shura*), including with members of the community they serve. The act of consultation (*mushawarah*) is an obligation in Islam, and the Holy Qur'an states:

> *Those who have responded to their lord, and established regular prayer; who (conduct) their affairs by mutual consultation; Who spend out of what we bestow on them for sustenance ...*[58]

Consultation is a way for directors to engage with stakeholders, and it encourages ethical behaviours.[59] Mutual consultation (*Shura*) helps boards steer away from egotistical behaviour in the boardroom, and through principles of righteousness (*birr*) and goodness (*khayr*) decision-making becomes centred on the needs of stakeholders.[60]

Moral leadership is an obligation that requires board members to provide continuous assistance and to seek support from the community. This process involves the principles of goodness (*khayr*), truth (*haqq*), equity (*qist*) and piety (*taqwa*) when engaging with stakeholders.[61] In a comparison of the Organisation for Economic Co-operation and Development (OECD) governance compliance guidelines with Islamic principles, Obid and Naysary[62] and Abu-Tapanjeh[63] identified 'extended obligations of compliance' for organisations that adopted the Islamic worldview in their governance framework. For Islamic school boards, this means that governance in these schools has extended obligations that need to be considered by directors when exercising their governance roles.

Governance in Independent Schools

Governance in the corporate sector proposes that the role of boards is to pursue the interests of the shareholders,[64] often ensuring an economic benefit for the owners. This is based on the agency theory of governance, under which the board acts as the agents of the owners, thus ensuring the separation of ownership from control of the organisation.[65] Boards that adopt the agency model focus on maximising wealth for all owners and stipulate higher levels of autonomy in directors' decision-making.[66] Boards may give less emphasis to the needs of other stakeholders.

Stakeholder theory, on the other hand, enables boards to consider the needs of a broader range of stakeholders during the decision-making process. This theory assists boards in creating sustainable governance frameworks that maintain the well-being of stakeholder groups.[67] The OECD report 'Governing Education in a Complex World' states: 'Effective modern governance [in the education sector] requires coordinated system-wide change involving a broad set of actors.'[68] These actors are stakeholders that exist at multiple levels and can influence the governance of modern education systems. The OECD provides a framework of potential stakeholders in education, which include[69]:

1. internal stakeholders—principals, teachers and students;
2. intermediate stakeholders—parents, the board, local authorities, local communities, private business, training providers, resource providers, inspectors, government agencies, non-government organisations and unions;
3. external stakeholders—researchers, international organisations and the media.

School stakeholders have specific needs, and the OECD suggests that nuanced approaches to the education system should be explored to cater for the complex needs of stakeholders, which can be achieved by adopting a stewardship model of governance.[70]

Stewardship encourages socially responsible management and care of resources by board members for current and future stakeholders.[71] Stewardship theory challenges the notion that organisations operate purely for economic gain to maximise wealth for shareholders.[72] Stewards provide service to the local communities they serve and give consideration to current and future stakeholder groups.[73] However, researchers argue that some directors may employ 'narrow stewardship' that aims to benefit their own interests.[74] This is particularly evident when founding members assume the role of stewards and become too closely aligned with the organisations they serve.[75] In this instance, stewardship may mutate into a type of ownership by founding members.

Literature on the governance of schools highlights the roles of directors, their responsibilities to stakeholders and the governance structures and frameworks that need to be adopted by boards.[76] The NFP status of schools means there are some differences in the way governance is practised in schools. However, some researchers suggest that changes in the way organisations operate in the independent schools sector have influenced the way directors of these schools exercise governance.[77] Boards in independent schools have a moral responsibility to exercise stewardship and are accountable to a wider range of stakeholders, which can include students, parents and other community members.[78] In this instance, board performance can affect the overall well-being of the school.[79]

Research suggests that school boards can experience a lack of coherent participation by directors due to the boards' composition and structure and that this can impact the way boards function as groups.[80] Most independent schools operate as 'systematic structures' and some boards appoint management committees that focus on specialised areas in regulation, funding and accreditation, although ultimately the board is liable for the overall decision-making.[81] Furthermore, the Independent Schools Council of Australia outlines the various levels of liability schools have to stakeholders and stresses the importance of boards and management considering their stakeholder obligations during the decision-making process.[82] Current literature on the governance of independent schools identifies the need for more empirical research in the sector,[83] including in Islamic schools. This is the impetus for this study.

Researching Governance in Islamic Schools

The Islamic worldview was used as the paradigm to frame and interpret the research data for this chapter. This worldview challenges the use of the Western sciences and the influences of cultural traditions to inform reality (*haqiqah*) and truth (*haqq*).[84] Research suggests that cultural traditions, patriarchal dominance and gender stereotypes often conceal the ontological essence of Islamic tradition.[85] Other researchers take the view that the Islamic worldview is a guide for a complete Muslim way of life.[86] Although scholars may differ about what constitutes an Islamic worldview, all agree that the belief in the one God (*tawhid*) is at the epicentre of this paradigm.[87] As stated by Badawi,[88] the essence of *tawhid* is formed by:

> firstly to believe in the one and only God (*Allah SWT*) as the sole Sustainer, Creator and Cherisher of the universe, secondly to believe that *Allah (SWT)* is the only one worthy of worship, and finally to believe in the unity of essence and attributes of *Allah (SWT)* which are all attributes of absolute perfection.[89]

The Islamic worldview also establishes the universal principles of stewardship, ethics (*akhlaq*), justice (*adl*), benevolence (*ihsan*) and mutual consultation (*shura*) as the pillars of social justice and responsibility.[90] These pillars form a framework of objectives (*maqasid*) that helps Muslims interact with one another and the wider community more generally.[91] For Islamic schools, this worldview assists boards and educators in establishing informed approaches that consider the needs of all current and future stakeholder groups.[92] For the purpose of this chapter, this worldview has been used as a paradigm for analysis and interpretation to develop the hybrid model of governance proposed for these schools.

Islamic Schools in the Study

The study of Islamic schools in NSW investigated the governance practices adopted by seven school boards. Using a case study method, data were collected by interviewing a sample of members of these boards and, through focus group discussions, a selection of teachers and parents of these schools' students. Many Islamic schools were founded by community-based Muslim charities or associations, and findings from the focus group discussions suggested that, in more recent times, some schools were

Table 4.1 Case studies of Islamic schools

Islamic school case study	Years of operation	Total number of board directors as of June 2016	Number of founding board directors as of June 2016
ISCS1	20–30	12	4
ISCS2	10–20	5	1
ISCS3	<10	5	5
ISCS4	10–20	7	2
ISCS5	10–20	7	0
ISCS6	10–20	11	1
ISCS7	10–20	9	2

founded by individuals or groups of individuals who had weak ties with these organisations.[93] Data from the study suggest that there were variations in the number of directors appointed to the school boards. Table 4.1 outlines the years of operation and the total number of directors on each school board.

Most boards had appointed five to twelve directors, including founding directors. In total, there were fifty-six members on these boards; however, only six of these were women. This suggests that a gender imbalance exists on the boards of these schools, and this may be connected to particular cultural traditions that are typically practised by dominant cultural groups.[94] The data show a tendency for founding directors to remain on the boards for extended periods of time. In terms of the structure of the boards, Islamic schools adopted board structures that were similar to those of other schools in the independent schools sector.[95] Some participants stated that they followed traditional systematic structures commonly used by organisations in the NFP sector, including a traditional board structure with a chairperson, treasurer and secretary. This type of structure was compatible with the requirements outlined by ASIC.[96]

However, differences were found in the process of board member selection. A number of participants stated that founding directors played an important role in the decision-making process and brought 'more passion and showed more interest' in the school[97]; as stated by one participant:

> when he deals with the school the school is part of his soul … I can see when someone has passion (BP4ISCS1).[98]

Other schools recruited board members who were 'like-minded' in terms of the vision for the school.[99] Some participants stated that directors were appointed internally by the board as they did not see any need to consult with the stakeholder community they served. A review of the company statements of each school board used in the study found that most boards reinstated their members to their positions from term to term.[100]

Stakeholder participants (parents) stated that a lack of transparency in school boards made them question the legitimacy and competence of directors.[101] These parents felt that boards were more concerned with the number of enrolments and the academic outcomes of the students, whereas parents were more concerned with the well-being of their children and the Islamic pedagogy taught at the school.[102] Stakeholders also raised a number of concerns on issues of ownership and often misunderstood Islamic schools as for-profit institutions.[103] In an analysis of these findings the study identified that transparency and accountability were key issues contributing to the ongoing dilemma in Islamic schools.

The Dilemma of Stewardship and Ownership

The reoccurring issues of compliance, accountability and transparency that continued to surface in the boards of Islamic schools in NSW indicated a dilemma of stewardship and ownership as a nuanced phenomenon in this study. The findings highlighted how board members, at times, misinterpreted their role as stewards in ways that had them operate as owners. This study also found that directors were reluctant to inform parents in matters that involved accountability and financial reporting. The data collected for this chapter are from a larger research study on the identity of board members in Islamic schools. As the data emerged, interviews with directors developed into discussions about stewardship. Board participants were asked, 'What is the difference between stewardship and ownership?' In their responses, several directors referred to stewardship as 'leadership' and 'service' and defined a steward as a person with 'professionalism and values' including trust, sincerity and integrity. Conceptually, stewardship is to serve the collective interest of current and future stakeholders.[104] According to Beekun and Badawi,[105] stewardship is a role of moral leadership where a steward is a servant who enjoins the good and forbids the evil (*al-amr bil maarouf wa al nahi anil munkar*).[106] These leaders are servant leaders whose role is to serve their communities and wider stakeholder groups for 'no personal gain'.[107]

Responses by board participants often varied when discussing ownership, although a number of themes emerged that indicated that board members had developed a sense of ownership toward their schools. Most participants reflected on ownership as a dilemma. For instance, the first theme identified in the data was cultural issues that influence board members who adopt cultural type behaviours in their decision-making. As stated by one board member:

> it is because of the generation problem, the generation of the people on the Board, they don't have the concept of accountability, they don't have the concept of fairness, they don't have a concept of honesty so they don't know Islam, from fathers and forefathers, but once you get educated you will find out you should be able to fix this (IBP1).[108]

This suggests that although the lack of knowledge about the roles and responsibilities of directors may be an underlying issue in this dilemma, the generational problem discussed by the participant was more relevant to the cultural discourses that existed within the Muslim community.

Some of the cultural issues experienced in Islamic schools elsewhere are evident in a study on Islamic schools in the United States where, according to DeCuir,[109] board members who established Islamic schools often had limited knowledge of how to operate a school and used cultural behaviours to control the operations of the school.[110] In the Australian context, board members appear to struggle to operate Islamic schools for two reasons. First, they seem to lack the knowledge of educational institutions and the nature of NFP enterprises. Second, their governance practice is sometimes hindered by cultural behaviours and attitudes that do not support good governance practice. These factors increase the risk of not meeting compliance requirements for registration and accreditation purposes. This may create tensions between the values of directors and those of stakeholders in the community.

In further discussions with the participant, these cultural behaviours appeared in the personal leadership style of the participant (IBP1). Ownership traits were identified in the type of decision-making that he adopted on the board when he stated: 'I am running the show, and it is my way or the highway (IBP1).'[111] This participant considered that his educational background and knowledge of community institutions gave him preference over other members of the board and the community. This type of cultural behaviour was evident throughout most of the interviews conducted for this study. When asked about the type of governance structure used by the board, participants stated that board composition and consultation among directors were all important factors of board structure and practice.

However, this seemed contrary to the statements made by participant IBP1 who talked about how the chair controlled the board. He said an overall sense of transparency was not typical of the chair's behaviour.

The issue of control is the second theme of this study. During the interviews, some participants displayed attitudes of control and dominance when explaining the way they operated on the boards. In the words of one participant: 'I'll be asked on the day of judgement … (IBP1).'[112] A common theme discussed by most participants was the issue of blame: 'The problem is with the people who want to take control, they think they can come in and do what they want and nobody will ask questions… (IBP1).'[113] These statements were often used to justify the type of decision-making that was practised. However, directors who engaged in this type of behaviour could use their position to dominate others around them, which may have contributed to the ownership-type behaviours in the form of controlling attitudes on the board. This is contrary to Islam, which discourages the use of position for control, as it may steer directors away from their mutual obligations towards others. In the prophetic sayings (*hadith*), Prophet Muhammad (Prayers, Peace and Blessings be Upon Him), said:

> Abd al-Rahman, do not ask for a position of authority, for if you are granted this position as a result of your asking for it, you will be left alone (without God's help to discharge the responsibilities attendant thereon), and if you are granted it without making any request for it, you will be helped (by God in the discharge of your duties).[114]

Ownership traits may also stem from control when founding directors of NFP organisations adopt for-profit structures in the board.[115] To avoid this, Islamic school boards would normally aim to operate for the interests of stakeholders, and directors' stewardship obligations would be focused on serving the public interest (*maslah*).

Stakeholders perceive control as a cultural issue in Islamic schools, and the themes of culture and control are interconnected. Several parents stated that boards failed to consult with parents and staff on the needs of students and did not show the intention to serve in the public interest (*maslah*) of the school community. Although parents stated that the main reason they sent their children to Islamic schools was to help them develop a Muslim identity,[116] they felt alienated from the schools their children attended. The following statement conveys a common sentiment among parents:

It reminds me of a dictator and government, chairperson and principals are the dictators and the Boards are the government: people's voices and concerns are not taken into account and whatever the dictator wants to happen, will happen (SP1ISCS3).[117]

This statement is relevant to the cultural discourses within the Muslim community more generally, and many parents felt this rhetoric was influenced by the cultural behaviours adopted by boards in Islamic schools. The issue of culture is a common theme in Islamic educational leadership, and researchers argue that cultural traditions overpower, and at times conceal, the Islamic from emerging as the framework for development and progression.[118]

Ownership behaviours can also emerge when founding directors adopt 'narrow stewardship'.[119] This form of stewardship occurs when board members exercise governance for personal interests.[120] For instance, one founding director described the ownership issue as

a very important area to consider on our Board and we were very mindful of that. We never thought that we could be effective on a Board over our lifetime: our lifetime, not the institution's lifetime, so we never set out and said listen, ok we will start and stay on the Board until we die (BP1ChairISCS3).[121]

Although this participant was mindful of his stewardship obligations, he also displayed a strong personal interest in the performance and outcomes of the school when he stated:

serving on the Board was deeper than just serving at the school because we put up a lot of money to get the thing started ... there is a lot of risk involved to get the job done right ... you need the founding people to be heavily involved in the setup years because they are all like-minded, you don't want any conflict in the Board ... (BP1ChairISCS3).[122]

Researchers have argued that founders often fall into an emotional trap when appointed as board members and abandon the stewardship principles of service.[123] Founders who become too emotionally aligned with the institution may overlook the need to add value to the strategic direction of the school.[124] In this study, directors who applied this 'narrow form of stewardship' contributed to the board's compliance and accountability. These boards were selectively transparent with their stakeholder groups.

This is the dilemma of stewardship and ownership—when the stewardship approach to the governance of boards mutates into a type of ownership, with the consequence that decision-making is based on ownership rather than stewardship. Stewardship theory proposes that boards of NFP organisations serve in the interests of current and future stakeholders and for the general will of the community.[125] Applying the Islamic worldview, we consider that the role of directors of these schools is to monitor their mutual obligations to others using self-discipline and right action (*adab*). This ensures they serve their communities rather than their own personal interests.[126] To do this, directors would need to engage in consultation (*mushawarah*) with the school's community and make connections with their religious obligations of service and justice.

From a broader perspective, some founding directors spoke about their struggles to keep the composition of their boards intact. Appointing people to the board involved strategic decisions to ensure that like-minded people joined the board. Audits completed on a number of Islamic schools found that some boards had appointed members for personal interest, which raised questions about compliance and accountability issues in these Islamic schools. Community debates on issues of transparency also contributed to these dilemmas. In governance research, independent school boards have been challenged with the compliance, accountability and transparency practices of directors.[127]

From this discussion, it would be safe to argue that Islamic school boards' compliance, accountability and transparency are impacted by several nuanced themes in governance research. These themes include board composition and structure; however, the dilemma of stewardship and ownership is influenced by cultural themes that include control, dominance and personal interests. A way forward for governance in Islamic schools may be to develop a model of governance that addresses the cultural and religious nuances in boards, and this can assist directors in fulfilling their mutual obligations to the stakeholder communities they serve. Through the lens of an Islamic worldview, an understanding of their Islamic obligations, including trust (*amanah*), justice (*adl*), benevolence (*ihsan*) and ethics (*akhlaq*), may help boards maintain compliance and develop accountable and transparent measures to bridge the gap between them and the multiple stakeholders of these schools.

A Hybrid Governance Model for Islamic Schools

This study has suggested a hybrid model of governance to overcome the complexity of compliance, accountability and transparency issues for these schools. This hybrid model adopts a holistic framework for Islamic school boards and can be adopted by organisations in the independent schools sector more generally.

From an Islamic perspective, these boards are required to exercise stewardship with the intention of service to the Muslim communities they serve. In his inaugural leadership speech, Abu Bakr (the best friend of the prophet Muhammad) As-Siddiq (May Allah be pleased with him) discussed his Islamic obligation in his stewardship role as a vicegerent (*Khalif*) and stated:

> I have been given authority over you although I am not the best of you. If I do well, help me; and if I act wrongly, set me right. Loyalty is to tell the truth to a leader; treason is to hide it. The weak among you will be powerful in my eyes until I secure his rights, if Allah so wills. The strong among you shall be weak in my eyes until I get the right from him. Obey me as long as I obey Allah and his prophet, and if I disobey them, you owe me no obedience (see *Abu Jafar al-Tabari, Tarikh al-Tabari, Vol.3 Cairo: Dar al-Ma'arif, 1969:224*).[128]

The main themes of his speech were the mutual obligations of accountability and transparency through principles of trust (*amanah*), justice (*adl*) and equity (*qist*). In the Holy Qur'an, Allah (*SWT*) commands Muslims to fulfil the divine obligations of worship and mutual obligations of service and moral leadership.[129] However, several issues of ownership in the governance models used by Islamic schools continue to prevent boards from fulfilling these obligations. Islamic schools are an important part of the formation of cultural and religious identity for Muslims in Western societies.[130] As leaders of Islamic institutions, directors have an obligation to ensure schools operate in the best interests of current and future stakeholders, government and non-government funding bodies that offer financial and curriculum support as well as employees and the Islamic community. The hybrid model addresses the complexity of this issue as outlined in Fig. 4.1.[131]

This model has been developed as a guide to assist in understanding the complexity of governance frameworks in Islamic schools. Under the

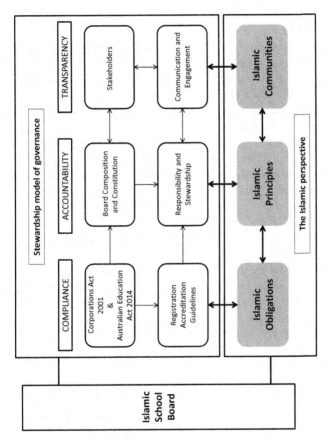

Fig. 4.1 Hybrid model of governance

'compliance' heading, independent school boards are required to operate as NFP institutions and develop a constitution that is compliant with the Corporations Act 2001 and the Australian Education Act 2014.[132] Additionally, under the 'accountability' heading, school boards are required to appoint directors who are responsible members of the community and whose role is to serve the interests of their stakeholders.[133] 'Transparency' involves communication and engagement with multiple stakeholder groups that include parents and the Muslim community.

The hybrid model can assist or guide boards to meet their Islamic obligations (as well as legal obligations expected of board members). To fulfil these obligations, governance adopts Islamic principles such as trust (*amanah*), justice (*adl*), ethics (*akhlaq*) and benevolence (*ihsan*). The hybrid element of transparency requires boards to recognise the public interest (*maslah*) of the communities they serve. This may assist them in pursuing and safeguarding the interests of stakeholders more generally. Islamic school boards would need to comply with the aforementioned Islamic principles that underpin these obligations for better standards of accountability and transparency to the multiple stakeholder groups outlined in this chapter.

IMPEDIMENTS TO THE HYBRID MODEL OF GOVERNANCE

Members of some of the boards studied appeared to be resistant to changing their current governance models. This may have been attributable to the cultural beliefs and attitudes of participants. However, as previously discussed, current issues in the governance of Islamic schools indicate a need for change for the well-being of these institutions. As Al-Attas[134] suggests, change influences development and development is progress.[135]

Based on the findings in this study and the literature reviewed, the governance of Islamic schools more generally remains an area that is under-researched. Further investigations to explore the nuanced phenomena of boards and governance are needed to better understand the problems of governance that exist in these schools. Although all boards of schools are required to be compliant, accountable and transparent, this process requires more complex interpretations as a result of the multiple dimensions of governance in the Islamic school sector.

Conclusion

An increase in the self-organisational nature of NFP organisations has required a more nuanced approach to governance research. In independent schools, governance practice has experienced periods of uncertainty and change due to the growth of this sector and changing compliance requirements by government funding bodies.[136] For these organisations, a new way of understanding governance is needed to align with these changes. The present chapter identified a number of issues in the governance of Islamic schools.

In contrast to past research on the governance of Islamic schools, this study identified an issue with the compliance, accountability and transparency processes of boards as a contributing factor to the problem of governance. The main issue affecting Islamic schools may be the confusion about stewardship and ownership among directors of school boards. Cultural issues that include control, dominance and personal interest among the founding members of boards in these schools contribute to ownership concerns. In addition to the compliance process for funding bodies, Islamic schools have a moral obligation to fulfil their divine and mutual duties to Allah (*SWT*) and to the communities they serve.[137] To address these issues, the study proposed that a hybrid model of governance is necessary to address issues of governance in Islamic schools. The study recognised that there could be impediments to the hybrid model, including challenges of control and resistance to change by boards in some of these schools.

A lack of understanding of the moral obligation of stewardship was evident among these Islamic school boards, including ensuring that the principles of trust (*amanah*), justice (*adl*), benevolence (*ihsan*) and ethics (*akhlaq*) are applied.[138] The Islamic worldview, as a framework, may help directors apply these principles through self-discipline and right action (*adab*).[139] Stewardship governance is a combination of 'good behaviour and good judgement',[140] and boards have a moral obligation to the current and future stakeholder communities they serve. For organisational governance, the hybrid model provides opportunities to sustain the quality of service to stakeholders and other community groups.

Notes

1. John Carver, "A Theory of Governing the Public's Business", *Public Management Review*, 3:1 (2001): 55.
2. William M. Klepper, *The CEO's Boss: Tough Love in the Boardroom* (New York: Columbia Business School, 2010).

3. 'Allah, Subhanna wa Ta'alah (SWT)' means 'God, the most glorified the most high.' (SWT) can also mean 'may he be glorified and exalted.' It is a matter of religious reverence and convention to include the words in parenthesis after a written reference to God (Allah). The written words in parenthesis have been included after each reference to Allah throughout the chapter.
4. Syed Muhammad Al-Naquib Al-Attas, "Islamic Philosophy: An Introduction", *Journal of Islamic Philosophy*, 1 (2005).
5. Syed Muhammad Al-Naquib Al-Attas, "Islamic Philosophy: An Introduction", *Journal of Islamic Philosophy*, 1 (2005); Syed Muhammad Al-Naquib Al-Attas, *The Concept of Education in Islam: A Framework for an Islamic Philosophy of Education* (Kuala Lumpur: Muslim Youth Movement of Malaysia (ABIM), 1980).
6. Abdullah Al-Ahsan and Stephen B. Young, *Guidance for Good Governance* (Malaysia: IIUM Press, IIUM and Caoux Round Table, 2008).
7. Rafik I. Beekun and Jamal Badawi, *Leadership an Islamic Perspective* (Maryland: Amana Publications, 1999).
8. Mark Blair and David Shortland, *Good Governance Principles and Guidance for Not-For-Profit Organisations*. Australian Institute of Company Directors, 2013.
9. Leo Shanahan, "Muslim School Rissalah College's Funding Frozen," *The Australian*, April 29, 2013; Natasha Bita, "Parents turn to Muslim Schools to Enforce Values," *The Australian*, May 25, 2015; Alison Branley, "Further Details Emerge of Alleged Mismanagement at Islamic Schools," *ABC News*, December 2015.
10. Association of Independent Schools (NSW), *Registration and Accreditation, Advice for NSW Independent Schools*, 2015, https://www.ais.nsw.edu.au.
11. *The Holy Quran, Al-Maida*, English translation of the "*Meanings and Commentary*". Completed at: The custodian of the two Holy Mosques King Fahd Complex for the printing of The Holy Qur'an, Al-Madinah Al-Munawarah under the Auspices of The Ministry of Hajj and Endowments. The Kingdom of Saudi Arabia, 5:1, page 276.
12. John Carver, "A Theory of Governing the Public's Business", *Public Management Review*, 3:1 (2001): 55.
13. *The Holy Quran, Al-Maida*, English translation of the "*Meanings and Commentary*". Completed at: The Custodian of the two Holy Mosques King Fahd Complex for the printing of The Holy Qur'an, Al-Madinah Al-Munawarah under the Auspices of The Ministry of Hajj and Endowments, The Kingdom of Saudi Arabia, 5:1, page 276.
14. Natasha Bita, "Parents turn to Muslim Schools to Enforce Values," *The Australian*, May 25, 2015; Leo Shanahan, "Muslim School Rissalah College's Funding Frozen," *The Australian*, April 29, 2013.

15. Ibid.
16. Alison Branley, "Further Details Emerge of Alleged Mismanagement at Islamic Schools." *ABC News*, December 2015.
17. Natasha Bita, "Parents turn to Muslim Schools to Enforce Values," *The Australian*, May 25, 2015.
18. John Hamilton, "Governance for School Boards." *McInnes Wilson Lawyers*, 2013.
19. Ibid.
20. Ibid.: 3.
21. Ibid.
22. Simon Birmingham, "School Compliance with the Education Act: *Media Release*", *Minister for Education and Training*, March 2, 2016.
23. Board of Studies, Teaching and Educational Standards, *Registration Systems and Member Non-Government Schools (NSW) Manual*, 2016, Updated January 2016 (incorporating changes from 2004 to 2016). Accessed 14 March 2016: https://www.bostes.nsw.edu.au.
24. John McCormick, Kerry Barnett, Seyyed Babak Alavi and Geoffrey Newcombe, "Board Governance of Independent Schools," *Journal of Educational Administration*, 44:5 (2006): 430; Independent Schools Council of Australia, *Independent Schooling in Australia: The Independent Schools Sector, Snapshot* (2015), Accessed 2 June 2016: http://isca.edu.au/wp-content/uploads/2011/07/ISCA-Snapshot-2015.pdf.
25. "The Good Schools Guide", last modified 2016, http://www.goodschools.com.au/?gclid=CMuQuPqwm88CFYGXvAodqWcOgQ.
26. Independent Schools Council of Australia, *Independent Schooling in Australia: The Independent Schools Sector, Snapshot* (2015), Accessed 2 June 2016: http://isca.edu.au/wp-content/uploads/2011/07/ISCA-Snapshot-2015.pdf.
27. Independent Schools Council of Australia, *Independent Schooling in Australia: The Independent Schools Sector, Snapshot* (2015), Accessed 2 June 2016: http://isca.edu.au/wp-content/uploads/2011/07/ISCA-Snapshot-2015.pdf. Independent Schools Council of Australia. *The Independent School Student: A Demographic Profile, An Analysis of the Australian Bureau of Statistics 2011 Census of Population & Housing Census*, September 2014, Accessed 21 April 2015: http://isca.edu.au/wp-content/uploads/2011/03/The-Independent-School-Student-A-Demographic-Profile.pdf.
28. Yasmin Hassen, "Making Muslims: the Politics of Religious Identity Construction and Victoria's Islamic Schools, *Islam and Christian-Muslim Relations*, 24:4 (2013), 10.1080.09596410.2013.813120.
29. Australian Bureau of Statistics. *Article: 4221.0 – Schools, Australia*, February 2016. Accessed 31 August 2016: http://www.abs.gov.au/ausstats/abs@nsf/PrintAllPreparePage?

30. David AC. Gonski, Ken Boston AO, Kathryn Greiner AO, Carmen Lawrence, Bill Scales AO and Peter Tannock AM, "*Review of Funding for Schooling-Final Report*", Department of Education, Employment and Workplace Relations, December 2011. Accessed 1 September 2016: http://www.schoolfunding.gov.au; Independent Schools Council of Australia. *The Independent School Student: A Demographic Profile, An Analysis of the Australian Bureau of Statistics 2011 Census of Population & Housing Census*, September 2014, Accessed 21 April 2015: http://isca.edu.au/wp-content/uploads/2011/03/The-Independent-School-Student-A-Demographic-Profile.pdf.
31. Allan K. Beavis, "The Governance of Independent Schools: An Autopoietic Systems Approach," *The International Journal of Learning*, 14:7 (2007).
32. David Gonski et al., "Review of Funding for Schooling-Final Report", 2011.
33. Independent Schools Council of Australia, *The Independent School Student*, 2014; David Gonski et al., "Review of Funding for Schooling-Final Report", 2011.
34. David Gonski et al., "Review of Funding for Schooling-Final Report", 2011.
35. Natasha Bita, "Parents turn to Muslim Schools to Enforce Values," *The Australian*, May 25, 2015.
36. Australian Charities and Not-For-Profit Commission, *2015 Research: Public Trust and Confidence in Australian Charities: Quantitative and Qualitative Report*, 2015, Accessed 31 August 2016: file://ad.uws.edu.au/dfshare/HomesPTA$/30032548/Downloads/Download%20 the%202015%20Public%20trust%20and%20confidence%20survey%20 report%20[PDF%202.4 MB].pdf.
37. Australian Securities and Investment Commission, *Obligations of Companies Limited by Guarantee*, 2016: 131, Accessed 5 September 2016: http://asic.gov.au/regulatory-resources/financial-reporting-and-audit/preparers-of-financial-reports/companies-limited-by-guarantee/obligations-of-companies/.
38. Australian Charities and Not-For-Profit Commission, *Guide to the ACNC's template constitution for a charitable company limited by guarantee*, 2014:5, Accessed 22 September 2016: file://ad.uws.edu.au/dfshare/HomesPTA$/30032548/Downloads/Download%20Guide%20to%20 the%20template%20constitution%20[PDF%201.6MB].pdf.
39. Ibid.
40. Australian Government, *Corporations Act 2001 – Act no. 50 of 2001 as amended*, Federal Register of Legislation, 2016:S182, Accessed 5 September 2016: https://www.legislation.gov.au/details/C2013C00003;

John Lessing, David Morrison and Maria Nicolae, "Educational institutions, corporate governance and not-for-profits," *Corporate Governance eJournal* (2012), ISSN 1836–1110, Accessed 15 January 2016: http://epublications.bond.edu.au/cgej/26.
41. John Carver, "A Theory of Governing the Public's Business", *Public Management Review*, 3:1 (2001).
42. Amaarah DeCuir, "A gendered interpretation of the roles and responsibilities of the women leading American Islamic schools," (Doctor of Education Diss., George Washington University, 2014).
43. Ibid.
44. Ibid.
45. Ibid.
46. Randa Elbih, "Debates in the Literature on Islamic Schools," *Educational Studies*, 48:2 (2012): 156–173, https://doi.org/10.1080/00131946.2011.647147.
47. Ibrahim Lawson, *Leading Islamic Schools in the UK: A Challenge for us all*, Spring 2005, Accessed 5 July 2016: http://www.ncsl.org.uk.
48. Ibid.
49. Rafik I. Beekun and Jamal Badawi, *Leadership an Islamic Perspective* (Maryland: Amana Publications, 1999).
50. Khaliq Ahmad and O.K. Ogunsola, "An empirical assessment of Islamic leadership principles," *International Journal of Commerce and Management*, 21:3 (2011).
51. Rafik I. Beekun and Jamal Badawi, "Balancing Ethical Responsibility among Multiple Organisational Stakeholders," *The Journal of Business Ethics*, 60:2, (2005), https://doi.org/10.1007/s10551-004-8204-5.
52. Tufyal Choudhury, *The role of Muslim Identity Politics in Radicalisation: A Study in Progress*, London: Department for Communities in Local Government, 2007, Accessed 5 September 2016: file://ad.uws.edu.au/dfshare/HomesPTA$/30032548/Downloads/1431_identity%20(1).pdf.
53. Syed Muhammad Al-Naquib Al-Attas, *The Concept of Education in Islam: A Framework for an Islamic Philosophy of Education* (Kuala Lumpur: Muslim Youth Movement of Malaysia (ABIM), 1980).
54. Syed Muhammad Al-Naquib Al-Attas, "Islamic Philosophy: An Introduction", *Journal of Islamic Philosophy*, 1 (2005).
55. Syed Muhammad Al-Naquib Al-Attas, "Islamic Philosophy: An Introduction", *Journal of Islamic Philosophy*, 1 (2005); Saeeda Shah, "Educational Leadership: An Islamic Perspective," *British Educational Research Journal*, 32:3 (2006).
56. Rafik I. Beekun and Jamal Badawi, *Leadership an Islamic Perspective* (Maryland: Amana Publications, 1999).
57. Ibid.

58. *The Holy Qur'an, Ash-Shuraa*, English translation of the "*Meanings and Commentary*". Completed at: The custodian of the two Holy Mosques King Fahd Complex for the printing of The Holy Qur'an, Al-Madinah Al-Munawarah under the Auspices of The Ministry of Hajj and Endowments. The Kingdom of Saudi Arabia, 42:38.
59. Sheikh Safiur-Rahman Al-Mubarakpuri, "*Tafsir Ibn Khathir (Abridged by a group of scholars under the supervision of Sheikh Safiur-Rahman Al Mubarakpuri)*," Volume 8: Parts 22 to 25 (Surat Al-Ahzab Verse 51 to Surat Ad-Dukhan) Darussalam, Kingdom of Saudi Arabia.
60. Khaliq Ahmad and O.K. Ogunsola, "An empirical assessment of Islamic leadership principles," *International Journal of Commerce and Management*, 21:3 (2011).
61. Al-Hasan Al-Aidaros, Faridahwati Mohd Shamsudin, Kamil Md Idris. "Ethics and Ethical Theories from an Islamic Perspective." *International Journal of Islamic Thought*, 4 (2013).
62. Normala Sheikh Siti Obid and Babak Naysary, "Toward a Comprehensive Theoretical Framework for Shariah Governance in Islamic Financial Institutions," *Journal of Financial Services Marketing*, 19:4 (2014): 315.
63. Abdussalam Mahmoud Abu-Tapanjeh, "Corporate Governance from the Islamic Perspective: A Comparative Analysis with OECD Principles," *Critical Perspective on Accounting*, 20 (2009), https://doi.org/10.1016/j.cpa.2007.12.004.
64. Chris Pierce, *The Effective Director* (London: Kogan Page, 2001).
65. Normala Sheikh Siti Obid and Babak Naysary, "Toward a Comprehensive Theoretical Framework for Shariah Governance in Islamic Financial Institutions," *Journal of Financial Services Marketing*, 19:4 (2014).
66. John McCormick et al., "Board Governance of Independent Schools," *Journal of Educational Administration*, 44:5 (2006).
67. Edward R. Freeman, *Strategic Management: A Stakeholder Approach* (Boston: Pitman, 1984).
68. Tracey Burns and Florian Koster (eds.), "*Governing education in a complex world*," Educational Research and Innovation (Paris: OECD Publishing, 2016): 11.
69. Ibid.
70. Ibid.
71. Donald Nordberg, "Unfettered Agents? The Role of Ethics in Corporate Governance", (2010), in Kent H. Baker and Ronald Anderson, "*Corporate Governance: A synthesis of theory, research and practice*" (New Jersey: John Wiley and Sons, 2010).
72. Donald Nordberg, "Unfettered Agents? The Role of Ethics in Corporate Governance", (2010), in Kent H. Baker and Ronald Anderson, "*Corporate Governance: A synthesis of theory, research and practice*" (New Jersey: John

Wiley and Sons, 2010); Lex Donaldson and James Davis, "Stewardship Theory or Agency Theory: CEO Governance and Shareholder Returns," *Australian Journal of Management*, 16:1 (1991).

73. James Davis, H. F. David Schoorman and Lex Donaldson, "Toward a Stewardship Theory of Management," *Academy of Management Review*, 22:1 (1997); Donald Nordberg, "Unfettered Agents? The Role of Ethics in Corporate Governance", (2010), in H. Kent Baker and Ronald Anderson, "*Corporate Governance: A synthesis of theory, research and practice*" (New Jersey: John Wiley and Sons, 2010).

74. Donald Nordberg, "Unfettered Agents? The Role of Ethics in Corporate Governance", (2010:182), in Kent H. Baker and Ronald Anderson, "*Corporate Governance: A synthesis of theory, research and practice*" (New Jersey: John Wiley and Sons, 2010).

75. Ibid.

76. John McCormick et al., "Board Governance of Independent Schools," *Journal of Educational Administration*, 44:5 (2006).

77. Ibid.

78. R. Herman and D. Heimovics, "Executive Leadership", in Herman, R (Ed.), *The Jossey Bass Handbook of Non-profit Leadership and Management* (San Francisco CA: Jossey-Bass, 1994), 137: 53.

79. June Kronholz, "Boot Camp for Charter Boards: Finding and Civic-Minded Leaders," *Education Next*, 15:3 (2015), ISSN-1539-96642015; Chris James, Jeff Jones, Michael Connolly, Steve Brammer, Mike Fertig and Jane James, "The role of the chair of the school governing body in England," *School Leadership & Management*, 32:1 (2012), Accessed 2 October 2015: https://doi.org/10.1080/13632434.2011.642356.

80. Independent Schools Council of Australia, *Factors Affecting School Choice*, ISCA Research Report 2008, Accessed 2 June 2016: http://isca.edu.au/wp-content/uploads/2011/03/ISCA-Research-Report-School-Choice-2008.pdf.

81. John McCormick et al., "Board Governance of Independent Schools," *Journal of Educational Administration*, 44:5 (2006).

82. Independent Schools Council of Australia, *Factors Affecting School Choice*," ISCA Research Report 2008, Accessed 2 June 2016: http://isca.edu.au/wp-content/uploads/2011/03/ISCA-Research-Report-School-Choice-2008.pdf.

83. John McCormick et al., "Board Governance of Independent Schools," *Journal of Educational Administration*, 44:5 (2006); Allan K. Beavis, "The Governance of Independent Schools: An Autopoietic Systems Approach," *The International Journal of Learning*, 14:7 (2007).

84. Seyyed Hossein Nasr, "Islamic Pedagogy: An Interview," *Islam & Science*, 10:1 (2012).

85. Saeeda J.A. Shah, "Rethinking educational leadership: exploring the impact of cultural and belief systems," *International Journal of Leadership in Education*, 13:1 (2010).
86. Jamal Badawi, "Islamic Worldview: Prime Motive for Development," *Humanomics*, 18:3/4 (2002): 3–4.
87. Jamal Badawi, "Islamic Worldview: Prime Motive for Development," *Humanomics*, 18:3/4 (2002): 3–4; Seyyed Hossein Nasr, "Islamic Pedagogy: An Interview," *Islam & Science*, 10:1 (2012).
88. Jamal Badawi, "Islamic Worldview: Prime Motive for Development," *Humanomics*, 18:3/4 (2002).
89. Ibid.: 3–4.
90. Samiul Hasan, *Philanthropy and Social Justice in Islam: Principles, Prospects and Practices* (Kuala Lumpur, Malaysia: A.S. Noordeen, 2007).
91. Muhammad Abdullah and Muhammad Junaid Nadvi, "Understanding the principles of Islamic World-View," *The Dialogue*, 6:3 (2011).
92. Muhammad Abdullah and Muhammad Junaid Nadvi, "Understanding the principles of Islamic World-View," *The Dialogue*, 6:3 (2011); Dylan Chown and Omaira Alam. "Towards Authentic Behaviour Management Models for Islamic Schools – A Framework Synthesising Research," *5th Annual ISNA West Coast Education Forum*, January 15–16, 2016.
93. SP1ISCS3 – Stakeholder Participant 1, Islamic School Case Study 3; FG1P1ISCS1 – Focus Group 1, Participant 1, Islamic School Case Study 1.
94. Saeeda J.A. Shah, "Rethinking Educational Leadership: Exploring the Impact of Cultural and Belief Systems," *International Journal of Leadership in Education*, 13:1 (2010).
95. Australian Securities and Investment Commission, *Registering Not for Profit or Charitable Organisations*, Accessed 5 September 2016: http://asic.gov.au/for-business/starting-a-company/how-to-start-a-company/registering-not-for-profit-or-charitable-organisations/.
96. Ibid.
97. BP4ISCS1 – Board Participant 4, Islamic School Case Study 1.
98. Ibid.
99. BP1ChairISCS3 – Board Participant 1-Chair, Islamic School Case Study 3.
100. Australian Securities and Investments Commission (ASIC), *Company Statements of Directors (History)*, Accessed September 2016: www.asic.gov.au.
101. FG2P2ISCS3 – Focus Group 2-Participant 2-Islamic School Case Study 3; SP2ISCS4 – Stakeholder Participant 2, Islamic schools case study 4.
102. Ibid.
103. Ibid.

104. Donald Nordberg, "Unfettered Agents? The Role of Ethics in Corporate Governance" (2010), in H. Kent Baker and Ronald Anderson, "*Corporate Governance: A synthesis of theory, research and practice*" (New Jersey: John Wiley and Sons, 2010).
105. Rafik I. Beekun and Jamal Badawi, *Leadership an Islamic Perspective* (Maryland: Amana Publications, 1999).
106. Ibid.
107. Saeeda Shah, "Educational Leadership: An Islamic Perspective," *British Educational Research Journal*, 32:3 (2006).
108. IBP1 – Independent Board Participant 1 – Chair of the Board.
109. Amaarah DeCuir, "A gendered interpretation of the roles and responsibilities of the women leading American Islamic schools," (Doctor of Education Diss., George Washington University, 2014).
110. Ibid.
111. IBP1 – Independent Board Participant 1 – Chair of the Board.
112. Ibid.
113. Ibid.
114. Centre for Muslim Jewish Engagement, "Kitab Al Imara" (The book on Government), *Sahih Muslim Book 20, Hadith number 4487*, University of South California, Accessed 15 August 2016: http://www.usc.edu/org/cmje/religious-texts/hadith/muslim/020-smt.php.
115. Chris James and Paul Sheppard, "The Governing of International Schools: The Implications of Ownership and Profit Motive," *School Leadership & Management: Formerly School Organisation*, 34:1 (2014), https://doi.org/10.1080/13632434.2013.813457.
116. Yasmin Hassen, "Making Muslims: the Politics of Religious Identity Construction and Victoria's Islamic Schools," *Islam and Christian-Muslim Relations*, 24:4 (2013), https://doi.org/10.1080.09596410.20 13.813120.
117. SP1ISCS3 – Stakeholder Participant 1, Islamic School Case Study 3.
118. Saeeda J.A. Shah, "Rethinking educational leadership: exploring the impact of cultural and belief systems," *International Journal of Leadership in Education*, 13:1 (2010): 374.
119. Donald Nordberg, "Unfettered Agents? The Role of Ethics in Corporate Governance" (2010), in H. Kent Baker and Ronald Anderson, "*Corporate Governance: A synthesis of theory, research and practice*" (New Jersey: John Wiley and Sons, 2010).
120. Ibid.
121. BP1ChairISCS3 – Board Participant 1-Chair, Islamic School Case Study 3; SP1ISCS3 – Stakeholder Participant 1 – Islamic school case study 3 is also part of this case study.

122. Ibid.
123. Stephen R. Block and Steven Rosenberg, "Toward an Understanding of Founder's Syndrome, An Assessment of Power and Privilege Amoung Founders of Nonprofit Organisations," *Nonprofit Management and Leadership*, 12:4, Summer (2002).
124. Ibid.
125. Donald Nordberg, "Unfettered Agents? The Role of Ethics in Corporate Governance" (2010), in H. Kent Baker and Ronald Anderson, "*Corporate Governance: A synthesis of theory, research and practice*" (New Jersey: John Wiley and Sons, 2010); Normala Sheikh Siti Obid and Babak Naysary, "Toward a Comprehensive Theoretical Framework for Shariah Governance in Islamic Financial Institutions," *Journal of Financial Services Marketing*, 19:4 (2014).
126. Zamir Iqbal and Abbas Mirakhor, "Stakeholders Model of Governance in Islamic Economic System," *Islamic Economic Studies*, 11:2 (2004).
127. John McCormick et al., "Board Governance of Independent Schools," *Journal of Educational Administration*, 44:5 (2006).
128. Abdullah Al-Ahsan and Stephen B. Young, *Guidance for Good Governance* (Malaysia: IIUM Press, IIUM and Caoux Round Table, 2008): 31.
129. *The Holy Qur'an, Al-Maida*, English translation of the "*Meanings and Commentary*". Completed at: The custodian of the two Holy Mosques King Fahd Complex for the printing of The Holy Qur'an, Al-Madinah Al-Munawarah under the Auspices of The Ministry of Hajj and Endowments, The Kingdom of Saudi Arabia, 5:1, page 276.
130. Yasmin Hassen, "Making Muslims: the Politics of Religious Identity Construction and Victoria's Islamic Schools," *Islam and Christian-Muslim Relations*, 24:4 (2013), https://doi.org/10.1080.09596410.20 13.813120.
131. The Hybrid model was developed by the authors of this chapter. It is a hybrid of a stewardship model of governance and the Islamic perspectvies of a stewardship model.
132. Australian Securities and Investment Commission, *Obligations of Companies Limited by Guarantee*, 2016; Australian Charities and Not-For-Profit Commission, *Guide to the ACNC's template constitution for a charitable company limited by guarantee*, 2014; Association of Independent Schools (NSW), *Registration and Accreditation, Advice for NSW Independent Schools*, 2015.
133. Australian Charities and Not-For-Profit Commission, *Guide to the ACNC's template constitution for a charitable company limited by guarantee*, 2014.

134. Syed Muhammad Al-Naquib Al-Attas, "Islamic Philosophy: An Introduction", *Journal of Islamic Philosophy*, 1 (2005).
135. Ibid.
136. John McCormick et al., "Board Governance of Independent Schools," *Journal of Educational Administration*, 44:5 (2006).
137. Rafik I. Beekun and Jamal Badawi, *Leadership an Islamic Perspective* (Maryland: Amana Publications, 1999); Abdullah Al-Ahsan and Stephen B. Young, *Guidance for Good Governance* (Malaysia: IIUM Press, IIUM and Caoux Round Table, 2008).
138. Rafik I. Beekun and Jamal Badawi, *Leadership an Islamic Perspective* (Maryland: Amana Publications, 1999).
139. Syed Muhammad Al-Naquib Al-Attas, *The Concept of Education in Islam: A Framework for an Islamic Philosophy of Education* (Kuala Lumpur: Muslim Youth Movement of Malaysia (ABIM), 1980).
140. Mark Blair and David Shortland, "Good Governance Principles and Guidance for Not-For-Profit Organisations," *Australian Institute of Company Directors*, 2013. Accessed 14 March 2016: http://www.companydirectors.com.au/~/media/b42bd5b5ca1445f582bb96adac752325.ashx.

Bibliography

Abdullah, Muhammad, and Muhammad Junaid Nadvi. "Understanding the Principles of Islamic World-View." *The Dialogue* 6, no. 3 (2011): 268–289.

Abu-Tapanjeh, Abdussalam Mahmoud. "Corporate Governance from the Islamic Perspective: A Comparative Analysis with OECD Principles." *Critical Perspective on Accounting* 20 (2009): 556–567. https://doi.org/10.1016/j.cpa.2007.12.004.

Ahmad, Khaliq, and O.K. Ogunsola. "An Empirical Assessment of Islamic Leadership Principles." *International Journal of Commerce and Management* 21, no. 3 (2011): 291–318.

Al-Ahsan, Abdullah, and Stephen B. Young. *Guidance for Good Governance, Explorations in Qur'anic, Scientific and Cross-Cultural Approaches*. Malaysia: IIUM Press, IIUM and Caoux Round Table, 2008.

Al-Aidaros, Al-Hasan, Faridahwati Mohd Shamsudin, and Kamil Md Idris. "Ethics and Ethical Theories from an Islamic Perspective." *International Journal of Islamic Thought* 4 (2013): 1–13.

Al-Attas, Syed Muhammad Al-Naquib. "Islamic Philosophy: An Introduction." *Journal of Islamic Philosophy* 1 (2005): 12–52.

———. *The Concept of Education in Islam: A Framework for an Islamic Philosophy of Education*. Kuala Lumpur: Muslim Youth Movement of Malaysia (ABIM), 1980.

Association of Independent Schools (NSW). *Registration and Accreditation, Advice for NSW Independent Schools*. 2015. Accessed 10 March 2016. https://www.ais.nsw.edu.au.

Australian Bureau of Statistics. *4221.0 – Schools, Australia*. 2015, February 2016. Accessed 31 August 2016. http://www.abs.gov.au/ausstats/abs@nsf/PrintAllPreparePage?.

Australian Charities and Not-For-Profit Commission. *Guide to the ACNC's Template Constitution for a Charitable Company Limited by Guarantee*. 2014. Accessed 22 September 2016. file://ad.uws.edu.au/dfshare/HomesPTA$/30032548/Downloads/Download%20Guide%20to%20the%20template%20constitution%20[PDF%201.6MB].pdf.

———. "*2015 Research: Public Trust and Confidence in Australian Charities.*" Quantitative and Qualitative Report. 2015. Accessed 31 August 2016. file://ad.uws.edu.au/dfshare/HomesPTA$/30032548/Downloads/Download%20the%202015%20Public%20trust%20and%20confidence%20survey%20report%20[PDF%202.4MB].pdf.

Australian Government. *Australian Education Act 2013 – An Act in Relation to School Education and Reforms Relating to School Education, and for Related Purposes*. Federal Register of Legislation. Accessed 2 June 2016. https://www.legislation.gov.au/Details/C2013A00067/Download.

———. *Corporations Act 2001 – Act no. 50 of 2001 as Amended*. Federal Register of Legislation. Accessed 5 September 2016. https://www.legislation.gov.au/details/C2013C00003.

Australian Securities and Investment Commission. *Obligations of Companies Limited by Guarantee*. Accessed 5 September 2016. http://asic.gov.au/regulatory-resources/financial-reporting-and-audit/preparers-of-financial-reports/companies-limited-by-guarantee/obligations-of-companies/.

Australian Securities and Investment Commission. *Registering Not for Profit or Charitable Organisations*. Accessed 5 September 2016. http://asic.gov.au/for-business/starting-a-company/how-to-start-a-company/registering-not-for-profit-or-charitable-organisations/.

Badawi, Jamal. "Islamic Worldview: Prime Motive for Development." *Humanomics* 18, no. 3/4 (2002): 3–25.

Beavis, Allan K. "The Governance of Independent Schools: An Autopoietic Systems Approach." *The International Journal of Learning* 14, no. 7 (2007): 83–92.

Beekun, Rafik I., and Jamal Badawi. *Leadership an Islamic Perspective*. Beltsville, MD: Amana, 1999.

———. "Balancing Ethical Responsibility Among Multiple Organisational Stakeholders: The Islamic Perspective." *The Journal of Business Ethics* 60, no. 2 (2005): 131–145. https://doi.org/10.1007/s10551-004-8204-5.

Birmingham, Simon. "School Compliance with the Education Act." *Media Release, Minister for Education and Training*, 2 March 2016. Accessed 7 March 2016.

http://www.senatorbirmingham.com.au/Media-Centre/Media-Releases/ID/2973/School-compliance-with-education-act.
Bita, Natasha. "Parents Turn to Muslim Schools to Enforce Values." *The Australian*, 25 May 2015. Accessed 27 November 2015. http://www.theaustralian.com.au/in-depth/community-under-siege/parents-turn-to-muslim-schools-to-enforce-values/story-fnubfp6c-1227367627130?sv.
Blair, Mark, and David Shortland. *Good Governance Principles and Guidance for Not-For-Profit Organisations*. Australian Institute of Company Directors, 2013. 14 Accessed March 2016. http://www.companydirectors.com.au/~/media/b42bd5b5ca1445f582bb96adac752325.ashx.
Block, Stephen R., and Steven Rosenberg. "Toward an Understanding of Founder's Syndrome, an Assessment of Power and Privilege Among Founders of Nonprofit Organisations." *Nonprofit Management and Leadership* 12, no. 4 (Summer 2002): 353–368.
Board of Studies Teaching and Educational Standards. *Registration Systems and Member Non-Government Schools (NSW) Manual*. Updated January 2016 (incorporating Changes from 2004 to 2016). Accessed 14 March 2016. https://www.bostes.nsw.edu.au.
Branley, Alison. "Further Details Emerge of Alleged Mismanagement at Islamic schools." *ABC News*, December 2015. Accessed 15 July 2016. http://www.abc.net.au/news/2015-12-02/details-emerge-of-alleged-mismanagement-at-islamic-schools/6995956.
Burns, Tracey, and Florian Koster, eds. *Governing Education in a Complex World: Educational Research and Innovation*. Paris: OECD Publishing, 2016.
Carver, John. "A Theory of Governing the Public's Business: Redesigning the Jobs of Boards, Councils, and Commissions." *Public Management Review* 3, no. 1 (2001): 53–72. Accessed 5 September 2016. https://doi.org/10.1080/14616670010009450.
Centre for Muslim Jewish Engagement. "*Kitab Al Imara*" *(The Book on Government)*. Sahih Muslim Book 20, Hadith Number 4487, University of South California. Accessed 15 August 2016. http://www.usc.edu/org/cmje/religious-texts/hadith/muslim/020-smt.php.
Choudhury, Tufyal. *The Role of Muslim Identity Politics in Radicalisation: A Study in Progress*. London: Department for Communities in Local Government, 2007. Accessed 5 September 2016. file://ad.uws.edu.au/dfshare/HomesPTA$/30032548/Downloads/1431_identity%20(1).pdf.
Chown, Dylan, and Omaira Alam. "Towards Authentic Behaviour Management Models for Islamic Schools – A Framework Synthesising Research." *5th Annual ISNA West Coast Education Forum*, 15–16 January 2016.
Davis James, H., F. David Schoorman, and Lex Donaldson. "Toward a Stewardship Theory of Management." *Academy of Management Review* 22, no. 1 (1997): 20–47.

DeCuir, Amaarah. "*A Gendered Interpretation of the Roles and Responsibilities of the Women Leading American Islamic Schools.*" Doctor of Education Diss., George Washington University, 2014.

Donaldson, L., and J. Davis. "Stewardship Theory or Agency Theory: CEO Governance and Shareholder Returns." *Australian Journal of Management* 16, no. 1 (1991): 49–64.

Elbih, Randa. "Debates in the Literature on Islamic Schools." *Educational Studies* 48, no. 2 (2012): 156–173. https://doi.org/10.1080/00131946.2011.647147.

Freeman, R. Edward. *Strategic Management: A Stakeholder Approach.* Boston, MA: Pitman, 1984.

Gonski, David A.C., Ken Boston AO, Kathryn Greiner AO, Carmen Lawrence, Bill Scales AO, and Peter Tannock AM. "*Review of Funding for Schooling—Final Report.*" Department of Education, Employment and Workplace Relations, December 2011. Accessed 1 September 2016. http://www.schoolfunding.gov.au.

Hamilton, John. "Governance for School Boards." *McInnes Wilson Lawyers*, 2013. Accessed 28 May 2015. http://www.mcw.com.au/page/Publications/Education/governance-for-school-boards-and-councils/.

Hasan, Samiul. *Philanthropy and Social Justice in Islam: Principles, Prospects and Practices.* Kuala Lumpur: A.S. Noordeen, 2007.

Hassen, Yasmin. "Making Muslims: The Politics of Religious Identity Construction and Victoria's Islamic Schools." *Islam and Christian-Muslim Relations* 24, no. 4 (2013): 501–517. https://doi.org/10.1080.09596410.2013.813120.

Herman, R., and D. Heimovics. "Executive Leadership." In *The Jossey Bass Handbook of Nonprofit Leadership and Management*, ed. R. Herman, 137–153. San Francisco, CA: Jossey-Bass, 1994.

Independent Schools Council of Australia. *Factors Affecting School Choice.* ISCA Research Report 2008. Accessed 2 June 2016. http://isca.edu.au/wp-content/uploads/2011/03/ISCA-Research-Report-School-Choice-2008.pdf.

———. *Independent Schooling in Australia: The Independent Schools Sector, Snapshot.* 2015. Accessed 2 June 2016. http://isca.edu.au/wp-content/uploads/2011/07/ISCA-Snapshot-2015.pdf.

———. *The Independent School Student: A Demographic Profile, An Analysis of the Australian Bureau of Statistics 2011 Census of Population & Housing Census.* September 2014. Accessed 21 April 2015. http://isca.edu.au/wp-content/uploads/2011/03/The-Independent-School-Student-A-Demographic-Profile.pdf.

Iqbal, Zamir, and Abbas Mirakhor. "Stakeholders Model of Governance in Islamic Economic System." *Islamic Economic Studies* 11, no. 2 (2004): 43–64.

James, Chris, and Paul Sheppard. "The Governing of International Schools: The Implications of Ownership and Profit Motive." *School Leadership &*

Management: Formerly School Organisation 34, no. 1 (2014): 2–20. https://doi.org/10.1080/13632434.2013.813457.

James, Chris, Jeff Jones, Michael Connolly, Steve Brammer, Mike Fertig, and Jane James. " The Role of the Chair of the School Governing Body in England." *School Leadership & Management* 32, no. 1 (2012): 3–19. Accessed 2 October 2015. https://doi.org/10.1080/13632434.2011.642356.

Klepper, William M. *The CEO's Boss: Tough Love in the Boardroom*. New York: Columbia Business School, 2010.

Kronholz, June. "Boot Camp for Charter Boards: Finding and Civic-Minded Leaders." *Education Next* 15, no. 3 (2015): 40–46, ISSN-1539-9664.

Lawson, Ibrahim. *Leading Islamic Schools in the UK: A Challenge for Us All.* Spring 2005. Accessed 5 July 2016. http://www.ncsl.org.uk.

Lessing, John, David Morrison, and Maria Nicolae. "Educational Institutions, Corporate Governance and Not-For-Profits." *Corporate Governance eJournal* (2012): 1–22. ISSN 1836-1110. Accessed 15 January 2016. http://epublications.bond.edu.au/cgej/26.

McCormick, John, Kerry Barnett, Seyyed Babak Alavi, and Geoffrey Newcombe. "Board Governance of Independent Schools." *Journal of Educational Administration* 44, no. 5 (2006): 429–445. Accessed 28 April 2016. https://doi.org/10.1108/09578230610683741.

Nasr, Seyyed Hossein. "Islamic Pedagogy: An Interview." *Islam & Science* 10, no. 1 (2012): 7–24.

Nordberg, Donald. "Unfettered Agents? The Role of Ethics in Corporate Governance, Chapter 10." In *Corporate Governance: A Synthesis of Theory, Research and Practice*, ed. H. Kent Baker and Ronald Anderson. Hoboken, NJ: John Wiley and Sons, 2010.

Obid, Siti Normala Sheikh, and Babak Naysary. "Toward a Comprehensive Theoretical Framework for Shariah Governance in Islamic Financial Institutions." *Journal of Financial Services Marketing* 19, no. 4 (2014): 304–318.

Pierce, Chris. *The Effective Director*. London: Kogan Page, 2001.

Ray, Chris. "Behind the School Gates." *Good Weekend, Sydney Morning Herald*, 24 October 2015: 16–19.

Shah, Saeeda. "Educational Leadership: An Islamic Perspective." *British Educational Research Journal* 32, no. 3 (2006): 363–385.

———. "Rethinking Educational Leadership: Exploring the Impact of Cultural and Belief Systems." *International Journal of Leadership in Education* 13, no. 1 (2010): 27–44.

Shanahan, Leo. "Muslim School Rissalah College's Funding Frozen." *The Australian*, 29 April 2013. Accessed 14 July 2014. http://www.theaustralian.com.au/national-affairs/policy/muslim-school-rissalah-college-funding-frozen/story-fn59nlz9-1226631197794?nk=dedea0cb3c3422.

Sheikh Safiur-Rahman Al-Mubarakpuri. "*Tafsir Ibn Khathir (Abridged by a Group of Scholars Under the Supervision of Sheikh Safiur-Rahman Al Mubarakpuri).*" Volume 8: Parts 22 to 25 (Surat Al-Ahzab Verse 51 to Surat Ad-Dukhan) Darussalam, Kingdom of Saudi Arabia.

"The Good Schools Guide." Last Modified 2016. Accessed 5 September 2016. http://www.goodschools.com.au/?gclid=CMuQuPqwm88CFYGXvAodqWcOgQ.

The Holy Quran. English Translation of the "*Meanings and Commentary*". Completed at: The Custodian of the Two Holy Mosques King Fahd Complex for the Printing of The Holy Qur'an, Al-Madinah Al-Munawarah Under the Auspices of The Ministry of Hajj and Endowments, The Kingdom of Saudi Arabia.

CHAPTER 5

What Else Do They Teach in an Islamic School?

Peter Jones

FORMING AN ISLAMIC IDENTITY

In 2003, when Brendan Nelson was Minister for Education in the Howard Coalition government, he was lobbied by 'concerned citizens' alleging that anti-Christian and anti-Western sentiments were being fostered among students at Islamic schools.[1] As a result, he wrote to state counterparts asking them to ensure Islamic schools were meeting curriculum requirements and not encouraging such sentiments. This move was to trigger the Australian Values debate but suspicion of Islamic schools continues and a number of proposed new schools, such as the one in Camden in 2007, have since been met with local community opposition.

Following the shooting of a police official in Parramatta in October 2015 by a Muslim teenager, One Nation leader Pauline Hanson appeared on the *Seven News Sunrise* programme demanding that 'we need to know what is being taught in Islamic schools',[2] although none of those visited by police had any connection with Islamic schools in the Sydney area. She came back to this theme after her election as Senator for Queensland in

P. Jones (✉)
Friends' School, Hobart, North Hobart, TAS, Australia

© The Author(s) 2018
M. Abdalla et al. (eds.), *Islamic Schooling in the West*,
https://doi.org/10.1007/978-3-319-73612-9_5

July 2016, when she again demanded greater transparency on what was being taught in Muslim schools.[3]

Despite these attacks on Islamic schools, the demand for places is steadily growing, as many Muslim families are eager for their children to be educated in such establishments, despite the criticism levelled against them. While one advantage is that their children are taught specific units in their faith, much like in church schools and the fast-growing Christian schools, there is also the wider issue of the broader curriculum and what is taught in these classes.

For Muslims, as for those of other faiths, values are considered to permeate the whole of life, as all books and articles on Islamic education point out. As Noha Sanjakdar notes,

> Parents are looking for a school that will immerse their children in an Islamic environment and study a curriculum underpinned with Islamic values and beliefs.[4]

It is this issue that raises a number of concerns regarding whether or not the Islamic schools in Australia are just teaching the normal curriculum with a faith component tacked on, or whether an Islamic ethos pervades the entire curriculum as well as the rhythm of the school year. In addition, there is the issue of what parents are hoping for when they save to pay the fees to send their children to an Islamic school rather than a public school. Students too may be more interested in getting good exam results to further their academic career, particularly when they get to Years 11 and 12, so the Islamic content of their education may be of less concern to them.

Giles argues that 'Islamic education prepares the child for the "outside", laying the foundations in terms of good values and educational achievement'.[5] It is this nexus of building character within an Islamic framework and, at the same time, providing a good academic education that seems to be at the centre of what parents are seeking when they opt for an Islamic education in Australia. However, they do not seek an education that is exclusive, given the effort made by almost all the schools to encourage involvement in extra-curricular and dialogue activities beyond their own school. In addition, a number of families move their children between the public system, other private schools and the Islamic schools, sometimes switching them to an Islamic high school after primary school, or starting them in an Islamic primary school and then opting for the state system. There are also students who themselves choose to move on to a college in the state system where they can study subjects not available in their Islamic school.

This was the case with one of the Somali mothers interviewed by Giles, who sent her five children to an Islamic school for their primary education but then enrolled them in the public system for high school. 'She explained that the children could get a better understanding of Australian values from their teachers and peers by enrolling in the public high school system. At the same time, it was an opportunity for the children to discuss their values and beliefs with mainstream children'.[6] However, Giles also mentions that for some parents, one of the reasons to send their children to an Islamic school is so that they are not bullied or teased by non-Muslim children, so obviously a great deal depends on the resilience of the child and the school concerned.[7]

For Muslims, the question is whether this satisfies their understanding of what constitutes an Islamic education, while for the critics, it is whether these Islamic values run counter to what they understand to be Australian values. While the schools themselves have constantly stressed Values Education in their promotional materials and annual reports, little research has been carried out on the content of the 'hidden curriculum' in Islamic schools, apart from stressing the importance of creating an Islamic space through dress codes, provision of halal food, observation of Muslim holidays and the fasting month of Ramadan, and limited gender segregation after puberty. In addition, school fundraising activities would not include any form of gambling, such as raffles, a form of raising extra money practised by many other Australian schools, but *haram* for Muslims. Some detail comes through in school yearbooks, with reference to school camps, visiting speakers and service programmes, but as my research interviews made clear, the ways in which an Islamic ethos permeates the rest of the school vary enormously.

What is clear, however, is that as far as the curriculum is concerned, Australian Islamic schools follow the same one as all other schools, and they take great pride in their pre-tertiary exam results. Following the national or state curriculum is obviously a prerequisite for government funding, and most Islamic schools employ a mixture of Muslim and non-Muslim staff, with only a few employing 100% Muslim teachers. Many of the non-Muslim staff teach subjects such as Maths, Science and English, or the normal range of subjects taught in primary schools, to each grade. Some schools also at times employ a non-Muslim as principal as it obviously takes time to build up a core of experienced Muslim teachers able to take on such a role. Converts to Islam also play a crucial role in a number of the schools, with perhaps the best-known example being Abdul Karim Galea, who taught at the first Islamic College in Melbourne from its inception in 1983 until he retired as principal in 2015.[8] Fijian Muslims, having grown up in Fiji with an English educational background, also play a prominent role.

The curriculum taught in these core subjects is the normal Australian curriculum, although literature is subject to the guidance of the school imam when it touches on subjects that might be of concern to parents, such as premarital sex or drugs and alcohol. There are now a number of books written by Australian Muslim authors such as Randa Abdel-Fattah,[9] while other popular class study books feature the migrant experience, such as *Looking for Alibrandi*.[10] All schools with Year 11 and 12 classes teach the normal exam curriculum and are proud of their results in terms of the percentage of their students going on to university.

Little has been written in Australia on some of the more controversial aspects of the 'hidden curriculum' in Islamic schools, such as physical education, health education, science and the arts, while the extent to which specifically Islamic values were integrated into the mainstream teaching subjects in the timetable varied enormously. This often depended on whether the teacher was a Muslim or non-Muslim, though one school did in-service professional development classes on Islam for non-Muslim teachers once a term. The curriculum development teacher at the school had circulated a form on how the teachers integrated an Islamic perspective into the secular subjects' curriculum. Commenting on this, one Islamic Studies teacher observed:

> It depends very much on who is teaching the subject. If a Muslim teacher is teaching the subject, he is able to incorporate a lot of these values in his teaching. I mean again in the real world is there a difference between Islamic and non-Islamic? I think that would be another topic to deal with but generally I sense and I feel that when a Muslim is teaching a SOSE subject or a Science subject, I know because they ask me sometimes for resources that incorporate values in Islamic teaching in their method. As well, it is more difficult for a non-Muslim. Though non-Muslim teachers who have been here a long time are able to easily adapt these in their courses, newer teachers feel more uncomfortable because they are not sure where these Islamic values are coming from so they'd rather not deal with them.

An example of this would be mathematics and whether teachers ever talked to students about Islam's historic contribution to the subject. Not surprisingly, maths teachers' responses to this question varied enormously. Most did not touch on it, though perhaps this was often because they were not Muslim. One teacher interviewed said there was a very superficial input on the history of maths when he taught Years 8 through 11, but he did mention the origins of algebra and the concept of zero. Another non-Muslim teacher said he followed the school syllabus he was given, which came from South Africa, in order to incorporate Islamic values into the course:

> We follow what is written, for example, when we talk about a straight line, we equate it with the hadith that says in the Qur'an that you need to take a straight path. When we talk about infinity, which is a huge concept, we talk about the Creator.

Worth noting was the comment of a former student who said how thrilled he and his class were to learn from their teacher about Islam's contribution to mathematics. However, although there are now a number of books in print on this topic, such as *The House of Wisdom: How the Arabs Transformed Western Civilisation*,[11] books of this kind do not seem to be used very often in conjunction with the teaching of maths.

One student who was critical of his school's approach said that when he was in Year 12 he asked his father why they didn't teach students about Islamic history and Islamic science. He could remember reading a quote at university from a well-known scientist who said, 'If it wasn't for Islam, there would be no science'. He added, 'So when I think about that, I think why we were not taught this because it would have brought us some pride?' He did, however, feel that this knowledge was now spreading as a result of the Internet, but thought it had not been projected well in his school 'considering it was an Islamic school'.

Another teacher of Maths and Science said that she taught her classes some of the facts that were mentioned in the Qur'an, then gave examples of early scientists during the Golden Age of Islam. She thought it important to give her students confidence in a subtle way about the contribution of Muslim scholars in geometry, trigonometry and algebra. She was in the process of preparing a science unit about light and would include the contributions of Muslim and Arab scholars. She felt this was a way of helping her students maintain their self-respect 'because if they can respect themselves, they can respect others', as it goes both ways.

Is There an Islamic Approach to Science and Creationism?

Science is mainly taught at the high school level by non-Muslim teachers, but the contentious issue is raised of differences over creationism and evolution, just as in conservative Christian and some Orthodox Jewish schools. This was the subject of an *SBS Insight* programme in which teachers and students from Jewish, conservative Christian and Islamic schools were interviewed on the subject of how evolution was taught at their schools.[12] One Muslim academic interviewed on the subject said it was not a big issue in most of their schools but that some Muslims felt very strongly about it. Students interviewed varied in their responses, with some saying they just followed the state syllabus and learned what Islam had to say on the subject in Islamic Studies, while others said their teachers pointed out that there were different theories and they should learn about them all.

One school dealt with the issue by following the state syllabus. However, an Islamic Studies coordinator then came as a guest speaker to give an Islamic perspective on evolution because the textbook only gave the Darwinian view, 'which is not an Islamic perspective'.

Another non-Muslim science teacher said he liked to use the creation of the earth as a discussion issue with senior students and that everyone could share in the discussion. He found the Book of Genesis a good starting point as he could refer to the Christian fundamentalist point of view and then the contradictions, seeing this as a great way to get the story rolling. On the Big Bang theory, he felt that he could explain or justify the creation of the universe by God and this could still be reconciled with the Big Bang concept, although it was harder to make a connection between humans and apes in evolutionary theory.

An examination of science books in the libraries was interesting, as quite a few overseas texts took a strident line against evolution, but it is impossible to assess how many students read them or accept their line of argument.

Another issue that comes up in science lessons is human biology. A non-Muslim teacher taught reproduction in science but realised it was a sensitive subject, so that in science classes they had men teaching the boys and a female teacher taking the girls so that they did not get into contradictions with Islamic teaching in this area.

Alcohol also comes up as an issue in chemistry. One non-Muslim teacher was asked by his class what beer tasted like and what he drank. He pointed out to them that alcohol was first made by Arabs and was a word derived from Arabic, adding that they would be using it in medical matters and that nobody had ever told him that they could not do this as they could not touch alcohol.

Although Al-Khalili, writing from England, acknowledges the ongoing tension between science and religion in some parts of the Muslim world,[13] there does not seem to be a problem with science teaching in the Australian Islamic schools, where many senior students are attracted to science subjects and a substantial number hope to study medicine at university. From discussion with science teachers, as well as students, the issue seems to be that either the non-Muslim teachers saw their job as simply to teach the state curriculum in science, or that reference to the contributions of Arabs to scientific learning a thousand years ago seemed peripheral or irrelevant. On the other hand, some students did mention the pride they felt when they were taught about this and realised that not all scientific advances came from the West.

Teaching English

The question of whether an Islamic perspective could be introduced into the English syllabus predictably elicited another wide range of responses. English was a subject where the majority of teachers were non-Muslims, but it was a key subject in which students needed to do well, especially at pre-tertiary level. Teachers, however, were aware of the difficulties in teaching English as their students were often likely to be speaking another language at home in addition to learning Arabic to read the Qur'an. A number of schools also have a high English as a second language (ESL) intake, while others said all their students were fluent in English.

For an Islamic school, one difference is inevitably the topics covered in literature, though once again this is not an issue unique to Islamic schools in Australia. Teachers observed that many recommended texts were viewed as unsuitable because, although Islam does not shy away from sensitive topics, they had to be in the correct context, usually meaning references to sex and drugs. One teacher said that when issues such as abortion or homosexuality came up, he asked his students to take it to their Islamic studies class to talk to the teacher about it.

One teacher had introduced Persian literature, which went down very well, but several others had used *Looking for Alibrandi*,[14] as it gave them a chance to focus a bit more on multiculturalism and also the migration gap between students' families and those still at home and how the students related to those sorts of things. One added that he felt more comfortable using older classic texts, for example *To Kill a Mockingbird* and *Animal Farm*, as he felt that contemporary texts dealt with too many issues with which the school was not comfortable. Many recent books for young people emphasise premarital sexual relationships, drugs and alcohol, gambling and homosexuality, all of which are haram for Muslims, so they found it easier just to avoid them.

Even Shakespearean literature had its issues. One student noted that since none of the English teachers at her school were Muslims, they wouldn't study *Romeo and Juliet*, but *Macbeth* and *The Merchant of Venice* were acceptable. If there was a kissing scene, the teacher would fast forward it or cover the TV set with a pencil case.

At primary school level, a Muslim teacher said she used *The Lion, the Witch and the Wardrobe* with a Year 4 class because the values and stories were based on the Islamic textbook she used and the idea of sacrifice was common to both faiths.

A non-Muslim head of English spoke of her efforts to find texts that stressed migrant viewpoints, mentioning *Does My Head Look Big in This?*[15] and the poems of Omar Khayyam, adding that there were not a lot of useful suitable resources in Australia. By contrast, another teacher said she didn't choose books that were specifically Islamic or that had anything to do with religion because she felt the students needed to broaden their awareness of cultural perspectives and see outside a bit. Her school had invited Randa Abdel-Fattah to come and talk about her book, *Where the streets had a name*,[16] but they had also invited Aboriginal speakers after reading *Sally's Story*.[17] She felt this was important for the students as they were very sheltered and she wanted to push them to think outside their culture.

Linked to English, drama presented other issues, for while often taught in other Australian schools, few Islamic schools taught it. Sometimes staff felt it was for cultural reasons, as students were too shy or lacked self-confidence. In other cases, the problem was in finding a suitable production or simply that they didn't have the opportunity to rehearse. This was because so many students caught school buses home as soon as school ended and it was impractical to come at weekends to rehearse. Where it was taught, self-confidence was stressed and at one school, the teacher said it was good for her ESL students because they found writing so hard but 'acting something out, they can do fairly easily and it shows me that they have the same understanding of a particular topic'.

Teaching the Humanities

Given that teaching of the humanities, especially history, is still tailored very much to a Eurocentric view of the world, plus some Australian content, it was a point of interest to enquire whether Islamic schools taught anything about Islam's contribution to world history and, indeed, Australia's history. The answers varied widely and again this was a subject where a high proportion of the teachers were non-Muslim.

Given the national curriculum in Studies of Society and Environment (SOSE), it is not easy to integrate an Islamic perspective into the content, and even harder for non-Muslim teachers who are unlikely to know anything themselves. In Victoria, there has been research on this in relation to SOSE textbooks, while Windle presented a paper on his research at the National Centre for Excellence in Islamic Studies conference at the University of Melbourne in December 2008.[18] Research is continuing at Monash University on how Islam is represented in Victorian textbooks.

Students interviewed on this subject gave a variety of responses. Some said it was rare to learn anything about Islam's contribution to world history:

> In SOSE, it was more the White history, we didn't intertwine it with Islamic history

Another student said she was lucky because although they had Australian textbooks, their teacher would add an Islamic perspective, so she had learned some Islamic history and about Islam in the West. This was because most of her teachers were Muslims so they had the relevant background knowledge.

However, some schools worked hard to bring in an Islamic perspective. One teacher referred to resources provided in the school library, adding that at her school they provided in-service professional development courses for non-Muslim teachers. The marked exception was a school where they had made a conscious decision in 2009 to include Islamic perspectives in the way history was taught. A non-Muslim teacher explained:

> So an example of this would be the Semester One unit for Year Ten students, which follows history from the end of the Classical Age to the end of the Enlightenment, sort of the 1800's. The focus of Islamic perspectives included studying the changes under the Caliphates in the Middle East and how a lot

of things they did with regard to jurisprudence and developing a legal system predated the Magna Carta. As well as that, we looked at Islam's contribution to the technical advances in Western societies, particularly Muslim societies and mathematicians. We had a specialist from the university and he came and gave a seminar to the students looking at some of the advances in science, arts and humanities in the Islamic world, how these were built on by Western civilisations. In particular, he highlighted the fact that if it were not for Islamic scientists translating the texts of the Ancient Greeks, much of that knowledge from the Classical Age would have been lost.

He added:

The kids were quite interested in that and many of them said when they reflected on the unit, they often felt a sense of inferiority when looking at some of their cultures and countries they came from in comparison to the way that a lot of Western nations progressed and they still feel they haven't advanced very much.

Asked about what texts they used, he referred to one national SOSE textbook in which essentially the only mention of Islam was in reference to the Crusades, and some of what was written there was not very religiously sensitive. As a result, they supplemented it with extra notes and extracts from *The History of Islam* in the school library.

From discussion with former students, it was fairly evident that they had had little opportunity to learn about Islam's role in world history, let alone study world history in general. However, as staff pointed out, in sticking to their state curriculum and textbooks, there wasn't much they could do about this, apart from adding a few perspectives of their own when relevant. One recent exception, however, was provided by the travelling exhibition put together by the South Australian Museum in Adelaide which covered the contribution of the Afghan cameleers to nineteenth-century Australia, which some schools had taken classes to visit.

Few texts on Australian history refer to the Macassars and their connections with Aboriginal people in Northern Australia prior to European contact, and a number of teachers were themselves unaware of it. The prominent Aboriginal activist Pat Dodson pointed out that this peaceful contact over a long period of time provided an interesting contrast to the impact of European arrival on indigenous people. In a keynote address to Muslim students at the Australian Universities National Conference in 2007,[19] he described the amicable nature of these encounters based on trading, when the Macassars arrived every year with the seasonal winds and stayed on, fishing for *trepang*, until it was the right time to sail home. They made no attempt to claim the land, and a number of the Yolngu people they encountered sailed back to the Celebes (now Sulawesi) and stayed with them there.

While there are now a number of books about Islam's contribution to learning, especially during the Golden Age,[20] they tend to be for college-level students rather than general textbooks. While some teachers were acutely aware of this issue, they said that at the moment there simply was neither the time nor the money available to release them for producing suitable texts, and libraries usually lacked the resources to obtain these more recent publications.

In some schools, SOSE incorporates units on citizenship and civics, which are at the heart of the values debate and allegations by hostile critics of the Islamic schools that students are taught intolerance and gender inequality. In civics, a number of schools are able to draw on the experience of their own students as new arrivals in order to help them understand and appreciate the plight of refugees and asylum seekers. In Southeast Australia, a number of schools organise visits to Parliament House in Canberra, while the ABC Compass programme featured a role play on democratic debate in an Islamic school where the students debated the issue of providing and financing items for their playground, modelled on parliamentary procedure.[21]

Music and Art: Areas of Contention

Two grey areas for Islamic schools are the teaching of Music and Art, which are of course a normal part of the curriculum in many other schools in Australia. Faith schools obviously censor some forms of modern music, and ultra-Orthodox Jewish schools share the same reservations about depicting the human form as the more conservative Islamic schools.

At the practical level, there is the question of providing facilities and adequate funding, especially for music, an issue which affects many other schools in Australia. Non-Muslim teachers would often check with the principal or imams if uncertain what was allowed. One Muslim primary school teacher with a wide experience of different Islamic schools reported that her current school was quite liberal so while they stayed away from stringed instruments, they allowed a bit of singing, especially of nasheeds and Islamic songs, in addition to the morning assembly when they all sang the National Anthem. Another said that she used a CD for her children to sing along to, adding that for her, Islamic songs were fine but Lady Gaga was not.

The sensitivity about music was illustrated by another teacher who reported that when their Islamic Studies teacher addressed a senior assembly on study skills and showed a short video with background music, two of the boys got upset and left the room. Several students commented on the lack of music, though they did not always know why it wasn't taught, while others realised it was controversial with some parents so the school decided it was easier not to teach it. Another student commented favourably on their music teacher who taught them the piano, how to sing in tune and how to create piano pieces, while the art teacher taught them how to paint and demonstrated different styles of painting, so they could pursue a career in painting if they chose to.

One interesting discussion with several former Islamic College university students focused on why Cat Stevens had given up music when he converted to Islam in 1978 but had then studied Islam's views on music and decided to return to it.[22] Another, when asked about music at her school, commented:

> I was at school before earphones and all that were really common. However, though we did not do music, we were never explicitly told that Islam did not approve of music or we were not allowed to listen to music. Students had their Walkmans and Discmans on the bus home and teachers were aware of it.

Art was encouraged at primary schools but what the students were allowed to draw was circumscribed by various rules. Arabic calligraphy was of course universally practised as an art form and all the schools had framed Islamic calligraphy on display, often in the entrance hall. Islamic art has come back onto the international agenda since 2001, and the National Gallery in Canberra hosted a display on Islamic Art and Civilisation in Southeast Asia in 2006, while the world's largest private collection of Islamic Art, *The Arts of Islam*, was on display at the Art Gallery of New South Wales in the winter of 2007.

Not surprisingly, the emphasis on art in Islamic schools reflects this particular perspective, though staff and students interviewed varied on what art was taught in their schools, if it was taught at all. Part of the reason was the need for special facilities and trained teachers, which was not always a priority for many schools, where the emphasis tended to be on getting good results in academic subjects and pride in doing well in the NAPLAN tests and Year 12 state result charts. Art was more often taught in primary schools, where class teachers sometimes included art lessons; one student spoke fondly of her principal who used to do lots of amazing things with her class, including clay work and screen printing, while at her high school they never did art.

While more schools did art than music, most art teachers were not Muslims but were aware of the limitations. Students stressed that while they could not draw humans, they did do lots of drawings. One student was particularly impressed by a teacher who introduced her to the Impressionists, including like Van Gogh, while another spoke about her fashion-conscious teacher who got her classes drawing and resigning dresses, including material work, as well as a little bit of calligraphy and lots of drawings of scenery. There were exceptions, as one school laid on art as a mainstream elective subject, then in Years 11 and 12 students could pick up Studio Arts and Visual Arts as options. Their Albanian-Australian teacher let them draw animals but not people, though other teachers did allow this. The school had a gallery display every year for Year 11–12 student work that included facial form and the human form, though obviously clothed.

Another non-Muslim primary school teacher who felt that creativity was important for children checked on her school outcomes statement to see what it had to say on art. As Arabic art was covered in Islamic Studies, she taught her Year 5 students about Aboriginal art. One student was so bitterly critical of her school's attitude to art, music and drama, that she went to a state college to repeat Year 12 and went on to study architecture at university. She argued that there was musicality in the Qur'an and a deep history of art in Islam, and she hated her school for ignoring this.

Sport and Physical Education

Sport and physical education (PE), including swimming, are contentious issues because of Islamic dress codes and sometimes cultural issues for girls. On the other hand, a lot of the constraints are due to limited facilities, like for so many other schools in Australia, and where possible use is made of public facilities near to schools. Physical education has improved enormously since the days of the early schools, when alumni said it simply did not exist. Now all the schools have PE teachers for boys and girls but the sports they play vary enormously.

PE teachers are often Muslim and stress to students how Islam and the Qur'an encourage people to be fit, to eat healthy food and to work together Islamically in sports and health. Obviously, some sports are segregated, including swimming, and much depends on access to pools where segregated facilities are provided, despite the opposition of right-wing shock jocks such as Alan Jones on 2GB in Sydney who jumped up and down at the idea of an Islamic school hiring the local pool at Auburn for girls-only sessions, forcing the school to drop the idea. Another Sydney Islamic school was more fortunate, as a local girl's school offered them use of their pool for the girls. Where a school did not have access to a pool, parents were encouraged to take their children to vacation swimming classes. Most Islamic schools are near the sea and older students commented wistfully that while they never went swimming, their younger siblings now get the opportunity.

Other sports on offer vary a great deal from school to school, often depending on the cultural background of the students. One PE teacher said that with students coming from thirty-five different cultures, soccer and basketball were very popular, but they had introduced AFL (Australian Rules Football League) in primary school and 'the kids love it'. They brought coaches and players from a local AFL team and the sport appealed particularly to the tall, fit Somali boys. He added that the boys from the Indian sub-continent preferred cricket, so they had started that too. Female teachers at the same school worked with girls in the school gym and the girls loved badminton and volleyball. Role models such as Bachar Houli and Usman Khawaja were seen as inspirational, and they feature in the display of well-known Australian Muslims at the Islamic Museum in Melbourne.

Some schools had girls playing cricket too, though always observant of appropriate dress codes on the field. One student said his school had a teacher who taught them Rugby Union. This was fairly typical, as so many schools seemed to depend on the interests and skills of particular teachers who were prepared to introduce new ball games.

Dress codes were dealt with at an Islamic level. Boys had to wear long shorts while girls playing netball had to wear trousers and long tops rather than short skirts. Girls taking part in athletics and cross-country running wore a hijab and skins or leggings. At primary school level, staff did not worry about a dress code for girls in their athletics carnival so that even when the older girls threw off their hijab in a race, no one worried.

One student reported that at her school the only chance to play sport was in Islamic classes, so in Beliefs and Values the girls had played soccer in the gym with a South African sheikh. At another school, the girls could do horse riding with their religion teacher, although the principal apparently thought that it was not suitable for girls 'because you could lose your virginity on a horse'. On the other hand, the Prophet Mohammed encouraged horse riding as well as archery so it was religiously sanctioned.

A more recent sport introduced for girls has been self-defence as well as tae-kwon-do, which they really enjoyed at the school where it was introduced.

Older female students said they usually had not taken part in athletics, either because they didn't like it or because the dress code made it awkward, but they acknowledged that attitudes were changing and it was much easier for girls now.

Health Education: A Difficult Subject for the Schools

Associated with health and well-being alongside physical education is the vexed question of a subject that comes under various names, such as personal and social development. In a secular society, state schools and many independent schools use these classes for educating students on sexuality, plus covering drug and alcohol issues. For faith schools with a strict moral code, this presents a number of problems, and Islamic schools line up more with the ultra-Orthodox Jewish, conservative Christian and Catholic schools, than with their more secular counterparts.

These schools all teach sexual abstinence before marriage and oppose teaching about homosexuality, though they differ on alcohol and abortion rights. In addition, the fear among parents is that if these issues are raised in the classroom, then students will be encouraged to experiment, despite the lack of evidence for this presumption. The general opinion in the Islamic schools is that all these matters are best discussed at home, though privately they acknowledge that this often does not happen and Muslim students are left in a vacuum when confronting some of these issues. Some imams double up as counsellors, as do some younger teachers, especially female staff.

Fida Sanjakdar's research on finding an appropriate sexual health education curriculum for Islamic schools was tried out at one of the schools working in conjunction with a small group of teachers.[23] She makes the point that the teaching and learning of sexual health is not only desirable in Islam but obligatory, while she acknowledges 'the failure of the schools to respond to this challenge'.[24]

English academic Mark Halstead makes the point that critics who oppose the introduction of sexual health education in schools fall back on three main arguments:

> Some sexual health education material offends the Islamic principle of decency and modesty;
>
> Sexual health education tends to present certain behaviours as acceptable, which Muslims consider sinful;
>
> Sexual health education is perceived as undermining the Islamic concept of family life.[25]

Co-Curricular Activities

As in other schools, there were a number of co-curricular activities besides sport that offered students a chance to mix with students from other schools, in particular debating and public speaking. Those students who had been involved in these activities spoke very positively about the experience, though the opportunities for social mixing were limited by time. One major disadvantage for many of the Islamic schools is that up to 90% of students come to school by bus, often travelling for over an hour each way every day, so this constrains their involvement in extra-curricular activities. On the other hand, a considerable number of students at Islamic schools have attended other types of schools over their educational years up to the age of 18 and so are used to social mixing anyway.

Conclusion

There is considerable variation in what is taught in Islamic schools in Australia, depending partly on the policies of the particular school and partly on whether or not it has the relevant staff available. Much also depends on the views of the principal, although there are still a number of Islamic schools where the principal is not a Muslim, in which case they defer to the school imam or their school board.

One related issue is reliance on Australian textbooks that are not likely to include a Muslim perspective, but as yet the schools are not in a position to remedy this situation, even at the level of faith teaching. At primary level, worksheets and simple publications can be easily put together, but high school classes will tend to rely on the normal Australian school textbooks that are available.

More contentious issues such as art and music bring up awkward issues because they reflect different opinions within the Muslim community, so principals tend to find it easier just to let the matter drop rather than upsetting more conservative parents. It is hoped that in the future some of these issues will be debated within educational circles, much as this discussion is under way in Europe and North America. With regard to health education, Fida Sanjakdar's innovative work may eventually bear fruit, but given the obstacles of conservative tradition and deeply embedded cultural restraints, only time will tell how long this will take.

Notes

1. Orietta Guerrera and Andra Jackson, *Minister urges watch on Islamic schools*. Melbourne: The Age, 28 March 2003.
2. *Sunrise* programme, 5 October 2015. Channel 7.
3. Nicole Hasham, *Defiant Hanson set to be a force in the Senate*, speech in Brisbane, 4 July 2016, *Canberra Times*, 5 July 2016, p. 1.
4. Noha Sanjakdar, *Why do Muslim parents choose King Khalid College of Victoria?*, unpublished M. Ed. thesis, University of Melbourne, 2000, p. 6.
5. Barbara Giles, 'Somali narratives on Islam, Education and Perceptions of Difference,' in Samina Yasmeen (ed.), *Muslims in Australia, The Dynamics of Exclusion and Inclusion*. Melbourne: Melbourne University Press, 2010, p. 180.
6. Ibid., p. 170.
7. Ibid., p. 173.
8. Originally King Khalid Islamic College in North Coburg but now the Australian International Academy (AIA).
9. *Does My Head Look Big in This?* and *Ten Things I Hate About Me*, both Pan Macmillan, London, 2005 and 2006.
10. Melina Marchetta, *Looking for Alibrandi*. Australia: Penguin Books, 1992.
11. Jonathan Lyons, *The House of Wisdom: How the Arabs Transformed Western Civilisation*. London: Bloomsbury, 2009.
12. *In Good Faith*, television programme, SBS Insight, 27 May 2008.
13. Jim Al-Khalili, *Pathfinders: The Golden Age of Arabic Science*. London: Allen Lane, 2010.
14. Melina Marchetta, *Looking for Alibrandi*. Camberwell, Victoria: Penguin, 1990.

15. Randa Abdel-Fattah, *Does My Head Look Big in This?* Sydney: Pan Macmillan, 2005.
16. Randa Abdel-Fattah, *Where the Streets Had a Name.* Sydney: Pan Macmillan, 2008.
17. Sally Morgan, *Sally's Story.* Fremantle: Fremantle Arts Press, 1987.
18. Joel Windle, *The Muslim Middle Ages in Victorian classrooms: an analysis of junior humanities textbooks.* 20 December 2008.
19. Access, Inclusion and Success, organised by the University of Western Sydney, 3–4 September 2007.
20. One good example is Lyons, *The House of Wisdom. How the Arabs transformed Western Civilization.* London: Bloomsbury Press, 2009.
21. *A Muslim Education.* Compass. 7 September 2008.
22. Cat Stevens said he originally gave up his musical career because he thought the music industry was incompatible with Islam and he believed that Islam did not approve of music. Later he realised that Islam's attitude to music was far more complex than he initially thought and, encouraged by other Muslims and his son, he decided to return to his musical career in 2005.
23. Fida Sanjakdar, 'The critical role of schools and teachers in developing a sexual health education curriculum for Muslim students' and 'Teachers struggle for an Islamically appropriate sexual health education curriculum at their school,' University of Melbourne, 2004 and 2004.
24. Linda Morris, 'Going by the book, Islamic schools can't offer sex education,' *Sydney Morning Herald*, 25 June 2003.
25. J. Mark Halstead, 'Muslims and Sex education,' *Muslim Education Quarterly*, vol. 26, no. 3, 1997, p. 319.

BIBLIOGRAPHY

Books

Abdel-Fattah, Randa. *Does My Head Look Big in This?* London: Pan Macmillan, 2005.

———. *Ten Things I Hate About Me.* London: Pan Macmillan, 2006.

———. *Where the Streets Had a Name.* London: Pan Macmillan, 2008.

Al-Khalili, Jim. *Pathfinders: The Golden Age of Arabic Science.* London: Allen Lane, 2010.

Ansari, Humayun. *The Infidel Within, Muslims in Britain Since 1800.* London: Hurst, 2004.

Foltz, Richard. *Animals in Islamic Tradition and Muslim Cultures.* Oxford: One World Publications, 2006.

Jenkins, Jean, and Paul Olsen. *Music and Musical Instruments in the World of Islam.* London: Horniman Museum, 1976.
Lyons, Jonathan. *The House of Wisdom: How the Arabs Transformed Western Civilisation.* London: Bloomsbury, 2009.
Marchetta, Melina. *Looking for Alibrandi.* Camberwell, Victoria: Penguin, 1990.
Morgan, Sally. *Sally's Story.* Fremantle: Fremantle Arts Press, 1987.

Chapter in a Book

Giles, Barbara. "Somali Narratives on Islam, Education and Perceptions of Difference." In *Muslims in Australia, The Dynamics of Exclusion and Inclusion,* ed. Samina Yasmeen, 180. Melbourne: Melbourne University Press, 2010.

Articles

Halstead, J. Mark. "Muslim Attitudes to Music in Schools." *British Journal of Music Education* 11 (2006): 143–156.
———. "Muslims and Sex Education." *Muslim Education Quarterly* 26, no. 3 (1997): 319.

CHAPTER 6

Islamic Worldview and Curriculum Development

Freda Shamma

INTRODUCTION

The theme of renewal is the major thread connecting all chapters and contributors in this book. Under the broad banner of renewal, it is the contention of this chapter that few greater challenges exist in Islamic schooling than those pertaining to matters of curriculum. This chapter sets out to address this significant issue for Islamic schooling, arguing that Islamic principles within an Islamic worldview represent the starting point and the guiding basis for curriculum development efforts and thus, as the title of the book suggests, pathways to renewal for Islamic schooling in the West.

The chapter begins with the history of Muslim migration to America and explores the early motivations, milestones and progress made in the establishment of Islamic schools in the American context. It next explores the underpinning features of the curricula commonly adopted in Islamic schools in Western contexts in which secular, humanistic and other ideas not necessarily aligned with an Islamic worldview dominate both curricula

F. Shamma (✉)
Foundation for the Advancement and Development of Education and Learning (FADEL), Cincinnati, OH, USA

© The Author(s) 2018
M. Abdalla et al. (eds.), *Islamic Schooling in the West*,
https://doi.org/10.1007/978-3-319-73612-9_6

and teaching resources. The author challenges the standard approach of accepting existing curricula with the aforementioned underpinning features and tweaking them to achieve an 'Islamic' curriculum. The chapter poses a number of key questions for further consideration for stakeholders in the field. What are the Islamic principles and Islamic worldview that should be the guiding basis of the curriculum? And within what worldview are teachers and curriculum developers operating? Finally, while it is acknowledged that great progress has been made across Islamic schooling in the West, it is argued that it is time to address the urgent need for curriculum development.

History

Before and after European colonisation, several waves of Muslims arrived in America: first as explorers starting with Abu Bakari II, brother of Mansa Musa of Mali, in 1312; then as refugees fleeing the Spanish Inquisitions of the fifteenth and sixteenth centuries: and from the fifteenth to the nineteenth century, the largest group arrived from West Africa as enslaved people.[1] Since most people of West Africa were Muslims, it is assumed that as many as 30% of those arriving in America were Muslim. Among them were literate, educated Muslims, a known number of whom wrote out at least parts of the Qur'an.[2] Labouring under severe repression, they were denied their language, their culture and their religion, so that over time Islam was lost to their descendants.

The next groups of Muslim immigrants were farmers from Pakistan and working-class Arabs who migrated in the 1800s. Islam was also lost among the majority of these immigrants. They were mainly unskilled workers who came hoping for financial success but did not realise until it was too late that their children and grandchildren would reject the old culture in favour of the new one, and that their Islam, presented to them as part of their old world culture, would be lost along with the old culture.[3]

The early half of the twentieth century saw significant numbers of African Americans rediscover Islam, with a determination to help their children remain within the fold of Islam.[4] The Nation of Islam called on members,[5] who were exclusively African American, to rebuild their self-respect by setting up businesses, joining together in prayer and building schools which would not ignore black history and culture, unlike the exclusively Eurocentric textbooks found in public schools.[6] The first Sister Clara Muhammed School was established in Atlanta, Georgia in 1965.[7]

Until 1975 the curriculum included Islam as taught by Wallace Fard and Elijah Muhammad. After the death of Elijah Muhammad, his son, Warith Deen Mohammed, took over and quickly moved the Nation of Islam and its schools toward orthodox Islam. Today there are thirty-eight Clara Muhammad elementary schools, a number of high schools and a teachers' college. They have also joined the Council of Islamic Schools in North America, an organisation representing all Muslim schools in America.

By the 1950s, Muslims who had enjoyed greater access to formal education were immigrating to North America, in part because they respected the results of an American education and sought to continue their university and post-graduate studies there. Failing to integrate with the Nation of Islam, these orthodox Muslim immigrants recognised the need to build mosques but were slower to see the need for separate schools for their children. They had a tendency to value and prioritise the public education curriculum and standards without question. As an English Literature graduate student stated in a conference I attended in 1996, 'English literature is value free so why shouldn't we Muslims teach it?'[8] In my years of experience with Muslim schools, I have found that even today, when new migrant parents put their children in Islamic schools, many insist that the public school curriculum and textbooks be used.

It is the graduates of American public schools, the descendants of the early African-American and immigrant Muslims, who call for a curriculum grounded in an Islamic worldview. From the author's experience, these groups are typically more aware of the detrimental results of the humanistic Eurocentric curriculum, and are determined to do better for their own children. There are now almost 300 Islamic full-time schools in the USA and Canada. They range from the long-established large Sister Clara Muhammad schools to start-up one-room schools.[9]

Problem

There have been a number of attempts in the North American context to develop an integrated Islamic curriculum, but almost all attempts have suffered from the same problem. Most Muslims who have graduated from schools, whether public or private, in the post-Industrial Revolution era, with separate classes for separate subjects and at most one period a day for religious education, are unaware that the curriculum has been underpinned by a 'secular' worldview which accepts humanistic and other ideas that may or may not align with Islam. Being thus unaware, they proceed to develop a curriculum starting with a 'good' public school text and adding bits and pieces to try to make it 'Islamic'. Adding one chapter on Islamic history or a biography or two of famous Muslims ignores the white elephant in the room, that is, textbooks which base all knowledge on the humanistic idea that there is no God, no Creator and no God-designed world—the implications of which are the assumption that science and man's own logic rule the classroom. Furthermore, it is assumed that history is linear, starting with primitive people and ending with Western civilisation, and that only the West has made improvements benefiting civilisation. In contrast, an Islamic worldview holds that logic is subservient to revelation and that history is best viewed cylindrically, which accounts for the rise and fall of civilisations and the lessons to be learned therein.

Table 6.1 illustrates some of the differences between principles informed by Islamic and secular worldviews.

Consider the distinctions and nuances in language adopted when textbooks present an exclusively Eurocentric narrative. In older history textbooks in Australia for example, past students would have studied the travels of Captain James Cook and his 'discovery of a new land'. Did he 'discover' Australia, and did subsequent European people in the main 'settle' the country?

Today in Australia there is an ongoing debate on whether to include curriculum content that mentions the taking of land unlawfully from Aboriginal and Torres Strait Islander peoples, the indigenous peoples of Australia, and whether to cover the disruption or loss of language, culture, education and religion. And would it be said that the loss of land and so on was to an 'invading' people? Returning to the issue of language and bias discourse amounting to an exclusively Eurocentric narrative, did the Europeans *defend* their land and *settle* in other lands to *help civilise* the people there? In contrast, did Muslim armies 'invade' and 'subjugate' other peoples' civilisations? Thus, even though the textbook might include a section on Muslim history, the vocabulary and language is very different according to whether the people were 'heroic' (white Europeans) or 'violent' (brown Muslims).

The result of a secular education with some Islam added on may have led to students attaining favourable academic results, but what about knowledge of Islam and *adab*. As Shaikh Abdul Mabud mentions in another Chap. 2 in this book, what is known as academic knowledge is not sufficient for an Islamic school. For knowledge to be termed as such in an

Table 6.1 Islamic or secular—some basic principles that orient teaching materials

Principle	Islamic	Secular
Who is in charge?	Allah	Nature/science/humankind's thinking
Humankind's place in the social system	The family is the basis of society	The individual is the basis of society
Role of the family	Within the family every individual has her/his needs met, including guidance and love. Everyone has her/his rights taken care of, but has corresponding responsibilities	Family is unimportant but is supposed to give the individual what he/she wants. Parents are optional. They are obligated to take care of the individual, but he/she has no obligation to them
Respect, seek and listen to parent's' advice	In order for the family to function as it should, every member has to accept responsibilities as well as her/his rights, which includes respect and accepting guidance and comfort	The individual is in charge of her/his own life—he/she owes nothing to her/his family. Most of the time he/she needs no one at all
Man/woman is a social creature	He/she seeks out the company of those who also accept the existence of God; and he/she is close to her/his family	He/she seeks out those who give her/him pleasure and allow her/him to do what he/she likes
History	History is cyclical, going up when people follow Allah, then down as they forget, then up when a prophet arises to bring them back on the right path, then down again as people forget	History is linear, starting with uncivilised barbarians and moving in a straight line to the most civilised—i.e. citizens of Western civilisation
School goals	Humankind has an obligation to learn in order to be of benefit to family, society, the world community and the environment	School has two opposite goals: (1) School should mold students into what the dominant society wants. (2) At the same time, subjects should be studied only if the individual is interested in the subject
School organisation	Everything is part of the unity which comes from the creation by the One God, and all areas of study are connected and based on Islamic perspectives	Every subject is independent of the others. All classes except religion are taught from a secular perspective

Islamic worldview, it requires 'the total development of students so that they become righteous servants of Allah'.[10] This cannot happen if the school has a 'split personality', when humankind is supreme for most of the time in classes where students are operating outside of an Islamic worldview and Allah is supreme in only a bare minimum of classes.

SOLUTION

Looking back at the history of Muslim education, we see that all the polymath geniuses of the 'Golden Age', 750–1300, began their education studying the Islamic foundational works, the Qur'an[11] and Sunnah[12] of Prophet Muhammad (peace be upon him), continued with the study of various religious sciences and then branched out into a myriad of fields: religion, medicine, astronomy, optics, philosophy, literary masterpieces, autobiography, chemistry and other sciences and various branches of mathematics. The first literary writer to support himself by his writings was Al Jahiz (776–868, Basra), who wrote not only literary works but also a commentary on the Qur'an. They all wrote from an Islamic perspective, acknowledging the existence of God and His definitive role in the creation.

What is needed today is that Islamic perspective in every subject, and in every teacher–student interaction. As Dr Ismail al-Faruqi, a contemporary Muslim scholar, says, 'The greatest calamity of the Muslim world is the existence of so many teachers without any Islamic vision'.[13] He goes on to explain that students graduating from Islamic schools arrive at college or university with 'an emotional, as opposed to a correct intellectual or ideological understanding of Islam. These sentiments and emotions are shipwrecked when they are confronted with the ideas, facts, and the objective judgments of science in modern disciplines.'[14]

In order to develop a curriculum based on Islamic principles, there are two major areas that need primary attention. First, what are the Islamic principles and what is an Islamic worldview that should be the guiding basis of the curriculum? Second, what worldview are teachers and curriculum developers operating within? Recently I was part of a group trying to develop a series of science textbooks for Islamic elementary grades. One popular opinion was that we should begin by identifying the best public school textbook available. Then we would add whatever was necessary to make it 'Islamic'. The underlying assumption in this instance would be that the secular book was an appropriate basis for Islamic schools, only in need of some tweaking here and there.

A worldview is the framework within which our mind operates. An Islamic worldview regards Allah as the Creator of all and the Unifier of all creation. Every idea begins with this acknowledgement. A humanistic or secular worldview, on the other hand, does not acknowledge the existence of God. Instead it is human logic and human made order of science that is the basis for all knowledge. How then can a secular textbook be in any way the foundation for an 'Islamic-oriented' science education? On what basis do we divide all subjects into independent units where English never ventures into the history class and biology does not intrude in chemistry and certainly anything religious is not to be found in the 'academic' classes? Often the religion class is not even considered deserving of its grades being included in grade point averages. Neither are future teachers ever required to take a course in religion. Elementary teachers in America are required to take courses in reading, arithmetic, social studies, art, physical education, music and science—but not religion. How then are they qualified to teach their subjects from an Islamic perspective?

Professor al-Attas, another modern scholar focusing on the idea of an Islamic worldview, states, 'Islamisation is the liberation of man, first from magical, mythological, animistic, national-cultural traditions opposed to Islam and then from secular control over his reason and his language'.[15] A worldview is formed by the individual in a casual manner. It is formed by our minds as a matter of habit that is dominant in our daily life. It is influenced by one's home life, television and the Internet, non-Muslim and Muslim friends, and to a very large extent by the schooling one receives six or seven hours a day, five days a week, thirty-six or more weeks a year, for twelve to sixteen, or even more, years, with perhaps an hour or two a week devoted to religion. When a school follows a humanistic or secular philosophy, Muslim students are taught that humankind is supreme and capable of discovering all and evaluating all moral decisions based on what the human mind decides is best for itself. To take one example, Islam promotes chastity outside of marriage and encourages respectful, supervised and appropriate parameters for interaction between genders. In contrast, starting with preschool books for 2 and 3 year olds, the mainstream reading material, and most if not all textbooks, feature boys and girls as best friends, and then by middle school as boyfriend/girlfriend, and by secondary school intimacy and sexual relations are viewed as acceptable in contrast to the values, beliefs and traditions of faith, family and positive cultural and community norms. Humanism encourages a person to act according to what *he/she* considers good, not what Allah says is good.

Educators must first examine their own worldview in order to reconcile it with Islam. They need to study Islamic principles and how they manifest themselves in every aspect of life. Then real change can begin to happen. Understanding the problems inherent in the secular worldview of a school's academic subjects (and reflected in the isolation of Islam as a completely separate subject), curriculum developers and teacher trainers can bring the Islamic worldview forward as the starting principle for curriculum development and for educating our students. One important step in this direction is an online course called the Islamic Teacher Education Program, which has been successful in reorienting teachers to think from an Islamic paradigm.

Making a truly Islamic school is a multidimensional task. It is of vital importance to provide appropriate teacher training options and to educate our present and future teachers with an Islamic view of education. It is also of vital importance to develop material that will help teachers in Islamic school classrooms. It is possible to use secular textbooks while pointing out every instance of secular misinformation, but this is hardly desirable. Students are more apt to accept what they read in a book rather than what someone tells them is wrong with it. Instead, we need to use teaching materials that are built on Islamic principles.

Treasury of Muslim Literature: The Golden Age 750–1250 CE[16] is an example of a textbook which is based on an Islamic perspective. As a Language Arts/English book it contains seventeen different genres of writing, and meets the requirements of the American Common Core Standards. The selections include some that are specific to religion, while most of the others are written by people whose foundational education was 'Islamic'. History is included through the selection of historians, geographers and travel writers; and science is included through the writings of Ibn Sina, Al Biruni and others. The authors are dealt with in chronological order, with an introduction to what was happening in the world of their time at three intervals in the book. It is aimed at middle school students but can be used in any grade beyond as well. This textbook offers several things that a text developed outside of an Islamic worldview cannot, including:

1. an orientation toward Allah and viewing His world as an interconnected whole;
2. an appreciation of Muslim scholars who wrote in the real world (as opposed to being isolated in a religious textbook), who dealt with the real-world problems of their time;

3. famous Muslim intellectuals, inventors, explorers, writers, poets, people of excellent character, and written pieces which entertain while delivering an important message;
4. an introduction to the history of Muslims as an integral part of the history of the rest of the world, not isolated as a minor part of the religion class.

In short, it is a book which shows the importance of the efforts of Muslims, interesting and important Muslim cultures, and how to live life as a practising Muslim.

Conclusion

As this chapter has shown, Islamic schooling in the West is still in its infancy. In the American as in other Western contexts, Islamic schooling has passed through the establishment phase, and the buildings and supplies are testament to the significant progress that has been made. The curriculum challenge, however, remains. It is time for stakeholders in Islamic schooling to take this challenge seriously and begin the greater project of curriculum development. It is the contention of this author that we need teachers qualified in Islam as well as in their subject matter. We need a curriculum based on Islamic principles within an Islamic worldview which unifies knowledge and prepares students for their purpose as this relates to the environments and contexts in which Allah has entrusted them. We also need to complement these efforts in curriculum development with the production of textbooks and other teaching aids which are based on the same Islamic principles and worldview. As this chapter has argued, Islamic principles within an Islamic worldview represent the starting point and the guiding basis for the necessary curriculum development effort for Islamic schooling in the West.

May Allah guide us all in the right path.

Notes

1. Islamic History Project. *A History of Muslim African Americans* (Calmat City, IL: WDM Publication, 2006).
2. Allan D. Austin, *African Muslims in Antebellum America: Transatlantic Stories and Spiritual Struggles* (New York: Routledge, 1997); Muhammad A. Al-Ahari (ed.), *Five Classic Muslim Slave Narratives* (Chicago, IL:

Magribine Press, 2006); and Jerald F. Dirks, *Muslims in American History: A Forgotten Legacy* (Beltsville, MD: Amana Publications, 1992), 35–38.
3. Abdo A. Elkholy, *The Arab Moslems in the United States: Religion and Assimilation* (New Haven, CT: College and University Press, 1966).
4. Sulayman S. Nyang, *Islam in the United States of America* (Chicago, IL: ABC International Group, Inc., 1999), 13.
5. The Nation of Islam was started by a Pakistani, Fard Muhammed, who came to America in 1931. His plea to African Americans was to became Muslim in order 'to achieve, money, homes and friendships'. His most faithful supporter was Elijah Poole, an African American born in Georgia in 1897 who later adopted the name Honorable Elizah Muhammad. He taught that Fard was God with 'a social and cultural plan to set the Black man on the road to freedom'. Clara Mohammed was his wife and partner. She took her own children out of public school and started the Sister Clara Mohammed schools in 1935. (All information taken from Islamic History Project's *A History of Muslim African Americans*, written under the guidance of Elijah's son W.D. Muhammad.)
6. Islamic History Project, *A History of Muslim African Americans*.
7. Aminah Beverly McCloud, *African American Islam* (New York: Routledge, 1994), 118–119.
8. English Literature in Muslim Schools Conference, Kuala Lumpur Malaysia, 12 May 1997. Unknown speaker.
9. Freda Shamma, "The Curriculum Challenge for Islamic Schools in America," in *Muslims and Islamization in North America: Problems & Prospects*, ed. Amber Haque (Beltsville, MD: Amana Publication, 1999), 276.
10. Shaikh Abdul Mabud, "The Emergence of Islamic Schools: A Conceptual Background".
11. The word of Allah transmitted without error from Allah to Arch Angel Gabriel to Prophet Muhammad (peace be upon him), which can be traced to this day via a chain of narration without error, addition or omission.
12. Any saying, action, approval or attribute, whether physical or moral, ascribed to the Prophet Muhammad (peace be upon him).
13. Muhammad Shafiq, *Growth of Islamic Thought in North America: Focus on Ismai'il Raji al Faruqi* (Beltsville, MD: Amana Publications, 1994), 96.
14. Shafiq, *Growth of Islamic Thought in North America: Focus on Ismai'il Raji al Faruqi*, 97.
15. Muhammad al-Attas, *Islam and Secularism* (Kuala Lumpur: ISTAC, 1978).
16. Freda Shamma, *Treasury of Muslim Literature: The Golden Age 750–1250 CE* (Beltsville, MD: Amana Publishers, 2012). Lesson plans are available at www.muslimlit.com.

BIBLIOGRAPHY

Abdul Mabud, Shaikh. "Are Islamic Schools Different from Secular Schools?" In *Islamic Schools in the West: Pathways to Renewal*. London: Palgrave Macmillan, 2017.

Al-Ahari, Muhammad A., ed. *Five Classic Muslim Slave Narratives*. Chicago, IL: Magribine Press, 2006.

Al-Attas, Muhammad. *Islam and Secularism*. Kuala Lumpur: ISTAC, 1978.

Austin, Allan D. *African Muslims in Antebellum America: Transatlantic Stories and Spiritual Struggles*. New York: Routledge, 1997.

Cincinnati Enquirer (Newspaper). 23 May 2012.

Dirks, Jerald. *Muslims in American History: A Forgotten Legacy*. Beltsville, MD: Amana Publications, 1992.

Elkholy. *The Arab Moslems in the United States: Religion and Assimilation*. New Haven, CT: College and University Press, 1966.

English Literature in Muslim Schools Conference, Kuala Lumpur Malaysia, 12 May 1997. Unknown Speaker.

Islamic History Project. *A History of Muslim African Americans*. Calmat City, IL: WDM Publication, 2006.

McCloud, Aminah Beverly. *African American Islam*. New York: Routledge, 1994.

Nyang, Sulayman. *Islam in the United States of America*. Chicago, Ill., ABC International Group. 1999.

Shafiq, Muhammad. *Growth of Islamic Thought in North America: Focus on Ismai'il Raji al Faruqi*. Beltsville, MD: Amana Publications, 1994.

Shamma, Freda. "The Curriculum Challenge for Islamic Schools in America." In *Muslims and in North America: Problems & Prospects*, ed. Amber Haque. Beltsville, MD: Amana Publication, 1999.

———. *Treasury of Muslim Literature: The Golden Age 750–1250 CE*. Beltsville, MD: Amana Publication, 2012.

Van Sertima, Ivan. *They Came Before Columbus*. New York Random House, 1976.

CHAPTER 7

Muslim Ethos Within Muslim Schools

Abdullah Trevathan

INTRODUCTION

Ulrike Schuerkens has identified a 'global management culture' which she claims pervades all areas of human society.[1] This 'managerialism'[2] is based upon (1) identifying objectives to meet the needs of consumers to ensure optimum financial gain; (2) developing and applying a professional bureaucracy to achieve the objectives; and (3) ensuring efficiency and standardisation to generate high rates of productivity. Ritzer believes that bureaucracy is so integral to managerialism that it[3] 'represents the ultimate form of rationalization',[4] basing this on Max Weber's (1864–1920) sociological concept of the 'iron cage of rationality'. The consequence of this is that people's lives are reduced to moving 'from rationalized educational systems to rationalized work places, from rationalized recreational settings to rationalized homes'.[5] Standardisation is a required and essential part of this, wherein the varied many are measured against singular criteria to achieve ultimate efficiency in productivity. With its origins within the business world, managerialism has nonetheless seeped into areas of non-profit-based human endeavour, including education[6] and religion.[7] The antithesis of managerialism, rationalism, standardisation and bureaucracy should be

---

A. Trevathan (✉)
International Green School of Benguerir, Benguerir, Morocco

© The Author(s) 2018
M. Abdalla et al. (eds.), *Islamic Schooling in the West*,
https://doi.org/10.1007/978-3-319-73612-9_7

immediately apparent in the form of religious modality and praxis embodying 'the mystical, the numinous, the unpredictable, and the non-rational (which is not, of course, the same as the irrational)'.[8]

In possessing a theology of an unquantifiable, indefinable and limitless God, one would presume that Muslims would counter the human tendency to constantly quantify and codify, of which managerialism is an optimum example—a type of conceptual idolatry. As such, Muslims could be expected to challenge this and other modern educational frameworks, reified on the back of calculative and rationalistic thinking. Should they do so, they would not find themselves alone for there is a growing body of people who are beginning to question various aspects of institutionalised education. However, managerialism seems even to have crept into the religious social realm through what is described by Cantwell Smith as a 'a process of reification: mentally making religion into a thing, gradually coming to conceive of it as an objective systematic entity'.[9] Karen Armstrong puts forward the argument that religious extremists 'have absorbed the pragmatic rationalism of modernity'.[10]

In attempting to address an aspect of the above, this chapter embarks upon an enquiry into a vague, frequently mentioned yet rarely questioned element found within the discourse of school improvement and development. School ethos is a thing frequently spoken of and actively sought after, yet there seems to be little questioning of the concept of ethos itself. Despite the fact that there is a small body of research on the matter, there is scant evidence of this discussion having trickled down to the practical level within schools themselves. Muslim schools are not exempt from this, as frequent presumptions are quite apparent regarding exactly what a 'Muslim or Islamic ethos' is, and these need some airing and challenging.

In the first part of the chapter, an initial attempt is made to clarify some of the apparent confusion around concepts of ethos, ethics and morality in order to clear a path to proceed. From there, the differences and tensions between positivist and non-positivist interpretations of ethos regarding schools are identified and discussed and a working definition is established for the purposes of the chapter. An argued justification for this definition follows that contends that the common understanding and usage of school ethos has been purloined as an educational tool and for the purposes of commodification, whereas authentically ethos describes things as they are rather than as they 'ought to be'. Having argued for the definition, a closer look at school ethos is embarked upon from this perspective. It is proposed that school management should give up the idea that they will ever be able to create the ethos of a school, though they might be able to influence it. Creating an inauthentic ethos will only increase the alienation of students and staff and be counterproductive, creating the opposite to the ethos desired. In the next section, an argument and some suggestions are made for simultaneously attempting a maximalist–minimalist approach to introduce virtues or principles in a school for their own sake as opposed to introducing them in order to establish an ethos. In the next section, a critical reflection on Muslim ethos, or Muslim 'distinctiveness', is embarked upon wherein an argument is made that prayers and clothing alone do not an ethos make. Moreover, through overuse, words describing a Muslim school ethos can come to lack depth, meaning and content. Some suggestions are made in the sections that follow, the first of which argues for a clearly thought through and articulated philosophy for behaviour management and the tone of school life for consistency. In the concluding part, some practical possibilities are discussed which could influence the outcomes and goals expected of students in Muslim schools.

What Is Ethos?

Though frequently referred to in educational, sociological and religious circles, the concept of 'ethos' remains indistinct. 'There does not appear to be a common language amongst researchers or research participants for talking about values, character development, spirituality or ethos; nor are there agreed definitions for these concepts.'[11] The word is derived from the Greek word ἦθος and is based upon on the idea of a customary disposition, bearing a relation to the Latin word *mores*, which denotes the habitual or customary and from which the word *morals* stems. However, specifically in the art of rhetoric (*al-balagh*) ethos refers to the conscious or unconscious self-portrayal of personal characteristics used for persuasive communication as part of the speaker's armament, which included *pathos* and *logos*. The question of whether the rhetorical ethos is prescribed by the content and thereby assumed for the event, or whether it is based on the natural moral character of the speaker, was a contested matter, with Aristotle arguing the former and Isocrates the latter.[12] The underlying divergence between these two views is still evident in approaches to ethos up to the present day, as we shall see when looking at positivist and non-positivist approaches to the matter.

Complexities arise in the fact that ethos arises through ethical activity yet can exist prior to ethics. In this way, the ethics of a person or group may even be based on an ethos, but an ethos may not necessarily be based on ethics. However, this is contradicted in Aristotle's interpretation, that ethos cannot arise within an ethical vacuum. The seeming paradox lies within praxis, for while ethos allows understanding, ethics is the naturally evolving practical expression of this understanding simultaneously combining understanding, evaluating and practice. Aristotle illustrates this pointedly: 'as in the Olympic Games it is not the beautiful and the strongest that are crowned but those who compete (for it is some of these that are victorious)'.[13] The beautiful and the strong sums up the ethos of sportsmen (within ancient Greek sensibilities), yet it is participation which brings things to fruition, and their being comparatively judged epitomises ethics.

The word *ethikos* (ἠθικός) or *ethics* stems from the word *ethos* and refers to the demonstration of moral character, essentially the philosophy of right and wrong. While ethics may be seen as the science of morality, it is linked with ethos, especially in the sense of descriptive morality (as opposed to the normative sense), and it does not indicate any objective right and wrong but simply describes rather than determines.

Descriptive morality and ethos elucidate the done thing or *mores* within any given group of people or even within the individual. However, the confusion between descriptive and normative morality or subjective versus objective morality is often mistakenly linked to ethos, more of which will be dealt with below. Despite close similarities, there is also a nuanced distinction to be made between descriptive morality and ethos. Descriptive morality describes the accepted *mores* within the collective, whereas ethos can be said to describe the qualitative character of the activity, the structure and the processes which occur within any given group of people or in relation to the individual. From this perspective, ethos is the more experiential as opposed to the cognitive. It is apparent that the lack of clear definitions and an ensuing blurring together of ethos, ethics and morality in common parlance is where the confusion lies.

Positivist and Non-Positivist Approaches to Ethos

Notwithstanding the differences between the Aristotelian and Isocratic perspectives outlined above, ethos is often viewed through positivist and non-positivist perspectives. The positivist view is inclined to perceive ethos as stipulating what is right and therefore what should be, and therefore what is closer to ethics and normative morality. In this interpretation, ethos is regarded as separate and independent from actuality as an objective truth and is imposed upon the organisation, just as a certain characteristic is adopted for the purposes of rhetorical delivery. It tends towards being an expression of an authority's aims and objectives and is usually considered as something that can be instrumental in improving the functioning of its organisation. Educational contexts lend themselves easily to illustrating this view, and Hogan describes a custodial ethos wherein school authorities or religious schools may understand their role to be preserving, defending and transmitting values.[14] Hogan explains that such an ethos might involve the attitude of being 'on the lookout for infringements',[15] a view he traces back to Plato and which continues to influence modern educational thought to this day. The practical expression of this would be an ethos that is outlined formally through policies to which teachers and staff are expected to adhere. Examples might be found in religious schools, wherein one may find an ethos 'to be driven by explicit, articulated and implemented concepts of a specifically Catholic ethos'.[16]

From the non-positivist view, ethos is neither something to be managed nor to be imposed, at least not directly, as it arises naturally from the social interaction which forms each separate environment. Rather than being something exterior to be applied within the institution, it is woven into its very fabric. As such, while policies may exist concerning what is expected of students, staff and parents, ethos cannot be formally prescribed as it is simply the combined feel of a place or what is popularly known as its 'vibe'. Such views are inextricably intertwined with concepts of culture, and as Oldfield et al. ask,[17] 'what is the difference, for instance, between a school's culture, climate and ethos?' So, while others have offered examples of schools supposedly utilising a non-positive ethos,[18] this seems to be a contradiction in terms, for the non-positivist ethos cannot, by its very nature, be described or prescribed. Consequently, where Donnelley observes that for one of the schools in her case study, 'ethos is a *negotiated* process whereby individuals come to some agreement about what should and should not be prioritised',[19] one could take issue with this.

The idea that ethos is reified to the extent that it is achieved through being 'negotiated towards',[20] pursued or 'captured' is problematic, as we simply replace the label 'Catholic' ethos with 'negotiated' ethos. It seems right to ponder whether any authentic grounds for 'negotiating' exist when the premise of our educational systems is compulsory, reducing the idea to a mere façade. Ultimately, there seems to be little difference between Donnelley's identification of an alleged non-positivist position in one school and the positivist (i.e., custodial) ethos in another. In both cases ethos emerges as something of an educator's utensil, whereas in fact, it is argued here, it is under no one's control, refuses any sharp definition and exists despite plans, arrangements or intervention. It is not that intervention will not influence ethos, but rather that *the outcome may not be what was intended* and in fact intervention can be counterproductive. The danger in imposing and establishing a formal school ethos is that it is so easily prone to being relegated as a set of rhetorical ideals set up by the institution. The greater the gap between the everyday reality and the prescribed 'ought to be', the greater the risk of the latter being perceived as artificial and pontifical by an increasingly cynical student and/or staff body.

Having worked through the above, a less reified perspective is put forward here, underpinned by a more sociological and existential definition. As a working model for this analysis, a possible definition of ethos is proffered as *the quality and characteristics of the unique ambience, social interaction, cultural overviews, practice and ritual within an organisation.*

THE ETHOS OF SCHOOLS

'If you have to plan, plan that you will not engage in planning'.[21] There is an inevitable yet universal factor that exists within the ethos of all schools irrespective of the best of intentions. This is the fact that most children would rather not have to undertake daily sessions learning things in which they may not be interested. It can be of no surprise that they would rather socialise, play or organise their own entertainment. As much as we may want to project upon them what we as adults think they should learn, they are not naturally disposed to this. A major part of the educational process is designed to divert children from their natural instincts and steer them towards what adults think best serves society.[22,23,24] Though awkward, it is important to recognise this as an underlying reality of a school's ethos.

While ethos may remain an ethereal concept, there is no doubt that there is a prevailing atmosphere to each school, manifested in things ranging from the overall school appearance to the students' interactions with adults. Some schools, usually but not necessarily the more privileged ones, seem to effortlessly exude a hallowed ambience based on a patina of accumulated educational exchanges over time, culminating in a calling to higher things. What role the passage of time plays in fomenting this type of venerable ethos is a moot question, but there does appear to be an element of sustained consistency. Following on from this, the common view is that schools with a 'distinctive' ethos tend to be successful which in turn precipitates questions concerning whether schools can 'achieve higher levels of pupil attainment by means of their superior "ethos"'?[25] or whether there is 'anything about the ethos ... of faith schools, which offers an educational advantage over non-faith or community schools?'.[26] If this distinctiveness is taken at face value, we can surmise that schools achieve success through striving to be distinctive. The first, rather obvious, rejoinder is that schools could be distinctive in a negative sense and therefore not be successful. What is clear in these statements is that there is a reification of ethos, and when ethos is reified to the extent of being something to strive towards with the objective of managing behaviour or raising academic standards, then something rings inauthentic. In approaching the matter in this fashion, are we not putting the proverbial cart before the horse?

Boyd speaks of an 'ethos of achievement' as existing in some Scottish schools, and it would be difficult to argue against its existence.[27] But it must be recognised that such an ethos will not exist in isolation as there will be other types of ethos concurrently existing, some of which may be directly counter to this. The ethos of achievement that he identifies undoubtedly will have come about through, among other things, worthy teaching on the part of teachers and highly motivated learning skills from the students and the overall quality of interactions between the two. Though policies and interventions may have advertently or inadvertently assisted in bringing this about, it is also possible to imagine that despite adverse conditions and in the absence of any formalised ethos, an ethos of achievement could come about. It is another thing entirely to consciously pursue an ethos of achievement in pursuit of its institutional and financial benefits. The objective of the interactions between student and teacher is projected out of the immediate encounter at hand, and into something unconnected and in the future. Attempting to establish an ethos in this way can breed inauthenticity, leading to possible innocuous 'celebrations of achievement' and eventually rendering them as 'Events that decrease perceived self-determination ... [which] will undermine intrinsic motivation'.[28] Mclaughlin distinguishes between an 'intended' ethos as opposed to an 'experienced' ethos.[29] The intention behind pursuing an ethos of achievement is institutionally self-serving in the Foucauldian sense and not actually about the individual students. Thus the idea of 'establishing an ethos' should not degenerate solely into a '*technē*, a process of reflection in service to doing and making',[30] or part of the contemporary trend to 'instrumentalize, professionalize, vocationalize, corporatize, and ultimately technologize education'.[31] The way this can be at odds with the educative process in schools, and especially in religious schools, has been dealt with previously at length elsewhere.[32] The 'in the moment' interaction of teacher and student wherein the pure process of teaching and learning takes place is integral to itself and not deviated from due to other concerns unrelated to the immediate encounter.

It is argued here that approaches to the question of deep ethos within schools should be first and foremost to look beyond the formally prescribed to what really exists as far as is possible, for 'the process of ethos is not static and operates on several levels'.[33] Ethos is the lived reality of the school rather than the prescribed one, which by necessity is closer to ethics. As such, we should recognise that we may never have full control of, or dominate, ethos and therefore our approach should be *intentive* as opposed to prescriptive, with educators aware of and prepared to take risks. In looking at the ethos of any school, the management should consciously think upon the matter with *phronesis* (practical, context-dependent wisdom). The *epistemic* (context independent and theoretical) and *technē* approaches (here meaning an envisioned accomplished concrete product) should be decidedly in the background.

MINIMALIST AND MAXIMALIST APPROACHES TO ETHOS

The contention here is not that there is nothing to be done about ethos but that it must be understood as an all-pervading and not easily manipulated presence. In helping to move some way towards a practical understanding, two possible approaches are raised by the question, 'is "ethos" connected to the classroom or school, or is it embodied in a broader philosophy of education?'[34] There seems to be no reason that it is not connected to both, existing simultaneously. Nonetheless, it is posited here that this *classroom* versus *broader philosophy* easily lends itself to a maximalist/minimalist approach that could be adopted in approaching the matter of ethos within a school. It is submitted here that the maximalist perspective would be more embedded within the broader philosophical context, while the minimalist approach would be more situated around the localised teaching–learning encounter.

A maximalist approach might involve deliberating and settling on general principles for their own sake, *as opposed to having principles for establishing ethos*. In this sense, it seems important that schools develop their own philosophy of education (i.e., the what, why and how of teaching and learning) and that teachers are called upon to participate in this philosophising.

An enormous blow was delivered to the Western educational system when, starting in the 1950s and through to the 1980s, the philosophy of education was axed from many teacher education courses. This was in parallel with, and probably a result of, the advent of the business model and its imposition upon the educational sphere. Yet the need for more philosophical thought within the practice of teaching is paramount and would certainly have an impact upon a school's ethos. In 1959, a prepared statement entitled 'The Place of Philosophy in Teacher Education' by the American Philosophical Association proposed the following:

> Consequently, if the teacher will inevitably need to reflect upon the nature and meaning of the process of education, taken in its relational totality, and to make and carry out professional decisions and programs in the light of that reflection, the necessity for at least a minimal philosophical experience seems quite clear.[35]

This is somewhat different to the current yet advantageous call for teachers to be reflective about their practice of education. An example of a considered approach might be to openly uphold the principle of trust as being of paramount importance within the school, leading to the management visibly and actively placing more trust in teachers and students. Questions of accountability and assessment for teachers, staff and students could be approached in a different manner than is currently the case within modern educational settings, where a basis of suspicion seems to be an underlying principle (and which must equally have an influence on the ethos of the school). David Sherrington, a headteacher of a school in London, sums it up thus:

- Public and political pressures dictate that Governments 'do something' about education because some people are unhappy; they make ever more highly centralised policy with a tough accountability-driven approach.
- Teachers, leaders and schools are under pressure to deliver; regardless of their actual strengths, there is a shared sense of being coshed; this breeds insecurity, leads to defensiveness and simultaneously forces teachers and schools to focus primarily on short-term measured outcomes.
- The inspection regime reinforces this—even if its Chief Inspector sounds utterly plausible and reasonable.[36]

The ethos emanating from this is palatable. Elsewhere, Sherrington interestingly compares the levels of trust given to teachers within a school as equivalent to the difference between a cage, a safari park and a game reserve. He admires the Finnish model whereby teachers are allowed more freedom in how they deliver, plan and assess. Clearly, this needs to be accompanied by a coherent appeal to personal integrity and a 'demand for high quality outcomes'.[37] The trust should be given over as being the best practical thing to do and not as a device to be employed for establishing an ethos—leave ethos to make of the situation what it will and hope for the best.

In the minimalist sense, more concentration upon the essential encounter between teacher and learner would be appropriate. This could consist of encouraging greater teacher self-awareness and personal integrity in addressing the countless unpredictable events of school life. A school-wide focus on supporting teachers to develop a heightened awareness of their social interactions with students could involve teachers developing a greater sense of presence, authenticity, active listening, awareness of body language, classroom manner and genuine respect for students. If the minimalist approach as outlined here or anything similar is pitched correctly, and if it is emphasised and followed through on with motivation and sincerity on the part of the teachers, something of this may be felt in the ambience of the school.

Muslim Ethos in a Muslim School

Trawling through Muslim school websites, it becomes apparent that 'Islamic ethos' is frequently tied to the performance of prayers, adherence to outward *sunnan* or the presence of Islamic books and posters throughout the school. Without wanting to minimise any of the above, and cognisant that there may be a very strong ethos within these schools, nevertheless it seems to state the obvious. We would expect a Muslim school to have some or all of these things, but how is this different from stating that an academic school ethos is evident in that it has desks and chairs? What makes up a Muslim ethos that will affect young people at any meaningful level? What is required is the inward *sunnan*, for the rest are resources and acts, empty vessels, to be filled with the required spirit.

Other sites speak of their ethos as consisting of 'wholesome quality learning' and use words such as 'aspirational', 'resilient', 'reflective', 'courteous' and 'charitable', encouragingly suggesting a move away from outward appearances to more inward qualitative dispositions. While this is certainly uplifting, it has more to do with ethics, possibly even a custodial ethos, wherein pupils who are not courteous or charitable will be identified. That is not wrong in and of itself, nor are ethics within schools to be rejected—quite to the contrary; but it must be made clear that this is not the deep ethos defined above which is worthy of consideration. The other issue is that secular schools make the same claims. Should there not be an apparent difference between a Muslim school and a secular school when they are based on very different doctrinal grounds?

Another problem lies in the articulation of ethos, especially in relation to virtues (i.e., resilience and courteousness). In our current educational environment, marketing has assumed a role that did not exist previously and words such as 'excellence' are bandied around so frequently that they have become devoid of meaning. Reifying an ethos for public relations or marketing purposes can result in vacuity, as indicated in some of the Socratic ruminations on the written word, for example 'the living word of knowledge which has a soul and of which the written word is properly no more than an image',[38] suggesting that the ethos of a school is authentically felt *in situ* rather than articulated. Equally, when a Muslim school claims an ethos and employs it for marketing purposes, the artificiality somehow seeps back into the Muslim body itself (i.e., the inanity of 'an ethos of excellence'), amounting to a mundane commodification of the sacred. It is appropriate to consider the words of the renowned polymath al-Kindi (801–873) who postulated, 'those who commodify religion thus have no religion—for he who trades in something, soon sells it and does not own it any longer'.[39]

A Qur'anic Ethos? *Tashbīh and Tanzīh*

Without contravening the preceding discussion, is it possible to explore what an authentic 'vibe' within a Muslim school might be, but to do so under Socrates' *proviso* that it must be explained—no empty words—yet also to accept that one may never arrive at any definitive position but at best some general orientation? In order to do this it seems relevant to go to some root Qur'anic concepts.

The self-referential description of the Divine within the Qur'anic text alternates between the twin poles of *tanzīh* and *tashbīh*, simultaneously interactive within the Divine mystery. Jumping from the sublime to the mundane, a discussion on the broad ambience of a Muslim school should occur preferably from the outset but retrospectively if necessary, with a deliberated stance on the ambient 'tones' of *tanzīh* or *ta<u>sh</u>bīh* within the school's cultural fabric. The first of these terms denotes the complete incomparability and transcendence of Allah from the world and human beings. It relates to the absolute distance between the Divine and creation—'Nothing is like Him'[40]—and is usually associated with the attributes of power (*al-Jabbar*), the Mighty (*al-ʿAziz*), the Abasing (*al Khāfid*) and the Judge (*al Hakīm*), amongst others. The second term relates to the identification with and the proximity of Allah with the human project, collectively and individually. The concept is associated with the Divine attributes that relate to nearness and mercy—'We are closer to him than his jugular vein'[41]—and is linked with the Compassionate (*ar-Rahmān*), the Merciful (*ar-Rahīm*), the Forgiver (*al-Ghafūr*) and the Friend (*al Walī*).

These two seemingly opposing yet interacting perspectives on the Divine nature could characterise the approaches to be adopted within the school. There is the individual's insignificance in the face of *tanzīh*, and on the other hand there is the human behavioural reflection of the care bestowed on the individual in relation to the *ta<u>sh</u>bīh*. These are combined to evoke what seems to be the epitome of the Prophet's behaviour, deemed as the 'Qur'an walking', which embodied humility: humility towards the Divine, towards others—enemies and friends alike, towards the surrounding world and towards the self. Therefore, it makes sense that Muslim schooling could be grounded in humility, but this, in turn, needs to be qualified.

Humility as a School Characteristic

A man came to the Prophet, praise and peace be upon him, and when he saw him began to tremble on account of timidity, but the Prophet, praise and peace be upon him, put him at ease straight away saying, 'Be calm, I am not a king, I am the son of a woman from the [tribe of] Koraysh who eats dried meat'.[42]

What follows is a basic exploration of the question of humility, which is intended to allow or to stimulate and possibly orientate the possibility of discussion for a Muslim school community. While it is undeniable that the question of humility is often referred to within the religious discourse of Muslims, is it nonetheless possible that frequent repetition decreases the power of the concept? It is felt that a conscious, practice-based, ongoing communal discourse around a philosophy of humility conducted amongst a core group of people within a school could have some effect on the internal interactions of a school.

The issues of humility, pride and arrogance are so fundamental to human existence that it is surprising how low a profile they present in the content of what is taught or is present within the educational dynamic of schools. One reason for this may be that focusing on humility flies in the face of social norms. Schools push 'academic excellence' and achievement is driven by the hope of success academically and beyond school. Within wider society the successful life is measured by levels of celebrity or material possession, and schooling reflects this and prepares one to compete for them. The refinement of character is pushed to the periphery in favour of measurable academic goals and targets being brought to the fore. Are we asking too much in thinking that religious schools, in particular Muslim schools, should promote values other than those reflected in a thoroughly consumerist society? The Prophet said, 'I was only sent to perfect good character'.[43] With this in mind, what is attempted here is to lay out a modicum of the complexities of humility to stimulate further enquiry leading to a possible philosophy of humility to be present in schools. This is with a view to stimulating something that Muslim educationalists might engage with and explore as an active group enquiry on the part of the school community. This could be carried out at different levels with the objective of a conscious commitment to taking this on in their lives and professional practice. Equally, what is proposed here inherently asks for consideration of the idea of demoting academic achievement as the primary aim of Muslim schools and replacing it with human refinement, and of the methods by which to communicate this pedagogically to students and pupils. To what degree the ethos of a school may be effected by these measures can only remain to be seen.

Educators are in direct competition with contemporary global youth culture, something that inevitably plays a large part in the ethos of schools across the world. Bly asserts that this global culture has affinitive ties among young people across the world that probably outnumbers the cultural ties they may have with their parents.[44] Within this youth culture, originating from American urban centres, humility is looked upon as a sign of a weak character. Humility is linked to humiliation, as opposed to comportment, and is seen as imposed by events or people that overwhelm or outdo the individual in the public arena so that one is forcibly humbled.

Within Muslim understanding, pride is part of the human psyche and is at ground level the need for self-admiration and the admiration of others. This need not necessarily be negative—a conscious yet measured degree of pride is humanly required to function effectively within the world. Yet a common human flaw is the tendency to seek admiration and approval and for this to become the primary motivator in one's life, rendering one inauthentic and self-centred. It also denotes forgetting (*ghaflah*) or covering (*kuru*) the Divine presence at every level of one's existence. At this level, the ego (*nafs*), based on individual pride, will resent and resist being shown to be wrong, being overshadowed or challenged. It will make concerted efforts to be shielded from the lurking suspicion, rightly or wrongly, that there may be little to be proud of, especially in relation to others. This defensiveness can lead to illusions of grandeur, with pride evolving to become arrogance, known as *kufr al kibr*, the root of cardinal sin within the Muslim faith, though more specifically manifesting as *shirk*,[45] the association or setting up of anything (including oneself) on a par with the Divine. Any and all abilities that one may have are of Divine origin and part of the planned unfolding of the world within the Divine consciousness. Describing the self as constituting the originary cause of anything puts one on a par with the Divine, which requires a degree of arrogance. The haughty depiction of Satan in the Qur'an, refusing to bow to human beings, demonstrates this poignantly.[46] The effect of not comprehending one's essential insubstantiality can manifest in conscious or unconscious opposition to the Divine way. One requires clear vision and self-awareness to see the plain fact that in the face of the Divine existence, one can be said to be non-existent, as a candle is to the sun. In Muslim terms, this is said to be the *haqā'iq* (reality) of existence; humility is recognising one's true status in the world.

Humility is the self-authentication and self-recognition of a person's humanity in its entirety, including its strengths and weaknesses. If the role of the Prophets was to call people to transcend common human impulses and thereby to become 'extra-ordinary' (i.e., out of the ordinary), then humility is probably the best embodiment of such a quest. It confronts head-on the desires within human nature itself. The understanding that leads to the comportment of genuine humility, the presupposition of one's lacking (as opposed to being humbled), is to fully comprehend the truth that one's *self* is an inadequacy. When one objectively sees norms which far supersede the norms of the self, then one has no choice but to assume the mantle of humility. One accepts that there is a human fragility that cannot be transcended, yet humility does allow transcendence over essential human norms. Equally, self-awareness also rounds this off, for along with one's better abilities there are other things at which one is not as good. In this knowledge, one should be prepared to promote others above oneself, though not in the exercise of humility (i.e., 'I humble myself by putting others before myself') but simply in recognition of the reality of the self and others.

Yet the matter is not as simple as it first appears for there is a paradoxical aspect to humility that sets it apart, and it is perhaps significant that Aristotle would not consider it a virtue. The paradox of humility lies in that it is in constant danger of being sabotaged in and of itself and converted into its direct opposite. Outward manifestations of apparent humility may, in fact, be at complete odds with appears; as Nietzsche says, 'He that humbleth himself wants to be exalted'.[47] As we recognise our humility, the element of pride can kick in, especially when this is witnessed and acclaimed by others, and we may experience pleasure in that. Yet humility should by its very nature reject the pleasure brought about by outward approval as this is the basic ingredient of pride. The complications of this can be discerned in the saying of Ibn Ataïlah: 'Whoever asserts that he is humble is in reality arrogant—as humbleness is a high state. And if you assert for yourself a high state, you are arrogant.'[48]

Humility is a very subtle and difficult balance to maintain and yet effectively penetrates to the very core of the human struggle with the self (*nafs*). It was this struggle for full self-integrity, the apex of the conflict for the salvation of the self, which brought about the famed *malāmatī* (the people of blame) movement of Nishapur of the ninth century.[49] With no set rituals, they set about eradicating their egos by ascetic practices in secret and by behaving in public in inappropriate ways to humiliate themselves by attracting the opprobrium of others.[50] Kierkegaard's Knights of Faith are indistinguishable from tax collectors, signifying that despite the grandeur of their inner spiritual states, to all intents and purposes they appear as ordinary citizens.[51]

Ironically, to be truly humble one may occasionally need to behave in ways that appear the opposite. The false humility so aptly depicted by Charles Dickens in the character of Uriah Heep is easily discerned, whereas genuine humility may be hidden from view when one might be required to take a strong and principled stand. Authentic humility need not denote passivity; one may need to influence, persuade or attempt to lead people towards what one believes to be right and yet inwardly remain detached from the outcome, always bearing in mind the possibility of being in error. When a child has stepped far over the boundaries of what is acceptable behaviour, would it be wrong to reprimand her/him as it would imply some sort of supremacy when in fact you are humble? There is also 'idiot humility', which is a self-deceiving and self-destructive attitude based more in fear and lack of confidence which does not allow one to take up opportunities, entertain any expectations or aspire to greater things.

To conclude this section, the purpose of exploring various aspects of humility is to focus on its meaning and nature and to foment further thought and discussion on the matter.

CONCLUSION

In *The Art of Memory*, Eickelman reports on the confrontation between classical Muslim education and modern systemised education at the Yusufiya, a renowned centre for religious education in Marrakesh in the 1930s[52]:

> The Yusufiya had no sharply defined body of students or faculty, administration, entrance or course examinations, curriculum or unified sources of funds. In fact, its former teachers related with amusement the frustrated efforts of French colonial officials to determine who its 'responsible' leaders were and to treat it as a corporate entity analogous to a medieval European University.

One of the main arguments of this chapter is that current modern education, strongly influenced by 'managerial culture', has become overly standardised and static. In this context, ethos has become a 'tool' to aid and abet school managers in creating a preconceived environment to further the ends of the institution. While one may not wish such a thing upon anyone, it particularly runs counter to the basic tenets of the religious way, and the context within which Muslims are educated should not be reified. The numinous is directly opposed to Weber's 'iron cage of rationality'. Despite the modern aberration of rationalist thought within the present Ummah, the early communities were generally characterised by a more flexible spirituality[53] wary of rigid idols of thought and theology.

As for Muslim ethos, humility has been identified as integral to Muslim 'beingness'. Though highly complicated, risky and running in contradiction to current youth culture, it has been suggested here that a concerted and thorough focus on authentic humility should be at the heart of Muslim education. Ethos should be allowed to develop in its own way and will do so regardless of efforts. For school managers, it is best to be aware, to carefully contemplate and subtly attempt to address matters wisely if required, ultimately giving over to the Divine will. Ibn Ataīlah refers to this Divine management of affairs when he says 'Give yourself a rest from managing! When Someone Else is doing it for you, don't you start doing it for yourself!'[54]

NOTES

1. Ulrike Schuerkens, *Global Forces and Local Life-Worlds: Social Transformations* (London: Sage, 2004).
2. Robert Locke and John C. Spender, *Confronting Managerialism: How the Business Elite and Their Schools Threw Our Lives Out of Balance* (London: Zed Books, 2011).
3. George Ritzer, *The McDonaldization of Society* (Thousand Oaks, CA: Pine Forge Press, 1996).
4. Ibid., xvii.
5. Ibid., 21.
6. Thomas Kilkauer, *Managerialism – A Critique of an Ideology* (London: Palgrave Macmillan Basingstoke, Hampshire, 2013).
7. John W. Drane, *The McDonaldization of the Church: Spirituality, Creativity, and the Future of the Church* (London: Darton Longman & Todd, 2000).
8. Ibid., 45.
9. Wilfrid Cantwell-Smith, *Traditional Religions and Modern Culture in Proceedings of the XIth International Congress of the International Association for the History of Religions* (Leiden: Brill, 1968), 51.
10. Karen Armstrong, *The Battle for God* (London: Harper Collins, 2000), xi.
11. Elizabeth Oldfield et al., *More than an Educated Guess: Assessing the Evidence on Faith Schools* (London: Theos, 2013), 46.
12. Thomas Cole, *The Origins of Rhetoric in Ancient Greece* (Baltimore, MD: Johns Hopkins University Press, 1991), and also see Niall Livingstone, "Writing Politics: Isocrates' Rhetoric of Philosophy", *Rhetorica: A Journal of the History of Rhetoric* 25, no. 1 (2007).
13. Aristotle, *Nicomachean Ethics*, trans. William David Ross (Ontario: Batoche Books, 1999), 13.
14. Padraig Hogan, "The Question of Ethos within Schools", *The Furrow* 35, no. 11 (1984): 695.
15. Ibid.
16. Caitlin Donnelley, "In Pursuit of School Ethos", *British Journal of Educational Studies* 48, no. 2 (2000).
17. Oldfield et al., 46.
18. Donnelley, 2000.
19. Ibid., 150.

20. Ibid.
21. Ibn Abbas Rundi, *Sharh al-hikam al-`Atā'iyya, The Guiding Helper Foundation*, 2004 [cited 29 December 2016]. Available at: http://www.filosofiaorientalecomparativa.it/foc15/wp-content/uploads/2015/06/Hikam-of-Ibn-Ata-Allah-commentary-by-ibn-Abbad-in-English.pdf.
22. James Taylor Gatto, *Dumbing Us Down – The Hidden Curriculum of Compulsory Schooling* (Canada: Gabriola Island, New Society Publishers, 1992).
23. John Holt, *How Children Learn* (New York: Pitman Publishing Company, 1967).
24. Ivan Illich, *Deschooling Society* (New York: Marion Boyars Publishers Ltd, 2000).
25. Oldfield et al., 40.
26. Ibid., 11.
27. Brian Boyd, "Scottish Schools: An Ethos of Achievement", *The Phi Beta Kappon* 79, no. 3 (1997).
28. Deci et al., "Extrinsic Rewards and Intrinsic Motivation in Education: Reconsidered Once Again", *Review of Educational Research* 71, no. 1 (2001): 3.
29. Terence McLaughlin, "The Educative Importance of Ethos", *British Journal of Educational Studies* 53, no. 3 (2005).
30. Ian Thomson, "Heidegger on Ontological Education, or How We Are", in *Heidegger, Education and Modernity*, ed. Michael A. Peters (Oxford: Roman & Littlefield, 2002), 218.
31. Ibid., 124.
32. Abdullah Trevathan, "Spirituality in Muslim Education", in *Philosophies of Islamic Education – Historical Perspectives and Emerging Discourses*, ed. Mujadad Zaman and Nadeem Memon (New York and London: Routledge, 2016).
33. Donnelley, "In Pursuit of School Ethos", 152.
34. Oldfield et al., 44.
35. American Philosophical Association, '*Philosophy in the Education of Teachers*' *Proceedings and Addresses of the American Philosophical Association*, 1959, 63, http://docslide.net/download/link/guidelines-for-accreditation-of-education-component-of-teacher.
36. Tom Sherrington, "Building a Trust Culture: It's not all hugs", *Teacherhead*, 2012, http://headguruteacher.com/2012/11/19/building-a-trust-culture-its-not-all-hugs/ [cited 24 September 2016].
37. Ibid.
38. Plato, *The dialogues of Plato, vol. 1, trans. Into English with analyses and introductions by B. Jowett, M. A. in Five Volumes*, 3rd edition revised and

corrected (Oxford: Oxford University Press, 1892), 485: 276d. http://oll.libertyfund.org/titles/111 [cited 11 November 2016].
39. Mohammed A. al-Jabri, *Arab-Islamic Philosophy—A Contemporary Critique*, trans. A. Abbasi (Austin: University of Texas, 1999), 55.
40. Qur'an 42:11.
41. Qur'an 50:16.
42. Qadi 'Iyad: 1992: 79.
43. Malik ibn Anas, *Al-Muwattah of Imam Malik*, trans. A. Bewley (Norwich: Diwan Press, 2014).
44. Robert Bly, *The Sibling Society: An Impassioned Call for the Rediscovery of Adulthood* (New York: Addison-Wesley, 1996).
45. Qur'an 4, 50.
46. Qur'an 34.
47. F. Nietzsche, *Human, All Too Human*, trans. R.J. Hollingdale (Cambridge: Cambridge University Press, 1996), 88.
48. Abdal Karim Ibn Ataīlah, *Sufi Aphorisms – Kitab al-Hikma*, trans. V. Danner and Brill Publishers (Leiden: Brill Publishers, 1978), 37.
49. Yannis Toussulis, *Sufism and the Way of Blame* (Wheaton: Quest Books, 2011).
50. Jong et al., "Malamatiyya", in *Encyclopaedia of Islam*, 2nd edition, ed. P. Bearman, Th. Bianquis, C.E. Bosworth, E. van Donzel, and W.P. Heinrichs, 2012. Accessed online at https://doi.org/10.1163/1573-3912_islam_COM_0643.
51. Soren Kierkegaard, *Fear and Trembling* (London: Penguin, 1985).
52. Dale F. Eickelman, "The Art of Memory: Islamic Education and Its Social Reproduction", *Comparative Studies in Society and History* 20, no. 4 (1978): 86.
53. Cantwell-Smith, *Traditional Religious and Modern Culture in Proceedings of the XIth International Congress of the International Association for the History of Religions*, 11 and also see Carl W. Ernst, *Following Muhammad: Rethinking Islam in the Contemporary World* (Charleston: University of North Carolina Press, 2003), 63.
54. Abdal Karim Ibn Atā'illāh, *The Hikam of Ibn 'Ata'llah*, trans. Aisha Bewley. [Online] 2011, http://bewley.vitualave.net/hikam.html.

Bibliography

Afsaruddin, Asma. "Muslim Views on Education: Parameters, Purview, and Possibilities." *Journal of Catholic Legal Studies* 44, no. 1 (2009): 163–166.

Al-Jabri, Mohammed A. *Arab-Islamic Philosophy-A Contemporary Critique*. Trans. A. Abbasi. Austin: University of Texas, 1999.

American Philosophical Association. '*Philosophy in the Education of Teachers*' Proceedings and Addresses of the American Philosophical Association 1959, 63. [Cited January 2017]. http://docslide.net/download/link/guidelines-for-accreditation-of-the-philosophy-of-education-component-of-teacher.

Aristotle. *Nicomachean Ethics*. Trans. William David Ross. Ontario: Batoche Books, 1999.

Armstrong, Karen. *The Battle for God*. London: Harper Collins, 2000.

Bly, Robert. *The Sibling Society: An Impassioned Call for the Rediscovery of Adulthood*. New York: Addison-Wesley, 1996.

Boyd, Brian. "Scottish Schools: An Ethos of Achievement." *The Phi Beta Kappan* 79, no. 3 (1997): 252–253.

Cantwell-Smith, Wilfrid. "Traditional Religions and Modern Culture." In *Proceedings of the XIth International Congress of the International Association for the History of Religions*. Leiden: Brill, 1968.

Cole, Thomas. *The Origins of Rhetoric in Ancient Greece*. Baltimore, MD: Johns Hopkins University Press, 1991.

Deci, Edward L., Richard Koestner, and Richard M. Ryan. "Extrinsic Rewards and Intrinsic Motivation in Education: Reconsidered Once Again." *Review of Educational Research* 71, no. 1 (Spring 2001): 1–27.

Donnelley, Caitlin. "In Pursuit of School Ethos." *British Journal of Educational Studies* 48, no. 2 (2000): 134–154.

Drane, John W. *The McDonaldization of the Church: Spirituality, Creativity, and the Future of the Church*. London: Darton Longman & Todd, 2000.

Eickelman, Dale F. "The Art of Memory: Islamic Education and Its Social Reproduction." *Comparative Studies in Society and History* 20, no. 4 (1978): 485–516.

Ernst, Carl W. *Following Muhammad*. Charleston: University of North Carolina Press, 2003.

Gatto, James Taylor. *Dumbing Us Down – The Hidden Curriculum of Compulsory Schooling*. Gabriola Island: New Society Publishers, 1992.

Glover, Derek, and Marianne Coleman. "School Culture, Climate and Ethos: Interchangeable or Distinctive Concepts?" *Journal of In-Service Education* 31, no. 2 (2005): 251–271.

Green, Elizabeth. *Mapping the Field*. London: Theos, 2009.

Hogan, Padraig. "The Question of Ethos Within Schools." *The Furrow* 35, no. 11 (1984): 693–704.

Holt, John. *How Children Learn*. New York: Pitman Publishing Company, 1967.

Ibn Atā'illāh, Abdal Karim. *Sufi Aphorisms – Kitab al-Hikam*. Trans. V. Danner. Leiden: Brill Publishers, 1978.

———. *The Hikam of Ibn 'Ata'llah*. Trans. Aisha Bewley. 2011. [Online]. http://bewley.virtualave.net/hikam.html.

Illich, Ivan. *Deschooling Society*. New York: Marion Boyars Publishers Ltd, 2000.

Jong, Frederic de, Hamid Algar, and Colin H. Imber. "Malāmatiyya." In *Encyclopaedia of Islam, Second Edition*, ed. P. Bearman, Th. Bianquis, C.E. Bosworth, E. van Donzel, and W.P. Heinrichs. Online. https://doi.org/10.1163/1573-3912_islam_COM_0643.

Kierkegaard, Søren. *Fear and Trembling*. London: Penguin, 1985.

Kilkauer, Thomas. *Managerialism – A Critique of an Ideology*. Palgrave Macmillan Basingstoke, Hampshire, 2013.

Livingstone, Niall. "Writing Politics: Isocrates' Rhetoric of Philosophy." *Rhetorica: A Journal of the History of Rhetoric* 25, no. 1 (2007): 15–34.

Locke, Robert, and John C. Spender. *Confronting Managerialism: How the Business Elite and Their Schools Threw Our Lives Out of Balance*. London: Zed Books, 2011.

Malik ibn Anas. *Al- Muwattah of Imam Malik*. Trans. A. Bewley. Norwich: Diwan Press, 2014.

Martel, Martin V. "'Dialogues with Parsons' (1973–74)." *Indian Journal of Social Research* 17, no. 1 (1976): 1–34.

McLaughlin, Terence. "The Educative Importance of Ethos." *British Journal of Educational Studies* 53, no. 3 (2005): 306–325.

Nietzsche, F. *Human, All Too Human*. Trans. R.J. Hollingdale. Cambridge: Cambridge University Press, 1996.

Parsons, Talcott. *Structure and Process in Modern Society*. New York: Free Press, 1959.

Plato. *The Dialogues of Plato*, Vol. 1. Translated into English with Analyses and Introductions by B. Jowett in Five Volumes. 3rd Edition Revised and Corrected. Oxford: Oxford University Press, 1892. [Cited 11 November 2016]. http://oll.libertyfund.org/titles/111.

Ritzer, George. *The McDonaldization of Society*. Thousand Oaks, CA: Pine Forge Press, 1996.

Rundi, Ibn Abbas. *Sharh al-hikam al-`Atā'iyya, The Guiding Helper Foundation*, 2004. [Cited 29 December 2016]. http://www.filosofiaorientalecomparativa.it/foc15/wp-content/uploads/2015/06/Hikam-of-Ibn-Ata-Allah-commentary-by-ibn-Abbad-in-English.pdf.

Schuerkens, Ulrike, ed. *Global Forces and Local Life-Worlds: Social Transformations*. London: Sage, 2004.

Series in International Sociology. Thousand Oaks, CA: Sage Publications, 2004.

Sherrington, Tom. *Building a Trust Culture: It's Not All Hugs*. Headguru, 2012. [Cited 24 September 2016]. https://headguruteacher.com/2012/11/19/building-a-trust-culture-its-not-all-hugs/.

Thomson, Iain. "Heidegger on Ontological Education, or How We Become What We Are." In *Heidegger, Education and Modernity*, ed. Michael A. Peters, 123–150. Oxford: Rowman & Littlefield, 2002.

Toussulis, Yannis. *Sufism and the Way of Blame*. Wheaton: Quest Books, 2011.

Trevathan, Abdullah. "Spirituality in Muslim Education." In *Philosophies of Islamic Education – Historical Perspectives and Emerging Discourses*, ed. Mujadad Zaman and Nadeem Memon, 57–57. New York and London: Routledge, 2016.

Wallace, David Foster. *This Is Water: Some Thoughts, Delivered on a Significant Occasion, About Living a Compassionate Life*. London: Little Brown and Company, 2009.

CHAPTER 8

Enacting a Vision in a Faith School: Putting Word into Action

Anne McDonald

INTRODUCTION

School renewal is about renewing the vision and mission of the school to bring about the continuous improvement that marks an effective school. All schools have as their focus quality student outcomes, but schools couched in a community of both faith and learning see renewal as that which enhances student learning outcomes in light of the shared beliefs and values of community members. Such schools are privileged to have an underlying vision that guides the work and focus of all involved—a vision that is far broader than learning outcomes alone. When a school's vision is renewed, all members benefit from a commitment to shared values and a collective ethos. When this is in place, students thrive.

A. McDonald (✉)
Catholic Education, Melbourne, VIC, Australia

A Case Study

Starting the Process for Continuous School Improvement

Vision and mission are two constants in any organization. When operating well, they guide an organization within an identified ethos or climate. However, how many of us actually understand the meaning and potential of these terms? From my own experience, there is a myriad of interpretations of these words and even more responses as to how they impact on daily practice. In this chapter, I intend to analyze these two words, seek to see if and where they impact on our school and share how my school has worked to ensure that our Vision and Mission impact on the culture, language and growth of staff, students and parents.

My own work over many years in Catholic education has enabled me to work with and for schools. I have held many leadership roles in Catholic secondary schools over many years, including my current role as principal. In my role as Educational Assistant to the Director in Catholic Education, Gippsland, I worked in the areas of School Review and Leadership Development.

In both roles, I had my own definition of the words vision and mission. To me, vision is the light that guides the work that we do. In my work with teachers, I often used a photo of a lighthouse to illustrate this concept of a light showing the way—lighting the path of our journey and giving clarity as to where we are going. On the other hand, mission in my thinking is the work that we do along our journey—work undertaken through the light of the vision. An organization needs both. Without the vision you are unable to see where you are going, and without the mission you are not doing the work needed to ensure your organizational health and growth. This mission is spelled out in the strategic plan with goals, targets and key indicators for achievement.

I am aware that many educational researchers and academics have offered their own explanations of these two terms. Barbara Brock and Madelyn Grady state that school success cannot be achieved by vision alone: "The Vision must be operational in a school Mission Statement. The Vision Statement expresses a dream of what a school can become; the Mission Statement provides a plan to achieve that dream."[1] Additionally, Caldwell sees vision as a "short statement on a desired future for the school. While it may be expressed in different ways, the key theme is transformation: significant, systematic and sustained change that leads to high levels of achievement for all students in all settings, thus contributing to the well-being of the individual and the nation."[2] It is within these definitions that I couch my work on school renewal through enacting Vision and Mission.

I have found in my own experience that the development of a vision in which everyone can understand both meaning and significance is most difficult. Stating goals and strategies within a strategic plan in light of this vision, or dream, is also difficult. However, most difficult is the "living out" of this Vision and Mission. For these to be more than words, members of the community must act on a daily basis in ways that *say this is who we are and what we do because we have a belief, a dream, a guiding light*. This requires constant evaluation and questioning of processes and practices to ensure both understanding of and adherence to Vision and Mission.

The Story of One School

The purpose of this chapter is to examine how one school has brought about renewal and worked to ensure that its Vision and Mission are alive, impacting on all aspects of school life. When I speak of Vision, I refer to that guiding light that shines on our preferred pathway and guides our daily activities. Vision is not a *destination* but an *aspiration* that, when linked with a strategic plan, with goals and strategies, enables our preferred future to become a reality. Melbourne Futurist Peter Ellyard speaks of futures as comprising four possibilities:

- our prospective future—what could happen?
- our probable future—what will happen?
- our preferred future—what could happen?
- our possible future—what can happen?[3]

We know that for renewal, Vision must be a shared vision, with language that all members understand, commit to and embrace—language articulated daily, and language that informs action. Our Vision must be realistic and achievable; if it is not, it is a mere frustration. In this section, I detail how Nazareth College is working to be on its preferred and possible pathways as a faith and learning community by sharing my story with the college. I commenced work at Nazareth College full of bright ideas and a firm belief that I could run the best school in the world. I had extensive experience as a leader in Catholic schools and ten years' experience as an educational consultant within the Catholic education system. I had a true sense of being called to Nazareth. My own Christian and Catholic faith was strong and was renewed during my study period in Jerusalem and Palestine, only a few months before the position of principal was advertised. I had spent time in the places that I had learned about in my own Catholic education—Jerusalem, Bethlehem, Galilee and Nazareth—the places where Jesus grew and became strong, and the lessons of my own Catholic education were reinforced as I walked in the footsteps of Jesus and heard the words of scripture through new ears and heart.

I was encouraged to apply for the position of principal, and was appointed as the first female principal of Nazareth College. It seemed incredible that less than six months after being in the Holy Land, I would be principal of a school that linked me with the town of Nazareth and with the community of Jesus—Jesus of Nazareth. I was elated with where I was and with the opportunities that lay ahead to build this community.

Nazareth College was established in 1986 in a south-eastern suburb of Melbourne, an area that was then a large suburban growth area—predominantly Anglo-Saxon. In those days, it had a student population of over 1000—today we work hard to keep 700. It is a Catholic co-educational school built to serve the families of four local feeder Catholic primary schools, but now attracts students from a variety of Catholic and non-Catholic schools. While the area is well served with government secondary colleges and Catholic single-sex schools, it is a non-growth area, making continued enrollments a constant area of focus and concern.

The school is owned by the Catholic Church but administered by Catholic Education Melbourne—a very large system educating 22% of primary students and 24.2% of secondary students in the Melbourne sector.[4] We are the youngest Catholic school in the southern and eastern corridors of Melbourne and happily boast a strong multicultural community of forty-two nationalities. It is a very happy, safe school where our students thrive. Each year in the School Improvement Surveys, parents and students rate their satisfaction with our school safety at around 97% and students tell me that they have a sense of belonging when they walk through the school gates each morning.

I have been principal for the past ten years and have enjoyed the challenges, relationships and opportunities that have come my way. As principal, I have significant autonomy as to the direction and daily management of the college. I have a Board of Management that allows me great freedom but oversees the annual budgets, buildings and major directions of the college. I am also very accountable to Catholic Education Melbourne and, like all schools, undertake Annual School Improvement Reviews and major Whole School Reviews every four years to meet both government regulations for re-registration, as well as system expectations and regulations.

I frequently give thanks for the fact that I am a leader in a faith school. In such a setting, we have the opportunity to go way beyond simply offering an education—we have the opportunity to offer our students a deeper understanding of their tradition, the tradition that tells them who they are, where they have come from and what their story is all about. Such schools can offer avenues for personal and spiritual growth that enable young people to live beyond the focus of a materialistic society. As schools of faith, this is our gift, the gift of tradition and values that we pass on to our students. Parents tell us this is what they expect for their children, regardless of their own faith commitment.

The Role of the Principal and School Improvement

The role of principal is crucial to the development of a school Vision that is alive and vibrant and provides the pathway to a preferred future. I soon realized that a school tradition takes a long time to build. Classrooms, facilities and staffing are all priorities and it is only when these are well established that the charism or climate of a school can begin to emerge—a focus that drives learning and achievement within a set framework or perspective. Central to the role of the principal are the notions of teamwork, partnership and empowerment of others. An effective principal does not work in isolation.

Stronge, Richard and Catano ask the following questions about determining the effectiveness of a school through the evidence of its climate:

> How does the school feel? Are the school's Vision, Mission and priorities clearly demonstrated? Do administrators and staff efficiently ensure that effective teaching and learning are taking place? Are members of the school community treated with respect? Is there a sense of pride in the school? Do staff members and stakeholders work as a team, a professional learning community? What level of community involvement is evident? When all is said and done is there a sense that this school is a great place to learn and work?[5]

These are vital questions and their answers give a good indication of the health of a school. In my first few years, I doubt I could have given positive responses to all of them and I know that I struggled to even identify ways that I could bring growth and development to these areas.

In 2007, I perceived Nazareth College to be a very happy and easy-going school. Teachers seemed confident in their work, with timetables and programs seemingly running effectively. However, there was little that marked it as a school with anything that was particularly its own. Learning outcomes were acceptable though not outstanding, and all members coasted along doing what they had always done. In 2008, we undertook a scheduled four-year review, developed our Strategic Plan and continued on our merry way. While we lifted out our Annual Action Plan (AAP) every year from our Strategic Plan, there was no strong link to it in what we did on a daily basis. In fact, our Strategic Plan, with the accompanying page-long Vision Statement, was an impressive document that sat on a shelf in my office. Things were going quite well and so we plodded along.

Building a Faith Community

In 2012, we undertook our subsequent four-year review—this time realizing that we were missing a soul and a vibrant Vision. We felt that, at last, the school was ready to verbalize who we are through prayer, actions and outcomes. We referred to the Bible for references to Nazareth—the home of Jesus. We found our gift. In Luke's gospel, we are told that Jesus "returned to Nazareth and became strong, filled with wisdom, and the favor of God was upon Him."[6] This was to become our guiding scripture, a sentence that would provide us with our Vision, our reason for being, our preferred pathway. We wanted more to accompany our scripture that would tell of who we are as a faith school. Our words had to be clear, succinct and achievable. They had to resonate with staff, students, parents and prospective families. It took quite a while to develop the two simple sentences that reinforced who we are as the community of Nazareth College:

Nazareth College is a learning community—centered on the person of Jesus Christ.

Through learning and teaching in the Catholic tradition, we foster a culture of faith, wisdom and knowledge.

Faith, Wisdom and Knowledge is our motto. It is interesting to note that a neighboring Islamic school—Minaret College—has the motto of Faith, Wisdom and Action, and so we are not that far apart. In order to have "action" as well as "words," we wanted something that would become ritual—a prayer that identified who we are as the faith and learning community of Nazareth College. We wanted to start each day—classes, meetings and interviews—with an expression of our faith, one that was specifically linked to our school, and so our college prayer emerged: "L: Holy family of Nazareth; R: Be our inspiration and our guide; L: Jesus of Nazareth; R: Help us to grow in faith, wisdom and knowledge."

Deep down I was skeptical—I really did not believe that anyone would say this prayer in a meaningful way or on a regular basis. All teachers of Religious Education were instructed to teach this prayer to their classes in preparation for daily praying. Usually, prayer is said in each Pastoral class at the beginning and end of each day, and often at the beginning of other classes or the beginning of lunch as our Thanksgiving Prayer. However, often this depended on the individual teacher. Each Friday morning prayer is said over the public address (PA) system so that each Pastoral class hears and prays the same words.

On one particular Friday, not long after we had launched the prayer, I was standing outside the office where the students were reading their prayers over the microphone. I did not know that a group of students was standing on the other side of the office just around the corner from me. When the students reading over the PA system said the first part of the prayer I certainly did not expect to hear the response—but to my incredible surprise and delight, I heard a strong and definite "Be our inspiration and our guide" followed by "Help us to grow in Faith, Wisdom and Knowledge." This was more than I could ever have hoped for—I swallowed hard to hide my emotion; things were changing. There was no teacher standing there instructing the students to respond with this prayer, they spoke the prayer of their own accord.

Between 2011 and 2013, we grappled with many aspects of our culture. If our Vision was to inform practice, we had many areas with which to deal. If we were truly to be a place where students were to grow in faith, wisdom and knowledge, then our emphasis had to be placed firmly on the student, and this was not really happening. When I look at the writing of Mazarno, Waters and McNulty, I can now see clearly that Nazareth College was not a *purposeful community*. The authors describe such a community as "one with collective efficacy and capability to develop and use assets to accomplish goals that matter to all community members through agreed upon processes." They describe "collective efficacy" as "that shared belief that we can make a difference."[7]

We were starting to take steps to "make the difference" but up until then that difference was in no tangible way linked to the light of our Vision. It was this realization that enabled us to take significant action and our emphasis was on building the faith and learning community of Jesus of Nazareth. This had to be more than prayer and philosophy and nice words, it had to be reflected in our structures and processes. It had to be *deliberate*!

Building Leadership for Change

There were some very obvious issues that had to be addressed if we were genuine in building our community of faith and learning. One example of change that needed to happen was in the area of timetabling. We had those who spoke strongly about our "family friendly" policy. This resulted in part-time teachers being given first choice as to their teaching load each time a new timetable was developed. Consequently, full-time teachers were allocated what was left, resulting in a timetable that did not always benefit our students and their learning. A change of focus to ensure that student needs came first initially brought criticism from some part-time staff, but the continued and often spoken emphasis on "students first" saw such negativity diminish. At the same time, my Leadership Team—all good people—were in their fifteenth year of their leadership roles. The energy was limited and new ideas and approaches hard to put into practice. While each member worked to his or her own capacity and understanding of leadership, there was no coherent and consistent approach to student needs. Despite advertising each time their leadership contracts expired, no one would apply for the positions as they had ceased to be school positions and had become particular people's positions.

Our ability to change the way in which we were acting out our motto and Vision was limited. While I had some very good support for change, there were also those who feared any change and blocked discussion and movement. I was in a state of frustration. Our Strategic Plan had moved from the bookshelf to the filing cabinet and while we had ticked the box for tabling our Annual Action Plan with Catholic Education Melbourne, in reality the AAP and our guiding scripture and Vision were in two different worlds. I knew that change had to happen and that the only way to achieve this was to break down the Leadership Team. As current contracts for the leadership positions were due to expire and there were no other applicants for the roles, I appointed them to a two-year contract only—half the period that others were given at the time.

In 2013, I was privileged to undertake a sabbatical that enabled me to study at both Boston College and Harvard University. The time away, the incredible intellectual and academic stimulation, and the distance from school enabled me to return refreshed, strengthened and resolved to take that brave step to implement change.

At that time my most senior leaders were:

- Assistant Principal, Pastoral
- Assistant Principal, Learning
- Director of Faith.

After many, many hours of dreaming and planning, I developed a new structure that I would implement at the beginning of the fourth term that year rather than waiting for the beginning of the following school year. I kept the Leadership Team in seeming operation until the end of that year as promised in their contract, but their influence and impact were significantly reduced. I then set up a new Executive Team that would work with me to bring about the much needed change. I had bitten the bullet!

The new structure promoted the Assistant Principal, Pastoral to the position of Deputy Principal, Strategic Management. I needed his skills and wanted to create a space for others to move. I then promoted the Director of Faith to the position of Assistant Principal, Faith and Wellbeing. It was very important for me to make the statement that our response to well-being must be through our faith—that our scripture and church teachings had to be at the core of all that we did to address student needs. Once this role was operational, our pastoral response took a new approach to student needs, one that put students first and encouraged relationships, restorative action, resilience and pride in self—just as our scripture states. At the end of that year, our Leadership Team was disbanded and the Executive took overall senior leadership and management decisions. In 2013, with the appointment of a new Assistant Principal, Learning and the inclusion of our Business Manager, the *Executive Team* was the most senior decision-making body in the college. We had a new understanding of our role as guardians of our students and a deep understanding of *Students First* was forged. Our Vision was coming alive in ways far greater than words. While we had always had our AAP within the setting of Catholic Education Melbourne, we revisited that structure and worked with staff teams to ensure their ownership of areas pertinent to them.

Student First Approach: An Outcome of Renewal

In 2014, we took the enormous step of planning for a new way of learning—of putting this Students First belief into our practice. Our plans were substantial and we ignored the predictable warnings that we were taking on too much and would fail. Brent Davis states, "If it does not affect the people within the organization, it will not be implemented."[8] These changes had to affect all staff and, in doing so, would also impact on students and parents. For me, our guiding scripture continued to say it all. Our students must have that sense of growth and nurturing in this Nazareth community, just as Jesus did. Our students must have the opportunities to grow in faith, wisdom and knowledge as our motto promised.

Our initiatives would change the way of learning, re-energize our staff and meet parents' concerns about some aspects of mediocrity at our school. To be honest, we were in a somewhat uncomfortable position. With sixteen competing schools at our doorstep and several select entry schools who scooped up the intellectual cream of our students, our numbers were declining and we found ourselves overstaffed. These initiatives had to change our culture and let the wider community know that we were, at last, alive and alert if we were to continue as a school of choice for our primary school parents.

We worked with a project developed and promoted by Catholic Education Melbourne—Performance and Development in Catholic Schools. This enabled us to do all that we had planned but also provided us with a consultant who walked with us at each stage of implementation and then arranged for a professional film company to capture our responses at the end of that year. Again, we were aware of the enormous steps we were taking, perhaps too many in one year, but encouraged ourselves to have faith in what we were doing.

We then implemented a Personalized Learning Program in Years 7, 8 and 9 that comprised:

- single gender classes in core subjects;
- iPad program and eLearning;
- acceleration program for high-achieving students.

We had already spent two years developing a House System that would give students a sense of belonging to something smaller within the school and would host a Vertical Pastoral Program across Years 7–12, thus breaking down the year levels and developing a community of care, growth and achievement—again prompted by our Vision. The Vertical Pastoral Program linked learning and well-being.

While we had already introduced a scholarship program, we now extended it across the school and in a number of areas—the most significant one being the development of an Acceleration Program that enabled students in Years 7, 8 and 9 to study science, mathematics and English at a deeper level, allowing them to then take on VCE Units 1 and 2 in Year 10, Units 3 and 4 in Year 11 and first-year university subjects in Year 12. We took a huge risk. Staff knew their jobs were on the line and slowly came on board. Bit by bit we were building a new culture of *us working together*. While many staff members were apprehensive about what was being asked of them, there was also a new sense of excitement emerging as their confidence was boosted by relevant and intensive professional learning in these new areas and evidence of success was seen.

Staff members are now very aware of the need for education to meet the challenges of a rapidly changing world. We had "sat on our laurels" for far too long, had been content to continue doing what we had always done—and in this way we were doing our students a disservice. While remaining faithful to our traditional values, our call is to respond to a diverse range of student needs and abilities so as to provide them with the skills and knowledge necessary to continue their personal growth.

Linking Vision and Mission

In 2015, the initiatives were introduced and embedded into our culture. Our Vision was alive and active. Our AAP stated specific goals linked to successful outcomes of this program. Goals were set by teachers in their own learning and pastoral areas, ensuring that they owned the targets and appropriate actions. At the end of the year, different teams analyzed the developments in their own area within the AAP and were delighted with the progress they saw.

When our Executive Team sat down to develop our AAP for 2016, we marveled at the ease with which we completed the document. What became very clear to us was the new clarity of our Vision, our ability to articulate what it is that will not be compromised and our knowledge of how we do this. Our goals and strategies were confidently tabled within the context of our Vision. Our focus on the *Student First* mantra was clearly evident in the document, distributive leadership was acknowledged and our preferred pathway was well and truly cleared. Our constant use of terms that reflect our faith, our hopes and our very realistic dreams are our guiding lights across our five strategic areas of:

- education in faith
- learning and teaching
- student well-being
- leadership and management
- college community.

Over the first year, we surveyed students, staff and parents and the feedback was then, and continues to be, encouraging. All three groups of stakeholders spoke positively of the learning that was taking place in the single gender classes. Parents of students in the accelerated classes, and students themselves, acknowledged the impact on learning of both the stimulation and challenge that the program provided.

Renewal and Well-Being: The Vertical Pastoral Program

Mr. Justin Duckett, Assistant Principal, Faith and Wellbeing at our school, had this to say:

> One of the strengths of the Vertical structure is that, not only do we see the Pastoral teacher, who is having that real shepherding role of the students, but we also see the other students in that group, particularly the older students, as being the big brother or big sister to the younger students. In this way, each student has the feeling of being known by both their teacher and by the other students in the group. Within our Nazareth community, we really desire for all students to experience the love and, in fact, the very person of Jesus of Nazareth. It is through the work of the Heads of House and the Pastoral Teachers in their shepherding role that all are made further aware of the Good Shepherd himself—Jesus of Nazareth.

Vertical pastoral programs are not new—many schools have had such structures for some years—but it provided us with a new way of growing, relating and building our faith and learning community. With an accompanying well-being program, the vertical structure enabled a greater emphasis on student well-being and personal growth—all aspects of renewal for continuous improvement.

Responses to Change

Teachers now have a greater understanding of their roles in bringing about continuous improvement and of being substantial in living out our Vision and Mission. It is their work that provides a pathway for students to achievement through a focus on faith, wisdom and knowledge. They have commented on the "power of our story and the message of Jesus of Nazareth" as well as on their own realization of their role as mentors. Their ability to lead and guide is based both on their professionalism and skills as teachers and on the student/teacher relationship that is enriched through Pastoral and Religious Education programs, and the climate or charism of the school.

It has been interesting to note how some teachers have responded very positively to the challenges of developing their skills, particularly in the areas of learning differentiation, eLearning, acceleration and student well-being. At the moment, we have four teachers who have undertaken Master's studies in Student Well-being and in Leadership. We are also undertaking a significant project to ensure the strength of literacy knowledge across all areas of our secondary curriculum. The Secondary Literacy Improvement Program, developed and delivered through the initiative of the Catholic Education Office Melbourne, gives teachers the skills to look at all aspects of literacy across the curriculum, supporting all students in their ability to understand sentence structure and to make meaning out of what is being read. This enhances the teacher's ability to support students in this method—thus enhancing learning. When students understand what they are reading, the content is more readily comprehended.

We now have a team of teachers in different faculties spending significant amounts of time in meetings and planning sessions developing these skills. Teachers are actively seeking professional development and the impact on student learning is significant. Michelle, a Year 12 student, says:

> Nazareth's multicultural community provides a sense of belonging among students, staff and families and our Vertical and House Pastoral program gives us the opportunity to strengthen this sense of belonging. Every day, students enter the school for an education, they greet their friends, greet

their teachers, get involved in classes and extracurricular activities. They mix with their friends across all year levels whom they know through their Pastoral Group and House. They have a sense of knowing others and of being known. This everyday lifestyle that these students live is one of family, supporting each other on good and bad days and working together to improve, learn and grow to be the best people they can be. This community is filled with young people who are constantly giving to the wider community by helping people with disadvantaged family situations, working with St Vincent De Paul Society, SCOPE, visiting nursing homes and a food kitchen for the homeless as well as making donations to the Blood Bank. The Religious Education program and focus of the school provides a better understanding of how we came to be who we are today and where we should go in the future.

Following the success of 2015, we celebrated an increase in our 2016 student numbers and retention across the year levels. Our 2017 Year 7 enrollment numbers are the highest they have been in four years. Prospective parents tell me they have heard great things about Nazareth and that our students are our greatest advertisement. In May of 2016, the college undertook our four-year Whole School Review. This is based upon a substantial self-reflection across the five spheres of review and is developed by a number of staff within the school. A further audit is carried out by external reviewers looking at a range of areas of school life including policies and protocols, documentation, learning outcomes, adherence to regulations, resources and financial health. While there are naturally areas for further development, our reviewers commented favorably on many areas of the school:

> The Reviewers concur with leadership's view that Nazareth is a community of Faith, Wisdom and Knowledge. The college's faith is strong and policies and practices are successful in developing a Gospel value based community that actively promotes the Catholic faith through curriculum, prayer, symbolism and care for the marginalized. Purposeful teaching has improved because of the interventions which the school has put into place ... There is evidence of increased personalized learning to meet each student's point of need and ... there has been significant growth in the sphere of wellbeing. The development of the whole person is fundamental to the college's philosophy.

It is from this review that our four-year Strategic Plan is written, identifying the goals and strategies that are needed to take the school forward. Finally, a word about our students, the focus of our Vision. Students refer to themselves as Nazarenes; assemblies and prayer services are led by proud students with skill, dignity and respect and the greeting is always "Good morning fellow Nazarenes." At every student gathering, I reiterate that to be a Nazarene means to be "the best person that you can be by following the teachings of Jesus of Nazareth, as well as by caring for others." When students graduate or leave the school their promise to me is "Don't worry—I will never forget that I am a Nazarene." Our Deputy Principal, Mr. Garry Giese, shares his reflection on this process of growth and development—a process of enacting a Vision in a faith school:

> It is very easy to meander along doing the day-to-day things that need to be done and appear to be effective in doing so. Operating that way does not provide unity, it does not give certainty, it does not give clarity and it certainly does not build community. When we became certain of our Vision at Nazareth, and when there was an almost universal commitment to it, the way that we needed to operate became very clear to us. It became much more apparent what structures needed to be put into place and what programs needed to run in our curriculum, to know where our focus with staff needed to be and to have consistency in the way that we care for our students. And, the remarkable thing is, once we had truly and energetically articulated our Vision, it seemed so natural and so clear, so obvious that it really was just the natural expression of our commitment to students and to their education which was growing out of our Faith.

By December 2016, the college's Year 12 results had shown enormous improvement. Between 2013 and 2016 our VCE median study score jumped four points; 40+ results improved by 3.5%; and A grade results increased from 8.6% to 16%. These results could only have been achieved through the very concerted efforts to link our vision of a faith and learning community to a mission of addressing the learning and well-being needs of every student. We still have much work to do—we are very much on a journey towards excellence in education—but staff and students have a clear understanding of the expectations of their membership of this college. I believe I can confidently say that the bar has been raised, our Vision is alive, Nazareth College is a place where students grow in their faith, wisdom and knowledge and, like Jesus, experience the favor of God.

Conclusion

From my experience, I am confident that change comes slowly, but I am also sure that change can only be effective and lead to renewal and to continuous improvement when the identity of the school is first clarified and then celebrated. Islamic schools have such a depth of culture, tradition and faith in which to immerse their schools. Such aspects assure all members of who they are within the tradition and provide avenues for growth and enrichment. All schools are accountable to stakeholders and government expectations, so learning outcomes and attention to programs, processes, outcomes and results is vital. This is not renewal—this is a legal requirement. Renewal takes us past this and enables our schools to thrive. Thus, in summary:

1. Celebrate your community—be up front and overt about who you are as an Islamic learning community.
2. Celebrate all members, giving them a sense of belonging.
3. Be clear and brave about stating expectations of all members.
4. Work to develop a four-year strategic plan that fits snugly in with your school's vision.
5. Ensure that you identify goals and strategies for each year of the four-year plan. Identify those responsible for each area and review progress regularly.
6. Build a language within the school that reflects who you are.
7. Place emphasis on learning for all.
8. Seek the support and encouragement of others—you are not in this alone.
9. Celebrate achievements.
10. Contribute back to your system so as to provide renewal and continuous improvement for yourselves and others.

Notes

1. Barbara Brock and Marilyn Grady, *The Daily Practices of Successful Principals* (Thousand Oaks, CA: Corwin Press, 2011), 13.
2. Brian Cladwell, *Re-imagining Educational Leadership* (Thousand Oaks, CA: Sage, 2006), 118.
3. Peter Ellyard, *Ideas for the New Millennium* (Melbourne: Melbourne University Press, 1998), 43–44.

4. Catholic Education Commission Victoria, "Victorian Catholic Schools at a Glance", accessed January 2016, http://www.cecv.catholic.edu.au/getmedia/64081c91-cd5b-4f6d-b81d-2e2b3d720d95/At-a-Glance-2016.aspx?ext=.pdf.
5. James Stronge et al., *Qualities of Effective Principals* (Alexandria, VA: ASCD, 2008), 16.
6. Luke. 2:45, NRSVCE.
7. Robert Marzano et al., *School Leadership that Works: From Research to Results* (Alexandria, VA: ASCD, 2005), 99.
8. Brent Davies, *The Essentials of School Leadership* (London: Paul Chapman Educational Publishing, 2005), 29.

Bibliography

Brock, Barbara, and Marilyn Grady. *The Daily Practices of Successful Principals.* Thousand Oaks, CA: Corwin Press, 2011.
Caldwell, Brian. *Re-Imagining Educational Leadership.* Thousand Oaks, CA: SAGE Publications, 2006.
Catholic Education Commission Victoria. "Victorian Catholic Schools at a Glance". Accessed January 2016. http://www.cecv.catholic.edu.au/getmedia/64081c91-cd5b-4f6d-b81d-2e2b3d720d95/At-a-Glance-2016.aspx?ext=.pdf.
Davies, Brent. *The Essentials of School Leadership.* London: Paul Chapman Educational Publishing, 2005.
Ellyard, Peter. *Ideas for the New Millenium.* Melbourne: Melbourne University Press, 1998.
Luke's Gospel 2:45. New Revised Standard Version Catholic Edition.
Marzano, Robert J., Timothy Waters, and Brian A. McNulty. *School Leadership that Works: From Research to Results.* Alexandria, VA: ASCD, 2005.
Stronge, James H., Holly B. Richard, and Nancy Catano. *Qualities of Effective Principals.* Alexandria, VA: ASCD, 2008.

CHAPTER 9

Islamic Pedagogy: Potential and Perspective

Nadeem A. Memon and Mariam Alhashmi

INTRODUCTION

The discourse around the term Islamic education needs to be broadened in order for the objective of Islamic schools today to be fully appreciated. Islamic education is commonly associated with teaching about religion. But to limit the term Islamic education to curriculum content, or rather the 'what' to teach, disregards how other essential educational aspects have been conceptualised in the writings and institutions in Muslim societies and communities past and present. The term Islamic pedagogy is a better-suited term because it lends itself more easily to the broader discussion required. In its simplest form pedagogy is a way of teaching, a methodology of instruction. But any methodology of instruction is rooted in a set of educational beliefs, values and perspectives that differentiate it from other methodologies of teaching.[1] Pedagogy in its full sense is based on big questions in education such as why teach (toward what end), whom

N. A. Memon (✉)
CITE-School of Education – University of South Australia,
Magill-Adelaide, SA, Australia
e-mail: Nadeem.memon@unisa.edu.au

M. Alhashmi
College of Education – Zayed University, Dubai, Dubai, United Arab Emirates
e-mail: Mariam.Alhashmi@zu.ac.ae

to teach, what to teach them, when, and where. To assume a teacher can impart religious studies in the absence of considering these questions more broadly is to do a disservice to the depth and perspective of education in the Islamic tradition.

In addition to replacing the term Islamic education with Islamic pedagogy, we also suggest another important conceptual nuance. We will use the term 'education in the Islamic tradition' in this chapter to refer to the specific references to education-related concepts, themes, ideas, and perspectives that have been written about, lived, and discussed within the expansive Islamic tradition. The Islamic tradition refers to the canonical texts to which all Muslims adhere, the Qur'an and the Prophetic tradition (Hadith), but also the expansive literature, both classical and contemporary, of interpretation and analysis of these canonical texts.[2]

The challenge for Islamic schools (of all varieties) today is articulating just what they mean by Islamic education or by the term 'Islamic schooling'.[3] By virtue of being observant, well-versed believers, while also being educators, most Islamic school leaders and teachers have an inherently ingrained sense that Islamic education is more than memorising verses of the Qur'an or facts about Islamic history. Most know that it is about nurturing *adab*, fostering a Prophetic ethic, and living Islam in its fullest sense. But Muslim educators know this in piecemeal, anecdotally, often reliant on a few educators in their school or community who are better versed in Islam. In the absence of an articulated pedagogy, some of the big questions mentioned earlier are articulated in school vision statements but not consistently reflected in practice, while other questions are addressed through conventional schooling best practices without an Islamic educational perspective.

In this chapter, you will find our attempt to succinctly capture the essence of an Islamic perspective on eight key areas discussed in the field of education: vision, stages of development, instruction, curriculum, assessment and evaluation, learning environment, the role of the teacher, and the role of the student. The intent is that each of these sections will provide clarity and a high level of appreciation to Islamic school educators about what makes their work distinct. It is also hoped that these sections will inspire further discussions, debates, and research into Islamic pedagogy toward a renewed sense of pedagogical practice.

Vision: The End Goals of Education in the Islamic Tradition

Every educational system is based on a distinctive philosophy that identifies its vision and its end goals. At the core of a vision of Islamic education is '*adab*', the differentiating feature of Islamic education.[4] *Adab*, as a process referred to as *ta'dib*, defines the profile of a student including their traits and attitudes that are to be fostered and inculcated. *Ta'dib* is also the key concept that lays out the principles of Islamic education. From a broad perspective, *adab* refers to the acquisition of an Islamic worldview as an underlying philosophy that guides all thoughts, sayings, and actions of a human being. According to this view, *adab* is defined as the 'recognition and acknowledgement of the right and proper place, station, and condition in life, and to self-discipline in positive and willing anticipation in enacting one's role in accordance with that recognition and acknowledgement'.[5]

In these senses, *ta'dib* is inclusive of, but not limited to, the training and the disciplining of the self. As a continuous end goal, *ta'dib* is a duty of every teacher.[6] It begins at a very young age, as soon as a child can distinguish between right and wrong, and there is no age or level at which *ta'dib* ends.[7] Teachers and parents are also directed in the Qur'an to practise *ta'dib* on their own selves by understanding what the self is, then training it. Stemming from the vision of *ta'dib*, the end goals of education in the Islamic tradition can be manifested in spiritual, moral, and intellectual aspects:

Goal 1: Spiritual Development

While most modern education systems separate knowledge from spiritual values,[8] reduce reality to the physical domain, and do not recognise the existence of non-scientific worldviews,[9] the purpose of education in Islam is characterised by a strong emphasis on spiritual development.[10] Due to the dualism of man, composed of soul and body in a harmonious integrative manner, both the material and the spiritual dimensions need to be addressed through a holistic growth approach.[11]

Goal 2: Moral Development

The cultivation of morality and good character is a prime purpose of Islamic education. Muslim scholars such as al-Ghazali and al-Zarnuji link moral values to all aspects of the educational process. Morality is considered in Islam to be a spiritual matter that is internalised and that results in righteous actions.[12]

Goal 3: Intellectual Development

Islamic education aims at achieving comprehensive growth towards acquiring knowledge and the ability to reason and analyse.[13] Unlike instruction that is focused on training the learner in skill acquisition and the efficient performance of a particular task, Islamic education aims at raising virtuous people in the holistic sense, which is inclusive of professional careers.

Every school should be clear on its guiding principles as well as the profile of the students it aspires to nurture. Such principles determine the school's overall approach that encompasses all the aspects of its educational process. The vision of education defines with clarity both the short-term and long-term goals of a school which, in turn, inform the practices that follow. The vision and the goals will act as a guiding compass which the school community uses to search for ideas or solutions in times of opportunities and challenges in regards to any aspect of the educational process.

Development: Learning and Spiritual Developmental Stages

Education theorists such as Vygotsky (1896–1934) and Piaget (1896–1980) emphasised the role of developmental appropriateness in relation to instruction and curriculum.[14] Muslim educators often wonder about Islamic guidance in regards to developmental stages. Practice and experience show that failing to consider and respond to the natural readiness and maturity of the learner can result in hindrances to achieving the ultimate *ta'dib* vision that reflects the purpose of Islamic education as defined in this chapter.[15]

In this section, we describe the developmental stages framework that was modelled by the Prophet Muhammad (peace be upon him), affirmed in the Qur'an, and alluded to by the Sunni scholars across the generations regarding the unique nature of each developmental stage. The nature of these stages, which have been considered a foundation of the tradition of Islamic education, is described in the Qur'anic verse: 'Know ye (all), that the life of this world is but play and amusement, pomp and mutual boasting and multiplying, (in rivalry) among yourselves, riches and children.'[16]

First Stage: Birth to Tamyeez *(Discernment)*
This stage includes the first two years of cradle and breastfeeding and ends at *tamyeez*. The age of *tamyeez* is determined based upon the child's consciousness, which reflects cognitive and comprehension abilities. Indicators

of *tamyeez*, which most children obtain around the age of 7, include differentiating between directions and comprehending speech and responding to it appropriately. It is the age when a child is able to discern things that are harmful and employs *haya'* (modesty) in holding back or being reticent.

During the first seven years guardians need to fulfil a child's need to play through games and toys that are closer to the *fitrah* (natural inclination) and to Islamic values, such as play with sand and in nature. Guardians also need to observe the particular interests of their children and allow them to pursue the kind of play they enjoy. Toys that represent something impossible in reality are not in line with our *fitrah* and could affect a child's affirmative understanding of the concepts of the obvious, possible, and impossible in life. Play that includes movement suitable to the child's age and that which is related to the child's physical health is particularly encouraged. Al-Ghazali notes that education of children from the early stages is a great affair.[17] Once a child shows readiness for speech, guardians can introduce words of *dhikr* (remembrance) such as Allah and Ya Allah. Memorisation can be introduced at this age through short Qur'anic chapters, Prophetic sayings, and poems in accordance with a child's individual readiness, motivation, and age appropriateness. The level of readiness for learning varies greatly within this first seven-year span.

Second Stage: Age of Tamyeez *(Discernment)*
The second stage starts once the child obtains *tamyeez* and ends once he reaches *bulough* (puberty), which takes place around the age of 14. Al-Ghazali says that at this age of *tamyeez* the first sign of the 'light of the intellect' is gifted to a child from God.[18] The first of these aspects is shame where a child, for instance, expresses the desire to cover their nakedness.[19] Shame and shyness are signs of goodness or beginnings of discerning between the deception of this world and *yaqin* (certainty) of the next.[20]

The child is now ready to embark upon the different stages of worshipping and obligations, hence the Hadith 'command your children to pray at seven'.[21] This should be accompanied with fostering love for Allah by introducing worship in connection with its inner meaning.[22] Although these might not be fully comprehended by children, they will nevertheless feel there is a purpose beyond the physical act.

During this stage children become interested in amusement, described in the Qur'an as '*lahou*'. Play at this stage remains important, but it is the responsibility of guardians to support children in making choices that are morally upright. Mixing with people of bad character and behaviour is harmful to children, particularly in this stage and the next. Successful consideration of the above results in children becoming intrinsically inclined to goodness and disapproving of immoral acts.[23]

Third Stage: Age of Taklif *(Accountability)*
Following *bulough* children enter the stage of *takleef*. During this third critical stage, which continues for around seven years, a young adult's perceptions of life and the hereafter are matured. Youth become particularly interested in their outlook and it is the role of parents to guide them towards that which is encouraged by Shari'ah (Islamic legal system). The aspects of outlook are referred to as *libas* (dress) and *zeenah* (outlook), which are included as chapters in all grand Hadith and *fiqh* (jurisprudence) texts.[24]

The young adult is prepared during this stage for understanding the purpose of life and of the Islamic way of living, the dangers of the world and why these are harmful, and the fact that life is short.[25] The role of the educator becomes that of helping the young person to focus on the ultimate purpose and to avoid distractions. A child who was raised as a person of *adab* during the first and second stages will mostly be accepting of guidance during the third stage.

Instruction: Teaching Methods Embodied by the Prophet Muhammad (Peace Be Upon Him)

Most schools around the world suffered from the negative influences of the eighteenth- and the nineteenth-century schooling 'factory model', and the majority of Islamic schools and institutions were no exception. In many Muslim-majority countries during the same period, these schools went through a change process in which they were reshaped to better fit the dominant modern model of the time.[26] This unfortunate change process was catalysed by the positivist paradigm which valued tangible 'quantitative' outcomes, resulting in an overwhelming focus on the cognitive domain of Islamic education.[27] The number of Qur'anic verses memorised and the number of books studied outweighed personality development, moral education, and spiritual growth. This quantification led to the decline of the *ta'dib* aspect embodied in the teaching practices of the Prophet Mohammed (peace be upon him).

In this section, light will be shed on the teaching methods embodied by the Prophet Muhammad (peace be upon him) in three key dimensions: *adab*, comprehension and action, and the place of memorisation.

Adab *Comes First*

The teachings of the Prophet Muhammad (peace be upon him) predominantly emphasised ethics and character building.[28] The essence of instruction in Islamic education is rooted in the importance of imparting, modelling, and learning *adab*. In the authentic practice of Islamic education, ethical conduct was embedded in the expectations and the practices of each element in the educational process.

Linguistically, the verb tense of *adab*, *adaba*, means to culture beautiful manners and includes the conduct of good manners in every aspect of life. Miskawayh insists that training of good character among children begins with good manners in eating.[29] Children should be taught from an early age that food is a means to keep our bodies healthy, to protect us from illness, and to sustain our lives—not a mere pleasure. Food should be considered a medicine with which we cure hunger and guard against disease. Children should be encouraged to eat the amount of food they need, not the amount they want, to not be gluttonous, to share food with others, and not to covet it. Children should also learn the etiquette of table manners when around guests: not to be the first to take food, not to stare at the courses of food, to share, to take moderately sized mouthfuls, to not eat in a hurry, to chew fully before taking another mouthful, to offer guests the food closest to them if it is food they themselves enjoy, and so on. Miskawayh also suggests that children should be taught to be content with simple foods every so often, such as dry bread with nothing else, to learn an appreciation for food.[30]

Character building had mistakenly led to physical punishment in certain centres of Islamic education in contemporary times. Abdallah et al. consider the punishment of students a chronic problem in the entire Islamic world.[31] Muslim scholars who have criticised the use of physical punishment in education settings include Ibn Khaldun, who argues that if the teacher exhibits a severe attitude, young children will suffer harmful consequences. Ibn Sahnun and al-Qabisi also describe the limits of punishment in great detail.[32]

Comprehension and Action

Nurturing *adab* should not be misconstrued as mandating or imposing a particular code of conduct or form of normative behaviour. In the practice of religious character, *taqlid* (imitation) is encouraged. But in *tawhid* (belief), *taqlid* is not appropriate.[33] It is for this reason that pedagogical practices in traditional *madrassas*[34] have often relied on debate, structured argumentation, and the encouragement of critical thinking. Burckhardt notes that in the Qarawiyin in Fez learning in the Middle Ages often took the form of 'legal discussions' where master and pupil debated legal positions through a combination of rationalistic and revelation-based arguments.[35] It was common in medieval Muslim societies to focus instruction on a single subject and work toward mastery to establish foundations before proceeding to subsequent learning.[36]

Several Muslim scholars have cautioned against knowledge that does not result in action. Al-Zarnuji warned that 'Man should try to provide what is useful while avoiding what is harmful to the [soul], lest his intelligence and his knowledge become weapons [arguments] against him and his punishment be increased'.[37] In his book 'O Son!', al-Ghazali dedicates a number of pages following the introduction of the book to detailing the importance of putting knowledge into action, describing the problems that result from acquiring knowledge without experiencing it, and quoting verses of the Qur'an and Hadith that describe punishment of those who acquire knowledge but do not apply it.[38] Action and increased consciousness have been underscored as essential fruits of acquiring knowledge. In one of Islam's earliest pedagogical treatises, *Kitab al-alim wa-l-muta'allim* (The Book of the One Who Knows and the One Who Wants to Know), a dialogue between master and student reinforces the critical interplay between knowledge and action when the master instructs the pupil: 'What a great decision of yours to search for what is of benefit to you. Know that actions follow knowledge like the body parts comply with eyesight. Therefore, learning knowledge with little action is better than ignorance with much action'.[39]

The Importance of Memorisation

The practices of memorisation have put Islamic education under continuous criticism by some who view memorisation as indoctrination.[40] However, accompanied with comprehension, memorisation is a tool towards embodiment due to its spiritual nature, which leads to an internalisation of knowledge through the oral transmission process.[41]

Additionally, memorisation has the potential to provide the learner with guidance and a moral compass, literally in the sense of meaning unfolding and in a metaphorical sense through its sacredness. The embodiment of the Qur'an deepens spirituality and awareness of the presence of God and leads to understanding and developing reason and discipline. It is important to adhere to balance in the employment of memorisation. Muslim scholars such as al-Ghazali, al-Jahiz, and Ibn Khaldun have criticised the consequences of a learning approach that overemphasises the role of memory. Therefore, Muslim educators should ensure a balance between employing memorisation and introducing it in consideration of the student's developmental readiness, interest, ability, and skills accompanied by *adab*, comprehension, and action.

Curriculum

Since the Islamisation movement of the 1970s, Muslim educators have voiced concerns about the secularisation of contemporary school curricula.[42] Muslim and other faith-based educators argue that public secular school curricula primarily focus on job-market preparation over moral development.[43] The basis for Islamising the curriculum is to promote a unified conception of knowledge with no demarcation between secular and religious studies, but rather bound by the belief that all knowledge comes from God.[44]

To rectify the secularisation of the school curriculum, there have been three key approaches attempted since the 1970s in Islamic schools.

1. *Append*: The initial curricular approach used in early Islamic schools was to adopt the state mandated curriculum wholesale while appending Islamic Studies as a single subject onto the school curriculum. In this way, accrediting bodies had less to be concerned about with respect to a school's ability to align with state standards, while parents achieved their objective of having their children introduced to religious fundamentals.
2. *Integrate*: Soon thereafter some schools grew dissatisfied with the appended approach and called for an integration of Islamic values and perspectives across the curriculum. This approach to date continues to be a work in progress, with individual schools attempting their own definition of the extent to which this integration can be achieved. Some schools have integrated Islamic character values as

themes into all subjects, others have integrated concepts and Islamic perspectives in key areas of contention (e.g., evolution), and yet others have gone so far as to remove Islamic Studies as a formal subject and to teach religion in each subject (e.g., canon of English texts are replaced with religiously oriented ones).

3. *Transform*: As schools have fumbled through attempts to integrate effectively, some educators have called for a transformative approach that is not integrated into an existing curriculum framework but rather begins afresh from an Islamic worldview. Contemporary schools derive their conceptions of knowledge, human nature, and existence from the Enlightenment period, excluding the relevance of religious worldviews and reducing religion to cultural practice.[45] The transformative view, therefore, calls for an overhaul of the curriculum with the epistemology of Islam as the foundation for studying all other subjects.

These three approaches represent three distinct attempts by contemporary Islamic schools to reconcile the adoption and adaptation of secular schooling curriculum conventions. However, to better appreciate the basis upon which the above approaches are founded, a brief explanation of how knowledge has been conceptualised in the Islamic tradition will be helpful. Muslim scholars historically have made three critical distinctions when debating what is necessary versus what is important to learn:

1. *Core knowledge vs branch knowledge*: 'Knowledge' within the Islamic tradition can be perceived according to two conceptual dimensions: *fardh 'ain* knowledge (core knowledge)[46] and *fardh kifayah* knowledge (branch knowledge).[47] *Fardh 'ain* knowledge is that which every single Muslim should acquire; it is obligatory knowledge that corresponds to the status and needs of the learner. Al-Zarnuji (2010) explains that if the person has to perform her/his prayers, then he/she will need to know as much of the prayer rituals as will help her/him fulfil this duty. Similarly, if he/she will be involved in commercial trade, then he/she should acquire the knowledge one needs for commerce. *Fardh kifayah* knowledge is that which does not become a requirement if a sufficient number of Muslims acquire it to an aptitude that suffices the needs of the community. *Fardh kifayah* knowledge becomes *fardh 'ain*, obligatory, on all capable individuals of a community if a certain speciality is not fulfilled by a sufficient

number of individuals in that community. Al-Zarnuji (2010) uses a metaphor to describe *fardh 'ain* as food that every individual needs and *fardh kifayah* as medicine that is needed at stipulated times.

2. *Religious sciences vs non-religious sciences*: There are a few classification schemes that an educator in Islamic schooling should be aware of. Al-Ghazali classifies knowledge as religious sciences (that which is based on revelation or by means of a prophet) and non-religious sciences. Al-Farabi classifies knowledge as either theoretical (e.g., language, logic, and mathematics) or practical (e.g., natural and political sciences). It is commonly understood by scholars that theoretical and practical sciences can be studied 'based on Islamic principles and will then be considered *shar'i* (religious). If they are approached on purely rational principles and means, excluding religious teachings as serving the fountains of their inquiry, then those same sciences are considered *ghayr al-shar'i* [non-religious sciences] ... It is the approach and framework adopted by the inquirer that determines whether the science is religious or rational.'[48]

3. *Beneficial knowledge vs non-beneficial knowledge*: What constitutes knowledge, what believers should learn, and the pursuit of knowledge itself have been of concern for Muslim communities since the time of the Prophet Muhammad (peace be upon him). Among the common themes in Islamic education is to learn that which is useful and refrain from that which has no benefit. For learning to be Islamic it must be beneficial. Benefit is defined as that which leads one closer to God. All knowledge, therefore, has the potential to be beneficial and at the same time unbeneficial. Al-Ghazali says that 'knowledge is never intrinsically blameworthy ... it is only in the harm that results from the science that is blameworthy'.[49] This is why the Prophet Muhammed (peace be upon him) made the supplication, 'O God, I seek your protection from knowledge that does not bring benefit'.[50]

The implications of these knowledge classifications is that within these broad categorisations there remains ample room for defining unique approaches in determining what to teach, how, and when. In the *Muqaddimah*, for example, Ibn Khaldun traces the ways that various Muslim societies in his time (the twelfth century) derived unique approaches to curriculum based on their social context.[51] He notes, for example, that what children were taught in the Maghrib versus Spain in the same time period was very distinct. In the Maghrib, learning for children focused on mastering the Qur'an and only the Qur'an, whereas in Spain children learned a broad range of foundational subjects that included handwriting, poetry, and composition.[52] This is one of many examples that he gives, but suffice to say that Muslim societies have employed unique curricular approaches to achieve similar ends.

Assessment and Evaluation

Contemporary conceptions of assessment focus on measuring academic learning and hence rely more heavily on tracking student progress in relation to prescribed curriculum outcomes. The terms assessment and evaluation are often used interchangeably but if they are to be distinguished, the former refers to an opportunity for students to receive feedback to improve learning, and the latter is a summative score that measures achievement in relation to set criteria. Assessing student behaviour or, more recently, what is commonly referred to as character education is also an aspect of overall student achievement.

Classical and contemporary writings on education in the Islamic tradition are less explicit about assessment and evaluation as a pedagogical category. That said, the development and refinement of character is a central theme and therefore assessing one's moral uprightness is discussed. Given that the essence of Islamic education is aimed at an embodiment of *adab*, lessons can be drawn from spiritually based forms of assessment that can then be applied to the way teaching and learning takes place in educational settings grounded in the Islamic worldview.

The most common theme in the Islamic tradition related to assessment focuses on *muhasaba* (self-assessment or taking account of oneself) toward spiritual perfection and moral uprightness. There is a Hadith of the Prophet that says 'He who knows himself knows his Lord'.[53] Another Hadith states: 'Take account of yourself before you are taken account of. Evaluate yourselves before you are evaluated.'[54] The beginning of knowing oneself is removing actions and thoughts that are displeasing to God—again, the recurring theme of character development or *ta'dib*.

Traditional conceptions of assessment in the Islamic tradition emphasised assessment for the purpose of self-development toward moral uprightness, social etiquette, and spiritual awareness and hence emphasised self-assessment because, apart from God, only we are aware of our own actions and thoughts. The end goal of *muhasaba* is to be in a constant state of self-reflection on one's thoughts and actions and how they pertain to the reality of death and *akhira* (hereafter). The larger goal of perfection of character is to always measure one's actions in preparation for readiness to face one's Lord after death. Vigilance in self-reflection is referred to as *muraqaba*, a concept derived from the Divine name *al-Raqib* (the all-seeing). *Muraqaba* is a state in which the heart and mind are tranquil, free of distractions, and where the heart is connected to spiritual perfection. It is the highest level of spiritual mastery.[55] Self-purification entails acts of spiritual perfection, such as guarding the limbs and organs against immoral acts, habitual practices of remembrance, almsgiving, and service. How one assesses is through keeping good company and measuring oneself against the uprightness and good character of those who exceed one in good acts and through imitating acts of goodness.[56]

The most critical implication for Islamic schools is the need to deeply embed the centrality of a '*muhasaba* mindset' in the ethos of the school. It is important for schools to foster an environment where all stakeholders (administrators, teachers, students, and parents) are constantly holding themselves to account for their interactions, thoughts, actions, and aspirations. Educators must model this for students in their own work, for example by reflecting on the quality of their teaching, correcting their actions, and being open about areas of their own improvement. Similarly, when teachers want to correct student behaviour they should encourage students to self-reflect on their own actions and reconcile mistakes or shortcomings in the best way they themselves see fit. *Muhasaba* is about attaining excellence in all that we do—spiritually and morally but also academically and socially. Students should be encouraged to become self-reflective even in assessing their own academic work, pushing themselves toward perfection, and questioning themselves about their own effort before submitting completed tasks, for instance. In the spirit of *muhasaba* it is also essential to not expose student errors or weaknesses publicly.[57] If a teacher senses that a student does not comprehend a concept, for instance, he/she should repeat explanations in a way that will maintain the student's motivation and not humiliate her/him. Using questions to draw out solutions will help students think for themselves and foster an ethic of thinking independently.

Environment: Learning Spaces' Ambience and Structure

Contemporary conceptions of what constitutes an effective learning space have evolved significantly over recent decades. Prior to the free school and deschooling movement in the 1970s, the push for experience-based education in the 1980s, play-based learning in the 1990s, and now twenty-first-century, exploratory-based learning, classrooms were very formal spaces. Classrooms used to be stringently organised spaces with seats and tables in rows facing the front of the classroom, instruction was teacher-centred and didactic, and students were expected to act with formal decorum at all times until they reached the playground for a break. Over the past fifty years, classrooms have evolved (and are still in the process of evolving) into collaborative learning spaces, with an array of seating arrangements to facilitate varieties of group work, where varying levels of noise are acceptable, and students are encouraged to innovate, create, and think constructively both individually and in groups about self-directed questions of inquiry.

Conceptions of learning spaces in the Islamic tradition would see value in both the teacher-centred and student-centred classroom organisation employed in conventional schooling globally. However, a religious nuance is emphasised in learning spaces that are Islamically oriented. Irrespective of how a classroom is structured or how teachers facilitate learning, a learning environment with an Islamic ethos should embrace learning as a sacred act and as a result require a high level of *adab* both in interactions and toward the tools of learning.

Al-Zarnuji says: 'Know that in the pursuit of knowledge, one does not acquire learning nor profit from it unless one holds knowledge in esteem and those who possess it. So one [must] esteem and venerate the teacher.'[58] Similarly, al-Zarnuji also emphasises having respect for the tools of learning. He gives the example of showing respect for the Qur'an by not stretching one's feet out toward it, or putting other things on top of it, or placing it on the ground.[59]

Classrooms or places of learning require a particular type of *adab*. The *adab* of a learning environment is not always explicitly mentioned in the writings of Muslim pedagogues but what is mentioned is the etiquette required in gatherings with elders and those with knowledge, for example. Social etiquette such as standing when guests, elders, or those with knowledge arrive, listening to those who speak and not interrupting the speech of others rudely in gatherings, and not boasting about one's achievements or possessions in public are all examples of the required etiquette of social gatherings. In classrooms, students should enter with salutations and greetings, with additional greetings to elders, listen attentively, not disturb others, sit upright, focus, not interject unless useful and relevant, be courteous and polite in speaking to peers and elders, pray for the teacher at the culmination of a lesson, begin the lesson in the name of God, avoid putting books on the ground or destroying or damaging books, respect all of the tools of learning, enter the class in a state of ritual purity, and put tools of learning in their place when completed.[60]

Ibn Jama'ah also notes that it is the teacher's responsibility to 'rebuke' bad behaviour in classrooms, such as when students act aggressively in discussions, have bad manners, or are 'quarrelsome' or unfair. Similarly, students who insult other students, think more highly of themselves than others, or laugh at or ridicule others must be addressed. But interestingly, Ibn Jama'ah concludes this advice by saying that rebuking students' bad behaviour 'should be done only if no greater evil ensues'.[61] In other words, the assumption here is that rebuking a student for bad behaviour should not come at the expense of a teacher's loss of *adab* or the loss of a student's intrinsic interest in learning. Respect for the learning environment must be maintained but this must be done with an awareness of its implications.

Among the means of creating a nurturing and positive learning environment is to encourage openness in discussion and questioning. Teachers should encourage questioning, even from those who are younger or less versed in the subject. Ibn Jama'ah writes: 'He [the teacher] should always be equitable in discussing and speaking. He should listen carefully to the student's question, even if the student is young. He should not disdain listening to him, thereby depriving the student of benefit.'[62] He goes on to say that if the questioner is unable to effectively formulate his or her question, either out of shyness or lack of clarity on the topic, the teacher should assist the student by trying their best to understand what the intent of the question might be, possibly reformulate the question in their own words, or even respond with answers to common questions that are generally asked related to the theme being raised.[63] The point being made here is that teachers should encourage students to feel comfortable to ask questions and to know they will not be demeaned or belittled for asking questions deemed unformulated.

The implications for contemporary Islamic schools is to foster learning environments that are undoubtedly fun and productive but within an ambience of *adab* where the opportunity to learn is coveted, student's appreciate each other, teachers, and the environment, while teachers equally espouse a deep sense of humility in the same way.

Teacher: Role and Responsibility of Educators

The role of an Islamic schoolteacher is similar to what is commonly termed in religious education as pastoral care. Teachers in religious education settings are considered role models of moral uprightness whose character in public and private is intended to positively influence students to be equally religiously observant in words and actions. The pastoral role requires teachers to see themselves as second parents who are concerned about a student's well-being, moral behaviour, personal choices, life decisions, and social etiquette, all guided by an Islamic ethic. A teacher's ability to foster moral uprightness in an Islamic educational setting is paramount.

A teacher's first responsibility in an Islamic education setting begins with establishing the right *niyyah* (intention). A teacher's intention should be to teach for the sake of God and 'for the spread of learning', for the welfare of the community, to receive blessings and merits from those whom they teach, to spread truth and remove falsehood, and to be connected in the 'chain of learning between the Prophet and his students ... for the teaching of knowledge is one of the most important matters of religion and one of the highest ranks of believers ...'.[64] Ibn Jama'ah notes that a teacher should not refuse to teach a student because of a student's bad intentions; the teacher should see their role as one who will nurture good intentions in the student over time. In this sense, teachers need to find ways to inspire and better understand the needs of unruly or unmotivated students. 'He [the teacher] should love for the student what he loves for himself, as stated in a Prophetic tradition, and loathe for the student what he loathes for himself.'[65]

Teachers should inspire students and encourage the pursuit of knowledge by reminding students of the benefits of learning and the nobility and high rank to which God has elevated scholars. Teaching is considered a position of high responsibility and a significant trust (*amanah*) given to an individual. Ibn Jama'ah, as well as other classical scholars, notes that the fundamental responsibility of a teacher is to be upright, God-conscious, and fearful of God outwardly and inwardly. Part of this responsibility is to also elevate and preserve the sanctity of religious knowledge.[66]

The second responsibility of a teacher is to strive to model noble character. *Husnul khuluq'*, translated as noble character or good manners, is what the Prophet Muhammad (peace be upon him) exemplified and what believers strive to embody. The role of the teacher is to model and strive to perfect, as much as possible, noble character because of the impact and influence educators have on their students. Al-Ramli says in his poem: 'Make him [a student] adhere to humility; And to not covet all that appears to him; For covetousness is one of the greatest afflictions'.[67] Struggling against internal desires, against one's *nafs* (inner self), is essential to striving toward the perfection of one's character. The role of the educator is to help students be morally upright, avoid lower desires, and continue to reflect on their actions.

The humility of a teacher is a common theme discussed as advice given to educators by classical Muslim pedagogues. If teachers are unable to answer a question, for example, they should feel confident in saying 'I don't know. ... Know that saying "I do not know" does not lower the esteem in which the person asked is held, as some ignorant people suppose; it raises his esteem because it is a great sign of his great rank, the strength of his religion, his fear of God, the purity of his heart, and the perfection of his knowledge'.[68] Nor should a teacher feel too proud to learn from someone who is less experienced or younger in age.

Combined with humility, a third theme that arises related to a teacher's responsibility is to show gentleness (*rifq*) in teaching and raising children. In al-Ramli's poem on raising children, he quotes the Hadith 'Whenever there is gentleness in something it shines and whenever there is harshness in something it dulls it'.[69] He also refers to the Hadith 'Whoever shows *rifq*, gentleness, to his nation, Allah will show *rifq* to him'.[70] In his advice to teachers, Ibn Jama'ah says they should be

> marked by generous traits of character: a cheerful countenance, effusive greetings, offering food, controlling his anger, averting harm from people, and bearing it from them. He should be beyond provocation; he should avoid selfishness; he should be equitable and not demand his due; he should be thankful for favors; he should create ease; he should strive to fulfill requests; he should show love to neighbours and relatives; and he should be gentle to students, helping and nurturing them.[71]

A fourth theme that comprises the role of teachers is to discipline students in a way that maintains their dignity. Miskawayh says that children should be praised and honoured for good traits and not exposed for shortcomings or ill-mannered behaviour, especially if they themselves have tried to conceal actions they know are inappropriate. The first time a parent or educator notices such behaviour they should 'feign not to have noticed it', as though the elder could not even fathom the child committing such an act. If a child repeats the behaviour, then the child should be 'reproached for it secretly, shown the seriousness of his action and warned against doing it again'.[72] If, however, a child's misbehaviour continues, becomes habitual, or the actions are deemed major moral transgressions, a parent/educator should give warnings and remind the student of their moral ramifications.[73] That said, the overriding theme remains that of gradually and patiently fostering good character with the same affection and compassion that a parent would show to their own children.[74]

The implications of these four themes concerning a teacher's role from an Islamic perspective is to consider ongoing professional development for teachers in Islamic schools about their pastoral role—what it means and what it should look like. These themes make explicit what most Islamic schools know but should continue to reflect on as a path to renewal.

Student: Role and Responsibility of Students

There is a significant overlap between the roles of teachers and students in an Islamic educational setting. The emphasis is on character and religious uprightness first as a foundation to learning prior to academic learning.

Similar to teachers teaching, student learning begins with the right intention. It is the responsibility of students to strive for knowledge with clear intentions (*niyyah*) for 'the pleasure of God, the abode of the Hereafter, the removal of ignorance from himself and from the rest of the ignorant, the revival of religion, and the survival of Islam'.[75] Among young students, teachers should be active in directing the right intention, while among older students, they should become accustomed to realigning their intentions regularly.

Humility is the second theme of a student's responsibility in learning similar to teachers. Students should be encouraged to believe deeply that knowledge comes from God alone. Feeling a sense of pride or boastfulness about one's accomplishments, intelligence, and opinions is a form of misguidance. Being in a constant state of 'gratitude for the blessing of intelligence' increases one's knowledge.[76] Nor should a student should be miserly with what they have learned. Coveting knowledge and assuming that if one shares what one knows it will somehow diminish one's own position or status 'no longer preserves the integrity of knowledge'.[77]

Good character and good habits for learning is the third theme. The beginning of learning is to cleanse the heart of ill thoughts, feelings, and vices. This is meant for older students in particular but it is an ethic that should be ingrained in students from a young age, not to hold grudges or form ill opinions of peers. Ibn Jama'ah says, 'If the heart is made fragrant for knowledge, the blessing of knowledge will emerge and grow, just as when the soil is made fragrant for the plant, the plant grows and thrives'.[78]

As students get older they should be encouraged to maintain good habits related to learning that reinforce the importance and privilege of learning itself. Ibn Jama'ah provides many practical examples, including to eat foods (both in quality and amount) that nourish and energize the mind and body rather than make one sluggish and lethargic, establish study spaces free of distractions, block off time for study, keep good company of pious people, and partake in regular physical exercise to stimulate the mind.[79] He also states good habits for classroom learning that students should embody, including respecting teachers, avoiding the company of peers who speak ill of the teacher, being well groomed, listening attentively, being polite in asking questions, and not pointing out the faults of others publicly.

The fourth theme raised about students is to have a high respect for teachers. 'Ali [ibn Abi Talib] said: "I am the slave of him who teaches me one letter of the alphabet."'[80] Having respect for teachers includes exhibiting etiquette as you would to an elder in speaking respectfully, asking questions in an inquisitive manner and not with the intent to demean someone, respecting the teacher's space, desk, books, and family. The emphasis here is not on obedience but respect. A teacher is not infallible or perfect but someone who has come to serve. Al-Zarnuji gives an example in which he compares a teacher to a physician and asks how helpful and caring a physician would be in addressing your ailment if you did not respect the physician.[81]

Fostering a school culture where students embody the right intentions, humility, good character, and respect is an ongoing process and one that is never quite complete. But through mentorship and modelling schools over time can create an environment where such behaviours and ways of being become commonplace. The essential means for achieving such an ethic is through consistent reinforcement and encouragement.

Implications for Islamic School Renewal

This chapter takes a comprehensive approach to articulating the potential conceptualisation of Islamic education rooted in the central concept of *adab*. Drawing from the Islamic tradition, eight key areas pertaining to Islamic schooling today are discussed. These include: vision, stages of development, instruction, curriculum, assessment and evaluation, learning environment, the role of the teacher, and the role of the student. It is hoped that these eight elements will provoke further discussion in regards to the applications of Islamic education in today's schools in a manner that transcends content, captures the essence of *adab*, and is manifested in the overarching concept of Islamic pedagogy.

The implications of the eight areas for Islamic school renewal are urgent and important. These eight areas can initially be used as a draft rubric for schools to self-reflect and consider areas of improvement. Although there will be overlap with many of the core standards of any national education framework, there are nuances in each of the areas outlined above that make the perspective of education distinctly Islamic. Secondly, the eight areas outlined can also serve as a guide for conceptual clarity as schools revise and renew mission, vision, and value statements or overall school development plans. It is hoped that the articulations above will provide the language and perspective necessary to distinctly articulate what makes an individual Islamic school unique. Finally, the ideas presented in this chapter should provide a road map for school renewal in two ways: by identifying less emphasised areas and by honing in on areas of interconnection. For example, an area of educational practice often implemented by relying on conventional practice is assessment and evaluation. With the articulation of the aims of assessment and evaluation in the Islamic tradition, schools can now consider new ways to introduce the importance and value of assessments to students. Similarly, considering the stages of development outlined in this chapter, schools can begin to ask deeper questions about the interconnectedness of what we teach and why we teach it at that particular time. The hope is that the ideas presented in this chapter will serve as fodder for the renewal of Islamic schools through more pointed questions and a more nuanced perspective.

Notes

1. William Hare and John P. Portelli (eds.), *Philosophy of Education: Introductory Readings 4th Edition* (Calgary, Alberta: Brush Education Inc., 2013).
2. Seyyed Hossein Nasr, *Traditional Islam in the Modern World* (USA: Kegan Paul International, 1990).
3. Islamic schools are of many varieties and depending on the context (e.g., Muslim-majority countries versus Western societies where Muslims are a minority) the term Islamic school can refer to a very distinct type of schooling. For a detailed typology of Islamic schooling refer to: Nadeem Memon, "Between Immigrating and Integrating: The Challenge of Defining an Islamic Pedagogy in Canadian Islamic Schools," in Graham McDonough, Nadeem Memon, and Avi Mintz (eds.), *Discipline, Devotion, and Dissent: Jewish, Catholic, and Islamic Schooling in Canada* (Wilfrid Laurier University Press, 2013).
4. Naquib Al-Attas, *The Concept of Education in Islam: A Framework for an Islamic Philosophy of Education* (Kuala Lumpur: ISTAC, 1999); Mohammed Al-Ghazzali, *The Book of Knowledge* (Kuala Lumpur: House of Revelation, 2013), 166.
5. Naquib al-Attas, *The Concept of Education in Islam. First World Conference on Muslim Education* (Mecca: Saudi Arabia, 1980), 22.
6. Abd al-Aziz Al-Qabisi. "A Treatise Detailing the Circumstances of Students and the Rules Governing Teachers and Students," in *Classical Foundations of Islamic Educational Thought*, ed. Bradley Cook (Utah, USA: Brigham Young University Press, 2010), 38–74.
7. Muhammad bin Ahmed al-Ramli, *Educating Children: Classical Advice for Modern Times (Riyadatul Sibyan)*, (United Kingdom: Kitaba—Islamic Texts for the Blind, 2013).
8. Seyyed Hossein Nasr, *A Young Muslim's Guide to the Modern World* (Kuala Lumpur: Islamic Book Trust, 2010).
9. Nasr, *Man and Nature*.
10. Nasr, *Man and Nature*; Bradley Cook, "Islamic versus Western Conceptions of Education: Reflections on Egypt," *International Review of Education* (1999): 346.
11. Ikhwan al-Safa. "The Seventh Epistle of the Propaedeutical Part on the Scientific Arts and What They Aim At," in *Classical Foundations of Islamic Educational Thought*, ed. Bradley Cook (Utah, USA: Brigham Young University Press, 2010), 20–37; Zahra Al Zeera, *Wholeness and Holiness in Education: An Islamic Perspective* (Virginia: The International Institute on Islamic Thought, 2001).

12. Abu Hamid Muhammad ibn Muhammad al-Ghazali, "O Son!," in *Classical Foundations of Islamic Educational Thought*, ed. Bradley Cook (Utah, USA: Brigham Young University Press, 2010), 88–107.
13. Abdullah Sahin, *New Directions in Islamic Education: Pedagogy and Identity Formation* (Turkey: KUBE, 2013), 194–198.
14. Allan Ornstein and Francis Hunkins, *Curriculum: Foundations, Principles, and Issues* (Boston, MA: Pearson, 2009).
15. al-Ghazzali, *The Book of Knowledge*, 178.
16. Qur'an 57:20.
17. al-Ramli, *Educating Children*, 16.
18. Mohammed Al-Ghazali, *Ihya Ulum al-Din, Book III* (Revival of Religious Sciences) (Beirut: Al-Maktabah Al-Asriyah, 2004), 95.
19. al-Ramli, *Educating Children*, 52.
20. al-Ramli, *Educating Children*, 52.
21. Narrated by Ahmed 11/369 number 6689 and 6756.
22. al-Ghazali, *Ihya Ulum al-Din, Book III*, 97–98.
23. al-Ghazali, *Ihya Ulum al-Din, Book III*, 95–97.
24. ∎.
25. al-Ramli, *Educating Children*.
26. See Sarfaroz Niyozov and Nadeem Memon, "Islamic Education and Islamization: Evolution of Themes, Continuities and New Directions," *Journal of Muslim Minority Affairs* 31 (2011): 12–13.
27. al Zeera, *Wholeness and Holiness in Education: An Islamic Perspective*, 84.
28. ∎.
29. Miskawayh. "From the Second Discourse of *The Refinement of Character*." In *Classical Foundations of Islamic Educational Thought*, ed. Bradley Cook, 75–87 (Utah, USA: Brigham Young University Press, 2010).
30. Miskawayh. "From the Second Discourse of *The Refinement of Character*." In *Classical Foundations of Islamic Educational Thought*, ed. Bradley Cook, 75–87 (Utah, USA: Brigham Young University Press, 2010), 83.
31. Amr Abdalla et al., *Improving the Quality of Islamic Education in Developing Countries: Innovative Approaches* (Washington, DC: Creative Associates International, 2006), vii.
32. See Ibn Sahnun. Ibn Khaldun, and others in Bradley Cook (ed.), *Classical Foundations of Islamic Educational Thought* (Utah, USA: Brigham Young University Press, 2010).
33. William Chittick, "The Goal of Islamic Education." In *Education in the Light of Tradition*, ed. Jane Casewit (Indiana, USA: World Wisdom, 2011), 90.
34. This applies to the period of madrassas establishment up to the sixteenth century before colonialism. See Niyozov and Memon, *Islamic Education and Islamization: Evolution of Themes, Continuities and New Directions*.

35. Titus Burckhardt, "Traditional Sciences in Fez." In *Education in the Light of Tradition*, ed. Jane Casewit (Indiana, USA: World Wisdom, 2011), 18.
36. Ibn Khaldun, "Selections from *The Muqaddimah*." In *Classical Foundations of Islamic Educational Thought*, ed. Bradley Cook, 208–242 (Utah, USA: Brigham Young University Press, 2010), 231.
37. al-Zarnuji, *Instruction of the Student: The Method of Learning*, trans. G.E. Von Grunebaum and Theodora M. Abel (USA: Starlatch Press, 2003).
38. al-Ghazali, "O Son!".
39. Quoted in Sebastian Gunther, "'Your Educational Achievements Shall Not Stop Your Efforts to Seek Beyond': Principles of Teaching and Learning in Classical Arabic Writings." In *Philosophies of Islamic Education: Historical Perspectives and Emerging Discourses*, ed. Nadeem A. Memon and Mujadad Zaman, 72–93 (New York, USA: Routledge, 2016), 73.
40. Discussed in Boyle, *Memorization and Learning in Islamic Schools*, 479–480; Eickelman, *The Art of Memory: Islamic Education and Its Social Reproduction*.
41. Glenn Hardaker and A'ishah Sabki, "Islamic Pedagogy and Embodiment: An Anthropological Study of a British Madrasah." *International Journal of Qualitative Studies in Education*, 2012.
42. See Cook, "Islamic versus Western Conceptions of Education: Reflections on Egypt," 342; Niyozov and Memon, *Islamic Education and Islamization: Evolution of Themes, Continuities and New Directions*, 14.
43. Wan Mohd Wan Daud, *Islamization of Contemporary Knowledge and the Role of the University in the Context of De-Westernization and De-Colonization* (Kuala Lumpur: Universiti Teknologi Malaysia, 2013); Wan Mohd Wan Daud, *The Educational Philosophy and Practice of Syed Muhammad Naquib Al-Attas: An Exposition of the Original Concept of Islamization* (Kuala Lumpur: ISTAC, 1998); al Zeera, *Wholeness and Holiness in Education*, 55.
44. See al-Zeera, *Wholeness and Holiness in Education*; Yusef Waghid, "Islamic Education Institutions: Can the Heritage Be Sustained?" *The American Journal of Islamic Social Sciences* 14 (1997): 35–49; al-Attas, *The Concept of Education in Islam: A Framework for an Islamic Philosophy of Education*.
45. Chittick, *The Goal of Islamic Education*, 85.
46. *Fardh 'ain* can also be referred to as 'personal obligation'. It is that which every single Muslim should acquire, obligatory knowledge that corresponds to the status and needs of the learner and is determined to be what a person may need in a certain situation.
47. *Fardh kifayah* can be referred to as 'collective obligation'. It is knowledge which doesn't become a requirement if a sufficient number of Muslims acquire it to an aptitude that suffices the needs of the community.

48. Omar Anwar Qureshi, "Disciplinarity and Islamic Education." In *Philosophies of Islamic Education: Historical Perspectives and Emerging Discourses*, ed. Nadeem A. Memon and Mujadad Zaman, 94–111 (New York: Routledge, 2016), 101.
49. Cited in Omar Anwar Qureshi, "Disciplinarity and Islamic Education," 106.
50. Cited in Omar Anwar Qureshi, "Disciplinarity and Islamic Education," 95.
51. Ibn Khaldun, "Selections from *The Muqaddimah*."
52. Ibn Khaldun, "Selections from *The Muqaddimah*," 231.
53. Jean-Louis Michon, *Introduction to Traditional Islam: Foundations, Art, and Spirituality* (Indiana, USA: World Wisdom Inc. 2008), 144.
54. Cited in Ramzy Ajem and Nadeem Memon, *Principles of Islamic Pedagogy*, 45.
55. Jean-Louis Michon, *Introduction to Traditional Islam*.
56. Abu Hamid Muhammad ibn Muhammad al-Ghazali, *On Vigilance and Self-Examination (Kitab al muraqaba wa'l muhasaba) Book XXXVIII of the Revival of the Religious Sciences (Ihya ulum al-din)*. Translated with introduction and notes by Anthony Shaker (United Kingdom: Islamic Texts Society, 2015).
57. Ibn Jama'ah, "A Memorandum for Listeners and Lecturers: Rules of Conduct for the Learned and the Learning." In *Classical Foundations of Islamic Educational Thought*, ed. Bradley Cook, 156–207 (Utah, USA: Brigham Young University Press, 2010), 193.
58. al-Zarnuji, *Instruction of the Student*, 13.
59. al-Zarnuji, *Instruction of the Student*, 16.
60. Ibn Jama'ah, "A Memorandum for Listeners and Lecturers," 192–198.
61. Ibn Jama'ah, "A Memorandum for Listeners and Lecturers," 168.
62. Ibn Jama'ah, "A Memorandum for Listeners and Lecturers," 168.
63. Ibn Jama'ah, "A Memorandum for Listeners and Lecturers," 168.
64. Ibn Jama'ah, "A Memorandum for Listeners and Lecturers," 170.
65. Ibn Jama'ah, "A Memorandum for Listeners and Lecturers," 171.
66. Ibn Jama'ah, "A Memorandum for Listeners and Lecturers," 160.
67. al-Ramli, *Educating Children*, 93.
68. Ibn Jama'ah, "A Memorandum for Listeners and Lecturers," 168–169.
69. al-Ramli, *Educating Children*, 76.
70. al-Ramli, *Educating Children*, 76.
71. Ibn Jama'ah, "A Memorandum for Listeners and Lecturers," 163.
72. Miskawayh, *The Refinement of Character*, 83.
73. al-Ramli, *Educating Children*.
74. Ibn Jama'ah, "A Memorandum for Listeners and Lecturers," 172.
75. al-Zarnuji, *Instruction of the Student*, 6.
76. al-Zarnuji, *Instruction of the Student*, 30.

77. al-Zarnuji, *Instruction of the Student*, 32.
78. Ibn Jama'ah, "A Memorandum for Listeners and Lecturers," 177.
79. Ibn Jama'ah, "A Memorandum for Listeners and Lecturers," 179–181.
80. al-Zarnuji, *Instruction of the Student*, 13.
81. al-Zarnuji, *Instruction of the Student*, 13.

Bibliography

Ajem, Ramzy, and Memon, Nadeem. *Principles of Islamic Pedagogy: A Teacher's Manual*. Toronto, Canada: Razi Education, 2011.

al-Attas, Naquib. *The Concept of Education in Islam. First World Conference on Muslim Education, March 1977*. Mecca: Saudi Arabia, 1980.

al-Ghazali, Abu Hamid Muhammad ibn Muhammad. *On Vigilance and Self-Examination (Kitab al muraqaba wa'l muhasaba) Book XXXVIII of the Revival of the Religious Sciences (Ihya ulum al-din)*. Translated with introduction and notes by Anthony Shaker. United Kingdom: Islamic Texts Society, 2015.

al-Ghazali. "O Son!" In *Classical Foundations of Islamic Educational Thought*, ed. Bradley Cook, 88–107. Utah: Brigham Young University Press, 2010.

al-Qabisi. "A Treatise Detailing the Circumstances of Students and the Rules Governing Teachers and Students." In *Classical Foundations of Islamic Educational Thought*, ed. Bradley Cook, 38–74. Utah: Brigham Young University Press, 2010.

al-Ramli, Muhammad bin Ahmed. *Educating Children: Classical Advice for Modern Times (Riyadatul Sibyan)*. United Kingdom: Kitaba—Islamic Texts for the Blind, 2013.

al-Zarnuji. *Instruction of the Student: The Method of Learning*. Trans. G.E. Von Grunebaum and Theodora M. Abel. Chicago, IL: Starlatch Press, 2003.

———. "Instruction of the Student: The Method of Learning." In *Classical Foundations of Islamic Educational Thought*, ed. Bradley Cook, 108–155. Utah: Brigham Young University Press, 2010.

al Zeera, Zahra. *Wholeness and Holiness in Education: An Islamic Perspective*. Virginia: The International Institute on Islamic Thought, 2001.

Amr Abdalla et al. *Improving the Quality of Islamic Education in Developing Countries: Innovative Approaches*. Washington, DC: Creative Associates International, 2006.

Burckhardt, Titus. "Traditional Sciences in Fez." In *Education in the Light of Tradition*, ed. Jane Casewit, 17–22. Bloomington, IN: World Wisdom, 2011.

Chittick, William. "The Goal of Islamic Education." In *Education in the Light of Tradition*, ed. Jane Casewit, 85–92. Bloomington, IN: World Wisdom, 2011.

Gunther, Sebastian. "'Your Educational Achievements Shall Not Stop Your Efforts to Seek Beyond': Principles of Teaching and Learning in Classical Arabic Writings." In *Philosophies of Islamic Education: Historical Perspectives and*

Emerging Discourses, ed. Nadeem A. Memon and Mujadad Zaman, 72–93. New York: Routledge, 2016.

Hardaker, Glenn, and Aishah Sabki. Islamic Pedagogy and Embodiment: An Anthropological Study of a British Madrasah. *International Journal of Qualitative Studies in Education*, 2012. Available at http://eprints.hud.ac.uk/12841/.

Ibn Jama'ah. "A Memorandum for Listeners and Lecturers: Rules of Conduct for the Learned and the Learning." In *Classical Foundations of Islamic Educational Thought*, ed. Bradley Cook, 156–207. Utah: Brigham Young University Press, 2010.

Ibn Khaldun. *The Muqaddimah (an Introduction)*. Damascus: Dar Ya'rub, 2004.

———. "Selections from *The Muqaddimah*." In *Classical Foundations of Islamic Educational Thought*, ed. Bradley Cook, 208–242. Utah: Brigham Young University Press, 2010.

Ibn Sahnun. "The Book of Rules of Conduct for Teachers." In *Classical Foundations of Islamic Educational Thought*, ed. Bradley Cook, 1–19. Utah: Brigham Young University Press, 2010.

Michon, Jean-Louis. *Introduction to Traditional Islam: Foundations, Art, and Spirituality*. Bloomington, IN: World Wisdom, 2008.

Miskawayh. "From the Second Discourse of *The Refinement of Character*." In *Classical Foundations of Islamic Educational Thought*, ed. Bradley Cook, 75–87. Utah: Brigham Young University Press, 2010.

Nasr, Seyyed Hossein. *Traditional Islam in the Modern World*. London and New York: Kegan Paul International, 1990.

———. *Man and Nature*. Chicago, IL: ABC International Group, 1997.

———. *A Young Muslim's Guide to the Modern World*. Kuala Lumpur: Islamic Book Trust, 2010.

Qureshi, Omar Anwar. "Disciplinarity and Islamic Education." In *Philosophies of Islamic Education: Historical Perspectives and Emerging Discourses*, ed. Nadeem A. Memon and Mujadad Zaman, 94–111. New York: Routledge, 2016.

Sahin, Abdullah. *New Directions in Islamic Education: Pedagogy and Identity Formation*. Turkey: KUBE, 2013.

CHAPTER 10

A Pedagogical Framework for Teacher Discourse and Practice in Islamic Schools

Muhammad Abdullah

INTRODUCTION

Prior to the 1970s, mosques were established in Australia by small communities, usually of the same ethnic background. These mosques served both the small number of migrants from diverse backgrounds and the generations born in Australia. Since the 1970s, Muslims have migrated to Australia from over seventy countries,[1] and although the representation in the popular media is of a uniform and homogeneous group, they come from a range of theological traditions and encompass different cultural, sectarian, linguistic and ethnic values.[2] A large number of these migrants come from countries that are in themselves culturally and religiously diverse. Like other migrants, they come for a multitude of reasons including economic advantages, educational opportunities, family reunion and escape from political oppression.[3]

Muslims have followed the patterns of other migrant groups in settling close to each other. Moreover, given the importance of family and the mosque in Islam, subsequent generations have continued this tendency.[4]

M. Abdullah (✉)
University of South Australia, Adelaide, SA, Australia

© The Author(s) 2018
M. Abdalla et al. (eds.), *Islamic Schooling in the West*,
https://doi.org/10.1007/978-3-319-73612-9_10

With the increased migration of Muslims from different linguistic, ethnic and cultural backgrounds, many of these individual communities became sufficiently large to construct their own mosques and centres. Although attendance and particularly management of these mosques tended to be dominated by people who shared the same language and/or ethnicity of the founders, the mosques were not exclusively for worshippers of those backgrounds. In addition to prayer gatherings, the mosques and centres were also utilised as places for children's religious education, particularly Qur'an recitation.

As with the Jewish[5] and Greek[6] communities, increased numbers of school-aged children prompted the development of a sentiment within the Australian Muslim communities[7] that a quality Islamic religious, cultural and Arabic/ethnic language experience could be more readily realised by the establishment of full-time Islamic schools. By 1983, the first Islamic schools had been established in Sydney, Melbourne and Perth. In the following thirty-three years more than fifty Islamic schools were established across Australia (this includes schools that do not necessarily label themselves as Islamic but cater for the Muslim community). During the same period a similar growth in Islamic schools was experienced in other migrant Muslim communities across North America and Europe.[8]

Importance of Culture

Cultural experience[9] is included above with religious experience because accepted indigenous cultural expressions within different Muslim communities over time have become harmonised with the universal norms of sacred law and, for those communities, essential parts of their Islamic and cultural identity.[10] The Qur'anic basis for this harmonisation is contained in the Qur'an (7:199):

> Accept (from people) what comes naturally (for them). Command what is customarily (good). And turn away from the ignorant (without responding in kind).

Eminent Muslim jurists have used this textual proof as a basis for legal decisions through the centuries. The Islamic cultural traditions of these countries have developed over time, and as Murad notes[11]:

The traditional Muslim world is a rainbow, an extraordinary patchwork of different cultures, all united by a common adherence to the doctrinal and moral patterns set down in Revelation. Put differently, Revelation supplies parameters (*hudud*)[12] rather than a complete blueprint for the details of cultural life.

Muslims from different parts of the world can therefore be recognised, at the same time, as both Muslim and members of a particular culture. It is important to note that the seeds for the emergence of a distinctive Australian Muslim identity have already begun to grow. A recent quantitative study found that Muslim students in Years 9–11 in Australian Islamic schools[13] identified most strongly with their religious affiliation, followed by their heritage culture and then with being Australian. However, their religious and cultural identification was not in opposition to being Australian, nor did it indicate a preference for separation from Australian society. The researchers proposed that the experience of negative public attitudes and racism weakened the students' feeling of belonging to Australia. This is reflected in the comments of some Australian-born female teachers at an Islamic school recorded by Watson and Chen"[14]

> Since the Cronulla riots we (Muslims) do not want to be seen as different ... We want to just melt into the background and disappear. We know this will not happen because we (a group of women) dress differently ... But we still don't want to write that we want this difference. We feel ashamed. We shouldn't feel like this ... We just want to be Australians like everyone else. We love our religion and we want to be Australians.

However, the previous school experiences of migrant Muslims arriving in Australia can pose a number of issues for Islamic schools. These issues go well beyond seemingly mundane decisions, such as the style of an Islamic school's uniform, in that they affect parental expectations as well as the curriculum and pedagogy of the school. One finds that most countries with large Muslim populations generally have two streams of education, the first being a government and private school system that tends to have an educational pedagogy[15] similar to those of previous colonial powers' systems,[16] and the second a more 'traditional' system for reading and memorisation of the Qur'an. Many of these countries also have an extension of the Qur'an school, which teaches the Islamic sciences at various levels and degrees. The traditional systems have underlying pedagogical strategies that are universal but they also display significant differences according to time and place.[17] Clyne conducted parental interviews to identify the reasons why Muslim parents send their children to Islamic schools in Australia.[18] She found that among the more important reasons were that the Islamic school curriculum reflects Islamic values; there is strong discipline; they prefer a Muslim environment; the teachers understand about Islam; Qur'anic studies are taught; and children will learn correct behaviour.[19] Sanjakdar adds that there is also a parental perception of a lack of quality education in Australian public schools.[20]

These expectations and the individual educational experiences influence perceptions of what an Islamic school should and should not be and can often be the cause for heated debate and dissatisfaction and occasionally the impetus for the establishment of new Islamic schools which are perceived by the founders and supporters to be 'more Islamic'. It is not surprising, therefore, that discussions in or about Islamic schools revolve around dress code, rules and regulations, curriculum, and the background, experience, quality, religiosity and/or piety of teachers. However, it is important to note that the Australian Institute for Teaching and School Leadership (AITSL 2017), in reflecting on the Australian Professional Standards for Teachers, points out that there is a broad national and international consensus 'that teacher quality is the single-most important in-school factor influencing student achievement' and that teacher quality is impacted by teachers' pedagogical knowledge[21] and the ability to adapt quality pedagogies to different school contexts.[22] Given the different understandings of the Islamic in Islamic schooling and the importance of pedagogy in student achievement, it is instructive to return to the Qur'an[23] and Hadith[24] as well as contemporary research to identify appropriate pedagogical solutions that will inculcate an Islamic worldview[25] and practice while fulfilling the expectations of parents and the community and meet the needs of students.

Islamic Education and Pedagogy

The Qur'an and Hadith are the original sources for all things Islamic, including the various concepts and applications of education in Muslim-majority countries today.[26] The first educational concept, known as *ta'lim*, refers to instruction and learning about things, which develops reason and trains the mind. Evidence for this is found in the Qur'an (2:31): 'And He [God] taught ("*allama*"[27]) Adam the names of all things', and the saying of the Prophet Muhammad (may peace and blessing be upon him), 'the best of you are those who learnt (*ta'allama*) the Qur'an and taught it ("*allama*")'.[28] The second concept, known as *tarbiyah*, refers to the development of human personality and the nurturing and rearing of a child (Qur'an 17:24), and the third concept, known as *ta'dib*, refers to the training of the mind and soul in terms of behaviour and ethical conduct. It encompasses the recognition and acknowledgement of one's right and proper place and the self-discipline to enact one's role in accordance with that place.[29,30] Each of these terms emphasises different aspects of the development of the whole person represented by the physical, intellectual, moral and spiritual dimensions.[31]

However, the opinion of Bin Omar is that an accurate definition encompasses all three aspects and is concerned with developing the essence of the human being (the soul-spirit, heart, self and intellect).[32] Memon sees immense value in the definitions discussed above but argues that limiting a definition to one or the other does not give justice to the expansiveness of the Islamic teaching tradition.[33] Although he does not explicitly follow Bin Omar in his synthesis to define Islamic education, the same elements are embedded in his discussion. Memon analyses Islamic education in relation to instances from the Prophetic tradition by using the famous Hadith Jibril.[34] This analysis follows on from a 2006 article in aiming to move away from a reliance on modern conceptions of education and to use educative moments from the Prophetic tradition to envision what such practices may look like.

The Hadith affirms the three aspects of the religion—Islam, *Iman* (faith) and *Ihsan*[35]—and it is this last aspect that Memon[36] proposes has been in the main neglected by Islamic schools. His explanation of the relationship of these aspects to the dimensions of reality correctly draw out that *Ihsan* is the depth of Islam. The Hadith describes the desired level of *Ihsan* as that state in which a person worships God as though he can see Him. At this point a person has attained *ma'rifah*,[37] and the resultant ability to fulfil the role of vicegerent (*Khalifa*). *Ihsan*, then, as the inner reality of worship, acts as the link between *ma'rifah* and vicegerency. The vicegerent has correct *adab*[38] in that their behaviour is appropriate and fitting for the occasion and has been performed in due proportion in a conscious state of being, as if seeing God. Memon argues that *Ihsan* needs to be lived, modelled and nurtured as part of the ethos of the school culture,[39] and needs to be exemplified by the teacher. The initial stage of *Ihsan* is to worship God with the knowledge that He sees and knows every act.

Muslim children are usually taught about this stage of *Ihsan* in any basic Islamic religious instruction during the lessons about *Iman* (faith), if not already at home prior to school commencement. However, Memon's expectation that teachers will exemplify *Ihsan* appears to be based on a more developed ideal of *Ihsan*. *Ihsan* is the inner quality of a person's worship, and the ideal is developed and nurtured over a lifetime and is the subject of an ongoing struggle for a Muslim. The level of attainment of *Ihsan* in any individuals' act of worship is not easily identified by others, and is often misread. To some degree, correct *adab* can be learnt and performed for specific acts and circumstances without necessarily emanating from any sense of *Ihsan*.

Beautiful character needs to be modelled for the students, but consideration of teachers' private lives when hiring, as proposed by Memon, is fraught with many potential pitfalls.[40] The reality for most Islamic schools in Australia, if not worldwide, is that there is generally a mixture of Muslim and non-Muslim staff. Muslim staff members themselves are very diverse in their practice and understandings of Islam and their spiritual development. Even within the community few people would claim that they have reached the desired level of *Ihsan* in even a small part of their worship. Consequently, any model of Islamic pedagogy, while necessarily in harmony with the purpose and guidelines of Islamic education, needs also to be responsive to the circumstances and environment of its implementation. The school, its ethos and pedagogy (which is the main concern here), can then foster the creation of a productive learning environment for all its participants. In such a pedagogical environment both teachers and students may then avail themselves of the opportunity to practise and evaluate ways of knowing and understanding in harmony with an Islamic worldview. The teacher is then a learner and 'a model of *adab*' as a participant in an organic process of change and improvement rather than 'the model of *adab*', in contrast with the Hadith Jibril (see note 8) which captures for us an instance of the Prophet as 'the model of *adab*' both as a learner and a teacher.

Memon discusses a further three Hadiths of the Prophet Muhammad (may peace and blessing be upon him) to deduce examples of prophetic pedagogical teaching techniques, including the use of examples relevant to context, questioning that engages the attention of the listener and the use of images to ingrain meaning.[41] As valuable as these techniques are, their value for Islamic education and pedagogy is not so much in their specific time and place applications, but rather in identifying the wisdom of what was taught and how, why, when, where and to whom it was taught.[42] The analysis of these and other examples in Hadith can assist in the identification of the underlying pedagogical principles of the Islamic tradition. It can be argued that a process of a fertile synthesis[43] of the pedagogical principles of contemporary educational thought and the underlying pedagogical principles of the Islamic tradition could enable the development of a more appropriate pedagogical model for Islamic schools. Consequently, some of the possible outcomes of this synthesis are that students of Islamic schools will attain a deeper understanding of Islam and confidence in their Islamic identity, and possibly will be prepared for rich and positive participation in society by serving humanity.[44] Of course, such a fertile synthesis may also lead to other outcomes conducive to the making of a more effective and productive Islamic schooling experience.

Memon does not attempt to model this synthesis but encourages each school to develop workshops for the professional development of their teachers in the pedagogical practices of the Prophet.[45] The three examples that are outlined above are based on the valuable work of Abu Ghuddah, who analysed over one hundred sayings of the Prophet to elucidate his character and teaching strategies.[46] The work of Abu Ghuddah is very important in the field but does not readily lead to the creation of a *framework* of Islamic pedagogical principles that may be utilised by teachers in Islamic schools in the West (and possibly in majority Muslim nations). Such a framework is important as it gives teachers a tool that provides a common metalanguage and the opportunity for collegial collaboration, evaluation and reflection on classroom practice. This in turn could then enable a classroom environment where ways of knowing and understanding are in harmony with an Islamic worldview and the enhancement of student outcomes.

Development of a Prophetic Pedagogy

A challenge in the development of a framework of the pedagogical practices of the Prophet Muhammad (may peace and blessing be upon him) is that pedagogy is implicitly embedded in each Hadith since it covers the sayings, actions and tacit approvals of the Prophet. Therefore, any conclusion(s) of what constitutes prophetic pedagogical principles that are derived from an analysis of Hadith are subjective and open to interpretation(s). However, this is not problematic, since the intent in identifying the principles is to construct a framework that may facilitate best practice within an Islamic schooling context. What follows is an exploration of how best one can derive pedagogical principles from the Prophetic example, followed by a proposed framework that synthesises these principles with productive pedagogies for teachers working within an Islamic schooling context.

To facilitate the emergence of a prophetic pedagogical framework from Hadith a number of methodological methods can be utilised. For this research, the inductive process of grounded theory was used to identify core pedagogical strategies in the practice of the Prophet Muhammad (may peace and blessing be upon him). Grounded theory, as a coding method, is deemed appropriate for our purposes because it is a bottom-up technique in relation to the data and begins at the word or sentence level.[47] It aims, in as rigorous and detailed a manner as possible, to identify categories and concepts that emerge from the text, and to link these concepts into substantive and formal theories. It is an iterative process by which the analyst becomes more and more 'grounded' in the data, enabling increasingly richer concepts and models of how the phenomenon being studied works.[48]

While there are multiple recognised and authenticated Hadith collections,[49] the author has chosen to work with Hadith found in the collection of Sahih Muslim. This compilation was chosen as it falls within the highest category of compilations for overall accuracy, reputation and acceptance.[50,51] In addition, the Hadith in Sahih Al Bukhari are often fragmented with different portions placed under different headings,[52] while in Sahih Muslim this is avoided. The analysis of a portion of a Hadith independent of the complete text could give a different emphasis and have implications for the pedagogical principles. The coding was commenced from the beginning of compilation using the Arabic text of the Hadith. The coding result for each Hadith and the codes were then recorded in English:

> From Abu Suhail from his father that he heard Talhah ibn Abdullah saying a man from Najd[53] came to the Messenger of Allah (may peace and blessings be upon him). He had unkempt hair and a loud voice which we could not understand until he drew near the Messenger of Allah (may peace and blessing be upon him). He was asking about Islam. The Messenger of Allah (may peace and blessing be upon him) said five *salah* in every day and night. He asked is there anything else than these. (The Prophet) said, no, except for voluntary prayers and fasting *Ramadan*. He asked is there anything other than this. (The Prophet) said, no, except for voluntary fasting and then the Messenger of Allah (may peace and blessing be upon him) mentioned *zakat*. (The Prophet) said, no, except

for voluntary charity. He then turned round leaving saying, 'I will not do more or less than this'. The Messenger of Allah (may peace and blessing be upon him) said (to us) indeed he has succeeded if he is true to this (or he has entered heaven if he is true to this).

The following codes with description were identified in this Hadith:

1. accessible not aloof;
2. patience with the mode of address;
22. addresses people at their level (however, the man is given possibility for extension).
24. clearly and concisely answers information;
28. takes great care to give very precise and clear information that includes only that which is necessary;
35. clearly sets out measurable minimum to be achieved or expected;
36. clearly sets out the criteria measurable by the individual for the required standard.

Based on analysis of the first 173 Hadith from the beginning of Sahih Muslim, a clear set of categories emerged (see Table 10.1). The resultant framework has been called a prophetic pedagogical framework (PPF) to emphasise that it should be understood as an enabling document rather than a prescriptive one. Memorisation was added as it has been a consistent part of Muslims' pedagogy since the inception of Islam.[54,55]

As coding proceeded, subcategories and later categories began to emerge. These categories became the elements and the subcategories descriptors within the elements (in italics below each element as sections). Up to five features were then listed for each descriptor that identified characteristics of a classroom supporting a prophetic pedagogy.

The PPF gives the teacher the opportunity when designing a unit or lesson plan to reflect on and consider the types of teaching practices, student activities and assessment that will support or hinder student learning. The PPF also gives a consistent framework for ongoing evaluation both during and after a unit or lesson plan and for future design. The PPF also facilitates consistent teacher collaboration in the design and evaluation. This is valuable not only for the students but also for teachers as it aligns our practice with accepted contemporary research as to what constitutes quality teaching and, an additional benefit for a Muslim teacher, with the practice of the Prophet Muhammad (may peace and blessings be upon him).

Table 10.1 A Prophetic Pedagogical Framework (PPF)

Elements	Features				
Building relationships					
Respect for others; humility; individual not shamed	All classroom members feel comfortable to take risks because there are no put-downs	Classroom input is presented without ostentation while counter-arguments and discussions are conducted calmly and address the issues and not the individual	All classroom members feel they may contribute if they wish to do so	A person's silence or deference to another's knowledge is respected	If a lack of respect is displayed by an individual he or she immediately acknowledges it and apologises where appropriate
Patient	Students are given time to consider their responses	Students are given time to self-correct	Contributors are not interrupted. Each waits their turn	Opportunity for understanding is given to those who are slow to grasp a point or concept	Classroom members are not angry with or sarcastic towards a person who makes a mistake
Just to both/all parties. Good expectation and interpretation of others' behaviour	There are clear and consistent consequences for inappropriate behaviour for all classroom members	Inappropriate behaviour is addressed and solutions sought without condemnation of the individual	A teacher who notices an instance of inappropriate behaviour does not immediately jump to conclusions	All parties involved in an incident are given a fair and equal opportunity to explain their perspective	A student is not labelled or stereotyped for any reason. All students are and feel accepted
Relates to people's environment and experience, concern for the welfare of the individual	Classroom members value others' life experiences	Classroom members value others' perspectives	Classroom members feel their circumstances are understood and given proper consideration	Classroom members listen to each other's concerns	Practical solutions are sought for classroom issues through class discussion

Relevance				
Relates to people's environment and experience; relevant material for listeners; use of stories and examples of others; responsive to circumstances; careful use of own and others' questions	Examples are used that readily facilitate investigation and understanding of difficult concepts	Structure of the stories facilitates understanding even if some aspects are outside the direct experience of the listeners	Stories of previous peoples are used to illustrate relevant points for the listeners. This permits sensitive issues to be dealt with more explicitly	Flexible presentation is utilised to give a more relevant learning experience	Questions and answers are used as teaching aids to focus on and emphasise relevant points
Deep knowledge What and why				
Direct and indirect indications to deeper knowledge; brief but encompassing information; readily accepts suggestions	Reasons for studying topics and the information within them are coherent	Lessons are coherent and facilitate students' access to deep knowledge of the different aspects of a topic	Students develop a deep knowledge of a topic's links with other topics and its place within the broader body of knowledge	Students' constructive suggestions are encouraged and readily accepted	Students learn to extrapolate logical corollaries and conclusions from a wide body of knowledge
Deep understanding How				
Direct and indirect indications to deeper understanding; broadens/ deepens understanding	Lessons are coherent and facilitate students' access to a deep understanding of the spiritual significance of all aspects of a topic	Students develop a deep understanding of a topic's spiritual links with other topics	Students learn to extrapolate practical implications of the topic's spiritual significance	Students learn to be conscious thinkers able to rigorously examine their own intentions	Students' spiritual development is manifest in their understanding and implementation of their responsibilities as members of their community, Australian society and humanity

(continued)

Table 10.1 (continued)

Elements	Features			
Differentiation				
Scaffolds the lesson addressing the listener according to their ability; varied techniques includes non-verbal strategies and appropriate examples	Lesson progresses in logical graduated steps	Lesson is presented in a manner such that all students are able to access aspects of the knowledge according to their ability	Teacher uses examples appropriate for the students that may be abstract, concrete, verbal, visual or performed	Teacher is able to change the teaching style within and between lessons according to the needs of the students
Clear and Unambiguous information and instruction for example; clear indication of standards; teaches strategies; gives reasons for direction	Information and particularly instructions are clear, unambiguous and coherent for all students	Required standards are clearly conveyed to all students	Teaching strategies allow all students to benefit from and contribute to the lesson	Teaching strategies maximise student learning
Engagement				
Strategies to aid retention for example; varied techniques for emphasis; explanation of negative consequences to discourage; draws attention from outset; builds interest and attention; maintains focus and attention on the matter being taught	Teacher uses various techniques to aid retention and emphasis, such as word repetition, rhyme, contrasts and practical demonstration	Attention is drawn from the outset, for example by posing rhetorical questions and raising curiosity by mentioning strange things beyond the reality of the listeners	Teacher maintains interest, for example through stories, deliberately incomplete information that begs clarification, silence and questioning	Positive emphasis is the norm but negative consequences of certain actions are occasionally given to show the enormity of particular behaviours	Teacher maintains focus on the objectives of the lesson despite disruptions and distractions

Authenticity of knowledge			
Link to source (authenticity—oral tradition)	The origins of the knowledge are recognised	Recognition is given of by whom and how the knowledge has been transmitted	The source and transmission of the knowledge is validated
Language precision				
Mastery of language	Words are chosen carefully to give precise meaning	Choice of words permits a consistent depth of meaning	Words are not chosen to merely embellish the conversation, that is, for ostentation	Words and structures chosen are accessible	Words and structures are regarded by language speakers as representing eloquence
Metalanguage	New concepts are given clear terminology	Words used for specific terminology with ongoing common usage are clearly defined	Terms are used consistently	Different nuances of terms are consistent	Different levels of meaning for terms are introduced logically
Memorisation as a key				
	Students learn the basic meaning of what is memorised	Students learn any additional information necessary to better understand what has been memorised	Students learn the links between what has been memorised and other topics	Students use what has been memorised and the links to topics as a tool to organise and access more extensive knowledge	Students use what has been memorised as a tool to store and recall important spiritual lessons

In Table 10.2 the features of the PPF are exemplified by Hadith from across the Sunnah.[56] For the sake of brevity, only the Hadith are included that exemplify some of the features from the first section, *building relations: respect for others, humility and avoidance of shaming individuals in class*.

An example of how the PPF in Table 10.1 may be synthesised with a contemporary pedagogical framework is demonstrated in Tables 10.3 and 10.4. This synthesis was developed in collaboration with a daily after-hours school for religious instruction. Since the school is in Queensland, the productive pedagogies framework was used as this is the framework that underpins the public school system in Queensland.[57] Other pedagogical frameworks can be used in place of productive pedagogies.

Tables 10.3 and 10.4 work together as one table. In Table 10.3 the first column gives the dimensions of productive pedagogies while the second

Table 10.2 Examples of additional Hadith

Building relationships	*Respect for others, humility, avoidance of shaming others in class*
Features	Hadith
All classroom members feel comfortable to take risks because there are no put-downs	Aayeshah Radiyallahu 'Anha[a] reports, 'A person asked permission to present himself before Rasulullah Sallallahu 'Alayhi Wasallam[b] while I was with him. Rasulullah Sallallahu 'Alayhi Wasallam said: "What a bad person is he among his community". After saying this, he gave him permission to enter. After the person entered, he spoke very softly to him. When the person left I said: "O Rasulullah, you said what you said before he entered, then you spoke so softly to him. Rasulullah Sallallahu 'Alayhi Wasallam said: "O 'Aayeshah, the worst person is that who stops speaking to one because of his indecency"'. (Shamaail-333) Anas bin Maalik Radiyallahu 'Anhu says: 'I remained in the service (of Rasulullah Sallallahu 'Alayhi Wasallam for ten years. He never once told me "Oof". When I did something, he never asked me, why did you do so? When I did not do a certain task, he never asked me why I did not do it. (Shamaail-328) From a narration of Hasan bin 'Ali Radiyallahu 'Anhu … the whole creation was equal before him as far as rights were concerned. His gatherings were the gatherings of knowledge, modesty, patience and honesty. (i.e., These four things were attained there or are a description of his gatherings). Voices were not raised therein, nor was anyone degraded or disgraced. If anyone committed a fault, it was not made known publicly … (Shamaail-319)

(continued)

Table 10.2 (continued)

Classroom input is presented without ostentation while counter-arguments and discussions are conducted calmly and address the issues and not the individual	From a narration of Hasan bin 'Ali Radiyallahu 'Anhu … Rasulullah Sallallahu 'Alayhi Wasallam would remain seated till that person began to stand up. Whenever one asked him for something, he kindly fulfilled that request, and did not refuse it, (if he did not possess the thing) he would give a soft and humble answer … (Shamaail-319) From Anas (may Allah be pleased with him) that a man was brought to (the Prophet) may peace and blessings be upon him who was very nervous from awe and respect of (the Prophet) may peace and blessings be upon him. He said be easy on yourself, I am not a King, I am the son of a woman from Quraysh who ate dried meat, the man then spoke about his need. Then (the Prophet) may peace and blessing be upon him said, 'O people it has been revealed to me that you should be humble until no person transgresses against another and no person is scornful of another and worshippers of Allah as brothers (Nabahani 2004:244)
All classroom members feel they may contribute if they wish to do so	Khaarijah bin Zayd bin Thaabit Radiyallahu 'Anhu says that a group came to Zayd bin Thaabit (his father) and requested him to describe to them some facts about Rasulullah Sallallahu 'Alayhi Wasallam. He replied. 'What can I describe to you of Rasulullah Sallallahu 'Alayhi 'Wasallam. (It is beyond my means to describe them). I was the neighbour of Rasulullah Sallallahu 'Alayhi Wasallam. (Therefore he was mostly present and knew many facts. He was also a writer of the wahi-revelation). When wahi was revealed to Rasulullah Sallallahu 'Alayhi Wasallam, he sent for me, I came and wrote it. (Sayyidina Rasulullah Sallallahu 'Alayhi Wasallam always showed kindness, and made us feel at ease). Whatever we discussed, he discussed the same. If we discussed some worldly affairs, he also spoke of it. (It was not that he only spoke about the hereafter to us,' and despised the talking of worldly affairs). When we spoke of the hereafter, he too spoke of the hereafter. (When we began speaking of the hereafter, he described its events etc. in detail). 'When we spoke of food, Rasulullah Sallallahu 'Alayhi Wasallam also spoke of it. (its etiquette, benefits, tasty foods, foods that are harmful, etc.) (Shamaail-326)

(*continued*)

Table 10.2 (continued)

A person's silence or deference to another's knowledge is respected	Ubayy Bin Ka'b (may Allah be pleased with him) said that the Messenger of Allah (may Allah's peace and blessings be upon him) said, 'O Abal Mundhir do you know which verse that you have memorised from the Qur'an is greatest'. I said, Allah and his messenger know better. He then asked the same question again. I said *Allahu laa ilaha illa Huwal-Hayyul Qayyum*.[c] He hit me on the chest and said may your knowledge be good (Riyadus Salihin Hadith 1020)
If a lack of respect is displayed by an individual he or she immediately acknowledges it and apologises where appropriate	Narrated Ma'rur: I saw Abu Zhar wearing a *Burd* (garment) and his slave too was wearing a *Burd*, so I said (to Abu Zhar), 'If you take this (*Burd* of your slave) and wear it (along with yours), you will have a nice suit (costume) and you may give him another garment.' Abu Zhar said, 'There was a quarrel between me and another man whose mother was a non-Arab and I called her bad names. The man mentioned (complained about) me to the Prophet. The Prophet (PBUH) said, "Did you abuse so-and-so?" I said, "Yes" He said, "Did you call his mother bad names?" I said, "Yes". He said, "You still have the traits of (the Pre-lslamic period of) ignorance." I said. "(Do I still have ignorance) even now in my old age?" He said, "Yes, they (slaves or servants) are your brothers, and Allah has put them under your command. So the one under whose hand Allah has put his brother, should feed him of what he eats, and give him dresses of what he wears, and should not ask him to do a thing beyond his capacity. And if at all he asks him to do a hard task, he should help him therein.'[d] (Sahih Bukhari Hadith 6050) The commentators of Sahih Bukhari note that the man who was insulted was Bilal (may Allah be pleased with him) and in some narrations the insult was that Abu Zhar (may Allah be pleased with him) called him the son of a black women. In some narrations it is said that Abu Zhar was so remorseful that he put his cheek to the ground and asked Bilal to step on it.[e] In this case Abu Zhar did not initially recognise his disrespect but was lastingly remorseful immediately it was pointed out to him.

[a]Transliteration of the Arabic equivalent of: may Allah be pleased with her

[b]Transliteration of the Arabic equivalent of: may peace and blessing be upon him

[c]This is the beginning of the verse of the throne, 'Allah, there is no God but him the everlasting, self-sustaining eternal'

[d]Translation from http://pdf9.com/hadith-bukhari-6050.html, accessed 20 January 2017

[e]The different narrations and commentaries are mentioned on http://www.alukah.net/sharia/0/53636/, accessed 20 January 2017

Table 10.3 A possible synthesis of Productive Pedagogies and a Prophetic Pedagogy (initial part of the framework)

Productive pedagogies	Items	Prophetic pedagogy	Planning critical questions
Intellectual quality	Higher order thinking	Why	Are students learning the thinking processes that develop their ability to analyse (*amal*), assess, extrapolate, synthesise, develop, revise, critique and plan (*Hal*)?
	Deep knowledge	What	Does the lesson cover the required depth and breadth of knowledge (including linkages to other concepts/themes and ideas)?
	Deep understanding	How	Does the work and response of students provide evidence of deep understanding of concepts/themes or ideas?
	Substantive conversation	Memorisation as key	Is there classroom conversation around the words, concepts/themes and/or ideas to be memorised?
	Knowledge as problematic	Authenticity of knowledge	Are students linked to the source of the knowledge?
	Metalanguage	Language precision	Are aspects of language, grammar and technical vocabulary being foregrounded?
Relevance	Knowledge integration	Link between source, why, what and how	Does the lesson integrate different fields/branches of knowledge?
	Background knowledge	Building the field	Is there an attempt to connect with students' background knowledge?
	Connections to the world	Context	Do lessons and the assigned work have any resemblance or connection to real-life contexts and challenges?
	Problem-based curriculum		
Supportive classroom environment	Student control	Individual students are not shamed	Are teachers responsive to students' needs, interests and abilities?
	Social support	Patient	Is the classroom a socially supportive environment?

(*continued*)

Table 10.3 (continued)

Productive pedagogies	Items	Prophetic pedagogy	Planning critical questions
	Self-regulation	Gives clear reasons for directions Behaviour self-regulatory	Does the teacher model appropriate behaviour? Are students responsible for their own behaviour? Is explicit direction about appropriate behaviour given when necessary?
	Explicit criteria	Scaffold Unambiguous/clear information and instruction Clear indication of standards	Are criteria for student performance made explicit?
	Engagement	Strategies to aid retention Varied techniques for emphasis Draws attention from outset Build the interest and attention Maintains focus and attention on the matter being taught	Are students engaged and on task?
Recognition of difference	Cultural knowledge	Relates to people's environment and experience Non-verbal strategies	Do teaching strategies allow for the diversity of the classroom?
	Inclusivity	Respect for others Humility Addresses students according to the ability of the listener	Are all students meaningfully included in the lesson?
	Narrative	Teaches by example	Are students engaged through narrative/stories?
	Group identity	Good expectations and interpretation of others' behaviour Teaches by example	Does teaching build a sense of community and identity?
	Citizenship	Concern for the welfare of the individual Just to all people	Do teaching strategies direct students toward their responsibility as a human being?

Table 10.4 A possible synthesis of Productive Pedagogies and a Prophetic Pedagogy (continuation of the framework)

Items	Prophetic pedagogy	Features				
Higher order thinking	Why	Students are aware that memorisation and application of knowledge and skills is for deeper understanding	Students are given opportunities to comprehend information where appropriate	Students are given the opportunity to apply knowledge where appropriate	Students are encouraged to analyse and synthesis knowledge	Students are engaged in reflective processes
Deep knowledge	What	Lessons are coherent and facilitate students' access to and deep knowledge of all aspects of a topic	Students develop a deep knowledge of a topic's links with other topics and its place within the broader body of knowledge	Students' constructive suggestions are encouraged and readily accepted	Students learn to extrapolate logical corollaries and conclusions from a wide body of knowledge	
Deep understanding	How	Lessons are coherent and facilitate students' access to and deep understanding of the spiritual significance of all aspects of a topic	Students develop a deep understanding of a topic and its spiritual links with other topics	Students learn to extrapolate practical implications of the topic's spiritual significance	Students learn to be conscious thinkers able to rigorously examine their own intentions	Students' spiritual development is manifest in their understanding and implementation of their responsibilities as members of their community, Australian society and humanity
Substantive conversation	Memorisation as key	Students learn the basic meaning of what is memorised	Students learn any additional information necessary to better understand what has been memorised	Students learn the links between what has been memorised and other topics	Students use what has been memorised as a tool to store and recall vast banks of knowledge	Students use what has been memorised as a tool to store and recall important spiritual lessons

(continued)

Table 10.4 (continued)

Items	Prophetic pedagogy	Features			
Knowledge as problematic	Authenticity of knowledge	Origins of the knowledge are recognised	Recognition is given of who and how the knowledge has been transmitted	The source and transmission of the knowledge is validated	
Metalanguage	Language precision	Words are chosen carefully to give precise meaning	Choice of words permits a consistent depth of meaning	Words are not chosen to merely embellish the conversation, i.e. for ostentation	Words and structures are accessible	Words and structures are regarded by language speakers as representing eloquence
		New concepts are given clear terminology	Words used for specific terminology with ongoing common usage are clearly defined	Terms are used consistently	Different nuances of terms are consistent	Different levels of meaning for terms are introduced logically
Knowledge integration	Link between source, why, what and how	Students integrate their knowledge of a topic with other topics and its place within the broader body of knowledge	Students link their knowledge Knowledge of the topic with the source			
Background knowledge	Building the field	The reasons for studying topics and the information within them are coherent				
Connections to the world Problem-based curriculum	Context	Examples are used that readily facilitate investigation and understanding of difficult concepts	Teacher uses examples appropriate for the students that may be abstract, concrete, verbal, visual or performed			

Student control	Individual students are not shamed Patient	All classroom members feel comfortable to take risks because there are no put-downs	Students are given time to consider their responses and self-correct	Contributors are not interrupted. Each waits their turn	Opportunity for understanding is given to those who are slow to grasp a point or concept
Social support					Classroom members are not angry with or sarcastic towards a person who makes a mistake
Self-regulation	Gives clear reasons for directions Behaviour self-regulatory	There are clear and consistent consequences for inappropriate behaviour for all classroom members	Inappropriate behaviour is addressed and solutions sought without condemnation of the individual	A teacher who notices an instance of inappropriate behaviour does not immediately jump to conclusions	All parties involved in an incident are given a fair and equal opportunity to explain their perspective
					A student is not labelled or stereotyped for any reason. All students are and feel accepted
Explicit criteria	Scaffold Unambiguous/clear information and instruction Clear indication of standards	Information and particularly instructions are clear, unambiguous and coherent for all students	Required standards are clearly conveyed to all students	Students, when directed, clearly understand the reasons for the direction	
		Lesson progresses in logical graduated steps	Lesson is presented in a manner that all students are able to access aspects of the knowledge according to their ability	Information in the lesson is presented in different ways, taking into consideration the different learning styles of students	Teacher is able to change the teaching style within and between lessons according to the needs of the students

(continued)

Table 10.4 (continued)

Items	Prophetic pedagogy	Features			
Engagement	Strategies to aid retention Varied techniques for emphasis Draws attention from outset Build the interest and attention Maintains focus and attention on the matter being taught	Teacher uses various techniques to aid retention and emphasis, for example word repetition, rhyme, contrasts and practical demonstration	Attention is drawn from the outset, for example by rhetorical questions and raising curiosity by mentioning strange things beyond the reality of the listeners	Maintains interest, for example through stories, deliberately incomplete information that begs clarification, silence and questioning	Positive emphasis is the norm but negative consequences of certain actions are occasionally given to show the enormity of particular behaviours	Maintains focus on the objectives of the lesson despite disruptions and distractions
Cultural knowledge	Relates to people's environment and experience Non-verbal strategies	Classroom members value others' life experiences	Classroom members value others' perspectives	Classroom members feel their circumstances are understood and given proper consideration		
Inclusivity	Respect for others Humility Addresses students according to the ability of the listener	All classroom members feel comfortable to take risks because there are no put-downs	Classroom input is presented without ostentation while counter-arguments and discussions are conducted calmly, addressing the issues and not the individual	All classroom members feel they may contribute if they wish to do so	A person's silence or deference to another's knowledge is respected	If a lack of respect is displayed by an individual he or she immediately acknowledges it and apologises where appropriate

Narrative	Teaches by examples	Structure of the stories facilitates understanding even if some aspects are outside the direct experience of the listeners		
		Stories of previous peoples are used to illustrate relevant points for the listeners. This permits sensitive issues to be dealt with more explicitly		
Group identity	Good expectations and interpretation of others' behaviour	Classroom members value others' life experiences	Classroom members feel their circumstances are understood and given proper consideration	
	Teaches by example	Classroom members value others' perspectives	Classroom members listen to each other's concerns	Practical solutions are sought for classroom issues through class discussion
	Concern for the welfare of the individual			
	Just to all people			

column gives the items/parts of each of those dimensions. The third column is the alignment of these items to the elements and descriptors of PPF. In Table 10.4 the first and second columns are exactly the same as the second, and third columns of Table 10.3.

However, it is the critical questions from Table 10.3 and the features from Table 10.4 when considered together inform and give tools for teachers in the design and evaluation process. When planning, the critical question directs teacher consideration to the techniques, strategies and activities that will facilitate the manifestation of the features described. When evaluating, the critical question and features should be used positively in assessing what has been achieved and what further improvements are required. A process necessarily both continuous and organic.

Conclusion

The efforts of various community members over the decades to establish Islamic schools should be, and indeed are, appreciated. In saying this, it is important for those currently involved in the education of our future generations to keep in mind the words of Umar (may Allah be pleased with him) from Ja'far Al-Zubraqaan. It reached me that Umar wrote a letter to some of the officials and at the end of the letter was written: "take account of yourself in ease before the difficult account (that is the day of resurrection)" (Hayatus-Sahabah 3:442). In order for evaluation to occur, processes, procedures and frameworks need to be in place to enable the ongoing renewal of practices both within and outside the classroom. This renewal of Islamic schools should take place in the light of research embedded in an Islamic worldview of education and pedagogy. These processes, procedures and frameworks can then enable a common discourse and a shared vision for all members of an Islamic school community and enhanced learning outcomes for our students.

Notes

1. Wise, A. & Ali, J. (2008) *Muslim Australians and Local Government*. Final Research Report for the Centre for Research and Social Inclusion 22 April 2008. Retrieved 17 June 2009, from http://www.immi.gov.au/media/publications/multicultural/grassroots/, 14.
2. Wise and Ali. *Muslim Australians and Local Governments*, 11.
3. Wise and Ali. *Muslim Australians and Local Governments*, 14.

4. Wise and Ali. *Muslim Australians and Local Governments*, 14–15.
5. Gross, Z. & Rutland, S.D. (2014) Intergenerational Challenges in Australian Jewish School Education. *Religious Education* 109(2), 143–161.
6. Tsounis, M.P. (1975) Greek Ethnic Schools in Australia. *The International Migration Review* 9(3), 345–359.
7. Clyne Donohoue, I. (2000) *The Struggle of Muslims to Educate Their Children in Australia*. PhD Thesis, University of Melbourne. Retrieved 18 May 2009, from University of Melbourne Library.
8. Merry, M.S. & Driessen, G. (2005) Islamic Schools in Three Countries: Policy and Procedure. *Comparative Education* 41(4), 411–432 and Parker-Jenkins, Marie. (2002) Equal Access to State Funding: The Case of Muslim Schools in Britain. *Race Ethnicity and Education* 5(3), 273–289.
9. Culture in this article is understood as defined by the Cambridge online dictionary, accessed 29 September 2016: the way of life, especially the general customs and beliefs, of a particular group of people at a particular time.
10. Abd-Allah, U.F. (2006) Islam and the Cultural Imperative. *Cross Currents* 56(3), 357–375.
11. Murad, Abdul Hakim (aka Timothy Winter) (1997). *British and Muslim?* Retrieved 25 May 2008, from http://www.masud.co.uk/ISLAM/ahm/british.htm, 6.
12. Limits or boundaries set by the Shari'ah: The knowledge of the practical religious laws (divine) as derived from their detailed sources.
13. Abu Rayya, M.H., Walker, R., White, F.A. & Abu Rayya, H.M. (2016) Cultural Identification and Religious Identification Contribute Differentially to the Adaption of Australian Adolescent Muslims. *International Journal of Intercultural Relations* 54, 21–33.
14. Watson, K. & Chen, X. (2008). Preserving Cultural Heritage: An Australian Islamic Perspective. *Pacific Asian Education* 20(1), 33–46.
15. Pedagogy can be conceived as encompassing the underlying philosophy and worldview of education, informing the creative and intuitive use of strategies and techniques by the teacher to facilitate the students' knowing, understanding, thinking and being.
16. Boyle, H.N. (2002, March 6–9) *The Growth* of Qur'anic *Schooling and the Marginalization of Islamic Pedagogy*. Paper presented at the Annual meeting of the Comparative and International Education Society. Retrieved 27 April 2007, from Proquest database.
17. Sabki, A.A. & Hardaker, G. (2013) The Madrasah Concept of Islamic Pedagogy. *Educational Review* 65(3), 342–356.
18. Clyne Donohoue, I. (2000) *The Struggle of Muslims to Educate Their Children in Australia*. PhD Theses University of Melbourne. Retrieved 18 May 2009, from University of Melbourne Library.

19. Clyne, *The Struggle of Muslims to Educate Their Children in Australia*, 199–200.
20. Sanjakdar, F. (2011) *Living Islam in the West, Counterpoints: Living West, Facing East: The (De)Construction of Muslim Youth Sexual Identities* 364, 22–46.
21. Guerriero, S. (2014) *Teacher's Pedagogical Knowledge and the Teaching Profession: Background Report and Project Objectives*, OECD Better Policies for Better Lives.
22. Zammit, K., Sinclair, C., Cole, B., Singh, M., Costley, D., Brown a'Court, L. & Rushton, K. (2007) *Teaching and Leading for Australian Schools—A Review and Synthesis of Research-Based Knowledge University of Western Sydney*.
23. It is important to note that no aspect of a Muslim's life is untouched by religion (Halstead 2004), not in the overt prescription of every detail of human activity by Shari'ah, but to the extent that the value of any act completed or not depends on the intention. This is based on the Prophetic saying: 'Indeed actions are based on intentions, and each person receives according to their intent' (An-Nawawi Hadith 1:9). The source of guidelines for this knowledge and action is the Qur'an (2:2, 6:155, 32:3).
24. A narration about an action or saying of the Prophet. It also refers to the whole body of these narrations and the life of the Prophet Muhammad (may peace and blessing be upon him) as a model for humanity. Aisha (may Allah be pleased with her) (The Prophet's wife) was asked about the character of the Prophet, to which she replied, 'have you not read the *Qur'an*? I said, 'yes' she then said, 'His character was the *Qur'an* (the embodiment of the *Qur'an*)', (Kandhalawi 1999 *Hadith* No. 2406) 'in the messenger of God you have an excellent model' (Qur'an 33:21), 'for this we have sent a messenger to you from amongst you reciting to you Our signs, purifying you, teaching you the Book and wisdom and teaching you what you previously did not know' (Qur'an 2:151).
25. An Islamic worldview is characterised by an authenticity and a finality that points to what is ultimate, and it projects a view of reality and truth that encompasses existence and life altogether in total perspective whose fundamental elements are permanently established (that is, constructed around Islamic beliefs about creation, existence, purpose and destiny) (Al-Attas 2005).
26. Although the extent to which the term 'Islamic' applies to the public education systems of these countries today is questionable, the terminology at least has some basis in Islam.
27. The root verb *'alima* encompasses a sense of knowledge, as does another trilateral verbal root, *'arifa*. However, an examination of the derivative shows a divergence in meaning: for *'alima*, there is *'allama* to teach, *t'allama* to learn, *a'lama* to let know and *ist'alama* to inquire, and for

'arifa; *'arrafa* to inform, to introduce, *ta'arrafa* to become acquainted with, to explore, to uncover, *ta'aarafa* to come to know, *i'tarafa* to confess, to acknowledge and hence *'ilm*, a noun derived from *'alima*, is generally knowledge about something or someone, whereas *'irfaan* and *ma'rifah* verbal nouns derived from *'arifa*, imply a more intimate knowledge of someone or thing.

28. An-Nawawi, Imam (2003) *Riyadhus Salihiin* Cairo: Daarul hadith. 1000:303.
29. Al-Attas, S.M. (1980) *The Concept of Education in Islam*. Kuala Lumpur: Muslim Youth Movement of Malaysia (ABIM), 22.
30. This is supported by statements of the Prophet Muhammad (may peace and blessing be upon him), for example, 'My Lord disciplined me in the best manner' (*Hadith* cited by Alwan 2005:592), 'That a man raises up his child on good manners is better for him than giving a measure of grain in charity' (*Hadith* cited by Alwan 2005:619), 'A father has never given his child anything better than bringing him up on good manners' (*Hadith* cited by Alwan 2005:619).
31. Boyle, H.N. (2004) *Qur'anic Schools: Agents of Preservation and Change*. New York: Routledge Farmer, 15.
32. Boyle, *Quranic Schools*, 15.
33. Memon, N. (2007) *The Prophetic Standard, Paper presented at ISNA Education Forum 2007*, Rosemont Illinois. Retrieved 2 May 2009, from http://www.isna.net/programs/pages/previous-education-forum-papers.aspx, 3.
34. Famous Hadith narrated by Muslim from Umar ibnul Khattab (may Allah be pleased with him): While we were sitting one day with the Messenger of God (SAW) a man appeared who had very black hair, wore extremely white clothes. No traces of a travelling were visible on him but none of us knew him. He sat on his knees with hands on his thighs and his knees touching the knees of the Prophet (SAW). He said, O Muhammad (SAW), inform me about Islam. The Messenger of God said, to bear witness that there is no god except God and that Muhammad is the Messenger of God, to establish *salah* (the five daily prayers), to give *zakat* (the compulsory charity for those fulfilling the conditions to pay), to fast the month of *Ramadan*, to make *hajj* (pilgrimage) to the house if you are able to undergo the journey. He said you have told the truth. We were surprised at him asking and then confirming the answer. Inform me about *Iman* (faith). He said, to believe in God, His angels, His books, His messengers, the last day and in fate its good and its evil. He said you have told the truth. He said inform me about *Ihsan* (see note 36). He said, to worship God as if you see Him, for though you cannot see Him yet He sees you. He said inform me about the Hour. He said, the one questioned knows no more that the questioner. So inform me about its signs. He said; that a slave girl will give birth to her

mistress, that you will see the barefooted, naked, destitute sheep herders vying one with another in raising lofty buildings. He then left. I waited a while and then he said, O Umar, do you know who was the questioner? I said, God and His Messenger know best. He said that was Jibril who came to teach you your religion.

35. The word *Ihsan* is derived from the verbal root *hasuna* encompassing a meaning of being beautiful and good. The verb *ahsana* from which *Ihsan* is derived encompasses the root meaning of doing or causing good.
36. Memon, *The Prophetic Standard*, 6–7.
37. The word *ma'rifah* is used in this chapter, rather than gnosis, as it better encompasses all the nuances of the Islamic concept.
38. *Adab* is right action that springs from self-discipline founded upon knowledge whose source is wisdom (Al-Attas 2001:16).
39. Memon, *The Prophetic Standard*, 7.
40. Memon, *The Prophetic Standard*, 7.
41. Memon, *The Prophetic Standard*.
42. Memon, *The Prophetic Standard*, 12–13.
43. Originally proposed by Abdul Hakim Murad (Memon 2007: 12).
44. Memon, N. & Ahmed, Q. (2006) *The Pedagogical Divide: Toward an Islamic Pedagogy*. Paper presented at ISNA Education Forum 2006 Rosemont Illinois. Retrieved 2 May 2009, from http://www.isna.net/programs/pages/previous-education-forum-papers.aspx, 2.
45. Memon, *The Prophetic Standard*.
46. Abu Ghuddah, A. (1996) *Al-Rasool Al-Muallim*. Beirut: Maktabatul Matbuaat Al Islamiyyah.
47. Urquhart, C. (2001) *An Encounter with Grounded Theory: Tackling the Practical and Philosophical Issues in E. Trauth* (ed.), Qualitative Research in Information Systems: Ideas and Trends (pp. 104–140). London: Idea Group Publishing, 107.
48. Ryan, G.W. & Bernard, H.R. (2000) *Data Management and Analysis Methods*. In N.K. Denzin & Y.S. Lincoln (Eds.), Handbook of Qualitative Research (2nd Edition, pp. 769–802) Thousand Oaks: Sage Publications Inc., 782–83.
49. These include but are not limited to:
    1. Sahih al Bukhari collected by Imam Bukhari (d. 870)
    2. Sahih Muslim collected by Muslim b. al-Hajjaj (d. 875)
    3. Sunan Nasa'i collected by an-Nasa'i (d. 915)
    4. Sunan Abu Dawood collected by Abu Dawood (d. 888)
    5. Jami at-Tirmidhi collected by al-Tirmidhi (d. 892)
    6. Sunan ibn Majah collected by Ibn Majah (d. 887)

50. Ali, S.B. (2003) *Scholars of Hadith*. Skokie: IQRA' International Educational Foundation, 37.
51. Kamali, M.H. (2005) *A Textbook of Hadith Studies*. Markfield: The Islamic Foundation, 42.
52. Ali, *Scholars of Haddith*, 104.
53. A large area in modern-day Saudi Arabia around Riyadh.
54. Sabki, A.A. & Hardaker, G. (2013) The Madrasah Concept of Islamic Pedagogy. *Educational Review* 65(3), 342–356.
55. Boyle, H.N. (2004) *Qur'anic Schools: Agents of Preservation and Change*. New York: Routledge Farmer.
56. The Arabic word *Sunnah* lexically means 'road' or 'practice'. In the language of the Prophet and the Companions it denotes the whole lawful practices followed in the Religion (*din*).

    In its technical sense *sunnah* has three meanings. In Hadith terminology it denotes any saying, action, approval or attribute, whether physical or moral, ascribed to the Prophet.

    In the terminology of *usul al-fiqh* or principles of jurisprudence, *sunnah* denotes a saying, action or approval related from the Prophet or issuing from him other than the Qur'an.

    In the terminology of *fiqh* or jurisprudence, *sunnah* denotes whatever is firmly established as called for in the Religion on the basis of a legal proof but without being obligatory.
57. This framework was developed from the Queensland School Reform Longitudinal Study (QSRLS) which is one of largest classroom-based research projects ever undertaken in Australia. The study was commissioned by Education Queensland, and commenced in 1997 with the submission of the final report in 2001. The QSRLS observational data led to the four dimensions of the productive pedagogies framework, which has been taken up widely in Australia and internationally as both a research tool and a metalanguage for critical teacher reflection (Mills et al. 2009). Productive pedagogies was adopted by Education Queensland in 2001.

Bibliography

Abd-Allah, U.F. "Islam and the Cultural Imperative." *Crosscurrents* 56, no. 3 (2006), 357–375.

Abu Ghuddah, A. *Al-Rasool Al-Muallim*. Beirut: Maktabatul Matbuaat Al Islamiyyah, 1996.

Abu Rayya, M.H., R. Walker, F.A. White, and H.M. Abu Rayya. "Cultural Identification and Religious Identification Contribute Differentially to the Adaption of Australian Adolescent Muslims." *International Journal of Intercultural Relations* 54 (2016), 21–33.

Al-Attas, S.M. *Islam and Secularism*. Kuala Lumpur: Muslim Youth Movement of Malaysia (ABIM), 1976.

———. *The Concept of Education in Islam*. Kuala Lumpur: Muslim Youth Movement of Malaysia (ABIM), 1980.

———. *Prolegomena to the Metaphysics of Islam*. Lahore: Suhail Academy, 2001.

———. "Islamic Philosophy: An Introduction." *Journal of Islamic Philosophy* 1, no. 1 (2005), 12–52.

Ali, S.B. *Scholars of Hadith*. Skokie: IQRA' International Educational Foundation, 2003.

Al-Nabahani, Y.I. *Wasaail al-Wusuul ila Shamaail al-Rasuul*. Jeddah: Dar Al-Minhaj 2004.

Alwan, A.N. *Tarbiyatul Aulaad fil Islam*. Cairo: Dar Al-Salaam, 2005.

An-Nawawi, Imam. *Riyadhus Salihiin*. Cairo: Daarul hadith, 2003.

Boyle, H.N. *The Growth of Qur'anic Schooling and the Marginalization of Islamic Pedagogy*. Paper presented at the Annual Meeting of the Comparative and International Education Society, 2002. Accessed 27 April 2007, from Proquest database, March 6–9.

———. *Qur'anic Schools: Agents of Preservation and Change*. New York: Routledge Farmer, 2004.

Buckingham, J. "The Rise of Religious Schools in Australia (Centre for Independent Studies (Australia)." *Policy Monograph* 111, 16 September 2010.

Clyne Donohoue, I. *The Struggle of Muslims to Educate Their Children in Australia*. PhD Theses, University of Melbourne. Retrieved 18 May 2009, from University of Melbourne Library, 2000.

Driessen, G.W., and J.J. Bezemer. "Background and Achievement Levels of Islamic Schools in the Netherlands: Are the Reservations Justified?" *Race Ethnicity and Education* 2, no. 2 (1999), 235–256.

Driessen, G., and M.S. Merry. "Islamic Schools in the Netherlands: Expansion or Marginalization." *Interchange* 37, no. 3 (2006), 201–223.

Du Pasquier, R. *Unveiling Islam*. Trans. T.J. Winter. Cambridge: The Islamic Texts Society, 2002.

Education Queensland. *Productive Pedagogies*, 2001. Accessed 23 September 2009. http://education.qld.gov.au/curriculum/learning/teaching/technology/pedagogy/index.html.

Glaser, B.G. *Theoretical Sensitivity: Advances in the Methodology of Grounded Theory*. Mill Valley: Sociology Press, 1978.

Gross, Z., and S.D. Rutland. "Intergenerational Challenges in Australian Jewish School Education." *Religious Education* 109, no. 2 (2014), 143–161.

Guerriero, S. *Teacher's Pedagogical Knowledge and the Teaching Profession: Background Report and Project Objectives*. OECD Better Policies for Better Lives, 2014.

Halstead, Mark J. "An Islamic Concept of Education." *Comparative Education* 2, no. 4 (2004), 5–17.

Hayes, D., M. Mills, P. Christie, and B. Lingard. *Teachers and Schooling Making a Difference*. Crows Nest: Allen and Unwin, 2006.
Holloway, I. *A–Z of Qualitative Research in Healthcare* (2nd ed.). Chichester: Blackwell Publishing, 2008)
Kamali, M.H. *A Textbook of Hadith Studies*. Markfield: The Islamic Foundation, 2005.
Kandhalawi, M.Y. *Hayaatus Sahabah*. Beirut: Dar ibn Hazm, 1999.
Marley, D. *Muslim Schools Prove Stars of the Higher-Performing Faith Family*. News Article Published in The TES on 19 December 2008.
Meer, N. "Muslim Schools in Britain: Challenging Mobilisations or Logical Developments?" *Asia Pacific Journal of Education* 27, no. 1 (2007), 55–71.
Memon, N. *The Prophetic Standard*. Paper presented at ISNA Education Forum 2007, Rosemont Illinois, 2007. Accessed 2 May 2009. http://www.isna.net/programs/pages/previous-education-forum-papers.aspx.
Memon, N., and Q. Ahmed. *The Pedagogical Divide: Toward an Islamic Pedagogy*. Paper presented at ISNA Education Forum 2006 Rosemont Illinois, 2006. Accessed 2 May 2009. http://www.isna.net/programs/pages/previous-education-forum-papers.aspx.
Merry, M.S. "Advocacy and Involvement: The Role of Parents in Western Islamic Schools." *Religious Education* 100, no. 4 (2005), 374–385.
Merry, M.S., and G. Driessen. "Islamic Schools in Three Countries: Policy and Procedure." *Comparative Education* 41, no. 4 (2005), 411–432.
Mills, M., M. Goos, A. Keddie, E. Honan, D. Pendergast, R. Gilbert, K. Nichols, P. Renshaw, and T. Wright. "Productive Pedagogies: A Redefined Methodology for Analysing Quality Teacher Practice." *The Australian Educational Researcher* 36, no. 3 (2009), 67–87.
Moes, M. *Islamic Schools as Change Agents*. Paper presented at ISNA Education Forum 2006 Rosemont Illinois, 2006. Accessed 2 May 2009. http://www.isna.net/programs/pages/previous-education-forum-papers.aspx.
Murad, A. *The Essence of Islamic Education*. Recorded audio lecture. Ihya Productions, 2001.
Murad, Abdul Hakim (aka Timothy Winter). *British and Muslim?* 1997. Accessed 25 May 2008. http://www.masud.co.uk/ISLAM/ahm/british.htm.
Parker-Jenkins, Marie. "Equal Access to State Funding: The Case of Muslim schools in Britain." *Race Ethnicity and Education* 5, no. 3 (2002), 273–289.
Raihani, D. Gurr. "Parental Involvement in an Islamic School in Australia: An Exploratory Study." *Leading and Managing Journal* 16, no. 2 (2010), 62–76. Accessed 22 January 2017. http://www.alukah.net/sharia/0/53636/, http://pdf9.com/hadith-bukhari-6050.html; Accessed 18 January 2017. http://www.aitsl.edu.au/australian-professional-standards-for-teachers/standards/development/the-crucial-roles-of-the-teacher.
Ryan, G.W., and H.R. Bernard. "Data Management and Analysis Methods." In *Handbook of Qualitative Research*, ed. N.K. Denzin and Y.S. Lincoln (2nd ed.), 769–802. Thousand Oaks, CA: Sage, 2000.

Sabki, A.A., and G. Hardaker. "The Madrasah Concept of Islamic Pedagogy." *Educational Review* 65, no. 3 (2013), 342–356.

Sanjakdar, F. *Educating Muslim Children: A Study of the Hidden and Core Curriculum of an Islamic School*. University of Melbourne, 2001. Accessed 27 April 2009. https://www.aare.edu.au/01pap/san01187.htm.

———. "Living Islam in the West, Counterpoints." In *Living West, Facing East: The (De)Construction of Muslim Youth Sexual Identities*, ed. Fida Sanjakdar, vol. 364, 22–46. New York: Peter Lang, 2011.

Shadid, W.A.R., and P.Sj. Van Koningsveld. "Islamic Primary Schools." In *Islam in Dutch Society: Current Developments and Future Prospects*, ed. W.A.R. Shadid and P.Sj. Van Koningsveld, 107–123. Kampen: Kok Pharos Publishing House, 1992.

Tauhidi, D. *Tarbiyah Project in Depth*, 2001. Accessed 17 June 2009. www.4islamicschools.org/tarbiyah.htm.

Tsounis, M.P. "Greek Ethnic Schools in Australia." *The International Migration Review* 9, no. 3 (1975), 345–359.

Urquhart, C. "An Encounter with Grounded Theory: Tackling the Practical and Philosophical Issues." In *Qualitative Research in Information Systems: Ideas and Trends*, ed. E. Trauth, 104–140. London: Idea Group Publishing, 2001.

Walford, G. "Classification and Framing of the Curriculum in Evangelical Christian and Muslim Schools in England and The Netherlands." *Educational Studies* 28, no. 4 (2002), 403–419.

Watson, K., and X. Chen. "Preserving Cultural Heritage: An Australian Islamic Perspective." *Pacific Asian Education* 20, no. 1 (2008), 33–46.

Wise, A., and J. Ali. *Muslim Australians and Local Government*. Final Research Report for the Centre for Research and Social Inclusion, 22 April 2008. Accessed 17 June 2009. http://www.immi.gov.au/media/publications/multicultural/grassroots/.

Zammit, K., C. Sinclair, B. Cole, M. Singh, D. Costley, L. Brown a'Court, and K. Rushton. *Teaching and Leading for Australian Schools* (A Review and Synthesis of Research-Based Knowledge University of Western Sydney, 2007).

CHAPTER 11

Attaining the 'Islamic' in Islamic Schools

Abdullah Elleissy

INTRODUCTION

Being part of an Islamic school and teaching for nearly two decades, one has come to learn through many interactions with key stakeholders the various reasons and motives behind parents opting for Islamic schools for their children's education. However, irrespective of the reasons and motives, there is a dire need to revisit the whole notion of what the 'Islamic' entails, what it should look like and how it can be attained so that its interpretation is not left to the mercy of individuals, cultural practices or common understandings in isolation from the facts.

A sincere and genuine approach to analysing the notion of the 'Islamic' in contemporary Islamic schools compels us to go back in history and contemplate the prevalent norms and methodologies that were embraced by our predecessors who played a significant role in shaping the society as a whole and in reforming individuals. The role of Islamic institutions was never solely confined to imparting knowledge; rather, institutions were a platform and a vehicle for a complete and thorough process of self-purification and transformation.

A. Elleissy (✉)
Darul Ulum College of Victoria, Fawkner, VIC, Australia
e-mail: abelleissy@dulum.vic.edu.au

Unfortunately, for many decades Islam has been portrayed as a religion of mere ideologies and legal commandments, whereby many attempts have been made to isolate the notion of spirituality from the actual religion, when the core of this faith is primarily based upon spirituality. The purpose of spirituality is to deliver and nurture an internal capacity to see so that one is able to read the signs of Allah (God) and to acknowledge the true identity of servanthood.

Therefore, it is imperative for educators to study and analyse the driving forces behind the success of the many classical Islamic institutions that have existed since the very early days of Islamic scholarship, when 'spirituality' was an integral part of such institutions, starting from the era of the circles of knowledge that dominated the Prophet's mosque in Medina to the widespread circles in the mosques of Baghdad, Basra, Qayrawan, Qurtuba, the *kuttaab* (elementary schools) in Cairo and Damascus, to mention only a few.

Today, the vision and mission statements of Islamic schools will usually include elements pertaining to students' well-being, students' growth, fostering education in an Islamic environment or the like. One can argue that achieving such outcomes is purely dependent upon the level of religious awareness and the willingness of all stakeholders to pursue the intended mission and vision.

The Interconnectedness Between Sacred Knowledge and Spirituality

An ideal of paramount importance among traditional Muslim scholarly circles was that the role of imparting knowledge was considered to be a sacred task and a noble exercise, provided that this role was affiliated with the core element of 'spirituality'. This understanding was substantiated by the many Qur'anic verses and prophetic traditions which ascertain the virtue of such knowledge that reinforces the relationship between the creation and the Creator. Consequently, self-reform and spiritual growth were always considered to be the ultimate objective and the desired outcome of education. To illustrate this point, Allah the Almighty states:

> Is one who is devoutly obedient during periods of the night, prostrating and standing [in prayer], fearing the Hereafter and hoping for the mercy of his Lord, [like one who does not]? Say, Are those who know equal to those who do not know?[1]

Given that 'knowledge' is a fundamental prerequisite for any educator, this verse draws our attention to the ultimate definition and succinct description of the people of knowledge, they are those who are those 'devoutly obdeint during periods of the night, prostrating and standing [in prayer], fearing the Hereafter'.

Islamic schools tend to take pride in the number of Islamic Studies periods that have been allocated (which often are minima in anycase), or perhaps a sense of satisfaction prevails when they identify the variety of strands covered by a so-called Islamic curriculum. Nonetheless, that alone does not necessarily help render an individual being observant of Allah the Exalted in all walks of life, nor will it equip future generations with the ethical standards and values that are an integral part of our schools' vision and mission.

Based on my personal expierence with Islamic schools, it seems that we tend to adopt a fragmented approach whereby our understanding of the 'Islamic' in our institutions is limited to the text and the content of the literature to which we are exposed, or perhaps to the apparent dynamics of the school and the like.

There is a pressing need for Islamic schools to free themselves from the superficial confinements of cultural practices and norms which have been intertwined with religion, and to reach out to the higher objectives and spiritual teachings of the Divine.

Reflecting upon my personal experience as a child being educated in an Islamic school in Victoria, the Islamic discourse that we were exposed to as young Australian Muslims was, to a variable extent, disengaging, and unfortunately, little progress has been made in recent years. Religious instruction is mainly about the Islamic Studies period whereby narratives of the Prophet and his companions are put before the students as pure historical events. Basic jurisprudence is taught essentially as the 'dos and don'ts, without much insight into the rationale for these laws, which leads to the understanding that true faith should manifest itself in all walks of life, including our personal dealings, social lives, and all types of interactions. The subtle message that is conveyed through this approach is that the teachings of Islam are predominantly confined to the parameters of worship, whereby the manifestation of our religious identity only becomes evident by attending the daily prayers, by paying the annual *Zakaat*, by observing fasting during the month of Ramadan or perhaps when pilgrimage is performed.

Under no circumstance does this advocate for being less considerate towards the sciences of religious and legal commandments; as Ibn Ashur declares, 'we can attain categorical knowledge that the *Shari'ah* aims at the acquisition of what is good and beneficial and the rejection of what is evil and harmful'. However, he explains that the attainment and achievement of this goal is dependent on the level of righteousness because 'Islam addressed itself to purifying the human psyche and uplifting the human soul, since it is the inner person that actually motivates one to righteous deeds'.[2] This compliments the Prophet's saying:

> Beware! There is in the body a piece of flesh, if it is good (reformed), the whole body becomes good, but if it is spoilt, the whole body is spoilt, and that is the heart.[3]

This leads us to the identification and distinction between *Ibadah* (worship) and *Ubudiyyah* (servitude or servanthood), and hence the clear separation between the two. All too often, as observant parents or educators, we are mainly concerned with teaching our youngsters the content and the text, but on the other hand, minimal consideration—if any—is given to facilitating the notion of *Ubudiyyah*. *Ibadah*, otherwise known as pure acts of worship, is clearly distinct from *Ubudiyyah*. In order for one to enjoy the ultimate connection with the Creator, one must acknowledge the identity of being human, and 'to be fully human is to realise our perfect servitude and to remove the veil of separative existence through spiritual practice'.[4] It is virtually impossible to reap the benefits of worshipping the Creator unless and until we realise the nature of our relationship with our Lord, whereby we acknowledge our complete servanthood to Allah, and this is what *Ubudiyyah* implies. This is precisely what our predecessors and scholars denote when they ascertain that the ultimate purpose of education and knowledge in Islam is the *ma'rifa* (cognisance) of Allah The Exalted. For example, Allah says:

> Recite, [O Muhammad], what has been revealed to you of the Book and establish prayer. Indeed, prayer prohibits immorality and wrongdoing, and the remembrance of Allah is greater. And Allah knows that which you do.[5]

We deduce from this verse that acts of worship ought to have an impact on an individual; however, we may all know of examples whereby a given person is observant of the prayer on the one hand, but on the other hand, that same individual may be immersed in faults and wrongdoings. Although Allah's words affirm that prayer shall prohibit a person from engaging in immorality, when this act of worship is attended to in isolation from its spiritual elements, the effect of such worship is compromised.

A classic example of this is the prevalent situation among many of our Muslim youth who have on the one hand often been educated in Islamic schools or nurtured by the common values of Muslim families, and are therefore observant of rituals pertaining to the daily prayers. However, on the other hand, one questions how much impact their worship has had on their overall conduct and their ethical standards? A split in personality is quite obvious when we compare their conduct in the mosque with their contrasting behaviour in the real world.

The Primary Role of Classical Islamic Institutions

There is a clear distinction between the role of curricula and syllabi and that of self-reform and purification. The number of *kuttaab* (elementary and secondary schools), which Salahuddeen al-Ayoubi (Saladin, 1138–1193) established in the twelfth century along the outskirts of Damascus, testifies to the fact that the role of Islamic institutions was not confined to imparting knowledge alone. Rather, the employment of a holistic approach implied that the primary role of such institutions was to nurture God-fearing individuals who were observant of the rights of their Creator and the rights of fellow humans simultaneously.

Soon after the establishment of the *kuttaab* during Salahuddeen's era, huge numbers of students were attracted to these schools. In the meantime, the Crusaders had conquered neighbouring Palestine and were committing atrocities and bloodshed. Given the large number of students and followers of Salahuddeen, he was requested by some of his close advisors to lead his students to Palestine and confront the Crusaders in an attempt to put an end to their oppression and bloodshed. However, Salahuddeen realised that these students' mere presence in the *kuttaab* did not necessarily mean they were well equipped with the prerequisites of gaining victory. He spent many years and much effort nurturing the spiritual growth of his students, training them in fasting during the day, spending the nights prostrating before God, and eradicating the love of materialism and worldly affairs from their hearts through the various means and practices of self-reformation. After several years had passed, and when he was confident that his students had attained a level of closeness with God by which the temptations of this worldly life had become trivial in their eyes and of no value when compared with the love of Allah and his Messenger, only then did he decide to march towards the Crusaders to put an end to their atrocities.[6] Hence, self-reformation and purification were the decisive elements in their success.

Moving towards a more holistic approach, doing justice to the notion of the 'Islamic' in our existing Islamic schools may entail further examining the biography of Prophet Muhammad (peace be upon him) and that of his companions. In doing so, we will appreciate that devotion to the Messenger of Allah (peace be upon him), which arguably is a core aspect of attaining the 'Islamic', consists of more than mere obedience to him; rather, the source and foundation of all such obedience is a heartfelt love for him, without which there would be no inward motivation to obey him in action. Those who assume that love for the Messenger of God means nothing but obeying him and following his example are in error; such people fail to realise that in order to emulate someone, we must have some motive for doing so, and that without a heartfelt love that takes possession of one's emotions, such motivation will be lacking.[7]

In a Hadith narrated by Anas, the Prophet (peace be upon him) said:

> None of you will have faith till he loves me more than he loves his father, his children and all mankind.[8]

Such sincere and genuine love of the Prophet, which is a criterion of faith, was manifested in the lives of the companions throughout their history. For example, in the Battle of Raji, which took place in the third year after the Prophet's migration, a companion by the name of Zayd Ibn al-Duthunna was held captive. Safwan Ibn Umayyah purchased him and when he was taken outside the city precinct to be killed, Aby Sufyan questioned him: 'Zayd, would you not prefer that Muhammad is beheaded in your place, and that you be at home with your family?' Zayd's response was a testimony of his true faith: 'By Allah, I would not want Muhammad being where he is at this moment to endure so much as a thorn pricking him while I enjoy the comfort and company of my family!' Abu Sufyan responded, saying: 'Never in my life have I seen people who love someone as much as Muhammad's companions love him.'[9]

Muslims in general, and more specifically Islamic schools, are all yearning for this religious emotion to play its role in our lives and in those of our youngsters. Such emotions have been obscured to varying degrees for many reasons, some of which may include the employed methodology of teaching religion in the context of ideologies, the prevalence of materialism and the mere absence of the emphasis on the spiritual realm of Islam.

Furthermore, when we consider the standard of Islamic scholarship which prevailed in previous centuries, we see that self-reformation and purification took precedence over all other factors. For example, Imam Abu Hamid al-Ghazali (d. 1111), otherwise known as *Hujjat al-Islam*, Arabic for 'Proof of the Religion', due to his contributions to protecting the Muslim world from the intellectual challenges that were facing it during the eleventh century. When he had reached the pinnacle of his career as a gifted intellectual with no equivalent in the entire region, al-Ghazali experienced a spiritual crisis, during which he began to doubt his intentions in teaching. He stated in his autobiography that his original intention 'was not directly purely to God, but rather was instigated and motivated by the quest for fame and widespread prestige'.[10] Recognising his spiritual dilemma, he abandoned his post at the Nizamiyya, a highly reputable Islamic institution at the time, and travelled to Damascus, Jerusalem and Arabia. During his travels, he focused on *tazkiya* (purification) of his soul. His search for purification lasted nine or 10 years, most of which time he spent in Damascus under the minaret of the Ummayad mosque, writing his renowned book *Ihyaa Ulum Aldeen* ("The Revival of the Religious Sciences"). This work of Islamic literature delves into all aspects of purification and self-reform. From al-Ghazali's perspective, there was a need to revive the religious sciences despite the unmatched level of scholarship that was prevalent at the time, and that was only achievable through the process of reviving the spiritual foundations of Islam.

One may ask how a scholar of such calibre could abandon his position of teaching and spreading sacred knowledge for nearly a decade, solely for the sake of purifying himself, when he had actually been immersed in the process of teaching and preaching Islam *per se*. Al-Ghazali's answer to this is summarised in his renowned saying: 'We sought this knowledge for other than the sake of Allah. But knowledge refused that it should be sought only for the sake of Allah.'[11]

The Importance of Nurturing a Heartfelt Love Towards the Messenger of Allah Along with the Pursuit of Knowledge

Confining our role as religious educators to the task of imparting knowledge in isolation from the core spiritual aspects of this knowledge will only further expand the existing gap between factual information and application.

Tapping into the hearts of our young learners, and creating opportunities and environments for the love of Allah and his Prophet to penetrate their hearts, is key to them embracing religion holistically and as a way of life—which is a primary aim of education in Islam. Such love is instrumental in facilitating the concept of *Ubudiyyah*, in order for us to be equipped with the ability to translate the acquired knowledge and factual information into real-life experiences.

Unfortunately, some would argue that mere knowledge is sufficient to facilitate a process of religious reformation, and by doing so, we would attain the 'Islamic'; hence, there is no need to engage in this spiritual training. This is easily refuted, as there are countless examples in which the intellect has led individuals to belief in the One Creator, but their conduct and ethical standards were in total conflict with the prerequisites of faith. Allah has described this phenomenon in numerous verses:

> And they rejected them (referring to the signs of the Creator), while their [inner] selves were convinced thereof, out of injustice and haughtiness.[12]

In another verse Allah says:

> Truly, it's not these eyes which are blind, what is blind is the heart, which is inside the chest.[13]

Hence, and from an Islamic worldview perspective, our hearts, which primarily dictate our emotions, play a considerable role in shaping our identity and our sense of being conscious of God or otherwise.

Scholars have addressed this issue at length, concluding that the reason for such contradiction between the logic of the mind and the actual conduct of a person is the fact that the intellect is not the main factor that influences a given person's acts. Rather, there are other instrumental factors that influence our conduct, most importantly the ego, emotions and the surrounding environment.

The Role of the Surrounding Environment

When we engage in a discourse pertaining to the existence of the 'Islamic' in our schools and how the 'Islamic' should manifest itself, we cannot be oblivious to nor unconcerned with the role that friendships and environments have in shaping students and young adolescents.

An interesting observation that has been made by several colleagues at Darul Ulum College of Victoria (where I teach) is how vulnerable our youth are in terms of peer pressure and the influence of the surrounding environment. With the support of the college's Student Well-being Department along with contributions from the Student Representative Council, the college has recently embarked on a mentoring programme whereby students who have displayed concerning behaviours are assigned to mentors who engage with them on a one-to-one basis. Despite the programme being in its infancy, the outcomes have been striking. Members of the college's Discipline Committee concluded that this process was much more effective and powerful in delivering the desired reformative outcome in comparison with the college's Discipline Policy, which is predominantly based on a punitive approach. Indeed, a mentoring programme of this type is considerably time consuming and demanding, but given the college's philosophy, the programme has gained the full support of the administration.

Interestingly, we ought to recognise that this approach was of considerable importance to our traditional scholars and the *Murabbeen* (spiritual mentors), who were mindful and vigilant of the role of companionship and its impact on individuals. For this very reason, the renowned scholar Ibn 'Ata'illah states in one of his maxims: 'Do not keep company with anyone whose inner state does not inspire you and whose speech does not lead you to God.'[14]

How often do we talk about inspiring our students and making a difference in their lives?! When the conduct of the righteous and observant individual attracts the mercy and blessings of Allah, such blessings will inevitably spread to the surrounding environment and find a place in the hearts of those in their company. In the context of Islamic schools, this puts the onus upon educators and administrators to hold themselves to the higher orders of spiritual reformation, as that is the fundamental prerequisite for genuinely nurturing and promoting righteous individuals and observant citizens. This concept is substantiated by the Prophet's words:

> The example of a good companion (who sits with you) in comparison with a bad one, is like that of the musk seller and the blacksmith's bellows (or furnace); from the first you would either buy musk or enjoy its good smell while the bellows would either burn your clothes or your house, or you get a bad nasty smell thereof.[15]

Islamic schools may need to consider the integration of ongoing spiritual development sessions and religious retreats aimed at inspiring zeal and passion among staff members and the school community alike, without which attaining the 'Islamic' in its true and actual sense may well remain beyond reach.

In addition to such in-house schemes or frameworks, it is also imperative to bring parents and the broader school community on board through a similar framework which targets the notion of the 'Islamic' and aims at reviving the concepts of spirituality and ethical standards in order for them to also play a constructive role in supporting the institution's vision and mission.

Conclusions

One can only appreciate the strong sense of responsibility that has been bestowed upon us when we claim that we are facilitating an Islamic institution, or when we make assertions that we are nurturing students in Islamic environments. The notion of the 'Islamic' cannot be based on a school's dress code nor can it be restricted to eloquent vision and mission statements. The 'Islamic' is not an outcome of the content being taught nor the immaculate resources and facilities on offer. A holistic and comprehensive approach may mean that as Islamic institutions we ought to exert more time and effort in reviving the spiritual realm of Islam on all fronts, and making it an integral part of our medium of instruction and interaction. In doing so, we ask Allah the Almighty to equip our future generations with the vital skills and qualities needed to survive their life-long adventures and the influences of modern-day society. On a final note, it should be noted that our approach in establishing the 'Islamic' and in inculcating it must be ruled and guided by the blessed and wise words of our beloved Messenger (peace be upon him):

> *Kindness is not to be found in anything but that it adds to its beauty, and it is not withdrawn from anything but it makes it defective.*[16]

Notes

1. Qur'an 39:9.
2. Ibn Ashur, 2006, pp. 94–5.
3. Sahih Al-Bukhari, Hadith 49.
4. Nasr, 2007, p. 13.
5. Qur'an 29:45.
6. Al-Bouti, 1997, p. 204.
7. Al-Bouti, 2010, p. 245.
8. Sahih Al-Bukhari, Hadith 16.
9. Albouti, 2010, p. 323.
10. Al-Musleh, 2012, p. 117.
11. Al-Bouti, 1999, p. 94.
12. Qur'an 27:14.
13. Qur'an 22:46.
14. Ibn 'Ata'illah, 2014, p. 211.
15. Sahih Al-Bukhari, 2008, p. 164.
16. Sahih Muslim, 2008, p. 1131.

Bibliography

Abu Abdallah Muhammad bin Ismail Al-Bukhari. *Mawsuatul Hadeeth Alshreef.* Riyadh: Darussalam, 2008, 164.

Abul Hasan Muslim Ibn Al-Hajjaj. *Mawsuatul Hadeeth Alshreef.* Riyadh: Darussalam, 2008, 1131.

Al-Bouti, M.S.R. *Al-Jihad fi al-Islam (Strife in Islam).* Damascus: Dar Al-Fikr, 1997, 204.

———. *Shakhsiyat Istawqafatni (Personages Caught My Attention).* Damascus: Dar Al-Fikr, 1999, 94.

———. *The Jurisprudence of the Prophetic Biography & A Brief History of the Rightly Guided Caliphate.* Trans. R. Nancy. Damascus: Dar Al-Fikr, 2010, 323.

Al-Iskandari, I.A. *The Book of Wisdoms—Kitab Al-Hikam.* Trans. V. Danner. London: White Thread Press, 2014, 211.

Al-Musleh, M.A. *Al-Ghazali, The Islamic Reformer: An Evaluative Study of the Attempts of Imam Al-Ghazali at Islamic Reform.* Kuala Lumpur: IBT, 2012, 117.

Ibn Ashur, M.A. *Treatise on Maqasid al-Shari'ah.* Trans. M.E. El-Mesawi. USA–UK: The International Institute of Islamic Thought, 2006, 94–95.

Nasr, S.H. *The Garden of Truth.* New York: HarperCollins, 2007, 13.

The Holy Qur'an.

CHAPTER 12

The Importance of Islamic Studies from an Islamic Worldview in Australia

Ibrahima Diallo

INTRODUCTION

The 2016 census data indicated that the Australian Muslim population represented 2.6% of the total population and that Islam was the second-largest religion in the country after Christianity.[1] The Australian Muslim population is one of the most ethnically and linguistically diverse communities in the country: at the state level, for example, the 2006 census in Bankstown in Sydney showed that 53% of Muslims were born in Australia, while in a number of other densely populated areas of Sydney and Melbourne the number was between 40% and 50%.[2] At the national level, figures confirmed the trend: in 2011, 62% of Australian Muslims were born overseas, whereas only 38% were born in Australia. Of those born overseas, around 42% were of North African or Middle Eastern origin and more than 58% were from elsewhere, including 25% from South and Central Asia, 10% from Europe and 4% from sub-Saharan Africa. In all, the Muslim population comprises individuals from

I. Diallo (✉)
School of Education, University of South Australia,
Magill-Adelaide, SA, Australia
e-mail: Ibrahima.diallo@unisa.edu.au

© The Author(s) 2018
M. Abdalla et al. (eds.), *Islamic Schooling in the West*,
https://doi.org/10.1007/978-3-319-73612-9_12

183 different countries of origin.[3] Another important feature of the Australian Muslim population is its extreme linguistic diversity: the Muslim population speaks a range of languages, including Arabic, Urdu, Turkish, Persian and Bahasa Indonesia, to name just a few. Given Australia's secular and liberal policies and practices, the current national and international debate on Muslim integration, Islamic radicalisation and anti-Muslim political attitudes and rhetoric, one could easily assume that these may have negatively impacted on and dampened the religiosity of Australian Muslims. A case study conducted among sixty-one members of the Islamic community in Adelaide and Darwin found that Australian Muslims show strong attachment to studying Islamic studies in their Islamic community schools in order to develop an Islamic worldview. For this reason, Islamic educational institutions in general, and Islamic schools in particular, continue to gain traction in Australia. According to Raihani and Gurr, in 2010, there were thirty Islamic schools accommodating more than 15,000 students.[4] In parallel with Islamic schools, Islamic community schools contribute significantly to the provision of Islamic education services for Muslim community organisations and educators. According to Clyne, '"education which is religious" is the most important educational need in Australia because it is a more comprehensive term than religious education, for it includes a belief that education will be infused with both religious teaching and practice, in all areas of the curriculum and of life".[5] This chapter is about the ways in which Australian Muslims show their affiliation with an Islamic worldview through Islamic studies. The chapter is divided into three sections. First, it begins with a discussion of the foundations and principles of the Islamic worldview primarily constructed on Qur'anic revelation and Prophetic traditions. The second section examines the context within which Islamic education, in general, and Islamic education in Australia, in particular, operate. The context is marked, on the one hand, by the prevalence of secular and liberal ideologies, and on the other hand, by prejudices towards Islam and Muslims. The third section describes and analyses the data collected for the case study. In addition to providing details about the sample represented in this case study, this section discusses the ways in which Islamic studies contribute to the Islamic worldview of Australian Muslims.

Islamic Worldview: A Snapshot

To start this discussion on Islamic studies in pursuit of the Islamic worldview in Australia, it is essential to understand the meaning of the word Islam. Islam is an Arabic word which encompasses the trilateral Arabic root *s.l.m.* and its derivatives are the meanings of peace, security and surrender. Translated into English, Islam has two distinct but complementary meanings. The first meaning is *salima*, or 'peace', while the second meaning is *aslama*, which means 'to submit or to surrender'. In simple words, a Muslim can be defined as a peace-loving person 'who surrenders to God's will, and the religion and society are based on this act of surrendering to God (or Allah)'.[6] Islam, as theorised and practised across the Muslim world, is fundamentally constructed on the Qur'an which was revealed to the Prophet Muhammad (Peace Be Upon Him). For this reason, the Qur'an occupies an extraordinary place in the minds and hearts of many Muslims and is the cornerstone of the Islamic worldview. According to Guessoum, 'The Qur'an plays a central role in defining the beliefs, the lifestyle, and the worldview of Muslims'.[7] In short, the Islamic worldview can be said to hinge on the Qur'an, the Prophetic traditions (Sunnah and Hadith)[8] and Shari'ah (divine Islamic law).

These foundations of the Islamic worldview are grounded on key Islamic principles. For example, 'the Islamic Worldview reflects the Islamic *tawhidic* paradigm: doctrine of divine unity/oneness of God. It represents two primary sources of Islamic religious law, belief and practice with (Sunni) Islam.'[9] This *tawhidic* principle of the Islamic worldview is tied to the principle of *aqidah* (religious creed) which stipulates that Islamic religious teaching and injunctions (as opposed to our understanding or application of them) remain unalterable and are not negotiable. At the same time, the principle of *aqidah* emphasises that faith must always supersede rational or scientific argument. Faith remains central and all-encompassing, and must therefore be used as a framework for reasoning and interpreting facts and events. In other words, the principle of *aqidah* 'details what a Muslim should know, believe and inwardly understand about God and religion as prescribed by the Qur'an, and the Sunnah, the way of the Prophet Muhammad'.[10] However, in an Islamic worldview, critical thinking, critical study and rational knowledge (secular or not) are encouraged; but, as argued by Halstead, these are only permitted as long as they do not contradict Islamic teachings.[11] In other words, learning and analytical processes must follow the principle of *tafakkur*, that is, 'thinking in the perspective of the revelation of the Qur'an and the teachings of the Hadiths and accepting every single Islamic truth'.[12]

The Islamic worldview is also constructed on the principle of *al-haqiqa al-mutlaqa* (absoluteness or absolute truth) which emphasises the existence of one God only and one absolute ultimate truth. This principle can be related to the principle of *aqidah* in the sense that faith is paramount in analysing and understanding the world. Truth, like God, is singular, and therefore the *tawhidic* paradigm, discussed previously, must supersede it and must lead to one ultimate truth that cannot be challenged. However, as highlighted by Annalakshmi and Abeer, 'the *tawhidic* worldview of Islam is a metaphysical view that places God at the nucleus, and holds Him as the Ultimate Reality, making the inevitable result for everything in creation return to Him'.[13]

Another important principle of the Islamic worldview is the principle of *Allahu a'lam* (only God knows). This intersects with the principles discussed previously, and means only God knows. In other words, absolute knowledge is not attainable by a simple human being; it is the privilege of God alone to know the ultimate truth. According to Halstead, in the Islamic worldview, 'knowledge must be approached reverently and in humility, for there cannot be any "true" knowledge that is in conflict with religion and divine revelation, only ignorance'.[14] He supports this view by emphasising that 'the appropriate use of knowledge from a Muslim perspective is to help people to acknowledge God, to live in accordance with Islamic law and to fulfil the purposes of God's creation'.[15] By indicating that knowledge is a divine prerogative, the Islamic worldview frames the methods and 'lends the eyes' through which knowledge, which emanates from God, is to be accessed.

These important principles of the Islamic worldview have in return influenced and shaped Islamic education in terms of its philosophy, teaching practices and curricula, so that Islamic education is in tune with the Islamic worldview. Therefore, in Islamic education in general, 'Islam was at the center and served as an overarching epistemological and ethical framework'.[16] Islamic education must reflect and embody the Islamic worldview as 'religion must be at the heart of all education, acting as the glue which holds together the entire curriculum into an integrated whole'.[17] According to Barazangi, Islamic education contributes to the process of shaping character within the Islamic worldview as well as exposing the individual to all knowledge as a means of understanding and forming a constructive relationship with God, other humans and nature.[18]

The spread of the Islamic worldview, which initially started in informal settings (e.g., houses and other circles of learning), shifted to more formal settings (e.g., *masjids, qutubs, madrasas*, colleges and universities). In many Western counties, Islamic (community) schools remain the best-known options for the provision of education for an Islamic worldview. For example, Islamic (community) schools in Australia focus on Islamic studies (e.g., study of the Qur'an) for the development of an Islamic worldview. The next section examines the challenges of Islamic education in general in Australia.

CHALLENGING CONTEXT FOR ISLAMIC STUDIES IN AUSTRALIA

To understand the challenges of Islamic education, in general, and Islamic studies in Australian, in particular, it is crucial to understand the broad context within which Islamic education institutions operate. In Australia, for example, the context is marked by the prevalence of the Western worldview constructed on secular and liberal ideologies and prejudices towards Islam and Muslims.

SECULAR AND LIBERAL IDEOLOGIES

Islamic education in the West in general, and in Australia in particular, operates within a particular epistemological context governed by the Western worldview which can be said to be constructed on secular grounds, liberal and capitalist ideologies and atheistic influences. With the influence of positivist thinkers and the philosophers of European Enlightenment of the eighteenth century, Western political and social structures espoused secular worldviews. For example, in Australia, the Constitution stipulates that 'The Commonwealth shall not make any law for establishing any religion, or for imposing any religious observance, or for prohibiting the free exercise of any religion, and no religious test shall be required as a qualification for any office or public trust under the Commonwealth'. In many countries of Judaeo-Christian heritage, similar worldviews govern or influence the laws, policies and practices.[19] As a result, in the area of education, this secularisation has impacted the ways in which knowledge is posited and education policies are conceptualised, designed and implemented. For example, knowledge, which was previously in the exclusive domain of religion (or God), was 'freed' from the grip of religion and 'liberalised'. Knowledge became attainable and demonstrable to all, and anyone could access it by following coherent, sensible and rational approaches. This led to a host of new perspectives as secular knowledge developed its own rationale and methods of inquiry. Subsequently, from the perspective of the Western worldview, education shifted to become (in principle) secular—that is, a deliberate, individual, conscious and active process that leads to knowledge-building and fact-finding outside a religious framework. In the secular Western worldview, multiple interpretations and views are encouraged and accepted as part of the rational and critical thinking processes of learning, but outside of a religious context. Zaman characterises Western education in contrast with the Islamic worldview:

> Western education is secular in outlook, skirts around moral issues central to Islam, and denies the idea that God is an active agent in human history. It is also highly Eurocentric, taking the key events in human history to be the Industrial Revolution in England and the French revolution, for example. It is built on a materialistic philosophy, stressing the primacy of physical objects over intangibles such as values, ideals and morals.[20]

Prejudices Against Islam and Muslims

The second-most significant challenge for Islamic education in general in Australia and elsewhere in the West is prejudice against Islam and Muslims, which has taken a new turn since the 11 September 2001 attacks in the USA, followed by the bombings in Europe (Spain, France and the UK) and elsewhere in the world (Bali in Indonesia, Mumbai in India).[21] The context of Islamic education in the West became more challenging as terrorist attacks in Western countries continued and became more violent and organised, for example the recent attacks in Paris (in 2014 and 2015) and Nice (2016), Brussels (2016) and Orlando, Florida (2016). In Australia, domestic events such as the Sydney Lindt café siege, which resulted in two deaths in 2014, and the killing of a police employee by a 15-year-old boy in 2015, have contributed to intensifying anti-Muslim portrayals, namely in the media. According to Kabir, in Australia, 'some print media reports Muslims news with provocative headlines often associated with the images that showed Islam as a violent religions'.[22] She adds that the Australian media associates veiled Muslim women and Muslim men with terrorism, violence and fanaticism,[23] and correlates Islam with chaos, brutality and violence.[24] These negative views of Islam are captured by Wike and Grim in their study on the attitudes of non-Muslims in five Western nations, including Britain, France, Germany, Spain and the USA, based on a survey conducted in 2006. The study examined the predictors of negative views toward Muslims and found that 'the strong impact of security-related threat perceptions is clear. Worries about the threats posed by Islamic extremism are by far the strongest drivers of negative attitudes across the five countries studies.'[25] This study also found several other variables that directly impact security threats and therefore affect attitudes towards Muslims. Among others predictors, the study mentions 'cultural threats perception, cultural non-integration and religiosity'.[26] Wike and Grim conclude:

> Those who believe Islam is incompatible with modernity and/or democracy are more likely to have concerns about Islamic extremism, and are more likely to voice concerns about Muslim identity and assimilation. *Cultural Non-Integration*, in turn, has direct and strong effect on security concerns.[27]

As a consequence of negative attitudes and negative media reporting, to many people in the West, 'Islam has been portrayed as a religion that breeds terrorism, violence, and a global threat'[28] and Muslims as the negative 'others'.[29]

In this general context, Islamic education in the West is regularly in the spotlight and draws considerable attention and suspicion because:

> in the Western World, some politicians and commentators[30] have linked some aspects of IREC [Islamic religious education curriculum] and the emergence of extremist Islamic groups. They think that IREC in some schools has encouraged students to engage in violent actions, labelled 'jihad'; this is because the curriculum itself is based on an ideology of hate towards the unbelievers, that is, Christians, Jews, Hindus and so on.[31]

In a study on Muslim schools in secular societies, Shah indicates that 'Muslim schools are subjected to suspicions of being potential breeding grounds for future extremists (*The Economist* cited in Judge 2001) in spite of a lack of evidence of association between Islamic schools in general and terrorist activities'.[32] She adds that 'even though none of the 9/11 attackers studied in such schools, [Islamic schools] are alleged to be incubators of militants in Pakistan and responsible for creating communities of support for militancy in the regions'.[33] Besides, Islamic schools face significant resistance from the wider community because 'by providing a sense of identity and belonging to an alienated and vulnerable community in the current hostile political climate, *[Islamic schools]* are struggling against the very phenomenon of "home grown terrorists", while people involved in recent terrorist activities have mostly been educated in the mainstream institutions".[34]

In Australia, suspicions of Islamic education have led to violent reactions against Islamic educational institutions. In June 2016, anti-Muslim messages were written on the buildings of an Islamic school in Perth following the fire-bombing of a car outside the Thornlie mosque.[35] Prior to this incident, in 2014, another Islamic education centre in Perth was also vandalised and profanities and anti-Muslim messages sprayed-painted on the walls of these institutions.[36] Australian Islamic schools have also been in the news over concerns about their curricula being perceived as incompatible with Australian secular values, for example for scrapping music and arts classes, maintaining gender segregation, focusing on the Qur'an in science classes and forcing all female teachers (Muslim and non-Muslim) to wear the hijab.[37]

As can be seen, Islamic education in Western countries in general, and in Australia in particular, operates in a complex environment marked by differences and divergences in worldviews. While the Western worldview remains informed by secular and liberal ideologies, the Islamic worldview 'defines God as the Creator and law-giver and considers worship and service in His way as the very object of life' (At Attas 2001).[38] Besides differences on ideological grounds, Islamic education in the West and in Australia faces prejudices, including negative media portrayals of Muslims and Islam, and violent attacks against and suspicion toward Islamic educational institutions. The next section discusses the findings of the case study.

Research Method

This section first discusses the research method used to collect data for this case study; second, it briefly describes the socio-demographic background of the sample; and third, it analyses the findings of the case study.

Data Collection Tools and Research Sites

The participants in this case study included sixty-one participants from Darwin and Adelaide. Both cities are important symbols for Australian Muslims. Darwin was the first point of entry of Islam in Australia, with contact occurring between Muslim Indonesians and Indigenous Australians in the 1750s.[39] Adelaide is the site of the first and still existing major mosque in Australia, built in 1880. As for data collection, questionnaires (self-administered) and face-to-face interviews (tape-recorded) were used.

Socio-Linguistic Background of the Sample

The sample of the case study is diverse in terms of geographic distribution, gender and age of the participants. Among the sixty-one respondents who participated in the research, 55.74% were from Adelaide and 44.26% from Darwin. Of these respondents, 57.37% were female and 42.63% were male. The ages of the participants ranged from 15 to 60 and above, with the largest group, aged 15–18, representing 29.56% of the respondents. The second-largest group was aged 31–45 (27.86%), the third largest was 19–30 (24.59%), the fourth largest 46–60 (13.11%) and the fifth largest 60+ (4.88%). The respondents included Muslim students, teachers, religious leaders (e.g., Imams) and school and community leaders, and general members of the Muslim community.

Data Analysis and Discussion

The data analysis and discussion focus on the views of the members of the Islamic community on the importance of the provision of Islamic studies in their Islamic community schools. Islamic studies are defined here as studying the Qur'an (developing Qur'anic literacy) as well as learning the Arabic language. The respondents were asked to rate the importance of Islamic studies on a four-point scale ranging from 'Not at all' to 'Extremely important'. The respondents were also asked to provide reasons to support their answers. This section focuses only on the ways in which Australian Muslims show affiliation with the Islamic worldview by pursuing Islamic studies in their Islamic community school.

For example, the first respondent expects Islamic community schools to provide the essence of what it means to be a Muslim in addition to developing basic religious skills (e.g., prayers). This respondent indicates that

'*It is important to teach children to pray, to continue the good deeds and humanity worldwide. It's an asset.*' For this respondent, providing Islamic studies has two main purposes. The first is to teach children to be able to perform their basic religious duties (to pray), and the second is to teach children to '*continue the good deeds*'. For this respondent, these are important goals, indicating that to be Muslim is not just about religious 'performance' but also doing good things—that is, to change students' characters and behaviours so that they follow Qur'anic teachings and emulate the prophetic teachings and life(style), which is expected from each and every Muslim. This respondent adds a powerful and meaningful phrase to their answer. They use the phrase '*humanity worldwide*'. They also expect the '*good deeds*' of Islam learnt at the Islamic community school to be expanded to the whole world. They see the good deeds of Islam as universal—that is, not just for Muslims alone. Interestingly, the respondent thinks learning to pray and continuing the good deeds of Islam and sharing them worldwide is an '*asset*'—that is, something very positive.

The next respondent provides an answer that is similar to the one provided by the first respondent. They indicate that Islamic studies are important for '*passing on Islamic knowledge to kids that provides guidance and rules for how to live and act in the world*'. For this respondent, Islamic knowledge provides '*guidance*' and '*Islamic rules*' to children. It is not just about learning to pray and performing Islamic rituals, but also about acquiring the Islamic knowledge that '*guides*' and provides the '*rules*' expected of Muslims so that they know how to '*live*' and '*act*' in the world. These '*rules*' to '*live*' and '*act*' clearly indicate the importance of following the Islamic path outlined in Qur'anic teachings and traditions.

The next respondent mentions that Islamic studies are important because they teach '*the history of Islam, the Qur'an, all the things that are important for being Muslim people, make them good Muslim, Islamic values. The Muslim rules, we want them to follow that, we are following so we want our kids to follow those rules too.*' For this respondent, both the history of Islam and the Qur'an are important. They clearly allude to the rich and varied heritage and traditions of Islam which have made a significant contribution to the modern world, but also believe it is important to learn the Qur'an. As discussed previously, for Muslims the Qur'an is the most important and the most influential book that ever existed, a comprehensive book sent by God to address all issues faced by mankind, because it is 'flawless and a timeless book'.[40] The centrality of the Qur'an is also supported by Murata and Chittick who argued that, 'the text [the Qur'an] is undoubtedly one of the most extraordinary ever put down on paper' (1994, xiv, xix).[41] For the respondent, the history of Islam and the Qur'an are important as they define the Muslim identity (being a Muslim) and Muslimness (what makes a good Muslim). The respondent does not discuss Islamic values, but it can be assumed that these are Islamic values contained in the Qur'an. Therefore, a good Muslim is one who knows (and certainly practises) those Islamic values. The respondent also indicates that the Islamic community schools teach the Islamic *'rules'*. These rules, as the Islamic values, are not discussed by the respondent, but it can also be assumed that these are the rules that guide Muslims on what *'to do'* and what *'not to do'* and how to act in life in conformity with the Islamic worldview contained in Qur'anic teachings and prophetic traditions. Therefore, the respondent wants the children to follow these *'Muslim rules'* as they are themselves following them.

The next respondent mentions that Islamic studies are important in order

> to maintain two things for my children in the future, the Arabic language and the Islamic culture or heritage. We believe they nurture unique characteristics in a person's uh personality um and I don't want my children to miss out on that opportunity, living in Australia, that's a privilege, but at the same time I don't want them to lose the privileges I had as well when I was a child.

The respondent highlights two important things: they want their children to learn the Arabic language, and to study Islamic culture or heritage. This idea is similar to the one expressed by the previous respondent, in the sense that they are about learning the Arabic language in order to understand and access the Qur'an, and learning the Islamic culture or heritage to know about the history and the teaching of Islam. These are both essential for any Muslim in their quest for an Islamic worldview. Similarly, while the previous respondent focuses on the ways in which the history of Islam and the Qur'an makes good Muslims, this respondent indicates that these two elements (the Arabic language and learning the history of Islam) *'nurture unique characteristics in a person's personality'*.

In fact, albeit in different ways, both respondents emphasise the same point: developing the *'characteristics'* of being a good Muslim, which are gained by following Islamic teachings. For the latter respondent, these are *'unique characteristics'*, which means characteristics particular to Islam, as the respondent sees Islam as a special religion.

The respondent adds that they don't want their children '*to miss out on the opportunity*', which is the opportunity to possess the important and unique Islamic characteristics (character) nurtured in Islamic studies, especially in the Australian context which is dominated by secular policies and liberal and capitalist ideologies. Therefore, for this respondent, it is important not to deny their children the opportunity they had when they were a child. In fact, they indicate that learning and having these characteristics was a '*privilege*' and they want to extend that '*privilege*' to their children. The phrase '*privilege*' in this quote is interesting, as it (may) suggest(s) that for the respondent, being a Muslim (in a secular context?) is a privilege because they think Islam is special because it helps develop special characteristics.

The next respondent indicates that pursuing Islamic studies is important because one learns '*to understand the whole Quran, which tells you what happened in the past*'. This respondent highlights the centrality of studying the Qur'an for an Islamic worldview. They say that when you understand the whole Qur'an, you will know everything about the '*past*', which means the history of Islam. This echoes the ideas already mentioned by previous respondents regarding learning the Qur'an and knowledge of Islamic history, but emphasises the importance and symbolism of the Qur'an for Muslims as a comprehensive book that covers all aspects of life and knowledge, including history.

Another respondent mentions the importance of pursuing Islamic studies in order to '*learn the morals of all prophets and learn from them*'. This is interesting because the respondent talks about studying the '*morals*' of the prophets and learning from them. As already discussed, the Islamic worldview is primarily informed by the Qur'an, but also by Prophetic Hadiths and Sunnah. Therefore, for Muslims the lives of the prophets exemplify and embody the highest moral standards to emulate when it comes to Islamic behaviours and values. The prophets are the perfect role-models for Muslims.

The next respondent mentions the importance of pursuing Islamic studies in order to '*do what Allah asks you to do*'. This is a broad response, but to '*do*' means to follow the Islamic teachings outlined in the Qur'an and to emulate the prophetic traditions, which include, among other things, putting into action Islamic codes of behaviour and performing one's religious and Islamic duties in accordance with the Islamic worldview: '*to do*' therefore means to do what Allah asked Muslims to do—to follow Qur'anic teachings and prophetic traditions.

The last respondent, like most others, highlights the centrality of the Qur'an and the implementation of Qur'anic teachings by all Muslims. The respondent indicates:

> '*You can just call yourself a Muslim, no one will stop you, but if you want to become a real Muslim; know what Islam means; what Islam actually means; and you want to implement that in your life, then the Quran is essential, there is no way around it.*' They state that anyone is free to call themselves a Muslim and no one can stop them, which is a right of anyone, but to be a '*real*' Muslim is different. A '*real Muslim*' is one who implements Qur'anic teachings in their life. The use of the word '*real*' is important as this respondent wants to highlight the connection between being a '*real*' Muslim and the essentiality of the Qur'an. If you are a Muslim you must know the Qur'an because it teaches what it means to be a Muslim and it teaches what Islam is too: to be a Muslim, you must implement and embody the Islamic values and teachings contained in the Qur'an and follow prophetic traditions (Shari'ah and Sunnah) and the Shari'ah in your life. The respondent clearly indicates that being a Muslim is a way of life rather than a self-proclamation. Therefore, the Qur'an is essential; as the respondent puts it, '*there is no way around it*'.

Conclusion

The chapter is based on a limited sample of sixty-one Muslim participants in Adelaide and Darwin. It shows that Islamic education in the West, including Australia, is marked by serious challenges for Islam and Muslims. On the one hand, Islamic education operates in a secular context shaped by liberal and capitalist ideologies and atheistic influences, while on the other hand, Islam in general, and Muslims and their institutions in particular, are faced with negative attitudes and experience prejudice. For example, in Australia, Islam is subject to negative media portrayals and there is suspicion towards Islamic educational institutions. As a result, Islamic institutions such as Islamic schools have experienced violent attacks. Despite this challenging environment, Australian Muslims show affiliation with the Islamic worldview through the provision of Islamic studies in their Islamic community schools. Based on the responses they have provided to support their views of the importance of Islamic studies, Australian Muslims express a strong attachment to Islamic studies, which are the gateway to the Islamic worldview. In their responses, they also indicate that Islamic studies provide the knowledge needed for Islamic religious rituals and for implementing the Islamic values contained in the Qur'an: in particular, to put into action '*the good deeds*' and the '*values of Islam*', to emulate the '*morals*' of the prophets and to develop the '*unique characteristics*' of Islam. Equally important is that Islamic studies includes humanity and universality as highlighted by the respondents: '*It is important to teach children to pray, to continue the good deed and humanity worldwide*' and to '*provide ... guidance and rules for how to live and act in the world*'.

Notes

1. Australian Bureau of Statistics, "Religion in Australia".
2. Amanda Wise and Jan Ali, "Muslim Australians and Local Government. Grassroots strategies to improve relations between Muslim and non-Muslim-Australians. Final Research Report for the Centre for Research and Social Inclusion," accessed 17 June 2009. http://www.immi.gov.au/media/publications/multicultural/grassroots/.
3. Riaz Hassan, *Australian Muslims: A demographic, social and economic profile of Muslims in Australia* (Adelaide: International Centre for Muslim and non-Muslim understanding, 2015), 44–47.
4. Raihani Raihani and David Gurr, "Parental involvement in an Islamic school in Australia: An exploratory study," *Leading and Managing* 1, no. 16 (2010): 2.
5. Irene D. Clyne, "Educating Muslim children in Australia," in *Muslim Communities in Australia*, ed. Abdullah Saeed and Shahram Akbarzadeh (Sydney: UNSW Press, 2001), 119.
6. Mesut Akdere, Darlene Russ-Eft and Natalie Eft, "The Islamic worldview of Adult learning in the workplace: Surrendering to God," *Advances in Developing Human Resources* 8, no. 3 (2006): 355.
7. Nidhal Guessoum, "The Qur'an, science, and the (related) contemporary Muslim discourse," *Zygon* 43, no. 2 (2008): 413.
8. Sunnah and Hadith are the second-most important sources of Islamic authority for Muslims. They both refer to actions and sayings of the Prophet Muhammad who lived and acted in accordance with God's teachings and, therefore, He represents the perfect model for all Muslims.
9. Narayanan Annalakshmi and Mohammed Abeer, "Islamic worldview, religious personality and resilience among Muslim adolescent students in India," *Europe's Journal Psychology* 7, no. 4 (2011): 721.
10. Ibid., 721.
11. Mark J. Halstead, "An Islamic concept of education," *Comparative Education* 40, no. 4 (2004): 520.

12. Rida Blaik-Hourani, Ibrahima Diallo and Alia Said, "Teaching in the Arabian Gulf: Arguments for the deconstruction of the current educational model," in *Teaching and Learning in the Arab World*, ed. Christina Gitsaki (Berne: Peter Lang, 2011), 345.
13. Annalakshmi and Abeer, "Islamic worldview," 721.
14. Halstead, "An Islamic concept of education," 520.
15. Ibid., 520.
16. Sarfaroz Niyozov and Nadeem Memon, 'Islamic education and Islamization: Evolution of themes, continuities and new directions," *Journal of Muslim Minority Affairs* 31, no. 1 (2011): 13.
17. Halstead, "An Islamic concept of education," 525.
18. Nimat Hafez Barazangi, "Religious Education", in *Oxford Encyclopedia of the Modern Islamic World*, ed. John L. Esposito (New York: Oxford University Press, 1995), 2.
19. In France, for example, Article 1 of the 1958 Constitution mentions 'France shall be an indivisible, *secular*, democratic and social Republic. It shall ensure the equality of all citizens before the law, without distinction of origin, race or religion [...]' (emphasis added).
20. Asad Zaman, "Developing an Islamic world view: An essential component of an Islamic education," *Lahore Journal of Policy Studies* 1, no. 1 (2006): 95.
21. Prejudice against Muslims is not recent in the history of Australia. Australia's first Muslims, known as the 'Afghan cameelers', faced systemic prejudice under Australia's White policy.
22. Nahid Kabir, "Representation of Islam and Muslims in the Australian media, 2001–2005," *Journal of Muslim Minority Affairs* 26 (2006): 314.
23. Ibid., 315–6.
24. Ibid., 320.
25. Richard Wike and Brian J. Grim, "Western views towards Muslims: Evidence from a 2006 cross-national survey," *International Journal of Public Opinion Research* 22, no. 1 (2010): 16.
26. Ibid., 18.
27. Ibid.
28. Emad A. Algamdi, "The representation of Islam in Western media: The coverage of Norway terrorist Attacks," *International Journal of Applied Linguistics and English Literature* 4, no. 3 (2015): 198.
29. Ibid., 203.
30. Bergen, Peter, and Swati Pandey. "The Madrassa Scapegoat." *The Washington Quarterly* 29, no. 2 (2006): 115–125.
31. Hazem Rashed, "Towards a common ground: Arab versus Western views about the challenges of Islamic religious education curriculum of the twenty-first century," *Compare: A Journal of Comparative and International Education* 45, no. 6 (2015): 954.

32. Saeeda J.A. Shah, "Muslim schools in secular societies: Persistence or resistance!," *British Journal Religious Education* 34, no. 1 (2012): 60.
33. Ibid., 60.
34. Ibid.
35. David Weber and Nikki Roberts, "Perth Mosque attack: Car firebombed, anti-Muslim graffiti sprayed in 'act of hate'," accessed 10 November 2016. http://www.abc.net.au/news/2016-06-29/firebombing-ant-islam-graffiti-attack-at-thornlie-mosque-school/7552394.
36. Charlotte Hamlyn, "Perth Mosques, Islamic School Vandalised in Weekend Attacks," accessed 5 November 2016. http://www.abc.net.au/news/2014-10-20/mosques-islamic-school-vandalised-in-perth-weekend-graffiti/5827552.
37. Sharri Markson, "Islamic school Al-Faisal College 'has never had a child who is gay'," accessed 14 November 2016. http://www.theaustralian.com.au/national-affairs/education/islamic-school-alfaisal-college-has-neverhad-a-child-who-was-gay/news-story/a79078065cc974276c9c0f8a50144e19.
38. Annalakshmi and Abeer, "Islamic worldview," 721.
39. Hassan, "Australian Muslims," 44–47.
40. Amy Nelson, "The Surrendering: An Introduction to Islam," in *Five Voices, Five Faiths: An Interfaith Primer*, ed. Amanda Millay Hughes (Cambridge: Cowley, 2005), 100.
41. Sachiko Murata and William C. Chittick, "The Koran," in *The Vision of Islam*, ed. Sachiko Murata and William Chittick (Minnesota: Paragon House, 1994), xiv.

Bibliography

Akdere, Mesut, Darlene Russ-Eft, and Natalie Eft. "The Islamic Worldview of Adult Learning in the Workplace: Surrendering to God." *Advances in Developing Human Resources* 8, no. 3 (2006): 355–363.

Algamdi, Emad A. "The Representation of Islam in Western Media: the Coverage of Norway Terrorist Attacks." *International Journal of Applied Linguistics and English Literature* 4, no. 3 (2015): 198–204.

Annalakshmi, Narayanan, and Mohammed Abeer. "Islamic Worldview, Religious Personality and Resilience Among Muslim Adolescent Students in India." *Europe's Journal of Psychology* 7, no. 4 (2011): 716–738.

At Attas, Syed Muhammad N. *Prolegomena to the Metaphysics of Islam: An Exposition of the Fundamental Elements of the Worldview of Islam*. Kuala Lumpur: International Institute of Islamic of Thought and Civilization, 1995.

Australian Bureau of Statistics. "Religion in Australia". Accessed 25 July 2017. http://www.abs.gov.au/ausstats/abs@.nsf/Lookup/by%20Subject/2071.0~2016~Main%20Features~Religion%20Data%20Summary~25.

Barazangi, Nimat Hafez. "Religious Education." In *Oxford Encyclopedia of the Modern Islamic World*, ed. John L. Esposito, 406–411. New York: Oxford University Press, 1995.

Bergen, Peter, and Swati Pandey. "The Madrassa Scapegoat." *The Washington Quarterly* 29, no. 2 (2006): 117–125.

Blaik-Hourani, Rida, Ibrahima Diallo, and Alia Said. "Teaching in the Arabian Gulf: Arguments for the Deconstruction of the Current Educational Model." In *Teaching and Learning in the Arab World*, ed. Christina Gitsaki, 335–355. Berne: Peter Lang, 2011.

Clyne, Irene D. "Educating Muslim Children in Australia." In *Muslim Communities in Australia*, ed. Abdullah Saeed and Shahram Akbarzadeh, 116–137. Sydney: UNSW Press, 2001.

Guessoum, Nidhal. "The Qur'an, Science, and the (Related) Contemporary Muslim Discourse." *Zygon* 43, no. 2 (2008): 411–431.

Halstead, J. Mark. "An Islamic Concept of Education." *Comparative Education* 40, no. 4 (2004): 517–529.

Hamlyn, Charlotte. "Perth Mosques, Islamic School Vandalised in Weekend Attacks." 2014. Accessed 5 November 2016. http://www.abc.net.au/news/2014-10-20/mosques-islamic-school-vandalised-in-perth-weekend-graffiti/5827552.

Hassan, Riaz. *Australian Muslims: A Demographic, Social and Economic Profile of Muslims in Australia*. Adelaide: International Center for Muslim and Non-Muslim Understanding, 2015.

Judge, Harry. "Faith-Based Schools and State Funding: A Partial Argument." *Oxford Review of Education* 27, no. 4 (2001): 463–474.

Kabir, Nahid. "Representation of Islam and Muslims in the Australian Media, 2001–2005." *Journal of Muslim Minority Affairs* 26 (2006): 313–328.

Markson, Sharri. "Islamic School Al-Faisal College 'Has Never Had a Child Who Is Gay'." 2016. Accessed 14 November 2016. http://www.theaustralian.com.au/national-affairs/education/islamic-school-alfaisal-college-has-neverhad-a-child-who-was-gay/news-story/a79078065cc974276c9c0f8a50144e19.

Murata, Sachiko, and William C. Chittick. "The Koran." In *The Vision of Islam*, ed. Sachiko Murata and William Chittick, xiv–xxiv. Minnesota: Paragon House, 1994.

Nelson, Amy. "The Surrendering: An Introduction to Islam." In *Five Voices, Five Faiths: An Interfaith Primer*, ed. Amanda Millay Hughes, 93–116. Cambridge: Cowley, 2005.

Niyozov, Sarfaroz, and Nadeem Memon. "Islamic Education and Islamization: Evolution of Themes, Continuities and New Directions." *Journal of Muslim Minority Affairs* 31, no. 1 (2011): 5–30.

Peter Bergen and Swati Pandey, "The madrassa scapegoat," Washington Quaterly 29, no. 29 (2006): 115–125.

Raihani, Raihani, and David Gurr. "Parental Involvement in an Islamic School in Australia: An Exploratory Study." *Leading and Managing* 1, no. 16 (2010): 62–76.

Rashed, Hazem. "Towards a Common Ground: Arab Versus Western Views About the Challenges of Islamic Religious Education Curriculum of the Twenty-First Century." *Compare: A Journal of Comparative and International Education* 45, no. 6 (2015): 953–977.

Shah, Saeeda J.A. "Muslim Schools in Secular Societies: Persistence or Resistance!" *British Journal Religious Education* 34, no. 1 (2012): 51–65.

Weber, David, and Nikki Roberts. "Perth Mosque Attack: Car Firebombed, Anti-Muslim Graffiti Sprayed in 'Act of Hate'." 2016. Accessed 10 November 2016. http://www.abc.net.au/news/2016-06-29/firebombing-ant-islam-graffiti-attack-at-thornlie-mosque-school/7552394.

Wike, Richard, and Brian J. Grim. "Western Views Towards Muslims: Evidence from a 2006 Cross-National Survey." *International Journal of Public Opinion Research* 22, no. 1 (2010): 4–25.

Wise, Amanda, and Jan Ali. *Muslim Australians and Local Government. Grassroots Strategies to Improve Relations Between Muslim and Non-Muslim-Australians.* Final Research Report for the Centre for Research and Social Inclusion, 2008. Accessed 17 June 2009. http://www.immi.gov.au/media/publications/multicultural/grassroots/.

Zaman, Asad. "Developing an Islamic World View: An Essential Component of an Islamic Education." *Lahore Journal of Policy Studies* 1, no. 1 (2006): 95–108.

CHAPTER 13

Islamic Studies in Islamic Schools: Evidence-Based Renewal

Mohamad Abdalla

Introduction

A number of the chapters in this volume have outlined the extent of the growth of Islamic schools in the West and the reasons for their establishment. We now know that some of these reasons relate to Muslim parents' desire to pass on 'valuable cultural, linguistic and religious traditions to their children in overwhelmingly non-Muslim environments'.[1] In one of the few studies conducted on Muslim parents' expectations of Islamic schools in Australia, Donohoue Clyne[2] found that parents wanted an education that was 'religious, teaches them [students] appropriate behaviour, respects Islamic culture and values, fosters their Muslim identity, and provides the skills and knowledge for a good future'. Clearly, a major aim for the establishment of Islamic schools pertains to the preservation of the 'Islamic' in terms of religious matters such as faith and practices. However, despite this noble aim, and the obvious significance of Islamic studies (IS) as a key learning area or subject in Islamic schools, no empirical research exists

M. Abdalla (✉)
University of South Australia, Adelaide, SA, Australia
e-mail: Mohamad.abdalla@unisa.edu.au

to date that examines the nature, scope, effectiveness and relevance of IS as taught *within* 'Islamic' schools. To find reliable answers, we have attempted to *begin* the process of filling this gap. Hence, and for the first time, qualitative research methods were used to gather data from an Australian Islamic school to explore the strengths and weaknesses of IS, the challenges faced in the teaching and learning of IS and the attitudes of *students* toward the relevance and effectiveness of IS to their lives as young Australian Muslims. The aim here is *not* to draw generalised conclusions but to *facilitate* a path to renewal based on empirical research, which can help us understand the status quo of IS in the context of Islamic schools.[3]

WHAT DO WE KNOW ABOUT ISLAMIC STUDIES IN ISLAMIC SCHOOLS?

The simple answer is that we do not have *any* academic research on IS (at primary or senior levels, though our concern here is with the latter without underestimating the significance of the former) in Islamic schools in the Western context. Research typically examines the possible reasons for the establishment of Islamic schools in the West, and this is often summarised under two categories: to protect students' faith and Islamic identity, and to improve the quality of their education.[4] Research on Islamic schools in the United Kingdom has focused largely on issues of identity, citizenship[5] and the legitimacy of Islamic schools with reference to Muslims integrating and functioning in wider society, as well as curriculum and pedagogy with reference to religion.[6] Research in North America, the Netherlands[7] and Belgium[8] focuses on the progress of Islamic schools, their aims and objectives and their success in mediating between academic standards and faith requirements.[9] In the Australian context, the focus has been on parents' expectations of Islamic schools,[10] teacher education programmes, reasons for establishment[11] and what is taught at Islamic schools.[12] None of these studies, however, examines IS in Islamic schools.

Halstead,[13] who writes predominantly within the context of the United Kingdom, investigates Islamic education as a concept but does not explore the status quo of IS, or the pedagogical approaches to teaching IS in Islamic schools. He notes that *ethics* and *morality* form a substantial core of Islamic education, with the development of rational and righteous human beings as important ideals.[14] He argues that

Islamic education can be seen in terms of (1) aiding individual development, (2) increasing understanding of society and its social and moral rules and (3) transmitting knowledge (p. 522). Furthermore, Halstead (1995) informs us that teaching is 'almost a religious obligation' for the learned (*ulamā*) in Islam, and the teacher is often 'accountable to the community not only for transmitting knowledge and for developing their students' potential as rational beings, but also for initiating them into the moral, religious and spiritual values which the community cherished'.[15]

Douglass and Shaikh[16] note that Muslim educators in the United States believe students must learn to internalise principles and practices of Islam and must be taught how to apply these in contemporary Western society. Merry and Driessen[17] explain the biggest concern of critics towards Islamic schools is 'the ability of Islamic schools to prepare children to live in a multicultural society', and the ability (or lack thereof) to reflect critically on their own cultural and religious norms. They note there is 'much dispute over the manner in which Muslims are to express themselves *qua* Muslims in a western context' (pp. 412–13). Despite the intended ideals that Islamic schools aim to attain, research informs us that Islamic schools vary and 'operate according to different pedagogical goals and with varying levels of administrative efficiency'.[18]

Memon (2007) has made significant contributions to the field of Islamic education in the West but focuses on the significant area of Islamic pedagogy to realise the 'Islamic' spirit in Islamic education.[19] He argues that while aspects of Islam and *Iman* (faith) are taught (to some extent and to varying degrees) at Islamic schools, *Ihsan* (excellence in faith) has been neglected and that this needs to be lived, modelled and nurtured as part of the ethos of the school culture (p. 7) and needs to be exemplified by the teacher. He further argues that for Islamic schools to prepare their students for the real world, 'curriculum and assessment need to be embedded in an authentic Islamic pedagogy', and a 'shift in effort from revisiting curriculum initiatives to teacher training' will 'enable improvements in standards'.[20]

The little work that has been done on IS in Islamic schools reveals some interesting findings. Merry and Driessen (2005) found that in the Dutch experience, IS is 'generally confined to lessons in Qur'an recitation and formalities expressed as rules and codes imposed by the board on staff and students'.[21] Walford (2002) arrived at similar conclusions regarding the British context, stating that IS is 'confined in the main to formalities and the introduction of Islamic and Qur'anic studies as subjects merely appended to a standard public education curriculum'.[22] Moes (2006, p. 11) found that in North America the 'prioritisation of academic excellence results in Islamic faith requirements being addressed merely by the addition of decontextualized courses in Arabic, Qur'an memorisation and Islamic studies'.[23] The danger of this, argues Moes (2006), is that it possibly 'creates a situation where at best the classes produce factually knowledgeable students uncommitted to Islam and at worst students who turn away from Islam'.[24]

Shamma (2011) has written and contributed significantly in the area of curriculum and Islamic schools in the North American context. She points to two approaches to curriculum, one being a 'traditional' approach whereby a curriculum (in this instance a text) is developed for the subject of IS and the second approach being the integration of Islam and Islamic perspectives across the entire curriculum.[25] The latter, Shamma (2011) argues, is a long way away and dependent on schools coming together with partners (*Fi-sabeel-il-lah*) who are willing to undertake this task voluntarily, or as a common good at no charge or cost. In her article 'An Overview of Current Islamic Curricula', Shamma (2011) identifies a number of textbook series adopted in IS classes in the USA as well as internationally.[26] A textbook, however, no matter its quality, is on its own not a substitute for a comprehensive IS curriculum and the article supports the argument that no such curriculum exists for Islamic schools in the West. She also shares from her experience in the field anecdotally that students in IS classes find the didactic approach of being taught from a text boring, repetitive and lacking in thought, resulting in them 'turning off'. No empirical research, however, exists to substantiate the strengths or weaknesses of IS in the North American context or the attitudes, perspectives and experience of students in IS classes.

It is clear that while there is some literature relating to Islamic education and its function within Western educational frameworks, particularly the UK and the USA, the subject of IS in Islamic schools (in these countries and in Australia) has not formed the basis of research or studies in the literature thus far. As we have seen, existing research demonstrates that a major aim for the establishment of Islamic schools pertains to religious matters such as faith and practices. Therefore, it seems appropriate to examine the extent to which these schools fulfil this major aim. This investigation would require a landmark and large study, but until then it seems appropriate to examine the status quo of IS at some of these

Islamic schools and see the extent to which it meets the needs and aspirations of Australian Muslim students. To fill this significant gap, we have undertaken this research to find answers to the following questions:

1. What are the strengths and weaknesses of IS at Islamic schools?
2. What are some of the challenges faced by teachers of IS?
3. What are the attitudes of students toward the relevance and effectiveness of IS to their lives as young Australian Muslims?

Methodology: Research Design

This project utilised two qualitative data collection methods, focus groups and classroom observations. Focus groups allowed us to gain rich and insightful data. Semi-structured questions were prepared to guide the discussions into more robust themes. The questions targeted the strengths and weaknesses of IS; the challenges faced by teachers of IS; and the relevance and effectiveness of IS to the lives of young Australian Muslims. Classroom observations allowed us to gain an understanding of how curriculum enactment and pedagogical approaches influence the learning environment as well as drawing out deeper understandings of the research questions. Ajem and Memon's principles of Islamic pedagogy were used as a rubric or tool for classroom observations.[27]

Focus groups are particularly well suited for conducting research among minorities and other vulnerable populations.[28] Glesne and Peshkin (1992) suggest that group interviewing at times proves very useful for people who are reluctant to talk individually.[29] One of the distinct features of focus group interviews is group dynamics. Hence, the type and range of data generated through the social interaction of the group are often deeper and richer than those obtained from one-on-one interviews.[30]

Six focus groups were conducted over three days across three monthly visits, each of which involved intensive discussions. The facilitator mediated these discussions in addition to introducing the project and explaining the process involved. The role of the facilitator was to keep the discussion focused on the intended topic and to give equal weight to views and participation. Another important role of the facilitator was to interact with participants and make the sessions as engaging as possible and to add value to the programme during the sessions.

Selection of participants took place prior to the focus group session dates. Invitations went out to those participants who could provide rich data on the success, weaknesses and challenges faced by teachers and the relevance and effectiveness of IS, including coordinators (each year-level coordinator in the college, from primary to secondary), IS teachers and students. Student participants were selected by the Head of Islamic Studies, based on equal gender representation, diversity of background and the likelihood that the participant would be information rich. This selection added value to the discussion as participants had different backgrounds and different sources of knowledge.

Information (participant responses) was recoded using two voice-recording devices. The time of the focus groups was dependent on availability of participants across three separate monthly visits. The venue for the focus groups was carefully selected to ensure mixed-gendered sessions were both comfortable and appropriate as well as providing maximum serenity and tranquillity for uninterrupted discussion.

Complementing the focus groups were classroom observations. Classroom observations offered insights into the life-world of the classroom and the interactions therein. 'Prolonged engagement and extensive observation are central to gaining an in-depth understanding of a classroom.'[31] Fasse (1993) cautions that classroom observation can be labour intensive and emphasises patience as the emergent design and its results unfold.[32]

Data Collection

Each focus group session was guided by semi-structured questions (such as 'can you tell me about the strengths of Islamic studies?'). These questions related to common themes although they varied slightly in wording depending on the participants' relationship and engagement with IS at the college. Each focus group session lasted between one hour and one hour and a half, allowing ample time to address the questions.

Each classroom observation was guided by a rubric incorporating Ajem and Memon's (2011) principles of Islamic pedagogy. The rubric proved to be very intricate and can be considered a methodology-in-progress. The rubric responds to Memon's (2013) call for a reframing of excellence in Islamic schooling, in this case narrowed to excellence in the IS classroom. Islamic pedagogy defined here encompasses all elements of the process of education beginning with the aims of education, and then subsequently curriculum content and instructional strategies as shaped by overarching educational values. Put simply, the rubric provided a framework of the principles of education derived from the Islamic tradition that influence, inform and in this case explain and shed light on approaches to teaching and learning. Distilling this down to the classroom, the rubric added value because of its explanatory power encompassing the *how*, *what* and *why* of teaching.

Analysis of Data

The data from the focus group discussions were first transcribed and then *thematically* analysed.[33] Freeplane Software was used to facilitate this process, proving effective in identifying and highlighting categories and themes. Each category once defined served to organise data by themes. Procedure-wise, the Freeplane Software presented the data in mapping form. The common categories across all focus groups were then included in a Report Findings table.

Participants and Sample Size

The study involved sixty-six participants, but this chapter focuses on data collected from forty-four participants (we also interviewed parents and primary students, but their views are not included here). Ten coordinators, fifteen IS teachers and nineteen senior students participated in the study. All IS teachers and student participants were Muslim. Six of the ten coordinator participants were Muslim and four were not. Four secondary IS classroom observations were conducted (Year 9 girls' and Year 10, 11 and 12 mixed-gendered classes). The participants in both the focus groups and the classroom observations were extremely diverse in terms of cultural, ethnic and linguistic markers.

FINDINGS

The following tables capture the views of the coordinators of IS, staff and senior IS students in terms of strengths of IS, the weaknesses of IS and the challenges faced in teaching IS, followed by their recommendations on how to improve the teaching and learning of IS.

Table 13.1 Views of coordinators of IS

Strengths

IS teachers	• Good mix of teachers
	• Very knowledgeable/very passionate/very enthusiastic
	• Share common beliefs and worldviews
Students	• Very passionate about Islam/love Islam
	• Curious about Islamic issues
	• Want to discuss contemporary topics
	• Want Islamic answers to problems in life
	• Want to know how IS topics relate to them
	• Willing to change/Islamic consciousness waking up from start of year
Staff and leadership	• Muslim and non-Muslim leadership supportive
	• Staff working as a team.
School context	• Context extremely positive
	• Staff coming on board/building holistic approach for everyone in school
	• Open for opportunity to grow/learn

Challenges/weaknesses

- Apparent lack of physical resources
- Booklets being created from bits of information for teaching
- No syllabus or curriculum for IS
- Diversity of teachers problematic to nurture Islam
- All teachers have input in Islamic nurturing so difficult for non-Muslim teachers
- Concern as to how behaviour management strategies can be employed that are conversant with Islamic principles
- Concern regarding staff without adequate knowledge imparting Islam into subjects other than IS; how to bring a consistent approach/staff on 'one page'
- Concern as to how can Islam be infused properly across all subjects by appropriately trained staff
- Lack of overarching approach encompassing aims/goals/plans/decision-making (DM) process/procedures/vision for IS
- Struggle to determine whether IS is a subject or a way of life
- Too many changes every year/resulting chaos and confusion in implementation
- Teaching approach/content problematic
- Could instil negative perceptions of Islam

Recommendations

- Physical resources should be prepared so teachers are not creating resources individually
- Creation of a syllabus or curriculum for IS
- Equip both Muslim and non-Muslim teachers for Islamic nurturing of students outside IS
- Consistent approach to behaviour management to implement discipline as a team
- IS needs more creativity in teaching approach to be useful/constructive
- Consider strands for IS like other subjects/carefully implement certain strands with non-IS teachers for holistic approach
- Lay out a five-year strategic plan that encompasses students' perspectives as they move through the year levels so staff know what the school wants to achieve with IS
- Limit amount of change every year to staff and IS subject/implement well-researched approach with fewer disruptions
- More positive outlook and encouragement for IS teachers to counter negativity

Table 13.2 Views of IS staff

Strengths

IS teachers	• Big and diverse team of religious teachers
	• Able to bring about changes in short period of time
Students	• Students are interested in IS/fuels discussion in class
	• Curious/desire Islamic knowledge
	• Senior students very keen/ask very critical questions
	• Primary students observed speaking Arabic words or common sayings or statements within the Islamic tradition
	• Students ask very challenging questions
	• Respect and love IS teachers (not at all times)
	• Students have respect for Islam
	• Students are multicultural and accepting of each other
	• Unity among students of different nationalities

Challenges/weaknesses

- No clear direction for studies
- Lack of systematic approach to IS subjects makes teaching difficult
- Absence of syllabus/curricula for IS makes teaching problematic
- No framework or direction for IS
- DM process fragmented and chaotic
- No strategic planning encompassing DM process and teacher training needs to successfully implement aims
- No consultation with teachers before decisions/changes
- Ineffective/insufficient/lack of communication
- Arabic is an isolated language for students
- Very hard to determine the Arabic level of students from different non-Arabic-speaking backgrounds
- Building genuine relationship with students not easy
- Challenging to draw the line between complacency and strictness
- Getting students to pray is a challenge/students run off during prayer time

Recommendations

- Properly infusing Islam should be a whole school response and all stakeholders/not response of only teachers
- Outline a vision of the desired outcome of IS
- Obtain help from specialists to research how system can be changed positively
- All stakeholders should be involved/present a united front to nurture students
- Training for parents/let them know what the school is aiming to develop within their children
- Professional development
- Provide workshops for communication skills and leadership skills
- Training on how to teach Islam in contemporary world
- Implementation of technology in teaching materials
- Learning ways to teach that are more creative/constructive
- Religion teachers should pray with students to make sure students pray properly

Table 13.3 Views of IS students (Years 10–12)

Strengths

Learning experience	• Important things they learn in IS
	• History of the Prophetic/Muslim way of respecting others/ punishment and consequences/power of *duaa'* (supplication)
	• How to respect parents in accordance with Islam
Teachers	• Some teachers equip students with real-life Islam
	• Teachers born and raised here more engaging and relevant to students
	• One teacher able to answer questions/is calm and does not make Islam seem so strict/makes jokes/enthusiastic

Challenges/weaknesses

Learning experience	• Not engaging or fascinating/not enjoyable
	• No discussion happening/only listening/students fall asleep
	• Not gaining new knowledge about Islam/no answers to questions/ repeating same things since Year 5/low-level info
	• Teaching approach is not practical
	• No depth in real-life issues
	• IS teachers do not showcase different schools of thought/points of view in Islam; only delve into their own school of thought
Outcomes and aims	• Outcomes not achieved in IS because they are not relevant to lives of students
	• Ways to achieve IS aims not working
	• Not teaching how to live in society/cannot apply what is being learnt
Curriculum	• Constant repetition/not practical/low-level
	• Teaching same basics into senior school
	• Contradictory information being taught
Teachers	• Behaviour and attitudes problematic
	• Show different faces to students and staff

Recommendations

- IS should go beyond what is *halal* and *haram* and go into 'why'; teachers should explain Islamic reasoning to students
- IS should help students navigate the real world and the society in which they live
- Teachers should work to address questions from students on practical issues in life where appropriate
- IS should explain various points of view within Islam
- Teaching needs to become more engaging and creative
- IS teachers should work on developing personable relationship with students, avoid harshness and strictness at all times
- Curriculum should advance as students progress through school years
- Should be a focus on theory *and* practice for young Muslims

IS' Overall Strengths, Challenges and Weaknesses, and Recommendations

Overall strengths

Staff and school leaders	Teachers	Students
• Supportive of IS as a whole • Work as a team together	• Good mix of teachers • Very passionate/knowledgeable/enthusiastic • Share things in common • Big/diverse team of IS teachers • Some teachers are good/open/patient/nice/helpful/really care • Some teachers equip students with real-life Islam • Teachers born and raised here more relevant to students • *One* teacher able to answer questions/calm and not strict • Teachers incorporating *Sunnah* into actions	• Very passionate about Islam/love and respect Islam • Want to discuss contemporary topics • Willing to change • Interested/curious/desire for Islamic knowledge • Senior students very keen • Senior students ask very critical/challenging questions • Respect and love IS teachers (not at all times) • Accepting of each other/diverse group

Overall challenges/weaknesses

Leading and governance processes	Curriculum	Learning experience	Outcomes	Teacher attitudes/behaviour/way of teaching
• Lack of overarching approach which encompasses aims/goals/plans/DM process/procedures/vision for IS • Struggle to determine whether IS is a subject or way of life • No framework or direction for IS • No strategic planning encompassing DM process and teacher training needs for more holistic approach to IS • Lack of role modelling for students	• No syllabus or curriculum for IS • Curriculum not helping achieve the aims of IS • Curriculum is irrelevant/repetitive/low-level • Present contradictory information to students • Lack of systematic approach to curriculum	• Learning experience is not good for students • IS not engaging/fascinating/enjoyable for students • Students not gaining new knowledge about Islam • Repetition of basics from primary into secondary • Students not gaining new knowledge about Islam • Teachers not answering students' questions on real-life issues • Teaching approach is not practical/relevant to lives of students • Too much time spent on irrelevant topics/students falling asleep in class • No depth into practical/real-life issues in Islam with older students • Questions from students often dismissed/ignored by IS teachers • Learning is not interactive/only involves listening to lectures	• Outcomes not achieved in IS because it is not relevant to society • Not teaching students how to live in society • Students unable to apply what they have learnt in IS to their own lives • Repetition of basics/not practical/low level	• Teaching approach/content problematic • Could instil bad perception of Islam and teachers among students • Diversity of teachers (culturally and levels of training) is problematic to nurture a consistent approach to teaching of Islam • Teacher attitudes/behaviours/ways of teaching/messages they convey are problematic and sometimes contradictory • IS teachers cannot handle disruption in class/ignore issues such as bullying in their classes • Behaviour and attitudes are problematic • IS teachers not enthusiastic about teaching • Some IS teachers are angry and harsh/make students feel bad • Too much emphasis on rigid approaches and rules and regulations of Islam and less on nurturing of knowledge and good manners • Lack of *akhlaq* (morals) and *adaab* (manners) • Teachers do not know how to teach • English proficiency poor

Overall recommendations

Leading and governance processes	Curriculum	Teachers	Enhance ways of teaching and learning
• System thinking should be embraced by everybody • Properly infusing Islam should be a whole school response and all stakeholders/not response of only teachers • Outline a vision of the desired outcome of IS • Making IS not just a subject but a way of life • Giving students skills to research problems on their own if lost/outcome intended of IS • Problem-solving knowledge • Physical resources should be prepared so teachers are not creating resources individually • Consider strands for IS like other subjects/carefully implement certain strands with non-IS teachers for holistic approach • Lay out a five-year strategic plan/strategic plan that encompasses students as they move through the year levels so staff know what the school wants to achieve with IS • Limit amount of change every year to staff and IS subject/implement well-researched approach with fewer disruptions	• Creation of a syllabus or curriculum for IS • Incorporate IS holistically into other subjects • Teaching should be more than multiple choice or ticking the 'right' answers • Focus on topics relevant to young people • Teaching of issues appropriate to age level of students • Outline aims and outcomes of IS • Should be a focus on theory *and* practice for young Muslims • Theory and practice from stories of the prophets for younger students • Bring more warmth to IS/has to be in the heart of students as much as the head to positively influence behaviour and *akhlaq* • Help foster love of Islam among students/good leaders for the future • Focus points each week shared with parents to develop students at home as well • Curriculum should advance as student progresses through school years	• IS teachers should interact with parents • Evaluation process for teachers from student point of view for improvement both ways • Better ways of teaching students • Teach more positives from Hadith/implement reflection among students on teachings and traditions • Make IS classes a place of happiness and relaxation as opposed to punishment • More control needs to be taken in class • Teachers need to role model to students/handle disruptions and bullying in proper Islamic manner • Put Sunnah into practice when dealing with students/stay calm and respectful/address issues properly • Foster a balance between home and school • More positive outlook and encouragement for IS teachers to counter negativity • IS teachers should work on developing personable relationship with students/avoid harshness and strictness at all times	• Implementation of technology in teaching materials • IS needs more creativity in teaching approach to be useful/constructive • IS should go beyond what is *halal* and *haram* and go into 'why'/teachers should explain Islamic reasoning to students • IS should help students navigate the real world and the society in which they live • IS should explain various points of view within Islam • Teachers should work to address questions from students on practical issues in life where appropriate

Discussion of Major Findings

This research aimed at exploring the strengths, weaknesses and challenges of IS as viewed by IS coordinators, IS teachers and senior IS students (especially their attitudes toward the relevance and effectiveness of IS to their lives as young Australian Muslims). What follows is an outline and discussion of some of the most salient findings.

Absence of an Islamic Studies Curriculum

It is evident that there is an absence of an IS curriculum and syllabus in this particular Islamic school (anecdotally we also know that this is the case across Australia). The coordinators of IS interviewed here declared that there is 'no syllabus or curriculum for Islamic studies', and therefore 'booklets were being created from bits of information for teaching'. Further, they argue that this has led to a 'lack of overarching approach encompassing aims, goals, plans, decision-making process, procedures and vision for Islamic Studies'. Consequently, there are 'too many changes every year resulting in chaos and confusion in implementation of Islamic studies'. Teachers of IS echoed similar sentiments and added, 'lack of systematic approach to Islamic studies subjects makes teaching difficult' and that the 'absence of syllabus or curricula for IS makes teaching problematic'. From the students' perspective, the absence of an IS curriculum leads to 'constant repetition' of information that is 'not practical' and of 'low level', and to the 'teaching of the same basics' learnt in primary years, and the knowledge conveyed to students is often 'contradictory'. This finding reflects similar anecdotal findings by Shamma in the North American context (2011).

These challenges are not peculiar to the school under study. Separate discussions with principals and teachers of IS from Islamic schools across Australia revealed that they also lack an IS curriculum.[34] Furthermore, whenever a school claimed to having an IS 'curriculum', deeper discussions revealed that: (1) there is confusion about the meaning, nature and scope of a 'curriculum', (2) most often schools (and their staff) either use imported IS books (or booklets but not a curriculum as such), or (3) 'booklets being created from bits of information for teaching'. Clearly, there is *no* national curriculum/syllabus for IS in Australia.

Renewal of IS within Islamic schools would require the development of a *national* IS curriculum that sets the *expectations* (which are discoverable only through empirical research that *asks* students about their *own* expectations of IS) for what all young Australian Muslims need to learn, regardless of their background. For effective implementation of the curriculum, learning areas relevant to students' lives, and support material for teachers needs to be developed. The development of a national IS curriculum that is cognisant of the needs of young Muslims growing up in the Australian (or other Western) context(s) would require an extensive and collaborative development *process*. The process should be guided by the Australian Curriculum, Assessment and Reporting Authority (ACARA) and the Melbourne Declaration on Educational Goals for Young Australians (MDEGYA). Furthermore, it is *not possible* for a single individual or school to produce a reliable IS curriculum; it must be a collaborative effort that: (1) involves high-level curriculum expertise nationwide, (2) provides opportunities for national consultation (with selected Islamic schools and experts in IS, in the sacred and academic traditions) and (3) ensures high-quality curriculum documents. Furthermore, the curriculum development process would need to involve four interrelated phases:

1. curriculum shaping
2. curriculum writing
3. preparation for implementation
4. curriculum monitoring, evaluation and review.[35]

Further details on each of these stages can be found in ACARA's document titled *Curriculum Development Process*.[36] What is important in the *process* of development of an IS curriculum is the *quality* of the product and process. Among other criteria, the quality of the curriculum would include:

- clarity about what 'is to be taught across the years or bands of schooling and the quality of learning expected of students as they progress through school'[37];
- flexibility in the curriculum so that is can:
    - 'accommodate the *reality* [sic] of student, teacher and school diversity'[38] (for example, this would include an awareness of the

various schools of thought—*madhahib*—operating within any given school and practices by students, and accommodating them, which helps avoid teacher bias that students often complain about);
- 'has high standards and expectations that are challenging yet realistic'[39];

- 'a strong evidence base'[40] (as the Islamic tradition would also demand).

We could also add to the list the following (but not exhaustive) criteria: that it be

- cognisant of Islamic worldview(s) (not discussed here, as it is the subject of other chapters in this volume and is beyond the scope of this chapter);
- pedagogically responsive to an 'Islamic' context (Islamic schools) and the needs of Australian Muslim students.

Our research found that the *absence* of a national (or even local) IS curriculum has resulted in a number of challenges (as exhibited by the school under study):

- aims and outcomes for IS (currently not defined, codified or written) not met under the current approach;
- lack of clarity and cohesion among staff and between coordinators about IS;
- an apparent lack of physical resources, resulting in the creation of teaching aids such as booklets by individual teachers. This is leading to increased pressure upon staff to supplement teaching in classes and is resulting in a fractured approach to teaching IS;
- IS content that is repetitive and low-level (no critical thinking or addressing of contemporary issues);
- feeling among senior students that they are deprived of the opportunity to develop skills and more in-depth Islamic knowledge as they progress through the years. Instead, students complained of repetition of basic knowledge from primary through to secondary school, leading to a perceived sense of stagnation in their study of Islam (contrary to ACARA's quality criteria (2) above).

The Role and Place of Islamic Studies

Undoubtedly, IS should hold a pivotal and central role in 'Islamic' schools. However, IS alone does not make a school 'Islamic'. Other chapters in this volume discuss ways to attain the 'Islamic' and what the central ethos of an 'Islamic' school may look like. Regardless of how one defines the 'Islamic', the role of IS in Islamic schools is indisputable. However, in the present study, we found that there is confusion among coordinators and teachers as to the *role* and *place* of IS.

In the absence of clearly articulated aims, expected outcomes and resources (because of the absence of an appropriate curriculum), IS teachers described their *inability* to deliver on the intended aims of IS as a learning area/subject. They were also confused about their *broader role* in facilitating a holistic approach to teaching 'Islam' across the school or attaining the 'Islamic aims' of the school. Further, they lacked clarity on the following questions: 'Is the teaching of Islamic studies isolated from the rest of the school, or should it be an integral part of the school?' In addition, how could the 'Islamic' be attained (however it is defined), when there is no clarity on *what* it is and *how* it should be implemented? It is counter-intuitive to assume or expect that the 'Islamic' can be attained, or IS can be effective, when no adequate IS curriculum exists that meets the highest standards and is responsive to the context of Islamic schools and the needs of young Muslim students. Coordinators stated that it was a 'struggle to determine whether Islamic studies is a subject or a way of life'.

However, the absence of an IS curriculum creates widespread confusion among staff and coordinators as to the role, priorities and overall approach of IS. ACARA's criterion demanding 'clarity about what is to be taught across the years or bands of schooling, and the quality of learning expected of students as they progress through school' is clearly missing in this Islamic school. Among other problems, the lack of 'clarity' about *what* is to be taught leads to a failure to engage in classroom discussions, especially on practical issues of interest to the students, as our research revealed. The absence of a national IS curriculum as a basis for what is to be taught has also constrained educators' efforts in the areas of responsive and appropriate pedagogy and quality assessment and reporting for the IS classroom.

Lack of Discussion on Practical Issues or Issues of Interest to the Students, Teacher Bias and Contradictions

Furthermore, for IS to be effective, it should 'accommodate the *reality*' of students' needs, have 'high standards and expectations that are challenging yet realistic' and be established on 'a strong evidence base' (as suggested by ACARA 2012 for quality national curriculum). Our research reveals that aside from *one* stand-out teacher (who has an engaging and open style in discussing Islamic issues with students), teachers ignore or refuse to discuss topics with students ('accommodating the reality' is absent) that do not form part of the core content of the lesson or unit (teaching methods are 'inflexible').

The problem with this approach, as expressed by student participants, is that it contributes to frustration because they 'expect deeper understandings' of Islam through inquiry as to the 'why', as well as the reasoning behind Islamic principles on a variety of issues relevant to their lives. Students told us they want 'depth in real life issues', to learn as Muslims 'how to live in society' (to become functional Muslims), and to gain the knowledge and skills to 'apply what is being learnt'. IS teachers argue that they are restricted in what they can teach because they lack the 'usual' learning area or subject information (provided for other reading key learning areas and subjects), guidelines or structures. Therefore, they do not have the tools to navigate outside of the content. In fact, teachers informed us that discussion or questions outside the narrowly focused content appears to be 'stressful' as it is perceived to 'take away from the lesson time, the assessment focus, and the sub-topics', which appear to act as a default for aims, learning intentions or learning area, content descriptions and elaborations.

Our classroom observations revealed a tendency to adopt a one-way question policy in several classes. That is, students were expected to answer teacher s' questions on command but were not permitted (or at the very least not encouraged) to ask their own questions. This led to frustration and disengagement by students. Secondary senior student participants also expressed disappointment that *some* IS teachers would provide them with content or answers to questions relating to *fiqh* (jurisprudence) that was either based on a narrow interpretation (biased), or what they described as the teacher's perspective that cannot be substantiated or validated (not evidence based). Students were aware of other Islamic perspectives (or were exposed to other viewpoints) and would follow this up with other IS teachers, or more commonly their parents, which resulted in confusion and loss of trust in the IS teacher as an authority or a source for learning. It is possible that this inflexibility, bias or lack of critical thinking in the teaching of IS is the result of the absence of an appropriate and contextual IS curriculum, and an appropriate pedagogy that is responsive to the needs of the students and the context (to be discussed later).

Furthermore, senior students reported that IS teachers seem to contradict each other on various Islamic issues/rulings (a complaint that we encountered in other Islamic schools). Instead of accommodating other valid jurisprudential viewpoints, students complained that the narrowness and/or tendency to dismiss them was a source of frustration. Interestingly, we found that the school under study does not have a policy or procedure for dealing with differences of jurisprudential opinions (in this case within the four Sunni acceptable schools of thought), perhaps due to the dominance of teachers (and school leaders) who belong to a particular Sunni school of thought. Clearly, the lack of discussion on practical issues relevant to the lives of the students or issues of interest to the students, teacher bias and contradictions, coupled with the absence of an appropriate pedagogy in IS classrooms, has led to frustration among students and staff alike.

The Absence of an Appropriate Pedagogy
In addition to the 'one-way question policy' described above, pedagogical approaches of IS teachers were a major concern across the focus groups interviewed, and as witnessed in the classroom observations. Coordinators, IS teachers and students all noted that while some teachers are viewed as having adequate knowledge of Islam, and are 'very passionate and enthusiastic', they are 'not doing justice' to this knowledge on account of the way the subject is being taught. Furthermore, students complained about 'unnecessary strictness, rigidity and authoritative teaching style of teachers'. They also complained about a lack of 'creative/interactive pedagogy' by IS teachers. While one teacher was praised for his 'engaging style', others were criticised for not being 'engaging, fascinating, or enjoyable', 'not being practical' and 'not creative'. This, they contended, is leading to 'disengagement in learning', which 'alienate[s] students from Islam as opposed to drawing them closer to it'.

Though IS teachers are often educated in the sacred sciences (to varying degrees in the study of the Qur'an, Hadith, Shari'ah and so on), they are usually *not* trained or registered teachers. Furthermore, 'despite the growth of Islamic schools, there exists no formal, research-based deliberation of the principles of an Islamic pedagogy and the training of teachers with a nuanced understanding of their teaching environment'.[41] Therefore, the problems associated with the teaching of IS are compounded. The absence of formal, research-based deliberation of the principles of an Islamic pedagogy and the training of teachers with a nuanced understanding of their teaching environment, and the absence of an adequate curriculum, leads to students' disengagement and disinterest in IS. Further research is required to assess the extent to which adequate teacher pedagogical training could lead to a better learning experience for IS students, and respond to the challenges expressed by IS teachers.

While research in finding 'appropriate' pedagogical methods is under way for Islamic schools (see, for example, Abdullah's prophetic pedagogy model outlined in Chap. 10 of this volume), Diallo[42] notes that assumptions are often made regarding the difference between 'Islamic' and 'Western' pedagogies. Diallo notes that Islamic pedagogy is criticised because it leads to 'passive learners who are not encouraged to develop questioning skills (outside religious conventions) or allowed to reject authoritative knowledge'. In other words, Islamic pedagogy is 'traditional, static and backward', and Western pedagogy and epistemology are 'modern, progressive and innovative because they advocate learners-centred approaches'. The problem with this argument is that it assumes that *existing* pedagogical approaches within Islamic schools are 'Islamic' or consistent with the Islamic tradition. Our research shows that existing pedagogies within the IS classes do not meet the criteria of 'Islamic' or 'Western' models. Though not the focus of this chapter, it is relevant to state that Ajem and Memon[43] argue that for pedagogy to be 'Islamic' (which one might expect in an IS classroom) it should:

1. not contradict the aims, objectives, and ethics contained in revelation (Qur'an);
2. closely reflect an Islamic ethos based on
    (a) revelation
    (b) the teachings and practices of the Messenger of God (peace and blessings be upon him)
    (c) the intellectual and spiritual heritage of his [Messenger of God] follower;

3. prove effective in developing the student's
   (a) intelligence (*aql*)
   (b) faith (*Iman*)
   (c) morality and character (*khuluq*)
   (d) knowledge and practice of personal obligations (*fard ain*)
   (e) knowledge, skills and physical abilities warranted by worldly responsibilities and duties.

Furthermore, Memon and Ajem argue that[44]:

1. Pedagogy is coherent when a teacher's practice is consistent with his or her theory and approach to teaching. This is the *How*.
2. Pedagogy is effective when a teacher's practice facilitates the aims and objectives of education, which includes curriculum. This is the *What*.
3. Pedagogy has purpose when a teacher's practice is rooted in a philosophy or belief, or reflects a particular ethos or worldview. This is the *Why*.

In the absence of adequate and appropriate teacher training, it would be counter-intuitive to expect highly developed and responsive pedagogical practices to be the norm (i.e., a whole school approach) in IS classrooms. The criteria outlined above by Memon and Ajem are mostly absent in the case of the school under study. This is further complicated because there is *no* IS curriculum which addresses the *how, what* and *why* described above.

Teachers' Conduct and Its Impact on Students' Learning

It is clear by now that IS teachers face multiple challenges that make it difficult to meet the demands of quality teaching and learning: the absence of an IS curriculum, lack of resources, unclear aims and objectives for IS, lack of quality assessment practices and absence of appropriate pedagogy are among the most salient challenges.

These challenges seem to have a negative impact on the conduct of most IS teachers. Students informed us that IS teachers 'raise their voices and discipline students harshly and/or publicly' and students viewed this 'extremely negatively'. Students reinforced this concern repeatedly. Students also complained that IS teachers' behaviours and attitudes are 'problematic' and that they are often 'angry', 'harsh' and make the students feel 'bad' about themselves.

Furthermore, both IS teachers and students have described a negative climate in which it is difficult to develop positive and nurturing relationships with the other during their studies. IS teachers feel students are increasingly misbehaving in their classes and are generally 'disrespectful' towards them. Students complain that IS teachers are 'unnecessarily harsh and rigid'. They also argue that teachers fail to overlook or move on, and subsequently refuse to interact and engage fully with students, after instances of student misbehaviour or past teacher–student conflict that the students consider had been resolved. Our research reveals that IS teachers who demonstrate patience, and who discuss issues with students in a relaxing and respectful manner, are the exception.

Not surprisingly, students informed us (unanimously) that they respected IS teachers who were able to teach them in a calm and relaxed manner. One particular IS teacher was respected for his 'calm and personable approach' within and outside his classroom. Students also complained that the issue of disruptive or inappropriate behaviour is more prevalent in their IS classes than in other classes in the school. There is a view among students that IS teachers cannot handle disruptions in class, or that these teachers handle misbehaviour poorly.

Conclusion

IS is a significant learning area/subject in Islamic schools because of its direct relevance to the vision, mission and aims of such schools. An understanding of best practice in the IS learning area, based on solid empirical research, is therefore necessary in order to understand its nature, relevance, effectiveness and how best to improve it. Until the present research, there has *never* been an independent expert review of IS anywhere in Islamic schools in Australia (or, as far as the author is concerned, in other Western countries). Given the significance of IS, the absence of a proper understanding of IS is not only problematic but also tragic and may have serious consequences for students of Islamic schools.

Given this predicament, the findings of this chapter are significant and timely. While the conclusions cannot be generalised, they can pave the way for further research in this field. This chapter was able to demonstrate empirically some of the strengths, weaknesses and challenges associated with the teaching and learning of IS at an Australian Islamic school. While there are strengths, the chapter also demonstrated that the most significant problem with IS is that it does not meet the needs of young Australian Muslims. Students expressed concern about the relevance and contextualisation of IS and its effectiveness in equipping them with the necessary knowledge and skills to navigate the modern world. IS is seen as an isolated subject that lacks a comprehensive curriculum or a curriculum commensurate with other key learning areas, direction and focus. Despite dedicated teachers and students wishing to learn, students were also dismayed with pedagogical approaches within the classroom and believed that (among other issues) lack of genuine and open engagement with students, and the ability to engage them with relevant issues that affect their lives, is a major problem.

Further research is required to assess the effectiveness and relevance of IS in Islamic schools in other Western contexts. Additionally, research is required to assess perceptions that the approach to IS in *primary* school is effective as opposed to the perceived ineffectiveness in secondary school. Findings could either inform best practice in secondary schools or ascertain whether later shortfalls are a manifestation of an ineffective approach at the primary level. The recommendations found in this chapter can inform the way forward for renewal in IS at Islamic schools, and lead to further research and engagement in this field to help improve the quality of IS in Islamic schools in Western contexts.

Notes

1. Rachel Woodlock, "Introduction," *The La Trobe Journal, Isolation, Integration and Identity: The Muslim Experience in Australia* (2012): 4.
2. I. Donohoue Clyne, "Seeking Education: The struggle of Muslims to educate their children in Australia" (diss., University of Melbourne, 2000).
3. This chapter is based on a comprehensive review and a written report undertaken by the author and Dylan Chown for an Australian Islamic school.
4. Geert Driessen and Michael Merry, "Islamic Schools in the Netherlands: Expansion or Marginalization," *Interchange*, 37(3) (2006): 201–223.
5. Nasar Meer, "Muslim Schools in Britain: Challenging Mobilisations or Logical Developments?" *Asia Pacific Journal of Education*, 27(1) (2007): 55–71.
6. Geoffrey Walford, "Classification and Framing of the Curriculum in Evangelical Christian and Muslim Schools in England and The Netherlands," *Educational Studies*, 28(4) (2002): 403–419.

7. Driessen and Merry, "Expansion or Marginalization."
8. Geert Driessen and Michael Merry, "Islamic schools in Three Western Countries: Policy and Procedure," *Comparative Education*, 41(4) (2005): 411–432.
9. Driessen and Merry, "Policy and Procedure."
10. Donohoue Clyne, "Seeking Education."
11. Donohoue Clyne, "Seeking Education"; Woodlock, "The Muslim Experience."
12. Peter Jones, "Islamic Schools in Australia," *The La Trobe Journal*, 89 (2012).
13. J. Mark Halsted, "Towards a Unified View of Islamic Education," *Islam and Christian-Muslim Relations* 6(1) (1995): 25; J. Mark Halsted, "An Islamic Concept of Education," *Comparative Education* 40(4) (2004): 517.
14. Halsted, "Concept of Education."
15. Ibid.
16. Susan Douglass and Munir Shaikh, "Defining Islamic Education: Differentiation and Applications." *Council on Islamic Education: Current Issues in Comparative Education, 7*(1) (2004): 1–12.
17. Driessen and Merry, "Policy and procedure," 428.
18. Driessen and Merry, "Policy and procedure," 412–3.
19. Nadeem Memon, "The Prophetic Standard: Incorporating the Instructional Methods of the Prophet Muhammad in Islamic Schools." Paper presented at the ISNA Education Forum Rosemont Illinois. http://www.isna.net/programs/pages/previous-education-forum-papers.aspx: Accessed 31 December 2011.
20. Cited in Muhammad Abdullah, Mohamd Abdalla and Robyn Jorgensen, 'Towards the Formulation of a Pedagogical Framework for Islamic Schools in Australia' 6(4) (2015), *Islam and Civilisational Renewal*: 7.
21. Cited in Muhammad Abdullah, Mohamad Abdalla, Robyn Jorgensen, "Towards the Formulation," 2.
22. Cited in Muhammad Abdullah, Mohamad Abdalla, Robyn Jorgensen, "Towards the Formulation," 3.
23. Cited in Muhammad Abdullah, Mohamad Abdalla, Robyn Jorgensen, "Towards the Formulation," 3.
24. Cited in Muhammad Abdullah, Mohamad Abdalla, Robyn Jorgensen, "Towards the Formulation," 3.
25. Freda Shamma, "An Overview of The Status of Islamic Curricula." Written 9 June 2004, revised January 2011. https://www.theisla.org/filemgmt_data/files/Shamma%20-%20An%20Overview%20of%20Current%20Islamic%20Curricula%20-%202011.pdf.
26. Freda Shamma, "An Overview."
27. Ajem and Memon (2011).
28. Calderon et al. (2000).
29. Glesne and Peshkin (1992).
30. MacMillan & Bond (1995).

31. Fasse & Kolodner (2000)
32. Fasse (1993).
33. I acknowledge the assistance of Dr Nezar Faris in the analysis of data.
34. This is the position of the Islamic Schools Association of Australia, an umbrella body representing a number of Islamic schools. This has also been a recurring theme at whole-of-field gatherings such as the Inaugural Australian Islamic Education forum where a unanimous call to come together to design and develop an IS curriculum was put forth.
35. ACARA (2012, p. 6).
36. Ibid., pp. 6–7.
37. Ibid.
38. Ibid.
39. Ibid.
40. Ibid.
41. Memon (2011, p. 289).
42. Diallo, op. cit. (2012, pp. 177–8).
43. Ajem and Memon, op. cit. (2011, p. 6).
44. Ibid., pp. 5–6.

Bibliography

Abdullah, M., M. Abdalla, and R. Jorgensen. "Towards the Formulation of a Pedagogical Framework for Islamic Schools in Australia." *Islam and Civilisational Renewal* 6, no. 4 (2015): 509, 510–511.

ACARA. *Curriculum Development Process*, 2012. https://acaraweb.blob.core.windows.net/resources/ACARA_Curriculum_Development_Process_Version_6.0_-_04_April_2012_-_FINAL_COPY.pdf.

Ajem, R., and N. Memon. *Principles of Islamic Pedagogy: A Teachers Manual*. Islamic Teacher Education Program, Canada, 2011.

Berber, M.G. *The Role of the Principal in Establishing and Further Developing an Independent Christian or Islamic School in Australia* (Doctor of Philosophy), University of Western Sydney, 2009.

Buckingham, J. The Rise of Religious Schools *Policy Monographs*: The Centre for Independent Studies, 2010.

Calderon, J.L., R.S. Baker, and K.E. Wolf. "Focus Groups: A Qualitative Method Complementing Quantitative Research for Studying Culturally Diverse Groups." *Education for Health* 13, no. 1 (2000): 91–91.

Chown, D. *Impacts on Educational Leadership: Enacting the Vision in an Australian Islamic School*. Master of Education, Griffith University, Brisbane, 2014.

Denzin, N.K., and Y. Lincoln. *Handbook of Qualitative Research*. Thousand Oaks, CA: Sage Publications, 1994.

Diallo, I. "Introduction: The Interface Between Islamic and Western Pedagogies and Epistemologies: Features and Divergences." *International Journal of Pedagogies and Learning* 7, no. 3 (2012): 175.

Donohoue Clyne, I. "Addressing Equity Issues in the Education of Muslims." In *Teacher Education for Equality*, ed. E. Befring. Oslo Norway: ATEE, 1996.

———. "Seeking Education for Muslim Children in Australia." *Muslim Education Quarterly* 14, no. 3 (1997): 4–18.

———. "Cultural Diversity and the Curriculum: The Muslim Experience in Australia." *European Journal of Intercultural Education* 9, no. 3 (1998): 279–289.

———. *Seeking Education: The Struggle of Muslims to Educate Their Children in Australia* (Doctor of Philosophy), University of Melbourne, Melbourne, 2000.

———. "Educating Muslim Children in Australia." In *Muslim Communities in Australia*, ed. S. Akbarzadeh and A. Saeed, xii, 244. Sydney: UNSW Press, 2001.

Douglass, S., and M.A. Shaikh. "Defining Islamic Education: Differentiation and Applications." *Council on Islamic Education: Current Issues in Comparative Education* 7, no. 1 (2004): 1–12.

Driessen, G., and M.S. Merry. "Islamic Schools in the Netherlands: Expansion or Marginalization." *Interchange* 37, no. 3 (2006): 201–223.

Fasse, B.B. *"No Guarantees": An Ethnography of Transition to Parenthood in Normative Lifespan Development*. Dissertation, Georgia State University, Atlanta, GA, 1993.

Fasse, B.B., and J.L. Kolodner. "Evaluating Classroom Practices Using Qualitative Research Methods: Defining and Refining the Process." In *Fourth International Conference of the Learning Sciences*, ed. B. Fishman and S. O'Connor-Divelbiss, 193–198. Mahwah, NJ: Erlbaum, 2000.

Gaižauskaitė, I. "The Use of the Focus Group Method in Social Work Research." *Social Work* 11, no. 1 (2012): 19–30.

Glesne, C., and A. Peshkin. *Becoming Qualitative Researchers: An Introduction*. White Plains, NY: Longman, 1992.

Halstead, J.M. "Towards a Unified View of Islamic Education." *Islam and Christian-Muslim Relations* 6, no. 1(1995): 25.

———. "An Islamic Concept of Education." *Comparative Education* 40, no. 4 (2004), 517.

Hussain, A. "Recent Western Reflections on Islamic Education." *Religious Education* 103, no. 5 (2008): 579–585.

Jones, P. "Islamic Schools in Australia." *The La Trobe Journal (Special Issue: 'Isolation, Integration and Identity: The Muslim Experience in Australia)* 89 (2012): 36–47.

MacMillan, Thomas L., E.J. McColl, C. Hale, and S. Bond. "Comparison of Focus Group and Individual Interview Methodology in Examining Patient Satisfaction with Nursing Care." *Social Sciences in Health* 1 (1995): 206–219.

Meer, N. "Muslim Schools in Britain: Challenging Mobilisations or Logical Developments?" *Asia Pacific Journal of Education* 27, no. 1 (2007): 55–71.

Memon, N. *The Prophetic Standard: Incorporating the Instructional Methods of the Prophet Muhammad in Islamic Schools.* Paper presented at the ISNA Education Forum Rosemont Illinois, 2007. Accessed 31 December 2011. http://www.isna.net/programs/pages/previous-education-forum-papers.aspx.

———. *From Protest to Praxis: A History of Islamic Schools in North America* (Doctor of Philosophy), University of Toronto, Canada, 2009.

———. Re-Framing Excellence in Islamic Schooling: Elevating the Discourse, 2013. Accessed 27 April 2013. http://razigroup.com/resources/2011/11/re-framingexcellence-in-islamic-schooling-elevating-the-discourse/.

Merry, M., and G. Driessen. "Islamic Schools in Three Western Countries: Policy and Procedure." *Comparative Education* 41, no. 4 (2005): 411.

Polat, C. "Gulen-Inspired Schools in Australia: Educational Vision and Funding," 2016. (date unknown). Accessed 30 March 2016. http://www.acu.edu.au/__data/assets/pdf_file/0004/223087/Gulen-Inspired_Schools_In_Australia_Educational_Vision_And_Funding_Conference_paper.pdf.

Shamma, F. "The Curriculum Challenge for Islamic Schools in America." In *Muslims and Islamization in North America: Problems and Prospects*, ed. Amber Haque. Kuala Lumpur: Amana Publications, 1999.

———. *An Overview of The Status of Islamic Curricula*, 2001. Written 9 June 2004, revised January 2011. https://www.theisla.org/filemgmt_data/files/Shamma%20-%20An%20Overview%20of%20Current%20Islamic%20Curricula%20-%202011.pdf.

Walford, G. "Classification and Framing of the Curriculum in Evangelical Christian and Muslim Schools in England and The Netherlands." *Educational Studies* 28, no. 4 (2002), 403–419.

Woodlock, R. "Introduction." *The La Trobe Journal, Isolation, Integration and Identity: The Muslim Experience in Australia* 89 (2012): 4.

CHAPTER 14

Arabic Teaching at Australian Islamic Schools: A CALL Framework

Nadia Selim

INTRODUCTION

Students take on a monumental task when they commit to learning a foreign language (FL). One of the first challenges is vocabulary acquisition. Research estimates indicate that a 5-year-old native speaker of English knows about 4000–5000 word families[1] and adds 1000 word families annually.[2] This means that a learner of English needs to master 5000 word families to have acquired the vocabulary knowledge of a 5 year old. Moreover, research suggests that to read with significant comprehension one needs to achieve 98% coverage of the vocabulary in a text, which has driven researchers to identify that core vocabulary figures are probably closer to 9000 word families.[3] This is clearly a daunting task with serious consequences for language pedagogy.[4]

As concerns Arabic, many questions about what constitutes a core Arabic vocabulary remain unanswered by research.[5] However, recently

N. Selim (✉)
CITE-School of Education – University of South Australia,
Magill-Adelaide, SA, Australia
e-mail: Nadia.selim@unisa.edu.au

© The Author(s) 2018
M. Abdalla et al. (eds.), *Islamic Schooling in the West*,
https://doi.org/10.1007/978-3-319-73612-9_14

Buckwalter and Parkinson statistically analysed a corpus of 30 million words to compile a dictionary of the 5000 most frequently occurring Modern Standard and colloquial Arabic words they deemed necessary for comprehension of written and oral discourse.[6] This means that learners of Arabic need to learn to read, hear, speak and write at least 5000 words while mastering the script, attaining a broader grammatical understanding and striving for *communicative competence*.[7] Furthermore, the US Foreign Service Institute (FSI) categorised languages according to their difficulty from the perspective of the native speaker of English and based their classifications on the number of hours needed to attain proficiency in the target language (TL).[8] The fourth category, which includes Arabic, Japanese, Chinese and Korean, is the hardest. For this category, some estimates indicate that at least sixty-eight weeks of full-time instruction are needed to attain fluency,[9] while others suggest the figure is closer to eighty-eight weeks.[10]

Given that young Australians are native speakers of English, these figures are extremely relevant, especially when coupled with the core vocabulary estimates, and ultimately call into question the two hours spent on Arabic study per week at Australian Islamic schools.[11] Moreover, they make the enhancement of the learners' experiences a priority, especially given that Standard Arabic is not generally accessible beyond the classroom, which means that Australian learners who are not from Arabic-speaking backgrounds are studying Arabic as a foreign language (AFL).[12] In this context, trained teachers, effective methodologies and informed textbook selection are critical to the success of the learning experience. However, when these are the very challenges facing the Arabic classroom today, an alternative must be found.

Known AFL Dilemmas

The first honest critique of Arabic teaching methodologies was made by the historian Ibn Khaldun, who died in 1406.[13] Ibn Khaldun distinguished between native speakers and non-native speakers, discussed the existing Arabic language teaching practices in various parts of the Islamic empire and analysed their varying degrees of success. However, the most important aspect of Ibn Khaldun's analysis was his distinction between Arabic proficiency and knowledge of Arabic grammar.

Ibn Khaldun noted that grammarians believed language should be taught through the introduction to grammar first, but he believed it should be taught by teaching language habits through interaction with Arabic speech.[14] In criticising the grammarians' view, Ibn Khaldun explained that teaching that focused on grammar only produced knowledge of Arabic, not an Arabic skill, and likened this to knowing the theory of sewing or carpentry but being unable to sew a garment or produce a single wooden item.[15] It has been emphasised that Ibn Khaldun argued against the traditional grammar-based methods explicitly, as he had discovered the futility of teaching language through rote memorisation of challenging passages or through the learning of grammar rules only.[16] Instead, Ibn Khaldun wanted to find ways of incorporating grammar teaching into a broader framework of teaching and admired the Spanish Muslims because they had distinct approaches and curricula for children and adults that used poetry rather than the Qur'an and led to a better grasp of Arabic.[17]

Unfortunately, it seems that we have made little progress since Ibn Khaldun's time. In fact, research on Arabic suggests that we are dealing with an AFL teaching scenario that is heavily invested in the nineteenth-century Grammar-Translation method. As implied by its name, this was a grammar-intensive way of learning languages and was often associated with classical languages such as Greek, Latin, Sanskrit and Arabic.[18] This method had no theoretical underpinnings[19] and focused solely on reading and writing,[20] to the extent that students were not required to speak or understand spoken language.[21] With the communicative aspect of language learning ignored, classroom time was reserved for translation, grammar drills and the rote memorisation of word lists.[22]

Although problematic, research suggests that the Grammar-Translation method still dominates many AFL classrooms today,[23] because it makes few demands on the teacher.[24] The teacher does need to be competent in the FL since the focus is on grammar drills and translation, and since some teachers of Arabic as a FL, particularly in some Islamic settings, are not themselves fluent users of the language,[25] a method that does not demand original language production presents itself as a natural fallback position.

This method is known to cause frustration for students,[26] particularly those who wish to speak the language, because they learn about the language and its rules but are unable to use it effectively. This method has often left learners who have studied the language for years unable to participate in the most elementary of conversations.[27] Moreover, this method bores the majority of students[28] and is often marked by a stern atmosphere. Accordingly, Grammar-Translation courses are still remembered with disfavour by thousands of students.[29] Somewhat ironically, the Arabic teachers who use this method do so because they believe that Muslim students only want to read the Qur'an and assume that scrutinising the grammar system and memorising words will enable learners to read with comprehension but often fail to achieve this objective.[30]

It is important to stress that many teachers of Arabic are aware of the existing issues and seek assistance in resolving them.[31] However, holding seminars, workshops and professional development programmes has not led to significant improvement. In fact, in a workshop held in the South African district of KwaZulu-Natal in 1984, it was made clear to the audience that inadequate teaching methods had been in use in secondary school Arabic classrooms since their inception and that as a consequence attrition rates were very high, and that there was now a need for rebuilding a love for Arabic.[32] In the following year, another attempt was made to orientate teachers at a local school, and the Association of Muslim Schools subsequently conducted numerous seminars, but despite all of these attempts, teaching methods had not changed to any significant degree, which led the researchers to conclude that the problem has not been tackled with seriousness nor have plans of action been actualised.[33] This stagnation is a curious phenomenon with a number of plausible explanations.

It is possible that the AFL profession is dealing with a number of deep-seated issues that are too hard to solve. It has been highlighted that the profession lacks adequate numbers of qualified teachers and is overwhelmed by demand for courses for which it cannot produce qualified teachers.[34] In some contexts the Arabic teaching situation is so erratic that breaking the cycle is difficult, as the teachers are products of a system that cannot produce effective teachers.[35] In fact, in South Africa and Botswana, many teachers of Arabic reported that they have limited oral-aural competency in the language.[36] This situation is further complicated by the scarcity of Arabic resources, especially those that are guided by second language acquisition (SLA) research, or that are relevant or suitable for FL learners.[37]

It is also quite evident that we lack clear objectives for Arabic courses offered in some Islamic settings. However, what is more concerning is that there is a lack of consensus on what the learning of Arabic involves or constitutes.[38] In fact, it seems the relationship between Arabic and

Islamic education is complicated.[39] While the basic literacy needed for daily religious practice is a priority for all stakeholders, among some learners this rudimentary literacy is equated with language learning. This leads to Arabic programmes being included for their tokenistic value, and to confusion between the goals of Arabic programmes and Qur'anic literacy courses. Conversely, for other learners, attainment of genuine linguistic ability across the four language macro-skills is desirable.[40] This desire may be growing among our younger non-Arabic-speaking Australian Muslims whose discerning nature and educational experiences leave them dissatisfied with Arabic programmes.[41] Furthermore, there is a misconception that the goal of preserving Arabic as the language of the Qur'an means the preservation of ineffective teaching traditions. This is highlighted by the fact that teaching at many schools is almost medieval in nature,[42] with students simply repeating things they do not understand.[43]

Another probable explanation for this stagnation is the lack of collaboration between schools and universities. This absence of coordination has become counterproductive and detrimental but is due to the fact that Arabic has no governing body and no institutions have risen to the international leadership role that is sorely needed. In the 1990s, regional coordination was suggested in Australia, with a recommendation that a body be formed in New South Wales to pool resources and expertise.[44] Similarly, the need for regional institutional leadership was emphasised in the USA, and it was suggested that the more established and successful programmes take on the role of regional leadership.[45]

Naturally, navigating partnerships among various religious and ethnic communities is a challenge and further emphasises the competing interests and objectives of various parties. Nonetheless, efforts have been made to form teachers' associations in Australia and the USA. In the Australian context, the Victorian Arabic Language Teachers Association (VALTA) was created in 1984 and is currently managed by Mr Khalaf Greis. VALTA is a small organisation that consists of about twenty-five to thirty teachers. VALTA conducts various professional development sessions but tends to cater for teachers in Victoria mainly and its reach remains quite small. In the American context, the American Association of Teachers of Arabic (AATA) has gained a significant degree of national ascendancy. AATA releases an annual journal and runs professional development sessions. However, there is limited evidence of a partnership between AATA and American Islamic schools to create an Arabic syllabus.

Therefore, despite recommendations for coordination and the creation of these two associations, no universally accepted standardised proficiency assessments or school syllabi exist for AFL.[46] Consequently, many teachers feel isolated and there are tendencies toward reinvention of the wheel, duplication of efforts and stagnation. However, while this stagnation endures, many classrooms continue to lack sufficient numbers of qualified teachers. This leads to teaching that is heavily invested in the Grammar-Translation method which is neither effective nor motivating, leads to high attrition rates[47] and inspires a lack of passion for the language.

To further complicate the situation, the absence of textbooks designed for AFL learners[48] means that many schools borrow books that are difficult, irrelevant and sometimes laden with pedagogical issues.[49] Ultimately, this creates learning environments that are saturated with decontextualised and inauthentic linguistic input that is administered in ways that do not foster *noticing*,[50] *interaction*,[51] *output*[52] or *vocabulary strategies*[53] which have a recognised role in facilitating language acquisition. Moreover, these students are deprived of the benefits of *motivational teaching*[54] and communicative approaches that do not exclude grammar but incorporate it into a broader framework that builds learners' grammatical, discourse, strategic and socio-cultural competence.[55]

Arabic at Australian Islamic Schools

The first Australian Islamic schools (AIS) were established in the early 1980s for the same reason that other faith-based schools were established: to provide an alternative to public secular schools.[56] Muslim parents wanted their children to excel academically in an environment that provides access to religious teaching, worship facilities and a religious language. Essentially, AIS teach the same curricula taught at other public schools with the only difference being the Islamic educational component, which includes Islamic and Arabic subjects.

While 80–90% of Muslim children attend public schools, the number of AIS has grown steadily since the 1980s. At least forty AIS are registered with the Islamic Schools Association of Australia and the Independent Schools Council of Australia's 2017 snapshot indicates that these schools cater for around 30,000 Muslim students.[57] Despite this notable growth trajectory, which makes research into AIS a matter of social and academic value, research into AIS is surprisingly limited and lags far behind research into other faith-based schools.[58] Research on Arabic studies at AIS is particularly limited.

However, it has been suggested that AIS have a critical role to play in the development and implementation of Arabic school programmes because of the many features that set them apart from other schools.[59] For instance, AIS are one of the few school domains where non-Arabic-speaking students study Arabic from Foundation to Year 12 and their environment provides opportunities for authentic language use beyond the classroom.[60] Additionally, it is crucial that Islamic schools take a leadership role in the maintenance and preservation of Arabic given its affinity with Islam. However, in a study of the compatibility of Islamic education with Australian values, insight into the AIS Arabic programmes suggests that this potential has not been realised, that AIS are not pioneering advancements and that student satisfaction with courses is divided along heritage lines, with students of non-Arabic-speaking heritage being dissatisfied with their learning experiences.

Peter Jones wanted to understand whether AIS created Muslims in Australia or Australian Muslims, and whether the faith topics and values being taught were compatible with Australian values. He visited ten Islamic Schools, held semi-structured interviews with fifty teachers and interviewed thirty-one alumni. He considered Arabic a faith subject and shed some light on AIS Arabic programmes and the opinions of teachers and students involved with AIS. Although, Arabic occupied a very small part of his thesis the findings are important and indicate that some of the dilemmas that constitute part of the global experiences of Arabic are present at AIS as well.

Peter Jones found that most schools taught Arabic for two hours a week from Year 1 to Year 10; that primary level lessons focused on the script to enable students to read the Qur'an; and that schools attempted to separate native speakers and non-native speakers in the later years. However, the teacher interviews suggested that programmes did not build language proficiency, that students generally remained at a beginner level of proficiency even if they came from an Arabic-speaking background, that teachers were untrained by Australian standards, that teacher turnover was high and that content repetition was common. The student interviews corroborated notions of slow progress, as it was identified that from Year 3 to Year 8 students learnt letters, how to form words and how to put words into sentences.

The most important finding related to the fact that the students' opinions of Arabic were influenced by their existing language proficiency, with the more favourable views being held by students who were of Arabic-speaking backgrounds and the less favourable views being held by students of non-Arabic-speaking backgrounds. For example, Student (F) was a Lebanese-Australian who joined the Islamic primary school in Year 4. Struggling to remember and maintain Arabic, this student found that teachers were good and helped him learn grammar rules and vocabulary. Similarly, Student (H), a fluent speaker of Arabic whose mother was a teacher of Arabic, said that he felt that his sheikh was suitably qualified and that he enjoyed studying the Qur'an under him. In contrast, Student (A), who was from a non-Arabic-speaking background, found that the lessons were unstructured, making it very difficult for students like herself who did not have Arabic as their first language. Student (A) also explained that her native-speaking teacher was not a good speaker of English which made things more challenging. This student explained that the only option left to her was to memorise everything. She emphasised that the schools needed teachers who were interested in seeing the students develop. In a similar vein, Student (K), also from a non-Arabic-speaking background, described a situation in Year 7 in which other students would attend Arabic Qur'anic classes and read aloud to the Imam if they wanted to, whereas she would mainly work on other things. This situation worsened for her in Years 8–10 because classes were segregated and the female teacher assigned to her class was not trained. In fact, this student, who could not receive support at home, found the teaching unsatisfactory.

This insight into some students' and teachers' impressions of Arabic at AIS is extremely valuable. These findings emphasise that the role outlined by remains unrealised, but more importantly, they imply that the programmes delivered by AIS may not be suited to FL learners. This may explain why non-Arabic-speaking students did not care when Arabic was dropped in Years 11–12. Additionally, this resonates with some of the findings on Arabic studies in Australian non-Islamic settings from the early 1990s, in which it was found that Arabic-speaking students were dissatisfied with their teachers and found the content difficult and therefore chose to drop their Arabic studies in Year 11, reflecting a very high 47.8% attrition rate.[61] Moreover, it is highly probable that the Grammar-Translation method is also in use at Islamic schools because survey of the chosen methods of Arabic teachers in ethnic schools conducted in the 1990s identified that teachers' preferred method was in fact the Grammar-Translation method.

While it is necessary to examine the efficacy of Arabic programmes at AIS in greater depth, it is crucial that we proactively use computer-assisted language learning (CALL) to facilitate the creation of a coordinating body for Arabic teaching and learning at AIS. Among its responsibilities would be the pooling of expertise and existing resources.[62] The body would assess the teaching and resource capital and fill gaps as well as lead professional development in order to cater for the needs of FL learners attending AIS. Ideally, this coordinating body would collaborate with centres dedicated to Islamic education, such as the Centre for Islamic Thought and Education based at the University of South Australia, but also with universities with well-established Arabic programmes such as Australian National University and the University of Melbourne.

Computer-Assisted Language Learning (CALL)

Reconsidering pedagogy in this newly digital world is the way forward.[63] However, before elaborating on how CALL can do this, we must address the nature of CALL and define it. CALL is defined as 'the search for and study of applications of the computer in language teaching and learning'.[64]

CALL has developed tremendously both in terms of research and the technology that is available to practitioners. These technologies have become more affordable especially since the advent of the Internet and its expansion. As such, CALL currently covers a host of tools ranging from simple word processing software such as Microsoft Word to task authoring tools and elaborate learning management systems (LMS) such as Blackboard.[65] In fact, CALL is an inclusive term that covers a range of technologies used in language teaching such as computer-mediated communication (CMC)[66] and mobile assisted language learning (MALL).[67]

However, CALL is not a methodology and does not subscribe to a theoretical model; in effect, CALL is neutral and mirrors the knowledge and philosophy of its practitioners.[68] Therefore, CALL design and implementation should draw on our knowledge of how languages are acquired.[69] In addition to being pedagogically guided, technological choices must consider learning contexts, students, the language, syllabus and the teachers administering it.[70]

This ultimately means that we should pedagogically interpret CALL for our particular Arabic teaching context in Australia and not misguidedly think that the incorporation of CALL automatically leads to successful teaching scenarios. It has therefore been noted that inexperienced teachers may assume that converting tasks from traditional formats to CALL formats will guarantee success, but this of course is not true.[71] Rather, activities and tasks that are not carefully planned and pedagogically sound will not produce satisfactory results even if they are enhanced technologically and seem visually appealing.[72]

Consequently, CALL materials are often designed by experienced teachers who develop tasks and courses, or adapt material based on an understanding of the needs and objectives of students.[73] Furthermore, CALL design stems from theories, pedagogical models, courses, syllabi, available technology, the nature of tasks, linguistic skills or a combination of all of these.[74] Naturally, CALL material development is constrained by feasibility,[75] and CALL materials follow a three-stage process of design, development and evaluation.[76] Evaluations of CALL vary in degrees of complexity but aim to judge the worth and efficacy of CALL materials.[77] These evaluations may be conducted using checklists or surveys or through qualitative and quantitative longitudinal evaluation studies.[78]

CALL materials include courseware, software, websites and online courses as well as activities and tasks. In this regard, a distinction is often made between CALL as a *tutor* and as a *tool*.[79] CALL tutors are programmes that can analyse, evaluate and provide learners with feedback about their responses to linguistic content or questions.[80] These range from the simple such as quiz game applications to the very complex where the aim is to provide individualised feedback.[81] In contrast, CALL tools are designed to be enabling devices and include online dictionaries, archives, databases and CMCs such as chat and e-mail.[82]

The value of using CALL has been empirically supported in many language domains, across a number of language macro-skills and in numerous contexts, which has led to four research journals being dedicated to CALL.[83] CALL research has covered many topics. For example, there have been investigations into the use of new technologies such as podcasting, blogging and text-to-speech in teaching,[84] use of CALL in language domains other than English[85] and CALL efficacy in tackling particular language skills.[86] Additionally, researchers have considered the value of

CALL for motivation and the promotion of learner autonomy,[87] the need for teacher development in CALL application as well as barriers to applying CALL in certain contexts.[88] Finally, the cognitive implications of CALL for vocabulary acquisition among right- and left-brain-dominant students have also been investigated.[89]

Furthermore, academic literature on Arabic teaching has suggested the need for CALL materials and addressed the fact that even if the teachers are chalkboard experts, today's students demand different modes of learning.[90] In fact, it was found that CALL was useful for Arabic vocabulary acquisition[91] and grammar acquisition.[92] Arabic research into CALL has assessed Arabic websites,[93] considered the use of audio-visual media in software programs[94] and looked at applications of automatic speech recognition.[95] Research has also sought the views of Arabic teachers on their use of CALL[96] and its applicability in their contexts.[97] Finally, research has supported the use of social networking for teaching Arabic.[98]

A CALL Framework for Arabic Language Teaching at AIS

This chapter does not need to argue for the efficacy and inclusion of CALL. The previous account of the research highlights the interest in applications of CALL to Arabic language teaching. However, while it is my view that we need CALL for resource development, I see CALL mediating cost-effective and strategic solutions for Arabic. These solutions include the launch of an Arabic coordinating body, minimising the number of teachers needed, addressing the communicative gap in our classrooms as well as permitting flexibility and rejuvenation.

Facilitating the Establishment and Management of the ACB

Collaborative efforts have become a necessity for Arabic language teaching and learning in Australia but also internationally. In this regard, CALL can play a significant role of facilitation, mediation and dissemination because CMCs have made communication and collaboration extremely easy on both the individual and organisational levels. This reduces potential costs of travel for members of the coordinating body whereby they can meet online to discuss issues and to brainstorm.

CMCs will also facilitate generous amounts of online training for teachers, allow online collaboration and facilitate dissemination of developed resources and guidelines. Furthermore, CALL will permit the creation of a national database and resource library for Arabic teachers and students. This would enable the coordinating body to pool resources, identify gaps and develop content while managing the teaching expertise as well.

Redefining the Roles of Teachers of Arabic

The first strategic advantage of moving Arabic into a more CALL-driven domain relates to the change in teachers' roles. Classically, one of the concerns that many teachers have is that technology will replace them,[99] and they are consequently wary of the introduction of CALL. It is important to note that technology does not threaten the teacher's job but redefines it. With the introduction of CALL, the teacher's role changes from that of the lecturer, information giver or tutor to that of the facilitator[100] or the designer.[101]

It has been identified that if technology is incorporated, roles are modified and assistants work with the main teachers, fewer numbers of qualified teachers will be needed.[102] Given that the estimates we have for fully qualified Arabic teachers in Australia range from fifty to one hundred,[103] this is a highly welcome notion. This would in effect constitute a paradigm shift that would hasten the move from the more teacher-centred classroom to the more learner-centred classroom.[104] This too is desirable given the dominance of the teacher-centred Grammar-Translation tendencies of Arabic courses in some contexts.

Moving teachers who are less trained, have limited language proficiency or are qualified but lack adequate English communication skills into facilitator roles immediately takes a lot of pressure off them. They are no longer the sole source of information and therefore they are less likely to feel insecure about their own abilities. If these teachers are presented with complete lesson plans, audio-visual material as well as various activities to conduct in class along with very clear instructions on how to administer these lesson plans, they are likely to achieve better results. Moreover, material can be designed to cater for the AFL learners specifically and follow the more contemporary communicative approach.

Naturally, CALL education and professional development becomes an issue to contend with.[105] Here it is highlighted that teachers need to undergo professional development sessions to learn how to use new tools.[106] Essentially, teachers incorporate various degrees of technology in their classrooms and with varying degrees of success.[107] However, in this interpretation of CALL, this matter would not pose a major problem because incorporation would be planned, uniform and accompanied by clear instructions. Additionally, administration would be closely observed until teachers felt comfortable with the CALL materials and lesson plans presented by the coordinating body.

The role of suitably qualified teachers will also change significantly as they move into leadership roles. Firstly, some teachers will become members of the coordinating body and work with other schoolteachers, academics and vocational trainers involved with the teaching of Arabic, while others will head Arabic departments at their schools. Secondly, some teachers will move into the role of designers of courses, textbooks and CALL content. These teachers may work on developing the syllabus using the ACARA syllabus as a point of departure.[108] However, teachers will also partner with information technology experts, graphic designers and animators in order to expedite the creation of content and improve its quality. Additionally, these partnerships will allow them to focus on the pedagogical aspects of the developed content.[109] Finally, these teachers will undertake training and professional development roles to guide teachers that have assumed facilitating roles.

Addressing the Communicative Gaps in AIS Arabic Classrooms

The value of interaction between native and non-native speakers for language acquisition is so well documented that it has moved from being a hypothesis to constituting an approach.[110] Therefore, ensuring that classrooms support interaction and communication is of paramount importance. However, Arabic students are often overwhelmed with grammar, repetition and translation and given few chances to interact with each other in communicative activities. In fact, research has shown that even in a Malaysian university course dedicated to speaking, students were not given opportunities to speak and practise with each other but were expected to memorise dialogues and deliver them from memory the following day, and that they spent time listening to the teacher translate its content.[111]

While the first advocate of a communicative approach to teaching, Ibn Khaldun, and contemporary advocates of communicative language teaching (CLT) do not argue for the exclusion of grammar form, they do emphasise the need for balance between the various aspects of language. CLT suggests the use of a communicative framework to enhance the learners' competence.[112] In this framework, teachers create activities that develop all macro-skills. Moreover, CLT does not prescribe a single methodology or set of techniques.[113] Rather, CLT argues that teaching should keep the communicative purpose of language in mind and allow for focus-on-form.[114]

This need for incorporating communicative aspects is particularly pronounced in the FL context where learners have very limited opportunities for interacting with native speakers outside of the classroom. In this regard, CALL can be used to fill the communicative gap. With the availability of various forms of recording, video and text creation software, some of which is free, language study can be made more communicative and indeed engaging and motivating.[115] Moreover, online platforms permit teachers and students to create *life-like speaking avatars, audio clips, videos, cartoon strips, animations, blogs* and *e-books*.

CALL options for communicative activities are limitless. For example, students can be presented with audio-visual material and then be asked to discuss this in various formats of pair and group work activities. Additionally, they can be asked to record and share their own content for class comprehension activities. Furthermore, students can use CMCs and social networking to communicate with each other both orally and in writing.

CMCs can also facilitate partnerships with students from the Arab world whereby language exchange activities can be undertaken. For example, a student in the Arab world can record a video about their school, family, friends and then this can be shared with students in Australia, who return the favour by creating similar videos in English. Or students can be paired up with Arabic-speaking students from other schools in Australia or the Arab world and engage in conversations, e-mail and audio clip exchanges. Communicative activities can also include projects that involve students reading online content available in encyclopaedias, e-zines or e-books and then presenting their findings in their own words either orally or in writing, or in activities that involve a combination of speaking and writing tasks. Students may then be asked to converse about these things.

Furthermore, CALL quizzes and games can be used in class to assess whether target items have been acquired or for revision without creating anxiety but in contrast by creating engaging class competitions. There are various formats such as *millionaire games, jeopardy* as well as interactive whole-class platforms such as *Kahoot* which allow students to use their own mobile devices to answer questions anonymously.

The crucial benefit of this aspect of the framework is that facilitating teachers will not need to create the material themselves but rather manage the sessions and activities by following the lesson plans and teacher instructions received from the coordinating body. Furthermore, the facilitating teachers will not need to model the target language if they are not comfortable doing so; rather, they can present the audio-visual material and manage the ensuing activities as they have been trained to do. Therefore, these teachers would not risk losing face because of mispronunciation or lack of fluency, and students would not be made to suffer due to these insecurities.

Flexibility and Rejuvenation of Arabic Studies

The most important benefit of using CALL in this framework is that it will permit flexibility and rejuvenation of courses, content and methodology. The flexibility of CALL will initially serve the purpose of urgency which will enable the coordinating body to pool, adapt or create content that is relevant, contains communicative components, while more comprehensive textbooks and resources are being developed.

CALL flexibility will also allow us to create digital textbooks that are easily editable, require shorter delivery lead-times and involve smaller financial commitments from school management boards. Additionally, by virtue of the ever-evolving nature of technology, CALL will allow for the constant reinvigoration of textbooks with more contemporary and relevant content and technological features. This would be in sharp contrast to the existing situation wherein books designed in the 1980s are still in use in the 2000s.[116]

CALL will naturally facilitate the assessment of programme efficacy through evaluations conducted at regular intervals throughout course and framework implementation. Additionally, because CALL assessments are easy to disseminate through e-mail and can take the form of online surveys, it will be easy to gather the responses of students, parents, teachers and school management frequently. Moreover, CALL will permit longitudinal investigations of the syllabus, textbooks, assessment methods and proficiency tests.

More importantly, because CALL does not subscribe to a particular method or approach, it will allow us to constantly revisit, rejuvenate and improve our methods. CALL will also enable us to mirror the advancements in the fields of cognitive linguistics, neurolinguistics, cognitive psychology, psycholinguistics, SLA and teaching. This is particularly important because we have entered the post-method era.[117]

Conclusion

The value of Arabic to Australia is communal,[118] economic[119] and strategic, making it one of the important 'languages other than English'. However, the learning of Arabic in Australia has been likened to a pyramid because enrolments diminish over the years of schooling.[120] Unfortunately, AFL teaching is gravely challenged internationally as well. However, it is possible to address many of the challenges by using CALL strategically.

This chapter has introduced a framework for the incorporation of CALL. It has identified that CALL can play an important role in facilitating the formulation of a coordinating body to manage the affairs of Arabic teaching and learning. Moreover, CALL can augment the existing supply of qualified teachers and alleviate some of the industry pressures caused by increased demand for Arabic courses. CALL will also support students and teachers by addressing the severe communicative gaps that exist in classrooms and content. Finally, CALL will allow for the continual rejuvenation of Arabic courses and methods.

In this regard, AIS have a particularly crucial role to play because they have become an important feature of the educational landscape in Australia, with at least forty schools currently servicing around 30,000 students.[121] Moreover, AIS are well positioned to champion the CALL framework being suggested in this chapter because AIS are managed by qualified educators, have access to sufficient funds and adhere to Australian standards of education as accredited institutions. Furthermore, AIS have an exceptional role to play in the development of Arabic language programmes due to the presence of high concentrations of teachers and non-native-speaking students that are not affected by the negative stereotypes of Arabs and Muslims that often deter other Australian students from taking up Arabic studies.[122]

Further to the role envisaged by Hall, AIS have a special responsibility towards Arabic, because in the context of Islamic education, Arabic should be seen as the key to the Qur'an and Sunnah and thus an *Amanah* (i.e., trust and responsibility) that should be safely delivered to the next generation of Muslims. As such, no efforts should be spared with regards to ensuring the effectiveness of Arabic courses being administered under their auspices. In fact, AIS should take a leadership role in addressing the challenges that have plagued the AFL industry for decades rather than allowing them to fester further.

Notes

1. In its simplest sense the term word family refers to a group of words that share a lexical relationship, such as *help, helper and helpful*.
2. Nation, Paul, and Robert Waring. "Vocabulary Size, Text Coverage and Word Lists." Chap. 1.1 In *Vocabulary: Description, Acquisition and Pedagogy*, edited by Norbert Schmitt and Michael M. McCarthy, 6–19. Cambridge, UK: Cambridge University Press, 1997.
3. Schmitt, Norbert, Xiangying Jiang, and William Grabe. "The Percentage of Words Known in a Text and Reading Comprehension." *The Modern Language Journal* 95, no. 1 (2011): 26–43.
4. Ibid.
5. Ricks, Robert. "The Development of Frequency-Based Assessments of Vocabulary Breadth and Depth for L2 Arabic." Doctor of Philosophy, Georgetown University, 2015.
6. Buckwalter, Tim, and Dilworth Parkinson. *A Frequency Dictionary of Arabic: Core Vocabulary for Learners*. Hoboken: Taylor & Francis Group, 2014.
7. Savignon, Sandra J. "Communicative Language Teaching: Linguistic Theory and Classroom Practice." Chap. 1 In *Interpreting Communicative Language Teaching: Contexts and Concerns in Teacher Education*, edited by Sandra J. Savignon, 1–28. New Haven, CT, USA: Yale University Press, 2002.
8. Blake, Robert J. *Brave New Digital Classroom: Technology and Foreign Language Learning*. Washington, DC, USA: Georgetown University Press, 2013.
9. Damron, Julie, and Justin Forsyth. "Korean Language Studies: Motivation and Attrition." *Journal of the National Council of Less Commonly Taught Languages* 12 Fall (2012): 161–88.
10. U.S. Department of State, "Language Assignments," 2015, published online: https://www.state.gov/documents/organization/247092.pdf. Retrieved on: 10/01/2016.
11. Jones, Peter D. P. "Islamic Schools in Australia: Muslims in Australia or Australian Muslims?", Doctor of Philosophy, University of New England, 2013.
12. Gass, Susan M., and Larry Selinker. *Second Language Acquisition: An Introductory Course*. 3 ed. New York, USA: Taylor and Francis, 2008.

13. Osman, Ghada. "The Historian on Language: Ibn Khaldun and the Communicative Learning Approach." *Middle East Studies Association Bulletin* 37, no. 1 (2003): 50–57.
14. Ibid.
15. Osman, "The Historian on Language", 53.
16. Ben-Ari, Shosh. "Language, Civilisation and Globalisation in the 14th Century: Historical Periodicity and the Evolution of Language at Ibn Khaldūn." *Acta Orientalia Academiae Scientiarum Hungaricae* 62, no. 2 (2009): 219–30.
17. Osman, "The Historian on Language", 52.
18. Patel, M. F., and Praveen M. Jain. *English Language Teaching: (Methods, Tools & Techniques)*. Jaipur, India: Sunrise Publishers and Distributors, 2008.
19. Richards, Jack C., and Theodore S. Rodgers. Approaches and Methods in Language Teaching. 2nd ed. Cambridge, UK: Cambridge University Press, 2001.
20. Patel and Jain, "English Language Teaching", 74.
21. Taber, Joan. "A Brief History of ESL Instruction: Theories, Methodologies, and Upheavals." In TESL Certificate Program – SCCC. Published online http://seattlecentral.edu/faculty/jgeorg/TESLSCCC/ABriefHistory.htm: Seattle Central College, 2006. Retrieved on 15/12/2015.
22. Ibid.
23. Mall, MA, and MM Nieman. "Problems Experienced with the Teaching of Arabic to Learners in Muslim Private Schools in South Africa and Botswana." *Per Linguam* 18, no. 2 (2002): 42–54; Campbell, Stuart, Bronwen Dyson, Sadika Karim, and Basima Rabie. *Unlocking Australia's Language Potential: Profiles of 9 Key Languages in Australia. Volume 1 - Arabic*. 1 vols. Canberra, Australia: National Languages and Literacy Institute of Australia 1993; Ismail, A.R.B.H. "The Teaching of Arabic in the Faculty of Islamic Studies in the National University of Malaysia." Doctor of Philosophy, University of Salford, 1993; Sirajudeen, Adam, and Abdul Wahid Adebisi. "Teaching Arabic as a Second Language in Nigeria." *Procedia – Social and Behavioral Sciences* 66 (2012): 126–35.
24. Richards and Rodgers, "Approaches and Methods in Language Teaching", 6.
25. Mall and Nieman. "Problems Experienced with the Teaching of Arabic", 42.
26. Richards and Rodgers, "Approaches and Methods in Language Teaching", 6–7.
27. Taber, "A Brief History of ESL Instruction", Retrieved on 15/12/2015.
28. Ibid.
29. Richards and Rodgers, "Approaches and Methods in Language Teaching", 6–7.

30. Mall, and Nieman. "Problems Experienced with the Teaching of Arabic", 50.
31. Mall, and Nieman. "Problems Experienced with the Teaching of Arabic", 53.
32. Mall, and Nieman. "Problems Experienced with the Teaching of Arabic", 44.
33. Mall, and Nieman. "Problems Experienced with the Teaching of Arabic", 45.
34. Al-Batal, Mahmoud. "Arabic and National Language Educational Policy." *The Modern Language Journal* 91, no. 2 (2007): 268–71.
35. Sirajudeen and Adebisi, "Teaching Arabic as a Second Language in Nigeria", 126.
36. Mall, and Nieman. "Problems Experienced with the Teaching of Arabic", 47.
37. Mall, and Nieman. "Problems Experienced with the Teaching of Arabic", 52; Morrison, Sally. "Arabic Language Teaching in the United States." ERIC Clearinghouse on Languages and Linguistics (Language link online) (2003). Retrieved from: Campus Watch, https://www.meforum.org/campus-watch/articles/2007/arabic-language-teaching-in-the-united-states. Retrieved on: 22/01/2016.
38. Cruickshank, Ken. "Arabic-English Bilingualism in Australia." In *Encyclopedia of Language and Education*, edited by Jim Cummins and Nancy H. Hornberger, 281–94. USA: Springer, 2008; Areef, Mohamed Kheder. "The Current Linguistic and Curricular Approaches in Teaching Arabic as a Foreign Language: Problems and Suggested Solutions." University of Southern California, 1986.
39. Jones, Sidney. "Arabic Instruction and Literacy in Javanese Muslim Schools." *International Journal of the Sociology of Language* 1983, no. 42 (1983): 83–94.
40. Ibid.
41. Jones, "Islamic Schools in Australia", 117–21.
42. Sirajudeen and Adebisi, "Teaching Arabic as a Second Language in Nigeria", 129.
43. Mall and Nieman. "Problems Experienced with the Teaching of Arabic", 43.
44. Campbell et al., "Unlocking Australia's Language Potential", v.
45. Al-Batal, Mahmoud, and R Kirk Belnap. "The Teaching and Learning of Arabic in the United States: Realities, Needs, and Future Directions." Chap. 30 In *Handbook for Arabic Language Teaching Professionals in the 21st Century*, edited by Kassem M. Wahba, Zeinab A. Taha and Liz England, 389–99. Mahwah, New Jersey, USA: Routledge, 2006.

46. Selim, Nadia. "Ibn Sahnun's Ninth Century Framework: A Guide for Arabic Language Curriculum Writing." *Islam and Civilisational Renewal*, 8, no. 4 (2017): 488–506; Berbeco, Steven. "Effects of Non-Linear Curriculum Design on Arabic Proficiency." Doctor of Education, Boston University, 2011.
47. Sirajudeen and Adebisi. "Teaching Arabic as a Second Language in Nigeria", 129.
48. Mall and Nieman. "Problems Experienced with the Teaching of Arabic", 52; Ismail, "The Teaching of Arabic in the Faculty of Islamic Studies in the National University of Malaysia." 99–100.
49. Schmidt, Richard. "The Role of Consciousness in Second Language Learning." *Applied Linguistics* 11, no. 2 (1990): 129–58.
50. Mackey, Alison, Rebekha Abbuhl, and Susan M Gass. "Interactionist Approach." Chap. 1 In *The Routledge Handbook of Second Language Acquisition*, edited by Susan M Gass and Alison Mackey. Routledge Handbooks in Applied Linguistics, 7–23. London, UK: Routledge 2012.
51. Swain, Merrill. "Communicative Competence: Some Roles of Comprehensible Input and Comprehensible Output in Its Development." Chap. 14 In *Input in Second Language Acquisition*, edited by S. Gass and C. Madden, 235-53. Rowley, MA, USA: Newbury House Publishers, Inc., 1985.
52. Takač, Višnja Pavičić. Vocabulary Learning Strategies and Foreign Language Acquisition. Clevedon, UK: Multilingual Matters, 2008.
53. Dörnyei, Zoltan. *Motivational Strategies in the Language Classroom*. UK: Cambridge University Press, 2001.
54. Savignon, Sandra J. "Communicative Language Teaching." *Theory into practice* 26, no. 4 (1987): 235–42.
55. Clyne, Irene Donohue. "Educating Muslim Children in Australia." Chap. 6 In *Muslim Communities in Australia*, edited by Abdullah Saeed and Shahram Akbarzadeh, 116–37. Sydney, Australia: UNSW Press, 2001; Jones, Peter D. "Islamic Schools in Australia." The La Trobe Journal 89 (2012): 36–47.
56. I.S.A.A. "Islamic Schools Association of Australia Website." http://www.isaahome.org.au/member-schools/. Retrieved on 26/03/2016; I.S.C.A. "Snapshot 2016." Independent Schools Council of Australia, isca.edu.au/wp-content/uploads/2011/07/ISCA-Snapshot-2015.pdf. Retrieved on 10/08/2016.
57. Jones, "Islamic Schools in Australia", 36–47.
58. Hall, Michael. "Arabic in Australian Islamic Schools [Paper Presented at the Australia Middle East Studies Association Conference (1994: Deakin University)]." Babel 31, no. 2 (July/September 1996): 28–31.
59. Ibid.
60. Campbell et al., "Unlocking Australia's Language Potential", 60–61.

61. Campbell et al., "Unlocking Australia's Language Potential", 32.
62. Campbell et al., "Unlocking Australia's Language Potential", v.
63. Beetham, Helen, and Rhona Sharpe. *Rethinking Pedagogy for a Digital Age: Designing for 21st Century Learning*. 2nd ed. New York: USA: Routledge, 2013.
64. Levy, Michael. *Computer-Assisted Language Learning: Context and Conceptualization*. Oxford: UK: Oxford University Press, 1997, 1.
65. Levy, Mike and Glenn Stockwell. *CALL Dimensions: Options and Issues in Computer-Assisted Language Learning*. ESL & Applied Linguistics Professional Series Edited by Eli Hinkel. Mahwah, New Jersey: USA: Lawrence Erlbaum Associates, 2006, 3.
66. Blake, "Brave New Digital Classroom", 4.
67. Stockwell, Glenn. Computer-Assisted Language Learning: Diversity in Research and Practice. Cambridge: UK: Cambridge University Press, 2012.
68. Blake, "Brave New Digital Classroom", 2.
69. Levy and Stockwell, "CALL Dimensions", 6.
70. Levy and Stockwell, "CALL Dimensions", 10.
71. Blake, "Brave New Digital Classroom", 11.
72. Ibid.
73. Levy and Stockwell, "CALL Dimensions", 10–40.
74. Ibid.
75. Ibid.
76. Levy and Stockwell, "CALL Dimensions", 40–84.
77. Ibid.
78. Ibid.
79. Fernández Carballo-Calero, Ma Victoria. "The EFL Teacher and the Introduction of Multimedia in the Classroom." *Computer Assisted Language Learning* 14, no. 1 (2001): 3–14.
80. Levy and Stockwell, "CALL Dimensions", 22–26.
81. Ibid.
82. Ibid.
83. Stockwell, Glenn, "Computer-Assisted Language Learning: Diversity in Research and Practice", 1.
84. Chan, Wai Meng, Ing Ru Chen, and Martin G Döpel. "Podcasting in Foreign Language Learning." Chap. 2, Part 1: New Technologies, New Pedagogies In *WorldCALL: International Perspectives on Computer-Assisted Language Learning*, edited by Mike Levy, Françoise Blin, Claire Bradin Siskin and Osamu Takeuchi. Routledge Studies in Computer Assisted Language Learning 19–37. New York, USA: Taylor & Francis Group, 2011; Kılıçkaya, Ferit. "Improving Pronunciation Via Accent Reduction and Text-to-Speech Software." Chap. 6, Part 2: In *WorldCALL: International Perspectives on Computer-Assisted Language Learning*,

edited by Mike Levy, Françoise Blin, Claire Bradin Siskin and Osamu Takeuchi. Routledge Studies in Computer Assisted Language Learning 85-96. New York, USA: Taylor & Francis Group, 2011; Domalewska, Dorota. "Technology-Supported Classroom for Collaborative Learning: Blogging in the Foreign Language Classroom." *International Journal of Education and Development using Information and Communication Technology* 10, no. 4 (2014): 21–30.
85. Barani, Ghasem. "The Relationship between Computer Assisted Language Learning (CALL) and Listening Skill of Iranian EFL Learners." *Procedia-Social and Behavioral Sciences* 15 (2011): 4059–63; Marzban, Amir. "Improvement of Reading Comprehension through Computer-Assisted Language Learning in Iranian Intermediate EFL Students." *Procedia Computer Science* 3 (2011): 3–10; Pirasteh, Parvin. "The Effectiveness of Computer-Assisted Language Learning (CALL) on Learning Grammar by Iranian EFL Learners." *Procedia, social and Behavioral sciences* 98 (2014): 1422–27.
86. Nachoua, Hassina. "Computer-Assisted Language Learning for Improving Students' Listening Skill." *Procedia, social and Behavioral sciences* 69 (2012): 1150-59; Zaini, Amin, and Golnar Mazdayasna. "The Effect of Computer Assisted Language Learning on the Development of EFL Learners' Writing Skills." *Procedia, social and Behavioral sciences* 98 (2014): 1975–82.
87. Mahmood, Asim, Salman ul Waheed, Muhammad Asif Ikram Anjum, and Rashda Majeed. "Computer Assisted Language Learning: An Instrument of Change for Boosting Motivation Level among the Students of Graduation in Pakistan." *Language in India* 13, no. 7 (2013): 159–70; Mutlu, Arzu, and Betil Eroz-Tuga. "The Role of Computer-Assisted Language Learning (CALL) in Promoting Learner Autonomy." *Eurasian Journal of Educational Research* 51 (2013): 107–22.
88. Dashtestani, Reza. "EFL Teachers' Knowledge of the Use and Development of Computer-Assisted Language Learning (CALL) Material." *Teaching English with Technology: A Journal for Teachers of English* 14, no. 2 (2014): 3–26; Hani, Nedal A. Bani. "Benefits and Barriers of Computer Assisted Language Learning and Teaching in the Arab World: Jordan as a Model." *Theory and practice in language studies* 4, no. 8 (2014): 1609–15.
89. Jevnaker, Birgit Helene, Brynjulf Tellefsen, and Marika Lüders. "Front-End Service Innovation: Learning from a Design-Assisted Experimentation." *European Journal of Innovation Management* 18, no. 1 (2015): 19–43.
90. Ditters, Everhard. "Technologies for Arabic Language Teaching and Learning". Chap. 17 In *Handbook for Arabic Language Teaching*

Professionals in the 21st Century, edited by Kassem M. Wahba, Zeinab A. Taha and Liz England, 239–52. Mahwah, New Jersey: USA: Routledge, 2006.

91. Gharawi, Mohammed A, and Azman Bidin. "Computer Assisted Language Learning for Learning Arabic as a Second Language in Malaysia: Teacher Perceptions." *International Journal of Information and Education Technology* 6, no. 8 (2016): 633–37.

92. Arrabtah, Adel, and Tayseer Nusour. "Using Technology for Teaching Arabic Language Grammar." *Journal of International Education Research* 8, no. 4 (2012): 335–42.

93. Achour, Hadhémi, and Wahiba Ben Abdesslam. "An Evaluation of Arabic Language Learning Websites." In *International Conference on Education and E-Learning Innovations*, 1–6. Sousse, Tunisia, IEEE Xplore Digital Library, 2012.

94. Samy, Waheed. "Instructional Media and Learning Arabic." Chap. 19 In *Handbook for Arabic Language Teaching Professionals in the 21st Century*, edited by Kassem M. Wahba, Zeinab A. Taha and Liz England, 263–74. Mahwah, New Jersey: USA: Routledge, 2006.

95. Terbeh, Naim, and Mounir Zrigui. "Arabic Language Learning Assisted by Computer, Based on Automatic Speech Recognition." arXiv.org: Operated by Cornell University Library 2012.

96. Al Musawi, Ali, Abdullah Al Hashmi, Ali Mahdi Kazem, Fatima Al Busaidi, and Salim Al Khaifi. "Perceptions of Arabic Language Teachers toward Their Use of Technology at the Omani Basic Education Schools." *Education and Information Technologies* 21, no. 1 (2016): 5–18.

97. Hani, "Benefits and Barriers of Computer Assisted Language Learning and Teaching in the Arab World", 1609–15.

98. Rahimi, Nik Mohd, Nor Azhan, Wan Normeza, and Harun Baharudin. "Students' Feedback Towards Using Facebook in Learning Arabic Language." *Asian Social Science* 11, no. 28 (2015): 170–74.

99. Blake, "Brave New Digital Classroom", 9.

100. Fernández Carballo-Calero, "The EFL Teacher and the Introduction of Multimedia in the Classroom", 3–14; Riasati, M, Negah Allahyar, and K Tan. "Technology in Language Education: Benefits and Barriers." *Journal of Education and Practice* 3, no. 5 (2012): 25–30.

101. Levy and Stockwell, "CALL Dimensions",10.

102. Ely, Donald P, and Tjeerd Plomp. "The Promises of Educational Technology: A Reassessment." *International Review of Education* 32, no. 3 (1986): 231–49.

103. Campbell et al., "Unlocking Australia's Language Potential", 48.

104. Riasati, Allahyar, and Tan. "Technology in Language Education: Benefits and Barriers", 25–30.

105. Levy, Mike. "A Rationale for Teacher Education and CALL: The Holistic View and Its Implications." *Computers and the Humanities* 30, no. 4 (1996): 293–302; Riasati, Allahyar, and Tan. "Technology in Language Education: Benefits and Barriers", 25–30; Fernández Carballo-Calero, "The EFL Teacher and the Introduction of Multimedia in the Classroom", 3–14; Nim Park, Chan, and Jeong-Bae Son. "Implementing Computer-Assisted Language Learning in the EFL Classroom: Teachers' Perceptions and Perspectives." *International Journal of Pedagogies and Learning* 5, no. 2 (2009): 80–101.
106. Nim Park, and Son. "Implementing Computer-Assisted Language Learning in the EFL Classroom", 80–101.
107. Almekhlafi, Abdurrahman Ghaleb, and Farouq Ahmad Almeqdadi. "Teachers' Perceptions of Technology Integration in the United Arab Emirates School Classrooms." *Educational Technology & Society* 13, no. 1 (2010): 165–75.
108. The Australian Curriculum, Assessment and Reporting Authority, designed a national Arabic syllabus for Foundation - Year 10 students. Which is a highly welcomed notion, however, the context statement notes that it is pitched at Arabic-background learners. Therefore, when designing content for AFL learners the ACARA syllabus may be used as a point of departure only but cannot be used in its entirety.
109. Levy, "A Rationale for Teacher Education and Call", 293–302.
110. Mackey, Abbuhl, and Gass. "Interactionist Approach", 7–23.
111. Haron, Sueraya Che. "The Teaching Methodology of Arabic Speaking Skills: Learners' Perspectives." *International Education Studies* 6, no. 2 (2013): 55–62.
112. Savignon, Sandra J. "Communicative Language Teaching: Linguistic Theory and Classroom Practice." Chap. 1 In *Interpreting Communicative Language Teaching: Contexts and Concerns in Teacher Education*, edited by Sandra J. Savignon, 1–28. New Haven, CT, USA: Yale University Press, 2002.
113. Berns, Margie S. *Contexts of Competence: Social and Cultural Considerations in Communicative Language Teaching*. New York, USA: Plenum Press, 1990.
114. Lightbown, Patsy M, and Nina Spada. "Focus-on-Form and Corrective Feedback in Communicative Language Teaching." *Studies in Second Language Acquisition* 12, no. 04 (1990): 429–48.
115. Dörnyei, "Motivational Strategies in the Language Classroom", 53.
116. Dawood, Shaukat. "Teaching of the Arabic Language in South African Schools: Nature of Language and Methodology." Master of Arts, University of South Africa, 2009.

117. Kumaravadivelu, B. *Understanding Language Teaching: From Method to Postmethod*. ESL & Applied Linguistics Professional Series Edited by Eli Hinkel Mahwah, New Jersey, USA: Lawrence Erlbaum Associates, Inc., Publishers 2006.
118. Cruickshank, "Arabic-English Bilingualism in Australia", 281–94.
119. Austrade, and DFAT. "Submission by Austrade and the Department of Foreign Affairs and Trade to the Joint Standing Committee on Foreign Affairs, Defence and Trade Inquiry into Australia's Trade and Investment Relationships with Countries of the Middle East", edited by Department of Foreign Affairs and Trade and Austrade, 1–56. Online Department of Foreign Affairs and Trade and Austrade 2014.
120. Campbell et al., "Unlocking Australia's Language Potential", 1.
121. I.S.C.A. "Snapshot 2016." Retrieved on 10/08/2016.
122. Hall, "Arabic in Australian Islamic Schools", 28–31.

Bibliography

ACARA. "Arabic: Context Statement." Australian Curriculum, Assessment and Reporting Authority. https://www.australiancurriculum.edu.au/f-10-curriculum/languages/arabic/context-statement/.

Achour, Hadhémi, and Wahiba Ben Abdesslam. "An Evaluation of Arabic Language Learning Websites." In *International Conference on Education and E-Learning Innovations*, 1–6. Sousse, Tunisia IEEE Xplore Digital Library, 2012.

Al Musawi, Ali, Abdullah Al Hashmi, Ali Mahdi Kazem, Fatima Al Busaidi, and Salim Al Khaifi. "Perceptions of Arabic Language Teachers Toward Their Use of Technology at the Omani Basic Education Schools." *Education and Information Technologies* 21, no. 1 (2016): 5–18.

Al-Batal, Mahmoud, and R. Kirk Belnap. "The Teaching and Learning of Arabic in the United States: Realities, Needs, and Future Directions." Chap. 30 In *Handbook for Arabic Language Teaching Professionals in the 21st Century*, ed. Kassem M. Wahba, Zeinab A. Taha, and Liz England, 389–399. Mahwah, NJ: Rouledge, 2006.

Almekhlafi, Abdurrahman Ghaleb, and Farouq Ahmad Almeqdadi. "Teachers' Perceptions of Technology Integration in the United Arab Emirates School Classrooms." *Educational Technology & Society* 13, no. 1 (2010): 165–175.

Areef, Mohamed Kheder. "The Current Linguistic and Curricular Approaches in Teaching Arabic as a Foreign Language: Problems and Suggested Solutions." PhD thesis – University of Southern California, 1986.

Arrabtah, Adel, and Tayseer Nusour. "Using Technology for Teaching Arabic Language Grammar." *Journal of International Education Research* 8, no. 4 (2012): 335–342.

Austrade and DFAT. "Submission by Austrade and the Department of Foreign Affairs and Trade to the Joint Standing Committee on Foreign Affairs, Defence and Trade Inquiry into Australia's Trade and Investment Relationships with Countries of the Middle East." Ed. Department of Foreign Affairs and Trade and Austrade, 1–56. Online Department of Foreign Affairs and Trade and Austrade, 2014.

Barani, Ghasem. "The Relationship between Computer Assisted Language Learning (Call) and Listening Skill of Iranian Efl Learners." *Procedia-Social and Behavioral Sciences* 15 (2011): 4059–4063.

Ben-Ari, Shosh. "Language, Civilisation and Globalisation in the 14th Century: Historical Periodicity and the Evolution of Language at Ibn Khaldūn." *Acta Orientalia Academiae Scientiarum Hungaricae* 62, no. 2 (2009): 219–230.

Berbeco, Steven. "Effects of Non-Linear Curriculum Design on Arabic Proficiency." Doctor of Education, Boston University, 2011.

Berns, Margie S. *Contexts of Competence: Social and Cultural Considerations in Communicative Language Teaching*. Teaching History. New York: Plenum Press, 1990.

Blake, Robert J. *Brave New Digital Classroom: Technology and Foreign Language Learning*. Washington, DC: Georgetown University Press, 2013.

Buckwalter, Tim, and Dilworth Parkinson. *A Frequency Dictionary of Arabic: Core Vocabulary for Learners*. Hoboken, NJ: Taylor & Francis Group, 2014.

Campbell, Stuart, Bronwen Dyson, Sadika Karim, and Basima Rabie. *Unlocking Australia's Language Potential: Profiles of 9 Key Languages in Australia. Volume 1 – Arabic*. 1 vols. Canberra, Australia: National Languages and Literacy Institute of Australia, 1993.

Chan, Wai Meng, Ing Ru Chen, and Martin G. Döpel. "Podcasting in Foreign Language Learning." Chap. Part 1: New Technologies, New Pedagogies. In *Worldcall: International Perspectives on Computer-Assisted Language Learning*, ed. Mike Levy, Françoise Blin, Claire Bradin Siskin and Osamu Takeuchi. Routledge Studies in Computer Assisted Language Learning, 19–37. New York: Taylor & Francis Group, 2011.

Clyne, Irene Donohue. "Educating Muslim Children in Australia." Chap. 6 In *Muslim Communities in Australia*, ed. Abdullah Saeed and Shahram Akbarzadeh, 116–137. Sydney, Australia: UNSW Press, 2001.

Cruickshank, Ken. "Arabic-English Bilingualism in Australia." In *Encyclopedia of Language and Education*, ed. Jim Cummins and Nancy H. Hornberger, 281–294. New York: Springer, 2008.

Damron, Julie, and Justin Forsyth. "Korean Language Studies: Motivation and Attrition." [In English]. *Journal of the National Council of Less Commonly Taught Languages* 12 (Fall 2012): 161–188.

Dashtestani, Reza. "Efl Teachers' Knowledge of the Use and Development of Computer-Assisted Language Learning (Call) Material." *Teaching English with Technology: A Journal for Teachers of English* 14, no. 2 (2014): 3–26.

Dawood, Shaukat. "Teaching of the Arabic Language in South African Schools: Nature of Language and Methodology." Dissertation, University of South Africa, 2009. http://hdl.handle.net/10500/1944.

Ditters, Everhard. "Technologies for Arabic Language Teaching and Learning." Chap. 17 In *Handbook for Arabic Language Teaching Professionals in the 21st Century*, ed. Kassem M. Wahba, Zeinab A. Taha, and Liz England, 239–252. Mahwah, NJ: Routledge, 2006.

Domalewska, Dorota. "Technology-Supported Classroom for Collaborative Learning: Blogging in the Foreign Language Classroom." *International Journal of Education and Development Using Information and Communication Technology* 10, no. 4 (2014): 21–30.

Dörnyei, Zoltan. *Motivational Strategies in the Language Classroom*. Cambridge, UK: Cambridge University Press, 2001.

Ely, Donald P., and Tjeerd Plomp. "The Promises of Educational Technology: A Reassessment." *International Review of Education* 32, no. 3 (1986): 231–249.

Fernández Carballo-Calero, Ma Victoria. "The Efl Teacher and the Introduction of Multimedia in the Classroom." *Computer Assisted Language Learning* 14, no. 1 (2001): 3–14.

Gass, Susan M., and Larry Selinker. *Second Language Acquisition: An Introductory Course*. [In English], 3rd ed. New York: Taylor and Francis, 2008.

Gharawi, Mohammed A., and Azman Bidin. "Computer Assisted Language Learning for Learning Arabic as a Second Language in Malaysia: Teacher Perceptions." *International Journal of Information and Education Technology* 6, no. 8 (2016): 633–637.

Hall, Michael. *Arabic in Australian Islamic Schools*. Paper presented at the Australia Middle East Studies Association Conference (1994: Deakin University). *Babel* 31, no. 2 (July/September 1996): 28–31.

Hani, Nedal A. Bani. "Benefits and Barriers of Computer Assisted Language Learning and Teaching in the Arab World: Jordan as a Model." *Theory and Practice in Language Studies* 4, no. 8 (2014): 1609–1615.

Haron, Sueraya Che. "The Teaching Methodology of Arabic Speaking Skills: Learners' Perspectives." *International Education Studies* 6, no. 2 (2013): 55–62.

Hassan, Ismail. *Teaching the Arabic Language: Problems in Languages or Speakers*. Paper presented at The II International Conference: Methods of Teaching Oriental Languages: Actual Problems and Trends, HSE School of Asian Studies in Moscow, 2014. https://www.hse.ru/data/2014/04/13/1320988201/Methods%20of%20teaching%20.

I.S.A.A. "Islamic Schools Association of Australia Website". http://www.isaa-home.org.au/member-schools/.

I.S.C.A. "Snapshot 2016." Independent Schools Council of Australia. isca.edu.au/wp-content/uploads/2011/07/ISCA-Snapshot-2015.pdf.

Ismail, A.R.B.H. "The Teaching of Arabic in the Faculty of Islamic Studies in the National University of Malaysia." PhD thesis, University of Salford, 1993.

Jevnaker, Birgit Helene, Brynjulf Tellefsen, and Marika Lüders. "Front-End Service Innovation: Learning from a Design-Assisted Experimentation." *European Journal of Innovation Management* 18, no. 1 (2015): 19–43.

Jones, Sidney. "Arabic Instruction and Literacy in Javanese Muslim Schools." *International Journal of the Sociology of Language* 1983, no. 42 (1983): 83–94.

Jones, Peter D. P. "Islamic Schools in Australia: Muslims in Australia or Australian Muslims?", University of New England, 2013.

Kılıçkaya, Ferit. "Improving Pronunciation Via Accent Reduction and Text-to-Speech Software." Chap. 6 In *Worldcall: International Perspectives on Computer-Assisted Language Learning*, ed. Mike Levy, Françoise Blin, Claire Bradin Siskin, and Osamu Takeuchi. Routledge Studies in Computer Assisted Language Learning, 85–96. New York: Taylor & Francis Group, 2011.

Kumaravadivelu, B. *Understanding Language Teaching: From Method to Postmethod.* [in English] Esl & Applied Linguistics Professional Series. Ed. Eli Hinkel. Mahwah, NJ: Lawrence Erlbaum Associates, Inc., Publishers, 2006.

Levy, Mike. "A Rationale for Teacher Education and Call: The Holistic View and Its Implications." *Computers and the Humanities* 30, no. 4 (1996): 293–302.

Levy, Michael. *Computer-Assisted Language Learning: Context and Conceptualization.* Oxford: Oxford University Press, 1997.

Levy, Mike, and Glenn Stockwell. *Call Dimensions: Options and Issues in Computer-Assisted Language Learning.* Esl & Applied Linguistics Professional Series. Ed. Eli Hinkel. Mahwah, NJ: Lawrence Erlbaum Associates, 2006.

Lightbown, Patsy M., and Nina Spada. "Focus-on-Form and Corrective Feedback in Communicative Language Teaching." *Studies in Second Language Acquisition* 12, no. 04 (1990): 429–448.

Mackey, Alison, Rebekha Abbuhl, and Susan M. Gass. "Interactionist Approach." Chap. 1 In *The Routledge Handbook of Second Language Acquisition*, ed. Susan M. Gass and Alison Mackey. Routledge Handbooks in Applied Linguistics, 7–23. London, UK: Routledge, 2012.

Mahmood, Asim, Salman ul Waheed, Muhammad Asif Ikram Anjum, and Rashda Majeed. "Computer Assisted Language Learning: An Instrument of Change for Boosting Motivation Level among the Students of Graduation in Pakistan." *Language in India* 13, no. 7 (2013): 159–170.

Mall, M. A., and M. M. Nieman. "Problems Experienced with the Teaching of Arabic to Learners in Muslim Private Schools in South Africa and Botswana." *Per Linguam* 18, no. 2 (2002): 42–54.

Marzban, Amir. "Improvement of Reading Comprehension through Computer-Assisted Language Learning in Iranian Intermediate Efl Students." *Procedia Computer Science* 3 (2011): 3–10.

Morrison, Sally. "Arabic Language Teaching in the United States." *ERIC Clearinghouse on Languages and Linguistics (Language Link Online)* (2003). https://www.meforum.org/campus-watch/articles/2007/arabic-language-teaching-in-the-united-states.

Mourani, Mishka Moujabber. "Arabic Teaching at Crisis Point." *The Guardian*, 18 (March 2004).

Mutlu, Arzu, and Betil Eroz-Tuga. "The Role of Computer-Assisted Language Learning (Call) in Promoting Learner Autonomy." *Eurasian Journal of Educational Research* 51 (2013): 107–122.

Nachoua, Hassina. "Computer-Assisted Language Learning for Improving Students' Listening Skill." *Procedia, Social and Behavioral Sciences* 69 (2012): 1150–1159.

Nation, Paul, and Robert Waring. "Vocabulary Size, Text Coverage and Word Lists." Chap. 1.1 In *Vocabulary: Description, Acquisition and Pedagogy*, ed. Norbert Schmitt and Michael M. McCarthy, 6–19. Cambridge, UK: Cambridge University Press, 1997.

Nim Park, Chan, and Jeong-Bae Son. "Implementing Computer-Assisted Language Learning in the Efl Classroom: Teachers' Perceptions and Perspectives." *International Journal of Pedagogies and Learning* 5, no. 2 (2009): 80–101.

Osman, Ghada. "The Historian on Language: Ibn Khaldun and the Communicative Learning Approach." *Middle East Studies Association Bulletin* 37, no. 1 (2003): 50–57.

Patel, M. F., and Praveen M. Jain. *English Language Teaching: (Methods, Tools & Techniques)*. [In English] Jaipur, India: Sunrise Publishers and Distributors, 2008.

Pirasteh, Parvin. "The Effectiveness of Computer-Assisted Language Learning (Call) on Learning Grammar by Iranian Efl Learners." *Procedia, Social and Behavioral Sciences* 98 (2014): 1422–1427.

Rahimi, Nik Mohd, Nor Azhan, Wan Normeza, and Harun Baharudin. "Students' Feedback Towards Using Facebook in Learning Arabic Language." *Asian Social Science* 11, no. 28 (2015): 170–174.

Riasati, M., Negah Allahyar, and K. Tan. "Technology in Language Education: Benefits and Barriers." *Journal of Education and Practice* 3, no. 5 (2012): 25–30.

Richards, Jack C., and Theodore S. Rodgers. *Approaches and Methods in Language Teaching*. 2nd ed. Cambridge, UK: Cambridge University Press, 2001.

Ricks, Robert. "The Development of Frequency-Based Assessments of Vocabulary Breadth and Depth for L2 Arabic." Georgetown University, 2015.

Samy, Waheed. "Instructional Media and Learning Arabic." Chap. 19 In *Handbook for Arabic Language Teaching Professionals in the 21st Century*, ed. Kassem M. Wahba, Zeinab A. Taha, and Liz England, 263–274. Mahwah, NJ: Routledge, 2006.

Savignon, Sandra J. "Communicative Language Teaching." *Theory into Practice* 26, no. 4 (1987): 235–242.

———. "Communicative Language Teaching: Linguistic Theory and Classroom Practice." Chap. 1 In *Interpreting Communicative Language Teaching: Contexts and Concerns in Teacher Education*, ed. Sandra J. Savignon, 1–28. New Haven, CT: Yale University Press, 2002.

Schmidt, Richard. "The Role of Consciousness in Second Language Learning." *Applied Linguistics* 11, no. 2 (1990): 129–158.

Schmitt, Norbert, Xiangying Jiang, and William Grabe. "The Percentage of Words Known in a Text and Reading Comprehension." *The Modern Language Journal* 95, no. 1 (2011): 26–43.

Selim, Nadia. "Ibn Sahnun's Ninth Century Framework: A Guide for Arabic Language Curriculum Writing." *Islam and Civilisational Renewal (ICR)* 8, no. 4 (2017): 488–506.

Sirajudeen, Adam, and AbdulWahid Adebisi. "Teaching Arabic as a Second Language in Nigeria." *Procedia – Social and Behavioral Sciences* 66 (2012): 126–135.

Stockwell, Glenn. *Computer-Assisted Language Learning: Diversity in Research and Practice*. Cambridge, UK: Cambridge University Press, 2012.

Swain, Merrill. "Communicative Competence: Some Roles of Comprehensible Input and Comprehensible Output in Its Development." Chap. 14 In *Input in Second Language Acquisition*, ed. S. Gass and C. Madden, 235–253. Rowley, MA: Newbury House Publishers, Inc., 1985.

Taber, Joan. "A Brief History of Esl Instruction: Theories, Methodologies, and Upheavals." In *TESL Certificate Program – SCCC*. Seattle Central College, 2006. http://seattlecentral.edu/faculty/jgeorg/TESLSCCC/ABriefHistory.htm.

Takač, Višnja Pavičić. *Vocabulary Learning Strategies and Foreign Language Acquisition*. Second Language Acquisition. Ed. David Singleton. Vol. 27, Clevedon, UK: Multilingual Matters, 2008.

Terbeh, Naim, and Mounir Zrigui. "Arabic Language Learning Assisted by Computer, Based on Automatic Speech Recognition." arXiv.org: Operated by Cornell University Library, 2012.

U.S. Department of State. "Language Assignments." https://www.state.gov/documents/organization/247092.pdf.

Zaini, Amin, and Golnar Mazdayasna. "The Effect of Computer Assisted Language Learning on the Development of Efl Learners' Writing Skills." *Procedia, Social and Behavioral Sciences* 98 (2014): 1975–1982.

CHAPTER 15

Conclusion

Mohamad Abdalla, Dylan Chown,
and Muhammad Abdullah

This book highlights, under the common theme of renewal, both challenges and opportunities for Islamic schools in the West. The intent of the book has been to further expand and build upon the contemporary intellectual, religious and spiritual rigour driving efforts towards renewal within Islamic schools. As this book demonstrates, the intellectual, religious and spiritual dimensions are entirely integrated because of the central principle of *tawhid* in an Islamic worldview. The preceding interconnected and interrelated chapter contributions from prominent scholars, academics and educationalists have thus intended to provide a powerful point of reference, an acquaintance with important principles, conceptualisations, theories and metalanguage in the field, and principally an impetus for renewal. This book coincides with the undeniable growth and maturation of local, national and global Islamic schools and, more broadly, Islamic education communities. The editors of this book and its contributors have thereby

---

M. Abdalla (✉) • D. Chown • M. Abdullah
University of South Australia, Adelaide, SA, Australia
e-mail: mohamad.abdalla@unisa.edu.au; dchown@razieducation.com

sought to address overarching questions within the field via a strength-based approach, offering pathways to renewal for Islamic schools.

THEMES

Several themes have arisen throughout the book that demand broader and deeper consideration. One such theme is the importance of respecting diverse perspectives. As Islamic schools in the West have developed, it is clear that despite characteristic similarities, and similar reasons for establishment and early challenges, distinct and diverse educational models are emerging under the broad Islamic school banner. This plurality of school models, albeit intending in the main to draw from an Islamic vision of education, is an area that can be celebrated and explored further. Islamic schools posting a vision, mission and strategy fitting to the era of renewal can facilitate this exploration. It allows each individual school to respond to a long-held criticism of Islamic schools: that they do not measure their success against their own vision.

A theme that is strongly related to vision, mission and strategy and embedded within them, which will add form and character to the continuum of Islamic school educational models, is the need to define purpose and subsequent pedagogy, which was emphasised repeatedly across chapters. Conceptualisations of pedagogy that are conducive to more nuanced and innovative educational models for enactment in Islamic schools are clearly a high priority. The themes associated with purpose and pedagogy also relate to a further theme of attaining the 'Islamic' in Islamic schools, as discussed in multiple chapters.

An Islamic worldview is of pivotal importance to renewal in Islamic schools. At every layer of school renewal—governance, character education, curriculum and pedagogy—the need for a clearly articulated and understood worldview has been emphasised. While discourse on the Islamic worldview is replete in Islamic schools and Islamic education literature, as in this book, it is unknown how clearly articulated, shared and understood this is 'on the ground' in schools. An Islamic worldview is the key to an orientation towards, as well as the agency for, renewal. Attaining the 'Islamic' and countering claims that Islamic schools are largely conventional demands deep consideration and operationalising of an Islamic worldview.

Spirituality is another recurring theme throughout many chapters in this book, reflecting its importance in Islamic schools and underlining the need for its broader and deeper consideration. Elleissy asserts that Islamic schools ought to exert more time and effort 'reviving the spiritual realm of Islam on all fronts, and making it an integral part of our medium of instruction and interaction'. Trevathan speaks of a more organic process whereby a focus on 'authentic humility', which he argues should be at the heart of education, would see a 'Muslim ethos' develop in its own way. Other contributors emphasise a more pedagogical approach to ethos.

A feature of the educational heritage across the breadth of Islamic civilisation has been the emphasis and focus on the educator or the teacher above and beyond the institution—people above bricks and mortar. This focus on educators is a strong theme in the book. Memon and Alhashmi speak of teachers' paramount role in Islamic schools to foster 'moral uprightness', emphasising claims by Abdullah, Chown and Alam that teachers are role models. They also speak of a pastoral role requirement for teachers in Islamic schools extending to concern about a 'student's wellbeing, moral behaviour, personal choices, life decisions and social etiquette', guided by an 'Islamic ethic'.

Abdullah, conscious of the climate of high expectations, high accountability and increased teacher burnout, and pragmatic about teachers' preparedness—spiritually or otherwise—argues that the teacher should not be seen as '*the* model of *adab*' but rather as a learner and '*a* model of *adab*', a participant in an 'organic process of change and improvement'. Chown and Alam equally emphasise, within the methodology of the Dignified Way, a reorientation in pedagogy whereby the teacher is immersed in the character development process in partnership with students as learners.

Finally, curriculum renewal is another theme arising throughout the book that demands broader and deeper consideration. This includes, but is not limited to, an urgent need to attend to curriculum development in Islamic schools as argued by Shamma, and the recognised absence of an 'appropriate' and 'contextual' Islamic studies curriculum as discussed in Abdalla's chapter. Earlier efforts to develop curriculum resources for Islamic studies, typically in the form of textbook series, are noteworthy; however, the shortfalls of this approach of bypassing usual requisites and processes for curriculum development are manifest. Abdalla demonstrates that in developing an Islamic studies curriculum, the *process* itself is significant.

Arguably, the curriculum was once seen as the pre-eminent concern for Islamic schools. However, given the proliferation of Islamic schools, the complexities and significant societal changes influencing local, regional and global contexts and other important structures affecting education, issues of well-being and pedagogy along with other factors are being examined along with the curriculum for renewal. Therefore, this book has upheld the view that curriculum is an important ingredient, although not the whole nor the driver, but rather an essential piece of the whole in the effort of renewal.

Key Aspects of Renewal

In exploring pathways, this book has shed light on several key aspects of renewal, the first of which is that robust governance models and processes are essential for Islamic schools to negotiate renewal, avoiding some of the concerns associated with neo-liberalism and corporatisation highlighted in Ali' and Abdul Mabud's chapters. Secondly, Succarie, Fallon and Coronado have underlined the role of an Islamic worldview as a framework for governance models for Islamic schools, again emphasising that an Islamic worldview provides the orientation and agency for distinct, responsive and potentially innovative education models to emerge in Islamic schools. Renewal must also reflect teaching and learning practices consistent with an Islamic worldview, an Islamic vision of education and appropriate pedagogy, and thereby inform all aspects of the school including character education, classroom management models and relevant, contextual Islamic and Arabic studies.

Challenges to Renewal

Renewal is focused toward the gap in intent (vision), ideal theory and practice. Renewal demands a purposeful synthesis of the tradition with contemporary educational practice and greater emphasis on empirical research substantiating best practices in Islamic schools. Challenges to renewal include explicit areas demanding attention such as governance, curriculum, pedagogy and language learning, particularly Arabic. More implicit challenges to renewal relate to the absence of clearly articulated and shared conceptualisations of the Islamic worldview and the absence of overarching aims and objectives for Islamic schools. The absence of an Islamic worldview has implications for all areas of an Islamic school, including perspectives on governance, educational leadership, Islamic school vision, views of children and child development theory, curriculum, pedagogy and assessment.

Other implicit challenges to renewal relate to access to appropriate professional learning. Staff within Islamic schools, whether they identify as Muslim or not, lack access to either teacher training, induction or quality ongoing professional learning that is grounded in an Islamic worldview and pedagogy and is responsive to Islamic school contexts and the needs of Muslim students. In the absence of foundational training and ongoing professional learning, Islamic schools can be become distracted from pathways to renewal. Educators within Islamic schools are often themselves by-products of various educational theories driving paradigms prevalent in contemporary schooling that are not necessarily aligned to Islamic educational theory. As such, Islamic schools and the educators within them may be less equipped to orientate themselves and hold their own position in the face of shifts that occur across schooling, including the impact of standardised testing, school ranking tables, data-driven instruction and the measurement of learning.

Another implicit challenge relates to the leadership capacity necessary to navigate renewal. The bridge between theory and practice, between this book and enactment of renewal on the ground, is dependent on strong educational leaders given their role at the interface between research and practice 'on the ground'. There are several concerns regarding educational leadership within Islamic schools, the first and obvious being an absence of research on educational leadership in Islamic schools in Western contexts. Another relates to the propensity of Islamic school communities to seek heroic leaders over and above distributed and shared leadership structures and processes. This serves to constrain the leadership capacity collectively of educators and staff within a school at every level. A further concern is the absence of professional learning and training for educational leaders cognisant of an Islamic worldview. The discussion around governance models and processes consistent with an Islamic worldview also demands a critical examination of the extent to which devolution of leadership to educational leaders and principals is occurring. Are educational leaders, particularly principals in Islamic schools, granted leadership along with the necessary support and autonomy to lead renewal? Do governing bodies of Islamic schools contain representation of educationalists, or a critical level of educational experience, and do they understand their role in relation to the principal and leadership activity?

Another significant challenge in the era of renewal relates to the need to develop whole-of-field structures beyond the school layer, impacting upon collective capacity and subsequently the mechanisms to facilitate robust collaborative efforts. This applies to local, regional and global Islamic school communities. Catholic education and other faith communities have developed whole-of-field structures aligned with their leadership structures, principles and processes. The intent could likely extend to increased continuity and coordination of efforts, increased collective capacity, and stronger advocacy and in some cases funding support. While Islamic schools should not necessarily operate under identical structures, an effort must be made to conceive of what whole-of-field structures and subsequently processes would entail for Islamic schools. This applies to renewal efforts internally within a school among collegial working teams as well as externally among school clusters and professional learning communities. The definitive example of this is the curriculum challenge, which has not and cannot be met by one school or one community in isolation.

Other challenges worthy of further deliberation relate to the impact of the 'external' and its implications for renewal. The 'external' relates to broad and often connected factors outside the precinct and the scope of control of Islamic schools. Examples include the terrorism narrative, increased surveillance in schools and the complex interplay between geopolitical, regional and local politics around citizenship, values and belonging and the subsequent impact on education policy. In some cases, the impact of the external can severely constrain leadership (Faris and Parry 2011; Faris 2014). It can also lead to disproportionate energy diverted to what Islamic schools are not instead of what they are, a seriously distracting threat to Islamic schools as they negotiate transition from the establishment phase to renewal. At the all-important level of children and young people, Islamophobia and the connected 'external' factors mentioned in this book by Ali, Diallo and Abdul Mabud and others can have a significant impact on identity, learning and overall schooling and post-schooling experience. It can also have a negative impact on the collective identity of Islamic schools. In the absence of the type of elucidation of Islamic education as framed in Memon and Alhashmi's conceptualisation of Islamic pedagogy, coupled with the negative impact of the external, Islamic schools can easily be distracted by theories, agendas and paradigms not necessarily aligned to the broadly conceived but largely unarticulated goals of the field of Islamic schooling. Significant examples include the impact of child development theory on views of children and early years education, and arguably most pervasively, in the era of standardised testing and its impact upon pedagogy, the holistic development of students and overall Islamic school renewal.

Beyond the school layer, in the absence of supportive bodies that serve the whole-of-field in addition to bodies at the level of regions, states and clusters—who is advocating for Islamic schools? If a collective effort towards renewal is sought within Islamic schools in Western contexts, representing vertical growth, what engagement with political discourse, educational policy, independent or other schooling sectors are Islamic schools contributing to? This would represent a form of horizontal growth and renewal whereby Islamic schools in the next phase would build structures, mechanisms and processes to add their voice and play an active role. Both forms of growth fit broadly within the challenges as well as the opportunities for renewal.

Future Research

Further research is necessary in the area of governance of Islamic schools answering Succarie, Fallon and Coronado's call for a 'more nuanced approach to governance research' and thereafter praxis. The same can be said of educational leadership, which is likely to be more complex and demanding than other educational contexts (Berber 2009). Educational leadership within an Islamic worldview is called upon to oversee an Islamic ethos, whole-school efforts associated with purpose and pedagogy, relating to a common theme of *adab* mentioned throughout the book, character development, teacher professionalism and relevant and appropriate assessment, pedagogical practice and curriculum enactment, to name a few.

Given the significant concern locally, nationally and globally around the curriculum in Islamic schools, further research is required around assessment practices in Islamic schools as touched upon by Memon and Alhashmi, Abdullah and Abdalla. What impact is standardised testing having on the enactment of curriculum, on the achievement of Islamic school visions, on the broader aims of Islamic schools? How can an Islamic worldview inform contemporary assessment of best practice and to what extent are Islamic schools engaging in such practice? What, as Abdullah has argued, can be borrowed from a prophetic pedagogy? Further research on assessment will be instructive for the curriculum challenges ahead as well as the urgent need to engage in further pedagogy research.

The absence of an Islamic studies curriculum in Islamic schools and of an Arabic curriculum for Islamic schools that is responsive to the diverse needs of students in Islamic schools in the West are arguably the most significant unachieved goals, and a most necessary milestone for renewal in the area of curriculum. Further research is needed to understand students' expectations of Islamic and Arabic studies, and teachers' views on the challenges and opportunities in teaching these in Islamic schools.

Bibliography

Berber, Mujgan G. "The Role of the Principal in Establishing and Further Developing an Independent Christian or Islamic School in Australia." Doctor of Philosophy, School of Education, University of Western Sydney, 2009.

Faris, N. "Embracing Basics: A Grounded Theory of Organisational Leadership in Islamic Organisation within a Western Society." Doctoral Dissertation, Griffith University, Australia, 2014.

Faris, N., and K. Parry. "Islamic Organizational Leadership Within a Western Society: The Problematic Role of External Context." *The Leadership Quarterly* 22, no. 1 (2011), 132–151.

Index[1]

A

ACARA, *see* Australian Curriculum, Assessment and Reporting Authority
Adab, 14, 64, 68, 77, 81, 120, 170, 171, 174–177, 180, 182–184, 188, 199, 200, 317, 321
African American Islamic schools, 118, 119
Akhlaq, 21, 64, 67, 71, 77, 80, 81
Al-Attas, S.M., 14, 68, 80, 82n4, 82n5, 85n54, 91n134, 91n139, 123, 126n15, 189n4, 189n5, 191n44
Al-Ghazali, 13, 171, 173, 176, 177, 179, 190n18, 190n22, 190n23, 191n38, 192n56, 233
Allah, 14, 15, 20, 39, 63, 64, 71, 78, 81, 121–125, 126n11, 140, 173, 185, 202, 209, 210, 218, 228–236, 241, 250
Al-Zarnuji, Burhan al-Din, 13, 28n12, 29n15, 171, 176, 178, 179, 182, 187, 191n37, 192n58, 192n59, 192n75, 192n76, 193n77, 193n80, 193n81
Amal, 14, 15, 21, 211
Arabic, 2, 3, 8, 26, 36, 41, 50–52, 103, 108, 109, 191n39, 196, 202, 210, 240, 241, 247, 249, 260, 265, 286–300, 301n7, 318, 321, 322
Arabic language, 36, 41, 50–52, 247, 249, 286, 295, 300
Arabic studies, 3, 286, 290, 292, 299–300, 318, 322
Australia, 4–6, 8n2, 35–52, 54, 55, 65, 66, 70, 98, 100, 103–107, 109, 112, 120, 195–198, 200, 239, 257, 260, 270, 278, 281n34, 289–291, 293–296, 298, 300
Australian Curriculum, Assessment and Reporting Authority (ACARA), 271–274, 297

---

[1] Note: Page numbers followed by 'n' refer to notes.

© The Author(s) 2018
M. Abdalla et al. (eds.), *Islamic Schooling in the West*,
https://doi.org/10.1007/978-3-319-73612-9

B

Baghdad, 228
Basra, 122, 228
Boards, 51, 52, 63–65, 67–78, 80, 81, 112, 154, 161, 236, 259, 264, 299

C

Catholic Church, 154
Catholic education, 19, 152, 154, 320
Chairperson, 72, 76
Challenges, 3, 4, 7, 8, 12, 16–18, 21, 65, 70, 71, 81, 112, 117, 118, 125, 130, 154, 161–163, 170, 172, 189n3, 201, 211, 233, 243, 244, 251, 258, 261–270, 272, 276–278, 285, 286, 289, 300, 301, 315, 316, 318–322
Character education, 3, 5, 180, 316, 318
Christian, 7, 8n2, 42, 66, 97, 98, 102, 111, 154, 245
Citizenship, 17, 20, 22–25, 27, 40, 107, 212, 258, 320
Classical, 2, 6, 105, 106, 144, 170, 180, 184, 185, 231–233, 287
Classroom management, 3, 5, 318
Cognitive development, 172, 174, 295
Commodification, 48–55, 130, 139
Community, 2, 3, 5, 6, 8, 12, 14, 17–20, 22–27, 36, 37, 39, 40, 44, 63–71, 73–78, 80, 81, 97, 113, 121, 123, 135, 140, 141, 144, 151, 153–158, 160–166, 169, 170, 172, 178, 179, 184, 191n47, 195, 196, 198, 200, 205, 208, 212, 218, 236, 239, 240, 243, 246–249, 251, 259, 289, 315, 319, 320
Compliance, 6, 64, 65, 67–69, 73, 74, 76–78, 80, 81
Computer assisted language learning (CALL), 8, 286–300, 301n7
Consultation, 68, 71, 74, 77, 265, 271
Context, 2–7, 8n2, 21, 25, 26, 42, 50, 51, 74, 103, 117, 119, 125, 133, 136, 144, 162, 179, 189n3, 198, 200, 202, 211, 214, 232, 235, 240, 243–245, 250, 251, 258–260, 264, 270–273, 275, 279, 286, 289, 293–295, 298, 300, 318, 319, 321
Contextualisation, 279
Corporate Muslim School Model, 5, 36, 37, 51, 52
Culture, 3, 6, 17–19, 21, 23–25, 27, 35, 36, 40, 43–45, 52, 75, 76, 104, 106, 110, 118, 120, 125, 129, 133, 141, 144, 152, 156, 157, 160, 161, 166, 175, 187, 196–199, 249, 257, 259
Curriculum, 5, 11, 12, 16, 19–22, 25–27, 36, 41, 43–45, 49, 78, 97–100, 103, 105–107, 111, 114n23, 117–125, 144, 163–165, 169, 170, 172, 177–180, 188, 197, 198, 211, 229, 240, 242, 245, 258–262, 264, 266, 270–277, 279, 281n34, 316–318, 320–322

D

Dignified way, 317
Discipline, 14, 25, 42, 43, 122, 177, 185, 198, 235, 264, 277

E

Environment, 17, 18, 27, 40, 42, 43, 49, 50, 98, 121, 125, 133, 139, 144, 170, 181–184, 187, 188, 198, 200, 201, 204, 205, 211, 212, 228, 234–236, 246, 251, 257, 261, 276, 290, 291

Ethical, 35, 45, 68, 131, 132, 175, 199, 229, 231, 234, 236, 242
Ethos, 4, 6, 11, 19, 20, 22, 26, 27, 35, 42, 43, 45, 52, 98, 99, 129–144, 151, 152, 181, 182, 199, 200, 259, 273, 276, 277, 317, 321
Eurocentric, 20, 26, 105, 118–120, 244

F
Faith school, 19, 20, 22, 41, 107, 111, 135, 151

G
Golden Age, 101, 107, 122
Governance, 5, 6, 46, 63–81, 316, 318, 319, 321

H
Hadith, 1, 21, 48, 75, 101, 170, 173, 174, 176, 180, 185, 198–203, 208, 210, 232, 241, 242, 250, 252n8, 276
Halal, 36, 49, 99, 266, 269
Humanism, 6, 123
Humility, 140, 142, 144, 184–187, 212, 242, 317
Hybrid governance model, 78, 80

I
Identity, 6, 17, 18, 20, 21, 25, 27, 35, 36, 40, 42, 44, 50, 67, 73, 75, 78, 97–101, 166, 196, 197, 201, 212, 228–230, 234, 245, 246, 249, 257, 258, 320
Ideology, 16, 46, 67, 228, 232, 240, 243–246, 250, 251
Ihsan, 15, 64, 67, 71, 77, 80, 81, 199, 200, 259

Ilm, 14, 19, 21
Immigrant Islamic schools, 119
Independent schools, 65, 66, 69, 70, 72, 77, 78, 80, 81, 111, 290
Integration, 12, 40, 43, 47, 177, 211, 214, 236, 240, 260
Islamic
  community schools, 8, 66, 240, 243, 247–249, 251
  education, 2, 3, 5, 7, 12–15, 19, 21, 25, 27, 36, 37, 41–46, 49–52, 55, 98, 99, 169–172, 174–176, 179, 180, 184, 188, 198–201, 240, 242–246, 251, 258–260, 281n34, 289, 291, 293, 300, 315, 316, 320
  identity, 17, 20, 21, 36, 50, 97, 201
  pedagogy, 7, 73, 169–188, 200, 259, 261, 262, 276, 320
  schools, 2–8, 8n2, 11–27, 35–52, 54, 55, 63, 97–113, 117, 119, 120, 122, 124, 157, 166, 169, 170, 174, 177, 178, 181, 183, 184, 186, 188, 195–218, 227–229, 231–233, 235, 236, 240, 245, 246, 251, 257, 286–300, 301n7, 315–321
  studies, 5, 7, 8, 26, 36, 41, 46, 49–52, 100, 102, 103, 105, 108, 109, 177, 229, 239–252, 257–279, 317, 321
  worldview, 3, 5–8, 63–65, 68, 69, 71, 77, 81, 117–125, 171, 178, 180, 198, 200, 201, 218, 239, 272, 315, 316, 318, 319, 321
Islamisation of knowledge, 36

J
Judaeo-Christian, 36, 243

K
Khalifa, 199
Knowledge, 1, 2, 5, 12–16, 18, 19, 21, 25, 36, 37, 44, 52, 54, 55, 63, 74, 101, 105, 106, 120, 123, 125, 139, 142, 156, 157, 160, 161, 163–165, 171, 172, 176–179, 182, 184–187, 191n46, 191n47, 198, 199, 205, 207, 208, 210–212, 214, 227–231, 233–234, 241–243, 248, 250, 251, 257, 259, 262, 264–267, 270, 272, 274–277, 279, 285, 287, 293

L
Learning, 14, 17, 22, 103, 158, 162, 180, 182, 187, 200, 263, 287, 318, 320
Liberalism, 48

M
Madrasa, 2, 11, 243
Maqasid, 71
Ma'rifa, 230
Media, 64, 66, 67, 69, 195, 244–246, 251, 295
Metalanguage, 201, 207, 211, 315
Mission, 6, 54, 64, 68, 151–153, 155, 161–163, 165, 188, 228, 229, 236, 278, 316
Moral development, 171, 177
Moral leadership, 68, 73, 78
Muhammad, Prophet, 1, 20, 39, 48, 75, 78, 122, 126n11, 126n12, 172, 174–177, 179, 185, 199–203, 241, 252n8
Muslim school, 5, 6, 8n2, 11, 12, 17, 18, 20, 22, 24, 35–59, 98, 119, 129–147, 245, 288
Mysticism, 130

N
Nazareth College, 153, 154, 156, 157, 165
Neoliberalism, 36, 46–48, 58n54, 58n57
Numinous, 130, 144

O
Organisation for Economic Co-operation and Development (OECD), 68, 69

P
Pedagogical framework, 7, 195–218
Pedagogies, 7, 198, 202, 208, 276
Philosophy of Islamic education, 7, 146n32, 191n39, 192n48
Positive learning environments, 183
Predecessors, 7, 227, 230
Prejudice, 7, 22, 240, 243–246, 251, 253n21
Principles, 5, 6, 12–14, 16, 17, 19, 21, 23–25, 36, 45, 48, 64, 67, 68, 71, 76, 78, 80, 81, 112, 117, 118, 120–122, 124, 125, 131, 136, 137, 171, 172, 179, 191n39, 201, 202, 240–242, 244, 259, 261–264, 274, 276, 315, 320
Productive pedagogies, 202, 208
Prophetic pedagogy, 7, 200–218, 276, 321

Q
Quran, 82n11, 82n13, 250, 251

R
Rationalism, 129, 130
Reformation, 3, 234, 235

Relevance, 178, 205, 211, 258, 261, 262, 270, 278, 279
Religious education, 7, 9n6, 11, 13, 15, 16, 42, 119, 144, 157, 163, 164, 184, 196, 240, 245, 253n18, 253n31
Renewal, 2–4, 6–8, 117, 151, 153, 160–163, 166, 186, 188, 218, 257, 271, 279, 315–318, 322

S
Saladin, 231
Secular, 4, 5, 11–18, 20, 22, 23, 26, 27, 35, 36, 40–44, 49, 100, 111, 117, 119–124
Secular education, 11, 13, 15–17, 22, 26, 42, 45, 120
Secular schools, 5, 11, 27, 139, 177, 178, 290
Sense of belonging, 20–21, 27, 40, 154, 161, 163, 166
Sociolinguistic, 247
Spiritual development, 21–22, 171–174, 200, 236
Stakeholders, 6, 49, 63–71, 73–78, 80, 81, 118, 125, 155, 162, 166, 181, 227, 228, 265, 289
Stewardship, 6, 65, 70, 71, 73–78, 81
Stewardship model, 6, 69
Students, 5, 13, 41, 75, 106, 122, 153, 160, 185, 197, 212, 228, 261, 266, 272, 273, 289, 291, 292, 317, 321, 322
Sufis, 13
Sunnah, 13, 18, 22, 122, 208, 241, 250, 251, 252n8, 267, 269, 300

T
Ta'dib, 14, 171, 172, 174, 180, 199
Ta'lim, 198

Tanzīh, 139, 140
Taqwa, 15, 68
Tarbiyah, 199
Tarbiyah project, 199
Tashbīh, 139, 140
Tawhid, 26, 71, 176, 315
Tawhidic, 13, 241, 242
Teacher, 156, 162, 184, 185, 187, 201, 203, 246, 261, 264, 268, 269, 275, 277, 291, 296, 299, 317

U
Ummah, 20, 21, 144
Utopian Muslim School Model, 5, 36, 37, 43–45, 52, 55

V
Values, 1, 5, 6, 8, 12, 13, 16, 17, 19, 21–23, 25–27, 36, 42, 43, 45, 48, 50, 52, 54, 55, 64, 73, 74, 76, 97–101, 104, 107, 111, 119, 123, 131, 133, 135, 141, 151, 155, 161, 164, 169, 171, 173, 177, 182, 188, 195, 198–200, 204, 229, 231, 244, 246, 249–252, 257, 259, 261–263, 289–291, 294, 297, 300, 320
Virtues, 15, 131, 139, 143, 170, 228, 299
Vision, 3, 5–7, 17, 19, 27, 40, 45, 48, 64, 67, 68, 72, 122, 142, 151–166, 170–172, 188, 218, 228, 229, 236, 265, 269, 270, 278, 316, 318, 321

W
Western context, 2–5, 117, 125, 258, 259, 271, 279, 319, 321

CPSIA information can be obtained
at www.ICGtesting.com
Printed in the USA
LVOW13*1604030618
579412LV00010B/424/P

9 783319 736112